Homeland Security, its Law and its State

This book assesses the impact of post-9/11 domestic counterterrorism policy on US political life. It examines political discourse, law, the institutional architecture of the state and its relations with the population, and shows that 'homeland security' is a project with wide-ranging implications for democratic institutions and culture. These implications are addressed through a novel approach which treats law and the state as social relations, and relates developments in law to those in the state and in social dynamics. On this basis, the book examines the new political representations in counterterrorism discourse, especially regarding the relation between the state and the population. It examines the form and content of counterterrorism law, the powers it provides, and the structure and functions it prescribes for the state. Moreover, by focusing on the new Department of Homeland Security and the restructuring of the intelligence apparatus, the book assesses the new, intelligence-led, policing model. Finally, it examines forms of popular support and resistance to homeland security, to discuss citizenship and state-population relations.

The author concludes that homeland security has turned the US into a hybrid polity; the legal and political institutions of democracy remain intact, but their content and practices become authoritarian and exclude the population from politics. These legal and political forms remain operative beyond counterterrorism, in the context of the present economic crisis. They seem to be a permanent configuration of power.

This book is an indispensable companion for students of (counter-)terrorism and security studies, politics, human rights, constitutional and criminal law, American studies and criminology.

Christos Boukalas is Law and Society Research Associate in Cardiff University Law School.

Routledge Research in Terrorism and the Law

Available titles in this series include:

The United States, International Law and the Struggle against Terrorism
Thomas McDonnell

Counter-Terrorism and Beyond
The Culture of Law and Justice After 9/11
Edited by Andrew Lynch, Nicola McGarrity and George Williams

Counter-terrorism and the Detention of Suspected Terrorists
Preventative Detention and International Human Rights Law
Claire Macken

Gender, National Security and Counter-Terrorism
Human Rights Perspectives
Edited by Margaret L. Satterthwaite and Jayne Huckerby

Surveillance, Counter-Terrorism and Comparative Constitutionalism
Edited by Fergal Davis, Nicola McGarrity and George Williams

Forthcoming titles:

Anti-Terrorism Law and Normalising Northern Ireland
Jessie Blackbourn

Homeland Security, its Law and its State
A Design of Power for the 21st Century

Christos Boukalas

LONDON AND NEW YORK

First published 2014 by Routledge

2 Park Square, Milton Park, Abingdon, Oxon OX14 4RN
711 Third Avenue, New York, NY 10017, USA

Routledge is an imprint of the Taylor & Francis Group, an informa business

First issued in paperback 2016

Copyright © 2014 Christos Boukalas

The right of Christos Boukalas to be identified as author of this work has been asserted by him in accordance with sections 77 and 78 of the Copyright, Designs and Patents Act 1988.

All rights reserved. No part of this book may be reprinted or reproduced or utilised in any form or by any electronic, mechanical, or other means, now known or hereafter invented, including photocoying and recording, or in any information storage or retrieval system, reserved. without permission in writing from the publishers.

Notices:
Product or corporate names may be trademarks or registered trademarks, and are used only for identification and explanation without intent to infringe.

British Library Cataloguing in Publication
British Library Cataloguing in Publication Data
A catalogue record for this book is available from the British Library

Library of Congress Cataloging-in-Publication Data
A catalog record has been requested for this book

ISBN 978-1-138-66650-4 (pbk)
ISBN 978-0-415-52631-9 (hbk)
ISBN 978-0-203-79771-6 (ebk)

Typeset in 10/12 Baskerville MT by
Servis Filmsetting Ltd, Stockport, Cheshire

To Foteini and Salomi

For Sherman Austin and all his friends who 'want to change the world'!

With thanks to David Sugarman, Bob Jessop, David Seymour, Helen Perkins, Maria Snell, Megan Webb, Chris Witter, Silvia Ferreira, and Telemachos Antonopoulos, for their sustained interest, support, and critique.

Contents

List of abbreviations   viii

1   Introduction: homeland security, the US polity, and social dynamics   1

2   Politics, the state and law: a strategic-relational approach   11

3   11 September 2001: a social, political and legal charting   27

4   Heralding a new politics: the *war on terror* discourse   46

5   A blueprint of power: legislating counterterrorism   67

6   Counterterrorism legislation and the law-form   90

7   The Act and the state: implementation, friction, resistance   102

8   Department of homeland security and police restructuring   117

9   Total intelligence, intelligence-led policing, 'totalitarian' state?   136

10   The political significance of intelligence: government by experts   151

11   Citizen corps: homeland security citizenship   169

12   Resistance to homeland security   184

13   Repression   196

14   Homeland security: capital in full armour   208

Bibliography   222
Index   251

List of Abbreviations

A&E	armaments and energy
ACLU	American Civil Liberties Union
ALA	American Library Association
AS	authoritarian statism
AUMF	Authorisation for the Use of Military Force, 2001
CCC	Citizen Corps Council
CDA	Critical Discourse Analysis
CDT	Center for Democracy and Technology
CERT	Community Emergency Response Team
CI	critical infrastructure
CIA	Central Intelligence Agency
CRS	Congressional Research Service
DARPA	Defence Advanced Research Projects Agency
DCI	Director of Central Intelligence
DHS	Department of Homeland Security
DIA	Defence Intelligence Agency
DCI	Director of Central Intelligence
DNI	Director of National Intelligence
DOD	Department of Defence
DOJ	Department of Justice
EAD-I	Executive Assistant Director for Intelligence (FBI)
EESA	Emergency Economic Stabilisation Act
FBI	Federal Bureau of Investigations
FEMA	Federal Emergency Management Agency
FISA	Foreign Intelligence Surveillance Act
FISC	Foreign Intelligence Surveillance Court
FLRA	Federal Labour Relations Authority
HR	human rights
HSA	Homeland Security Act 2002
HSC	Homeland Security Council
HSAS	Homeland Security Advisory System
HSC	Homeland Security Council
HSIN	Homeland Security Information Network

HSLRB	Homeland Security Labour Relations Board
IAIP	Informantion Awareness and Infrastructure Protection (Directorate, DHS)
IACP	International Association of Chiefs of Police
ICT	information and communication technologies
IMC	Indipendent Media Centre
ISP	Internet Service Provider
IT	Information Technology
IMF	International Monetary Fund
IC	Incident Commander
ICS	Incident Command System
IRTPA	Intelligence Reform and Terrorism Prevention Act
ISP	Internet Service Provider
IT	information technology
JTTF	Joint Terrorism Task Forces
LA	Los Angeles
LAFD	Los Angeles Fire Department
LAPD	Los Angeles Police Department
MCA	Military Commissions Act
MLAT	Mutual Legal Assistance Treaty
MOUT	Military Operation in Urban Terrain
MRC	Medical Reserve Corps
NCTC	National Counterterrorism Centre
NDAA	National Defence Authorisation Act
NIAC	National Infrastructure Advisory Council
NSA	National Security Agency
NSL	National Security Letter
NIAC	National Infrastructure Advisory Council
NYPD	New York Police Department
OHS	Office of Homeland Security
ODNI	Office of Director of National Intelligence
PIRA	Patriot Reauthorisation and Improvement Act
SAR	Suspicious Activity Report
TARP	Troubled Asset Relief Program
TIA	Terrorism Information Awareness
TSA	Transportation Security Administration
TTIC	Terrorist Threat Integration Centre
UA	Universal Adversary
VIPS	Volunteers in Police Service
WEF	World Economic Forum
WoT	War on Terrorism
WTC	World Trade Centre

1 Introduction: homeland security, the US polity, and social dynamics

This book raises the question of *how counterterrorism policy affects the ability of the US population to participate in politics*. To provide some answers, it explores US domestic counterterrorism in the wake of the attacks of 11 September 2001 (9/11). It examines the forms counterterrorism takes in political discourse, legislation, institutional design and practices, the organisation of popular support to homeland security, the forms of resistance to it, and the repression it seems to entail for certain kinds of political activity. Based on this examination, it argues that homeland security effectuates important changes to the overall shape of the law (the 'law-form') and to state institutions and powers (the 'state-form'). These changes affect, in turn, the ways in which the population can participate in politics. Therefore, homeland security introduces a new design for power relations. This study outlines some main features and modalities of this new design, and observes that the homeland security modalities are also employed to manage the current economic crisis. This implies that the state- and law-forms set by homeland security outlive the context of 9/11 and constitute a (relatively) permanent paradigm for doing politics. In this manner, this book seeks to raise the question – and provide some (partial and provisional) answers – regarding the overall effects of counterterrorism on US political organisation and culture. In simple, and agonising, terms, this question can be summed up as: *is the twenty-first century US a democracy*? In what sense?

Before explaining how the book grapples with this question, it would be useful to declare what this book does *not* do. This will help highlight its difference from other security-related studies, and will save the reader time and effort by informing her what she should not expect to find in its pages. This negative introduction will also help to outline some aspects of this study.

What this book is *not* about

This book is not concerned with, or interested in, *terrorism*. Nowhere will the reader find information on, or analysis of, the organisational structure, the operational modes and capabilities, or the leading personnel, their habits and idiosyncrasies, of Al Qaeda or any such organisation. There are two reasons for this. First, because the author (and, it may be said, the reader too, however well informed) knows nothing about terrorist groups and their plans, and activities. Everything we know about terrorism derives from the state: from politicians, security and terrorism experts, and secret agents. The knowledge which the mass media disseminates, and even the analyses of independent scholars, is based on material deriving from the state, which we have no means to either verify or falsify. Even the all-enlightening 'leaks' derive from the vaults of some secret agency and are done by its personnel. They are more telling as symptoms of intra-state malfunction or conflict, rather than the 'real truth' about terrorism. As knowledge on terrorism is monopolised and selectively disseminated by the state, it can be argued that official knowledge about terrorism is a conspiracy theory turned on its head. I am not claiming that all state-derived knowledge on terrorism is false; I claim – and this is precisely the point – that we have no way of knowing whether it is false or true. We can only take (or leave) it on the basis of faith.

Indeed, the common refrain of those in the loop (high-clearance security and political personnel) sounds conspiratorial: 'If you had seen what I have seen ... you would not complain about the intrusiveness of security measures, or worry about their (un-)constitutionality'. This justification seems to derive straight from the pages of Leo Strauss, whereas the Truth is so 'terrible' that only a chosen few 'State Leaders' should be able to access it. The rest of us – the herd – will turn into stone upon beholding it, so we should therefore put our mind at ease and do as the leaders tell us (Strauss 1968: 25–26; 1983: 178–188; see also Drury 1988: 133–181; McAllister 1996: 202–204, 211, 219–220). This apocalyptic Platonism (based on the knowledge of Evil rather than Good) constitutes a platform for government based on blind faith, where those in possession of an alleged political expertise can (and must) tell the herd how to live, and the herd has no option but to believe them and obey – for its own good. So, the knowledge of terrorism is monopolised by select state personnel, and is thoroughly concealed from the population. Policy based on this knowledge is profoundly anti-democratic, for democracy is a political organisation where the people decide on the basis of full knowledge of all available facts relevant to the decision.

The second reason terrorism is out of the remit of this study is that it does not affect our lives. The extraordinary effort, resources and discourse dedicated to the subject by individual citizens, states and international organisations make this statement appear odd. Yet, it is more likely that people like us will lose our life in an accident in our bathroom than in a terrorist assault – and the possibilities of either happening are insignificant (Schneier 2006: 26–31, 238). The only way in which terrorism affects us is through counterterrorism.

As all knowledge of terrorism derives from the state; and as all relevance of terrorism resides in state policy against it, this book ignores the terrorism shadow-play and cuts straight to the question of the state and its counterterrorism policy. A brief exposition of how it does this can be found below. Before that, an explanation should be given about another omission.

The second thing this book does not do, is provide advice on *how to improve counterterrorism policy*. Recommendations for improving counterterrorism mainly fall into two categories: enhancing its effectiveness, or making it more democratic and/or constitutional. It is impossible to make recommendations on the effectiveness of counterterrorism, as we do not know what terrorism is. To suggest how security can do more and better, when we do not know to what threats it is meant to respond, is absurd. It will also be avoided for another reason. Counterterrorism, like every state policy, is not a technical problem demanding a 'better' solution. It is a strategy devised by state actors on behalf of certain social forces and representing their interests – possibly to the detriment of other social forces and interests. Thus, the question of 'improvement' cannot be answered in general, but only from the point of view of social forces and interests. Simply put, both the author and the reader may have an interest in enhancing the effectiveness of counterterrorism if we think it is something that would save us from a likely, violent, death. If, on the contrary, we think that counterterrorism considers us as suspects and monitors our daily activity, we may not want it 'improved' at all. In other words, the question of effectiveness conceals the political character of counterterrorism, and reduces it to a technical issue. The question of how to make it 'work better' precludes the discussion about whose interest does it primarily serve, whether we really want such policy, and on what terms.

The question of democratising counterterrorism, and making it abide to legal standards and constitutional rules, is part of this (political) discussion. While this book is, essentially, a prolonged assessment of the democratic character (or lack thereof) of counterterrorism, it does not suggest how to make it (more) democratic or constitutional. We have already noticed a profoundly anti-democratic element at the very core of counterterrorism policy: it is determined on the basis of knowledge and information which are sealed from the population. Thus, the population is, from the very start, excluded from having a say in determining policy, or control its operations. As long as this condition holds, any attempt to democratise counterterrorism is just rearranging deckchairs. Moreover, even the democratisation question is usually dealt with in a mechanical manner, as if it were a mere technicality – making any police practice 'democratic', as long as there is some judicial overview or congressional review. In this manner the question of democratisation abstracts legal and political institutions and practices from the social dynamics and political strategies which create, reproduce and alter them. Due to its formalism, the question of democratisation is reduced to concerns about the 'balance between security and liberty'.

Finally, a third omission of this book is that it does not consider US counterterrorism policy beyond its borders. The reader will not find here a discussion of the Iraq and Afghanistan wars, or of the manners in which the US conducts its international counterterrorism policy – in the United Nations (UN), the North Atlantic Treaty Organization (NATO), or through multi- and bilateral agreements with other countries. This is the least defensible of this book's omissions, resulting only form the need to limit the scope of the study, and the time and space of writing. I therefore made the (arbitrary) decision to artificially separate an exterior branch of counterterrorism policy ('global war on terrorism') from a domestic one ('homeland security'), and focus exclusively on the latter. This cancels the opportunity for a discussion about the role and ability of the US to define international law and the policy of international organisations; and on the relative gravitas of such institutions in comparison to *ad hoc* multi- and bilateral agreements and impromptu alliances. Stressing, perhaps, the artificial character of the separation, some developments in the 'foreign' front will be considered in this study, as they reverberate in 'domestic' affairs – the Iraq war, for instance, is present in this book to the extent that it influences resistance to homeland security, or helps galvanise power relations among different fractions of capital.

With these omissions confessed and, to some extend, explained, it is time to take a look at what this book actually is about.

What this book does – and how (and where)

In a sense, this study attempts to answer one question only: *how does counterterrorism affect the ability of the US population to participate in politics?* The simplicity of this question is deceptive. In order to answer it with the slightest claim to adequacy, the political organisation and culture – the polity – of the US must be considered, together with the changes counterterrorism affects on it.

A first factor complicating this question is that 'politics' is not only the activity of professional politicians and state managers, but every activity, individual or collective, which attempts to influence the way we live communally; every activity which refers to the questions of the institution, organisation, direction and administration of society. Thus, the question of the population's participation in politics is far from limited to voting or party membership. It includes a vast range of issues regarding the (formal and actual) possibilities to form and express opinions, to organise and act politically, and to influence, take, and implement decisions.

The question of political participation is further complicated because the 'population' is not a uniform entity. It comprises different groups and fractions (or 'social forces'), which may have differing ability to influence politics. The reader would acknowledge that her capacity to influence politics is probably less than that of Bill Gates, despite both being equal before the law and having one vote each.

Moreover, different groups and fractions of the population may have conflicting views regarding social organisation, and therefore develop opposing political objectives and strategies. It has, I think, not occurred in history that a single group has determined the political question (the question of institution, organisation, direction and administration of social life) all by itself. Politics is a contingent, antagonistic process which involves, to a varying extent, degree and role, the entire population. In promoting a political view, different social forces seek to negotiate and forge alliances with other forces, to secure the support or the tolerance of others, and confront and repress others still. In modern societies, most of this work happens in and through the state. The modern state claims to be an institutional entity situated outside and above the antagonisms of (civil) society, and to guarantee its peaceful reproduction in the face of tensions which threaten to tear it apart. The state digests political input from different fractions of the population, and on its basis organises official policies which are meant to represent the common good of the entire society. On this basis, the state becomes the terrain where political antagonism is played out and, with the same token, a most powerful political agency: the political views, strategies, projects and agendas of social forces can only become part of the fabric of social life inasmuch they are endorsed and promoted by the state; and the state is a key factor in (co-)determining the political views, strategies, and projects of social forces. Thus, the state claims the monopoly of legitimate politics.

Thus, the question of the population's participation in politics is transformed into one about the capacity of different social forces to influence the state. The state here is seen not as an institutional system possessing power and acting according to the volition of its top custodians. On the contrary, it is conceptualised as a social relation: as a creation of social forces, a terrain where their antagonism is played out, and a key agency in social antagonism. The access of different social forces to the state is largely determined by its institutional layout and the ways in which it exercises power. Given that the state's power and institutional design are largely provided by, and codified in, law, the study of law is a central, indispensable part of the study of the state. Again, law is not (just) the sum total of legal texts and institutions, but a social relation, a relation of power among different forces, mediated by the institutionality of the legal system. These acceptances regarding the nature of law and the state describe a 'strategic-relational' approach to the state and law as social phenomena. In a nutshell: society creates its state and law; and law and the state are crucial in making society.

In this manner, the innocent question of counterterrorism's impact on the population's ability to participate in politics has turned into one concerning the impact of homeland security on the institutional design of the state, the way in which it exercises power, and it relates to society 'outside' it – what I will be calling the 'state-from'. This question includes, like a babushka doll, one concerning how homeland security affects law: its content and institutions, its production and implementation, its effects upon different sectors of the population and their capacity to access justice, and its gravitas as a mode of government – in short, the 'law-form'.

The study of the law-form examines counterterrorism legislation, its production, implementation, the relative weight of law in state practice and the importance of the legal system among state institutions. The study of the state-from includes that of the law-form, and expands to address political discourse, the restructuring of state institutions and power modalities, and state-population relations.

As the study of homeland security's impact on the state- and law-forms is guided by the question of popular political participation, and occurs under an understanding of the state and law as social-relational phenomena, it develops a unique, holistic approach to domestic counterterrorism.

Its holistic character derives from three interlinked features. The first one is the guiding question regarding the impact of homeland security on popular participation in politics. The question runs like a red thread across the different areas which comprise the study of the law- and state-forms, and provides this wide-ranging examination with conceptual unity – it permits a unified vista of the homeland security landscape.

The second feature is its strategic-relational approach to the phenomena it investigates. The conceptualisation of law and the state as social creations and agencies, ultimately pertaining to social dynamics, helps relate developments in law to those in the state (and vice versa), and to relate developments in both these areas to occurrences (actual, anticipated or designed) in the broader society 'outside' their institutional cluster. A new piece of legislation, for instance, is connected to the strategy of the state which produces and implements it. State strategy is, in turn, connected to relations between social forces (e.g. labour vs capital; men vs women), which it tries to maintain, adjust or alter.

Combined, these two features – the guiding question and the strategic-relational approach – provide a rich analytical tapestry, able to relate legal, state, and social dynamics to each other. Thus, the examination of a specific development, for instance, a new Bill, results in an account not only of its content, but also of its implications for the legal system; its indications about, and its impact on, the state; and the interests it promotes (and undermines) in the realm of social dynamics. In doing so, it goes some way to address the 'why?' question – *why did counterterrorism take this form after 9/11?* – and also the 'so what' question – *why should we care about it?*

The third feature which permits this study an holistic scope is the conceptualisation of politics not as a determined, institutionally located activity, but as a broad social work pertaining to the institution, organisation, direction and administration of social life. The study of homeland security transverses state institutions and power, law, citizenship and social dynamics. To do so it draws from state-theory, political philosophy, jurisprudence and legal studies, political economy, discourse analysis, sociology, and security studies. This wide range of influences derives from seeing homeland security as a political phenomenon, and understanding politics in a broad, inclusive sense. Thus, rather than trans-disciplinary, this study can instead by seen as 'pre-disciplinary': by adopting an amplified understanding of politics, it overcomes the separation of the study of the social into distinct (often entrenched) disciplines. In this manner, it avoids the self-referential assessment of counterterrorism developments within each area of social study (where, e.g. the analysis of counterterrorism law refers back to the legal system or, at most, to the separation of powers). Lastly, by adopting a strategic-relational approach, and thus understanding institutions as social creations, it avoids formalism and abstraction (where, e.g. surveillance technologies are discussed as apparitions of 'governmentality' or 'power'). Instead, it understands institutional developments as related to social dynamics, and looks there for their (ultimate) origins and effects.

At this point, I must confess an important limitation. While it conceptualises the state and law as institutional condensations of the relationship between social forces, and upholds that all institutional developments pertain to social dynamics, the discussion here concerns, mainly, class forces and dynamics. There is little doubt that homeland security has important effects on the gendered constitution of the state, and on social dynamics informed by gender – and, possibly, similar effects regarding sexuality or race. And its impact along the lines of religion and ethnicity are obvious and well documented. The focus on class is due to issues of personal competence (I am not well-equipped to discuss in depth issues of gender, sexuality or race), but is also an attempt to emphasise the class aspects of homeland security, and show that what is often framed as a 'clash of civilisations' along religious lines is, in fact, a frontal attack of capital on the subordinate classes. Still, even though a primarily class analysis, it does not focus on economic antagonism (as one would expect from a class analysis), but on politics. In this sense, the selectivities, biases and prohibitions homeland security inscribes in the fabric of the state and law may have similar effects on the capacity for political organisation and action along the lines of either gender, class or race.

A last peculiarity of this study is that, while it focuses exclusively on US domestic policy, its theoretical framework hails from 'abroad'. The broad, socio-centric definition of politics, along with conceptions of democracy and considerations about the capacity of the population to create politics, derive from Cornelius Castoriadis, a Greek political philosopher mainly active in France. A similar trajectory (from Greece to France, passing through Germany) was followed by state-theorist Nicos Poulantzas. From him, and his younger, British colleague, Bob Jessop, I adopt (and adapt) the 'strategic-relational' approach to the state – an approach which I attempt here to apply to law – which sees the state (and law) not only as an institutional system, or as a subject-like agency with its own will and power, but as an institutionally mediated relation among social forces. Both these theorists draw from the work of the Italian communist leader, Antonio Gramsci, and, of course, of German revolutionary philosopher, Karl Marx. Therefore, this is, in a sense, a study of the US through a European lens. This was not done by design, and I am not sure if it is a good or a bad thing. But it might be interesting.

Having thus provided an idea of how this book goes about its business, we can look at what it specifically does – and where.

The understanding of politics and the strategic-relational approach to law and the state are developed in Chapter 2. This chapter sets out the theoretical framework for the study; it provides general definitions of the state and law, and introduces the concepts of the 'type of state' and 'type of law', and those of the state-form and the law-form, which are the main subject of analysis and discussion in this study.

Chapter 3 assesses the law-form, the state-form and social dynamics on the eve of 9/11 – thus providing a basis for comparison with homeland security. It relates them to capital accumulation during that period. And, it introduces the term 'power bloc', which refers to power relations among different sectors of dominant capital, largely organised in and through the state, and having important effects on the state- and law-form. The eve of 9/11 was marked by severe crisis, combining power bloc infighting, popular unrest and a collapse of accumulation, which put the state-form under pressure.

In Chapter 4, the examination of homeland security begins in earnest, by considering its first, chronologically, apparition: Presidential discourse. This chapter employs analytical tools from Critical Discourse Analysis to decipher the political meanings instilled by the President in the wake of 9/11: the relations between the US and the terrorist Enemy, the relations among different entities of the state and, most importantly, the relations between the state and the population in the new political reality of the 'war on terror'. It further examines the President's success in conveying the new political meaning to the population, and the persistence of these early representations of political relations and roles in time.

Chapter 5 is the first of three chapters concerned with counterterrorism law. It discusses key pieces of relevant legislation (the Patriot, Homeland Security, and Intelligence Reform Acts, and their epigones) and para-legislation (Executive and Military Orders). While retaining considerations of constitutionality and the rule of law, the analysis is also concerned with what counterterrorism law implies for the relations between the Executive, Congress and the courts; the structure and operation of the policing mechanism; the spatiality and temporality of policing; and the power-relations between the state and the population – whether citizens, 'aliens' or 'enemy combatants'. Attention is given to trends towards intelligence, surveillance and pre-emption, and to 'domestic terrorism', a crime that is inherently political. This analysis provides new angles for understanding counterterrorism law, offering both a counterpoint and a supplement to more conventional legal analyses. Lastly, this chapter exceeds the remit of counterterrorism. By discussing the reaction to the current economic crisis, it notes that the legal modalities introduced to fight terrorism are replicated to manage an economic emergency.

The slightly unconventional character of the legal analysis results from its gearing towards an assessment of the law- and state-forms. This takes place in Chapter 6. This chapter discusses whether counterterrorism legislation pertains to (or constitutes) a 'state of exception'. Based on the legal analysis in Chapter 5, it argues that homeland security signifies the introduction of a new, 'normal' (i.e. not exceptional) law-form, characterised by a radical expansion of the legal powers of state vis à vis the population and their concentration at the hands of the Executive. Law loses it unique, specifying logic, and increasingly becomes a mere instrument for political pursuits – something highlighted by its pre-emptive turn and its political targeting.

Chapter 7 is concerned with the dynamics around the legislation. It examines the way in which legislation is implemented by Executive entities. It also looks at challenges to the legislation posed by Congress and the courts, as well as those posed by lawyers' associations (e.g. the American Civil Liberties Union) in the name of constitutionality. By constructing a meaning of American nationhood based on constitutional values, civil-libertarian lawyers mounted a *tout-court* (political rather than solely legal) challenge to homeland security. Their resistance is assessed, and evaluated as limited (and ineffective) due to the very platform from where it drew its strength: constitutionalism.

The next three chapters examine how legal provisions materialise in institutional practice. Chapter 8 discusses the newly founded Department of Homeland Security (DHS). It examines its structure, its place within the federal Executive, its role and its relations to other Departments. It explores how the DHS inscribes sub-national (state and local) governments in the (federally defined) homeland security endeavour, implying that the autonomy of sub-national governments is curtailed. It also looks at how the DHS involves private sector entities into homeland security, through the distribution of contracts to private capital, and the creation of a heavily subsidised 'homeland security economy'. Lastly, it investigates the working relations in the DHS, which are set to constitute a model for the entire public sector.

Chapter 9 follows a persistent theme in legislation, to see how the stirring of police towards intelligence occurs in practice. It examines the re-invention of the Federal Bureau of Investigation as an intelligence agency, and the restructure of the intelligence mechanism of the US, which, with the introduction of the Director of National Intelligence, took a turn towards unification and centralisation. Moreover, the chapter appreciates that the scope of intelligence is becoming total: subject to intelligence is the totality of individuals in the totality of their interactions, and especially their political activity. Finally, it argues that the turn to intelligence gives rise to a new policing model, one which predominantly operates outside legal considerations.

Chapter 10 examines intelligence as a mode of government. It investigates its impacts on democracy and on state-population relations. The chapter examines the colour-coded terrorism warning system (Homeland Security Advisory System): the way decisions to alter the threat level are made, their impact on social life, the intelligence which informs them, and the role ascribed to the population during alerts. It notes that intelligence-led government is based on (allegedly) scientific decision-making, on the basis of knowledge thoroughly concealed from the population. Drawing form ancient and modern political philosophy, it sees this as 'government by experts': a mode of (biopolitical) government, based on effectiveness and incompatible with democratic principles.

The next three chapters explore the ways in which homeland security relates to the population. Chapter 11 examines how the state organises bases of popular support to homeland security. It discusses the Citizen Corps: volunteers' programmes initiated by the federal and administered by sub-national governments. It examines their structure, functions and the place of the volunteer in them. It concludes that these programmes describe a new form of citizenship pertaining to a new, authoritarian, form of state.

Chapter 12 examines the main forms of popular resistance to homeland security: the 'community resolutions' movement, and the resistance of librarians to legal powers and police practices targeting their work. It assesses the peculiarity of these movements, which are excessively informed by legal considerations, values and objectives; tries to explain the reasons they have concealed their political character; and shows their limitations.

Finally, Chapter 13 examines what happens when everything else fails: when all the hurdles which homeland security poses on popular politics are overcome, and popular political antagonism breaks into the public sphere. This chapter describes a kaleidoscope of repression of popular politics. It is effectuated mainly by the state (several branches and types of personnel), but also elements in civil society. It is mainly based on the multitude of post-9/11 provisions which criminalise popular politics, but also, occasionally, on whim. And it systematically targets antagonistic popular movements (anarchist, anti-war, Occupy, ecology), but also individuals expressing dissent in a piecemeal fashion. It claims that the principal target of policing is the political activity of the population; and that this constitutes the US a double polity: democratic for dominant capital, dictatorial for everyone else.

While Chapters 6 to 13 provide updated accounts of the emerging state-form, based on their respective findings, the last one – Chapter 14 – offers its full account. It claims that homeland security establishes a new configuration (a third phase) of the 'authoritarian statism' form. Authoritarian statism is marked by expansion of state powers over social life, combined with exclusion of the population from influencing the state. It is a normal-democratic (not exceptional-dictatorial) state-form, marked by the proliferation of authoritarian elements in its democratic institutional shell. It is a state-form which results from the need of the state to combat economic and political crises – but it is also a form which generates crises. This chapter compares the homeland security state-form to the pre-9/11 one, to claim that a new (third) phase of authoritarian statism is established. Connecting with the discussion in Chapter 3, it claims that the homeland security reconfiguration of authoritarian statism occurred in response to the – political and economic – crisis on the eve of 9/11. The current (post-2008) crisis is an aggravated reoccurrence of the 1999–2001 one, resulting from the political exclusion and economic dispossession of the population. Hence, the state-form which homeland security set in place is, with some modifications, still operational and managing the present crisis – and it does it, thus far, successfully. Thus, the state-form which homeland security has established has outlived it. In its context, the crisis is managed, but the conditions which generate it are being aggravated. As this leads to recurring crises, it seems that this configuration of authoritarian statism is set to persevere – possibly setting the design of power for this century.

2 Politics, the state and law: a strategic-relational approach

The social – inclusive sense of 'politics'

This book is about politics: the politics of US counterterrorism, and the effects of counterterrorism on US politics. I should therefore clarify what I mean by this word, especially as its meaning here is significantly different from that construed by politicians, the mass media and political science. Throughout this book, 'politics' refers to the collective work of: producing the norms governing the life of individuals in a society; creating the meanings and worldviews which give society a sense of coherence and direction; construing the forms and mechanisms of societalisation and interaction; setting objectives for collective activity; and determining the means, methods and resources mobilised for their achievement. In short, politics is the collective work of instituting, organising, directing and administrating communal living, a work which is co-extensive with society and involves everyone therein (Castoriadis 1983a; 1983b; 1994; Contogeorgis 1985: 15–24).

Unwrapping this simple definition, we see, first, that society can be said to exist only inasmuch as it is instituted, i.e. as it acquires a political form. Second, the institution of society involves everyone acknowledged as a 'member' and no one from 'outside'. The distinction between 'member' and 'outsider' is made by society itself, it is necessarily arbitrary, and is constitutive of each society. 'Outsiders' and events 'abroad' can, of course, influence society. But they can do so only in two ways: either through their incorporation in/by the institutions of society, or through violation and force. It is obvious that certain 'outsiders' can influence the politics of a society much more than even the majority of 'members' can. This indicates the development of channels of incorporation of dynamics 'external' to society into it; and that in some ways and levels society may expand beyond the national scale which, in modern times, we recognise as par excellence platform for societalisation. Third, a society extends as much as its political organisation does. A historical example helps to highlight this point: while generalised inter-national and inter-regional trade recurs several times in history, and while the 'world market' is the ultimate horizon of capitalism, the interconnection of social life in a global scale is actualised – and gives rise to perceptions of 'globalisation' etc – only to the extent that institutions are developed for the organisation, regulation and strategic direction of the world-wide market; i.e. only to the extent that the global economic framework is organised *politically*, and its political mechanisms carry weight comparable with those of the national scale in determining social life. Social organisation anchored on the nation (rather than the tribe, clan, of feud) is another example of the historically variable co-expansiveness between society and its political organisation. In short, '[s]ociety does not exist as an objectively given totality, but as the complex and unstable result of multiple political articulations' (Buckel 2011: 165). And, fourth, this definition of 'politics' signifies that there is no other source for social institution than society itself. As their sole creator, the social is also the sole modifier and destroyer of institutions. This is so because, while the social is exclusively responsible for all institutions, it is not exhausted in them. Social dynamics exceeds the institutions, and can be the driving force for their abolition and change (Castoriadis 1965).

By acknowledging society *per se* as the sole creator of its institution, and by conceptualising politics as undertaken by society in its entirety, this 'expansive' and 'inclusive' definition of politics provides a forceful argument for democracy at an ontological level. At the same time, it permits a crucial distinction between 'state' and 'politics', showing that, either as agency or as an area of activity, there is something in politics which exceeds the state. This distinction, largely present in classic modern political theory, has been increasingly abandoned by political science, which tends to collapse the category of 'politics' to that of the 'state', with 'power' being the currency which specifies both. By contrast, the inclusive definition of politics would indicate that any separation between the state (or 'political society') and a 'civil society' is, alongside the very institution of these spheres, the historically contingent work of the social (Contogeorgis 2011).

The definition of politics as the collective work of everyone in society does not inform on the modes in which political activity occurs. Two crucial factors elaborate, and condition, the initial definition: the self-consciousness of political work, and the division of political labour.

First, while the institution, organisation, direction and administration of society are by definition its own work, society is usually not conscious of this. This raises a distinction between autonomy and heteronomy. Autonomous societies recognise the social – themselves – as the instituting force; heteronomous societies (the vast majority of historical formations) perceive their institution as the work of an extra-social source (e.g. divinity). Consequently, politics is undertaken by those who claim 'knowledge' of the instituting source (Castoriadis 1980; 1983b). Autonomy has close affinity to democratic polity: self-government entails explicit self-institution (Castoriadis 1988a). Heteronomy constitutes an estrangement of society from its institutions and organs, and is akin to government by experts. In modern societies, the two tendencies are in tension. While recognising politics as pertinent to the human sphere, they resurrect heteronomy in the form of objective 'laws' (of nature, the economy/market, history, etc) which determine social life. Accordingly, there is constant tension between self-government and government by experts.

The impact of counterterrorism on the balance between autonomy and heteronomy is discussed in Chapter 10, but it is also an undercurrent running throughout the book. It helps assess the political role which state leaders ascribe to the population, and informs the evaluation of resistance gestures. Lastly, while my conception of politics is influenced by Castoriadis, it diverges from his in an important way. While throughout his work Castoriadis insists on the social as the sole creator of social institution(s), he reserves the term 'politics' for activities which are lucidly and explicitly directed to the social institution as such – politics pertains to autonomous societies (Castoriadis 1988b; Tassis 2008: 76–77). By contrast, I consider all activity refereeing to the institution, organisation (etc) of society as essentially political, even when its political character is concealed behind the veil of theology, science or technocracy.

Second, the common work of politics can be subject to a division of labour between a political directorate which formally undertakes all instituting and directing functions, and the mass of the population, formally reduced to executants of the decrees issued by the political directorate. A distinction is necessary here between political *process* and political *power*. Political process is a constitutive element of society, referring to the condensation of general objectives through contestation and struggle. Its claim to a collectively binding outcome stems from its aspiration to collective action. Political power refers to the particular organisation of this process as one whose outcome is compulsory. The inability of political science to differentiate between a 'binding' and a 'compulsory' character of a decision is symptomatic of the banishment of the social from the political process through a system of prohibitions and exclusivities. The process is appropriated by an 'autonomised' political system which 'acts upon' society (Contogeorgis 1985: 17–23). While this authoritarian settlement is a socio-historically specific formulation of the political process, it is so predominant (in social reality and its theory) that 'politics' is identified with the exercise of power upon the population by a political directorate. This monopolisation of effective social power divides the population into directors and executants, rulers and ruled. It takes shape in the institution of 'the state'. I should clarify how I use this term.

The state as a social relation: a parameter in social antagonism

General definition and type of state

While politics cannot be anything but an affair involving the entire society, this does not mean that everyone is involved in it equally. The institution of the state introduces a radical differentiation of political roles. It causes a division of the collective undertaking, and the monopolisation of formal political labour by state managers ('politicians'). Nonetheless, the state is a part of politics. Hence it itself involves the entire society, also in differing roles and degrees.

Society is neither uniform nor passive, but a dynamic field defined by complex interrelations and groupings. Such groupings become *social forces* when they develop a set of suggestions (agendas) for the institution, organisation and direction of society – when they become political. Political agendas do not develop in isolation, but in relation – concurrence or opposition – to others. The process of their formation and the actions for their advancement constitutes the field of *social dynamics*. The state occupies a critical position in this field. Given that the social field is differentiated and dynamic, and that all institutional (self-)creation is a work of society as such, I conceptualise the state as a social institution which is shaped by social dynamics, constitutes a terrain in which they are played out, and is an important agency therein. Epigrammatically, I adopt a 'strategic-relational' approach to the state and, following Poulantzas and Jessop, I conceptualise it as a social relation (Jessop 1982: 252–258; Poulantzas 1975: 125–129; 1978: 129). The emphasis on the social character of the state helps avoid the fetishisation of the state inherent in its predominant conceptualisations: the instrumentalist one, which focuses on the materiality of the state mechanism or the personnel who run it (e.g. Lenin 1932; Miliband 1969); and the perception of the state as an (anthropomorphic) subject, separated from society, and replete with its own will, interests, capacities and objectives (e.g. Block 1987; Krasner 1978; Nordlinger 1981; Skocpol 1979).

The definition of the state as a social relation that effectuates a division of political labour provides the general framework for its understanding, but does little to help the analysis of 'actually existing' states. It would be absurd to discuss, say, the 1970s Argentina with the same analytical tools we discuss the Persian Empire, seeing that they both are 'states'. Even the author of the most famous definition of the modern state was weary of general theorising, claiming that there is no activity which states always perform, and none which they have never performed (Weber 1948: 77–78). A general theory of the state promises to be a highly improbable undertaking, and an ungrateful one, returning very little fruit in terms of our understanding of any concrete historical reality. What is called for is a typology of states, so that the discussion can focus on specific types thereof (Poulantzas 1973: 142–167).

Distinct from historically anterior (e.g. feudal, oriental despotic, absolutist, theocratic), and pertinent to the discussion of the contemporary US, is the *capitalist type of state*. This type is defined in judicial terms, especially on the basis of the pubic-private distinction. The latter permits it to claim it represents the unity of an otherwise atomised society, and to monopolise coercive means. Its administrative functions are based on law and on bureaucratic rationality. The specifying characteristics of this type are that, operationally, the overarching purpose of the state is to secure the social conditions for continuing capital accumulation, while, institutionally, it is constituted as separate from, and external to, the economic sphere. In this manner, (political) domination is separated from (economic) exploitation and the organised force of the state cannot violate property relations. Thus, the capitalist state is charged with managing something (capital accumulation) at the heart of which (private property) it cannot intervene (Jessop 1990: 355–358; 2002: 37–42; Poulantzas 1973: 187–152). This disjunction is the source of dynamism and flexibility of the overall social configuration, but it can also cause crises (Offe 1984; Poulantzas 1978: 190–194).

In operational terms, the state plays a catalytic role in imposing and maintaining capitalist relations of production (Neocleous 2000). At the same time, it relies on revenue for the development of its capacities and the implementation of policies. This makes it dependent on capital accumulation. The logic, objectives and calculus of the economy predominate the activity, planning and institutional logic of the state, and the economy becomes 'ecologically dominant' over the entire society (Jessop 2011).

Regarding social forces, the capitalist state unifies the judicially atomised individuals of civil society into a 'general interest' defined by the state. Its normal forms provide a smooth way for settling intra-capital frictions, and for incorporating the demands of dominated classes into a political arrangement which guarantees the maintenance of capitalist relations (Poulantzas 1965; 1973: 130–135, 190–194, 274–278).

In this manner, the capitalist state is defined as a type of state operationally and institutionally inclined to guarantee the continuing accumulation of capital. Its various morphological features (territoriality, command structures, power modalities, mechanisms and capacities) are largely determined by the perceived needs of accumulation in conjuncture with its own capacities and strategies; and both these are over-determined by social dynamics.

In this context, the key social relations are those of class. Other social relations and antagonisms (e.g. gender, religious, linguistic or racial cleavages or the treatment of the environment) are, strictly speaking, considerations foreign to it. The capitalist mode of production abstracts the individual from its social attributes, makes it an independent entity defined by its ownership of commodities (including labour power), and engaging in contractual relations of commodity exchange. Thus, cleavages along the lines of gender, sexuality, religion, etc are formally indifferent. The capitalist state acknowledges legal equality among its citizens, who are differentiated only on the basis of their property. Non-class considerations are taken up by the capitalist state only inasmuch as they affect accumulation, and hence are, partly, incorporated into class dynamics, as opportunities of its expansion (e.g. introduction of women in the labour force), or as antagonisms which threaten to disrupt it (e.g. race, youth and women's struggles).

In this manner, the capitalist state becomes the manager of all social antagonism. It is able to do so because the capitalist type of state does not exist in pure form. Just as the capitalist mode of production does not, and cannot, exist alone in any society, but it co-exists with (and depends upon) non-capitalist relations (Koch 2011: 108–109; Poulantzas 1973: 70–73), the capitalist state is an abstraction. Actually existing states attain considerations which exceed those directly related to accumulation, and manage dynamics which do not pertain to class. But they largely do so by inscribing them into an (ever expanding) problematic of accumulation.

State-form

While indispensable for describing core socio-political arrangements, the notion of the 'type of state' is too blunt an instrument for the analysis of specific states.

States as different as eighteenth-century Britain and twenty-first-century Britain, or 1990s Sweden and 1990s Kenya, are all capitalist states and would fall under the same analytical treatment. In order to analyse socio-historically specific ('actual') states, the notion of the type of state recedes in the background, and that of the state-form becomes the main analytical framework.

By 'state-form', I refer to the *historically specific articulation* among: (a) state structure and state strategy; (b) the state apparatus and state power; and (c) the state and society outside its institutional framework. As each of these components is a social relation, the state-form is seen as the historically specific articulation of a relation of relations. I shall briefly unwrap each of these relations, to present the state as a complex, peculiar, matrix of social interaction whose stake is politics: the institution, organisation, direction and administration of society. In the old aphorism 'the state is the official resume of society' (Marx 1936: 156), the 'official' needs some explaining.

The state apparatus and state power

The state is an institutional ensemble. As such, it is neither a depository nor a producer of power – it neither possesses nor generates power of/by its own. 'Power' refers to the capacity of social forces to advance their interests in opposition to the capacity of countervailing forces to advance theirs. Nonetheless, power is only conceivable insofar it materialises in practices, mechanisms and institutions. Hence, the state mechanisms are sites of contestation and elaboration of power-relations among social forces. Far from being a mediating mechanism transforming the 'input' social dynamics into 'output' state power, the state apparatus – through its forms of representation, its internal structure and its actions – contributes to the shaping of social forces, and is itself shaped by their interplay (Poulantzas 1973: 104, 129; 1978: 44–45, 147–152; Jessop 2008: 37–45).

State structure and state strategy

The state is a terrain, a generator and an outcome of political strategies. As a *terrain* where strategies are enacted, it is characterised by selectivity: each state formation is favourable to some types of strategy and unfavourable to others (Jessop 1990: 260; 2008: 45–49; also: Offe 1974).

As a *generator* of political strategy, the state is heavily involved in influencing the balance of power among different social forces; elaborating the strategies of certain forces; and, in some instances, even defining the forces as such (Jessop 1985: 124–125; 2008: 36–37; Poulantzas 1978: 136–142). The involvement of state managers in developing strategies on behalf of certain forces, whilst taking into account competing ones, contributes to the coherence of state activity: 'This strategic field is traversed by tactics which […] intersect and conflict with one another, finding their targets in some apparatuses or being short-circuited by others, and eventually map out that general line of force, the State's "policy", which traverses confrontations within the State' (Poulantzas 1978: 136; also:

Jessop 1990: 260–261; 2008: 36–37). Thus, state power(s) and their coherence result from the selective incorporation of social dynamics in the state apparatus.

Finally, the state is the *outcome* of political strategy. Strategies originating either within the state or at a distance from it, implicate its structure. Their advancement shapes the structural assemblage of the state (its institutions and their hierarchical configuration), and its mode of operation. So, at any given moment, the state structure is the condensed outcome of past strategies, in interaction with developing ones (Jessop 1985: 340–341; 1990: 261–262; 2008: 42). Thus, social dynamics and its codification into political strategies shapes the state apparatus, and determines state power.

State and society

Instituted as identical to the public sphere, the state is represented as the expression of the general interest, in juxtaposition to the individual interests that rule the private sphere of ('civil') society (Bratsis 2007: 27–50; Fine 2002: 12–13; Foucault 2007: 233; 2008: 310–311). Its monopoly over institutive authority is based on the twin claim to represent the 'general interest' and to possess the knowledge of political science. On the pinnacle of the legitimate monopoly of violence, sits the legitimate monopoly of *logos*, and this, in turn, lies on the legitimate monopoly over valid meaning (Castoriadis 1957: 51–52; 1983b: 274–277; 2012: 39; Poulantzas 1978: 218–219). On this basis, the state is paradoxically instituted on the claim to represent the whole of society, while being only a part of it. It thus has to synthesise the, often conflicting, demands, agendas and strategies of different fractions of society, as they enter its uneven institutional terrain (Jessop 2008: 7–8, 79; 2012: 59, 61–63). The incorporation of social struggle in the state mechanism defines the expanse of this mechanism, its jurisdictional limits and spheres of competence – the borderlines between state and society. It also hinders the development of uniformity in the state mechanism and power. Finally, from a point of view 'external' to the state, the political strategies of social forces only come to fruition insofar they are incorporated in state power. Even when strategies of social forces are not directed to the state, they become inscribed into its matrix. Whether by being accommodated by the state, or by being seen as antagonistic and, hence, devaluated and repressed, they reverberate in the state and affect its institutional and strategic outlook (Brand and Heigl: 2011: 246–249; Poulantzas 1976a; 1978: 140–141).

These relations are broadly pertinent to all capitalist states. The notion of the state-form refers to their historically specific content and articulations. It describes the state, in every given historical moment, as determined by, and co-determining, social dynamics.

In this manner, we have moved from an abstract definition of the state (applicable to every state, and analytically meaningful to none); to an ideal-typical categorisation of states according to their essential attributes corresponding to types of social organisation; to actual, socio-historically specific, configurations of the capitalist state: the state-form. This downward spiralling in terms of abstraction (from universal-abstract, to actual-specific) involves increasing temporal specificity. The abstract definition is virtually trans-historical (or historically empty); the type of state covers entire eras, is susceptible to immense internal variation, and does not exist in pure form; the state-from pertains to a periodisation of concrete socio-political developments within the framework of the capitalist state, and can be further concretised through the identification of different phases within a given state-form. A key argument of this book is precisely that counterterrorism policy indicates a shift to a new phase of a given state-form.

Finally, coming full-circle, it must be noted that an inclusive conception of politics is a necessary pre-requisite for the development of a strategic-relational approach to the state. The latter's assertion that the state is a social relation, that its power is a particular condensation of the balance among social forces, and that its institutional framework is the contingent outcome of social struggles, cannot be upheld without prior acceptance of politics as an affair which exceeds the state and involves, to differing degrees, society in its entirety. Even though this premise underlies a strategic-relational approach, and is sometimes hinted to by its main authors (e.g. Poulantzas's (1978: 149–152) assertion that social struggles always have predominance over state institutions), it has not been explicitly acknowledged.

Law as a social relation: social and state dynamics

General definition – law as politics

Turning to law, I would, very loosely, define it as a set of collectively binding and socially enforceable norms that guide and regulate social life. This definition deliberately ignores the (crucial) questions regarding who and how produces these norms; who and how enforces them; their level of coherence and systematisation; the basis of their validity; or their field of application – the expanse and limits of the aforementioned 'social life'. Yet, even this minimalist definition shows law as strongly related to politics. Indeed, if politics is conceived not as a clearly demarcated, institutionalised or professionalised area of social activity, but as the process of instituting, organising, directing and administering social life, then law is an essentially political phenomenon (see also Loughlin 2000: 112–113). While it by no means exhausts the field (the practices, logics and institutions) of politics, law certainly belongs therein: even its lesser provisions affect the work of instituting, organising, directing and administering society; while its source, the degree of its institutionalisation and its very conceptualisation as a distinct, more or less autonomous, sphere of social activity, are elements of the political organisation of a society. Law is (and 'does') politics.

As the introduction of the state causes radical realignments in the field of politics, it also has profound effects on law. Concomitant to the state's monopolisation of political labour, is its claim to monopoly over the production of (valid) law, which owes a lot to its monopoly over the means of enforcement. This twin monopoly means that the collectively binding character of legal norms assumes, under statehood, the form of compulsory imposition (see Colombo 2011: 67–77; Loughlin 2000: 113). To be sure, much of law – notions of justice, provisions, procedures, legal concepts, etc – originates 'somewhere' in society outside the state. Still, in order to acquire or maintain its social validity, law has to be statalised, to become part of the fabric of state-law. Even when social law is not incorporated into state-law but remains parallel to it, it can survive and flourish only inasmuch as it is somehow sanctioned by the state: encouraged, exploited, co-opted, overviewed, guaranteed, or merely tolerated. Similarly, regarding enforcement, mechanisms parallel to the police and judiciary, ranging from patriarchal or religious councils to businessmen forums, may be active, but only as sanctioned by the state, as delegates of its monopoly of force. (For key contributions to legal (neo-)pluralism, see Santos 2002; Teubner 1997; for critical review, see Roberts 2005.) The perseverance of parallel legal orders is symptomatic of a lack of reach of state power to spaces in its territory (Ehrlich 1936) or to specific practices and relations. This lack of reach may be a sign of weakness or even decomposition of the state; it may also be a strategic withdrawal.

Thus law is not only a creation of the state, but also indicates its capacities and competence vis à vis society. But this inter-relating between law and the state is mechanistic and a-historical. To overcome the former malaise, we should recall that the state is neither an instrument nor a subject, but a social relation. Hence, the creator, guarantor, over-viewer and enforcer of law, is a social creation. The state *per se* and its relation to law are ultimately determined by social dynamics. In short, much like the state, *law is a social relation*. At any given historical instance, law is a particular *expression* of social dynamics, mediated through the legal framework: its code, logic, culture, processes, rhythms and rituals. The legal framework is, in turn, the outcome of past developments in the field of social dynamics, and their (selective) incorporation into the then existing legal framework – and so on. At the same time, law is a *terrain* in which social dynamics unfolds, as different social forces press for the institutionalisation of different, often contradictory, moral, political and economic aspirations, interests and viewpoints. Finally, law is an important *means* for strategic intervention in social dynamics, as it selectively endorses certain social interests, aspirations and viewpoints, and thus recalibrates the balance of power between different social forces. In short, law is both created by social dynamics, and a key factor in their (re)shaping.

Capitalist type of law

While this describes a strategic-relational contour of thinking about law, it does very little for the analysis of legal phenomena, anywhere and at any time. My initial definition emphasises the inherent social character of law but, as it strives to encompass 'all' law, it remains silent regarding law's content, its institutional framework, its functions, sources of authority, modes and mechanisms of implementation, etc. It ignores, in other words, everything that matters. Indeed, like the hypothetical general theory of the state, a general theory of law would have to accommodate not only vastly different, mutually irrelevant legal frameworks (again, Argentina and the Persian Empire); but, moreover, to account for fully fledged legal systems in stateless societies, let alone the endless variety normative systems whose designation as law is contested. As was the case with the state, if a study seeks to account for the legal field of any specific society, a general theory of law would be of little analytical value, and hence abandoned in favour of socio-historically sensitive analytical frameworks (Poulantzas 1964: 26–28).

To do so, I once again revert to a typology of legal regimes and, again, through a variety of historical ideal-types I describe exclusively the type which seems more pertinent to contemporary US society: the type of law set out clearly in high modernity – largely through the French and American revolutions – which I will call 'the capitalist type of law' (or 'capitalist law'). Law is represented as an autonomous sphere, separate from political, economic or other social relations, and subject to its own, internal logic, traditions, codes and relations; the 'juridical field' is constituted as an autonomous institutional outfit and logic (Bourdieu 1987). It has universal and egalitarian character, it applies equally and to all. In doing so, it abstracts the individual from all its social (and, pathological cases aside, psychological and physiological) characteristics (Fine 2002: 49–50, 57, 81).

The decision to speak of a 'capitalist type' of law, rather than of modern law more broadly, is informed by the correspondence between the capitalist mode of production, the capitalist state, and law. In formal terms, the abolition of, and dissociation from, privilege and dependency in law corresponds to the separation of economic exploitation from political coercion, a differentiation also expressed formally in the separation between the state and the economy (Fine 2002: 46–47). Moreover, the establishment, protection and expansion of private property as the central social relation is fundamental in the development of core juridico-political categories (Fine 2002: 105; Kinsey 1979; Loughlin 2000: 164–165, 169, 177; Poulantzas 1964). First, private ownership becomes a constitutionally protected right, and therefore untouchable by majority rule. Second, the character of ownership divides the social world – institutions, practices, and relations, including property – into public and private. The public largely coincides with the state; the private constitutes the civil society. Third, the private/social realm is legally instituted as atomised. It consists of abstracted entities (individuals or legal 'persons') who are nominally equal, deprived of social characteristics, and interact on the basis of contractual relations. Fourth, the contractual relation also connects the social field with the state, a relation codified in law as rights (Loughlin 2000: 161–162, 169–173, 198–214). Also, the notion of the legal subject as independent, rights-bearing and free to associate on a contractual basis in relations of equal exchange of properties, corresponds to capitalist relations of exchange and production – the legal form is related to the commodity from (Fine 2002: 57, 107–110, 142; Jessop 1990: 52–54; Kinsey 1979: 60; Miéville 2008: 106–109; Pashukanis 1987; Poulantzas 1964).

In operational terms, law is crucial in organising the sphere of circulation; and its predictability, publicity and orderly change help provide the clarity, stability and calculability necessary for capital accumulation, thus defining an 'elective affinity' between capitalism and the rule of law (Weber 1978: 162; see also Buckel

2011; Hayek 1979; Hirsch 1978; Jessop 1990: 57, 62; Neumann 1937; Poulantzas 1964; Unger 1977).

Finally, regarding relations among social forces, the abstraction of the legal subject from its social attributes tends to fragment and atomise individuals; the predominance of contractual relations tends to organise the association of individuals in a capitalist framework (the contract relation defers from relations of dependence, but also from relations of mutual aid); and the universality and neutrality of law, as well as the freedom and equality it endows its subjects, help naturalise property relations, obfuscate the actuality of coercion and power differentials, and dissolve the unity of subaltern social forces. Still, at the same time, it helps impose limits on domination, and secure liberties for those dominated (Bourdieu 1987: 830; Buckel 2011; Fine 2002: 21–22, 100, 142, 145; Jessop 1990: 62; Neumann 1937; Poulantzas 1978: 82–84).

The overall effect of the (perceived) independence and closure of law, is precisely the concealment of its nature – and of all its institutions and provisions – as social relations: '*social relations* congeal into a materiality imbued with its own dynamic, which at the same time obfuscates the fact that they are social relations' (Buckel 2011: 163, original emphasis). And, to come full circle, the formal autonomy of both the law and the state is the result of social antagonism between capitalists and subordinate classes, but also among capitalists. This calls for the administration of law to be handled by an entity distinct from the various agents of 'private' interests, and results in the forging of the state as an autonomous, legal subject, entrusted and empowered to implement the law through a monopoly of force (Jessop 1992: 208).

Moreover, a juridical ideology reserves a privileged position in capitalist societies (largely replacing the prominence of religious ideology in earlier social organisations). For expanded periods, it even claims the predominant position among all ideologies (religious, scientific, nationalist, etc), and therefore law becomes a determinant factor in the justification of political organisation, and in its very shaping, giving rise to constitutionalism, the rule of law (*état du droit*, *Reechstsaat*), etc.

This points to a tight inter-weaving between the capitalist state and law. Indeed, adherence to law is the typifying characteristic of the exercise of power of the modern state (including its capitalist type), as opposed to despotic forms of rule. Modern state power is exercised through, and *as*, law: the object of law is politics, and politics is largely codified in legal terms. The state is constituted through (and largely *as*) law, it is a legal subject. Law materialises through the state, but the state is also defined and limited by law. Thus, the state is not an agent of arbitrary force, but of *power*: its authority stems from, and is codified in, law (Contogeorgis 2007: 30; Fine 1984 (2002): 21; Kriegel 1995: 40–42, 58; Loughlin 2000: 28; Neumann 1986: 16).

Furthermore, law sketches out the institutional architecture of the state, defines the modalities, scope and limits of its powers, and describes the relations between the state and society. It provides a *design* of the *state-mechanism* and a *blueprint* for exercising *state power*. Still, despite its instituting function vis à vis the state, law does not have primacy over the latter (Loughlin 2000: 162). The capitalist state is never purely *état de droit*. It creates and changes the law, while much of its activity is not subject to legal sanctions. It can curtail and withhold its implementation, circumvent it and even cancel it altogether through invocation of *raison d' etat*, 'state of emergency', etc (Hirsch 1978; Poulantzas 1978: 84–86).

The above show the importance of law for organising and maintaining a capitalist organisation of society, and portray it as socially biased and selective. This has led Marxist legal theorists to proclaim law as a phenomenon exclusive to capitalism (Tuschling 1976, cited in Jessop 1990: 54); or as a phenomenon that will eclipse with capitalism (Miéville 2008: 131; Pashukanis 1987). Even non-Marxist theorists declare that 'most of our law is political economy' (Clune 2011: 197). These pronouncements tend to erroneously identify law with the capitalist type of law, or to recognise the latter as the (Hegelian) perfect form of law.

Finally, a key formal affinity between capitalist type of law and state is representation. The individual partakes in the processes of both the political and the legal system through representatives. Legal representation is founded on the expertise of the lawyer-representative, designating the legal system as un-navigable by, and incomprehensible to, the common people. Political representation is founded on the need to synthesise the individual wills and interests of the represented (and then of their delegates), into higher, collective ones. Still, a foundation of expertise is not foreign to political representation, and it is gaining prominence. While in the legal realm we are dealing with first-order representation (mainly one-to-one relations, where the represented can have important, even decisive, input in their representation), in the political realm representation is merely nominal, as the represented merge into an amorphous mass. They constitute a subjectivity only through their representative, and their wills and interests are defined by the latter without possibility of effective control by the 'represented'. These important differences aside, both systems are characterised by formal exclusion of open and direct participation by the population.

In strategic-relational terms, we see that, as state power is a condensation of the balance of social forces mediated by the materiality of the state mechanism; and the process of legal production and distribution is monopolised by the state, law is a codification of *social* dynamics. Furthermore, law also constitutes a codification of *state*-dynamics: it forms a particular structure and logic within the state, with distinctive institutional culture, ritual, history, reference, jargon, rhythm and biases; and, of course, a distinct state 'branch' is dedicated to its production, and another to its distribution. Thus, law constitutes a doubly codified expression of social dynamics – codified once through their inscription in the institutions and strategic calculus of the state, and twice though their inscription in the legal framework and its logic. Much like the state, law pertains to the part-whole paradox, as a particular activity which claims to embody the good for the entire society. This makes law a recipient of conflicting demands, hence a terrain of social struggle. Law also displays a 'part-whole' syndrome vis à vis the state: while it is only part of state-activity, it is expected to define the state as a whole, making it recipient of diverse demands and hence a terrain of intra-state struggles. This makes law the *outcome* of social dynamics as incorporated into state dynamics; an (uneven) *terrain* of confrontation of social forces through their representation by state personnel (managers, departments, parties, etc); and a key *strategic means* by which state actors intervene in social dynamics: both directly, and by using law to redirect state power or reshape the institutional biases of the state, including those of the legal system.

In summary, capitalist law is a *political activity* referring to the institution, organisation, direction and administration of society, and does the same regarding the state, of which it (officially) constitutes exclusive competence. Far from being an autonomous force or a self-referential field, it pertains at once to both social and state dynamics, of which it is the contingent outcome, but also a terrain, and a means for strategic intervention.

Law-form

While helping produce an abstract description and identify the specifying characteristics of a legal organisation, the type of law is too blunt a tool for socio-historically specific analysis. Once again, the legal organisation of, say, nineteenth-century France and twenty-first-century South Korea would be dealt with in the same analytical framework. This would flatten the important variations 'internal' to the capitalist type of law. For instance, is the institution of the state as a legal subject inscribed onto a written constitution? How is the separation of powers organised? What are the legally guaranteed rights, and what aspects of social life and parts of the population do they cover? In what ways does the law provide for state intervention in the economy? Does the law impose a minimum wage, social benefits, environmental protections, workplace safety standards? What area of law carries more weight (e.g. contract vs administrative law) and how does it affect the overall legal system? Are there parallel (quasi-)legal orders? What areas of life do they regulate, and how they relate to state-law? In order to address the myriad of questions of this kind, it is necessary to overcome abstract typology and focus more on the actuality of law. To do this, I propose to call 'law-form' the socio-historically specific articulation among: (a) the legal system and the content of law; (b) law and the state; and (c) law and society.

The legal system and the content of law

While the content of law constitutes an expression of social dynamics and an intervention therein, it is also defined by the structures through which it is produced. Law's content is *not* directly determined by state-strategy, but through the introduction of the latter in the mechanisms and procedures which produce law. It is conditioned by the temporality, tradition, and logic that prevail in the legal field, and by the degree of systematisation of law, its source of authority (e.g. constitution) and the ideological importance thereof. Hence, law's content is not just any odd expression of social dynamics, but their particular codification in, and through the mediation of, the legal system. In turn, the content of law contributes to a reshaping of the legal system, whether directly (e.g. adjustments to the institutional shape of the Judiciary) or indirectly (e.g. the introduction of class action; the permission for pre-emptive arrests, which implicate elements of legal logic like the singularity of the case or the presumption of innocence; or the growth of administrative law, which implicates the Legislature's role as the main law-producer). Thus, the content of law is the outcome of the inscription of social dynamics in the legal system, and the latter is, in turn, co-determined by the content of law.

Law and the state

However produced, law does not exhaust state dynamics, nor is it the only means for intervening therein. The degree to which law is the predominant means for state intervention (instead of, e.g. custom or fiat); and the main mediator of state dynamics (instead of inter-agency arrangements, inter-branch cliques or interpersonal relations between state and non-state actors), is the result of established practices, and strategic or tactical calculation in specific conjunctures. In every case, a key factor is the relative weight and power the judiciary wields within the state. At the same time, the position of the judiciary among state mechanisms, its relative autonomy and power vis à vis the other branches, and the adherence to its specific rhythm and logic, is concomitant to the importance of law in codifying social and state relations.

Law and society

This relation refers to the articulation between the ways in which the law relates to the population, and the population relates to law. The former comprise the historically variable 'expanse' of law: the areas of social activity regulated (primarily) by it; and the modality through which it is applied – whether predominantly punitive, corrective, accommodating, hortatory, etc. These vary across time, and across the social activity they regulate. The population's relation to law refers to the 'intensity' of the law, the degree in which it is inscribed in the mentality, social outlook, and subjectivity of individuals, and the way it does so (e.g. legal-moral conflation, constitutionalism, law-and-order vigilantism). The legal sublimation of individuals depends partly on the area of social activity in question, the degree and kind of legal regulation of said activity, and the depth of time for which it is inscribed in legal practice. Legal intensity is partly determined by the relation between law and other normative orders: parallel legal frameworks, religions, political convictions, moral and tribal codes, social mores, etc. Finally, at the intersection between law and society is 'access to justice', the (nominal *and* substantive) capacity of the population to make use of the legal system. The procedural, financial, linguistic and substantive exclusions and inclusions which selectively filter the access of different social fractions to law is of crucial importance for the justification of the entire legal and political system – for 'access to justice' is also 'access to state'.

In this manner, the notion of the law-form populates the abstract 'type of law' by outlining the articulation of its main features in any given historical period and society. It provides a middle-range level of analysis, which can address legal regimes and trends in their socio-historical specificity, but is also able to aggregate, generalise and compare the main features of legal arrangements across different societies within a period, and their change across different periods.

The relation between law-form and type of law can be illustrated by an example. The most enduring and informing configuration of a capitalist *type of law* is in the context of the liberal *law-form* – the latter constitutes indeed the archetypal form of the former. There, the public-private, state-society duality is expressed in the legal code as rights. This legal trope reproduces the antagonistic balance of market relations; and it is reproduced in the institutionality of the state: a tri-partite arrangement, where each branch seeks to limit the others, creating space for checks to state power. Legal provisions are impersonal, impartial, public and universal, something allowed (but not determined) by the abstracted – and therefore interchangeable – nature of the individual in capitalist law. While this arrangement (interwoven with the liberal state-form) has historically been the predominant configuration of capitalist law, this liberal *law-form* should not be confused with the capitalist *type of law*. The latter can take, and has taken, different forms: the predominance of (various areas of) public law in the context of Keynesian interventionist/welfare state-forms; or a withdrawal of (state) law in the context of neoliberal deregulation.

Two incidental points stem from this, and call for clarification. First, a strong operational and structural coupling between law and the accumulation process has been established by several authors (e.g. Balbus 1977; Hirsch 1978; Kinsey 1979) who attempted to derive the form of law from that of the commodity as analysed by Marx in *Capital*. Among them, the initiator of the trend Evgeny Pashukanis (1924) and Bob Fine (1984) use the term 'legal form' in order to refer to law. Their derivation of the legal form from the commodity form shows that they are engaging in an analysis at a high level of abstraction, attempting to establish relations valid in capitalism in general. Hence, what they call 'legal form' would mainly correspond to the 'type of law' in the terminology I developed above.

The second point is that the above interrelation between type and form indicates the possibility of a plurality of forms within any given type, meaning that shifts of form do not necessarily signify substitution of one type by another. Hence, our analysis does not need to leap into identifying 'states of exception' every time some serious diversion from the liberal form occurs, for we may be still dealing with another normal form of capitalist law. Moreover, normal and exceptional forms are not natural, trans-historical phenomena, as Agamben (2005) seems to suggest when he only identifies two modalities of law and (state) power – normality and exception – throughout human history. Both normal and exceptional forms pertain to specific types of law. Thus, the exception in one type (say, Imperial Roman law) may have preciously little in common with the exception in another type (say, capitalist law), and their comparison should be conscious that it traverses different legal constellations, pertaining to different social organisations.

Finally, there is significant inter-relation between contemporary state- and law-forms. As law is produced by the state, and describes its institutions, powers, and relations to society; and the law-form constitutes a condensation of state dynamics, it follows that the law-form is a key part of the state-form, one which can provide crucial insights regarding the latter. Nonetheless, legal logic and institutionality do not fully coincide with those of the broader state. Therefore, there is no guarantee that the state- and the law-form will fully correspond to one another. The elaboration, in certain conjunctures, of social dynamics in the state may result in state strategies which are hindered or even undermined by the existing law-form (or even the existing state-form). In such cases, the existing forms will stifle the 'unfitting' state strategy; or the latter will modify the forms so that it can be accommodated. This adjustment may be done, in the case of the law-form, either through restructuring the legal system and content (e.g. New Deal); or through systematically bi-passing legal formalities, thus weakening the law (e.g. neoliberal governance). In every case, the new configuration constitutes an element of the adjusted law-form. Importantly, as both law and the state are complex, contingent outcomes of social dynamics, they tend not to be unitary, monocot things, but assemblages of personnel and agencies often antagonistic to one another. The degree to which a potentially chaotic assemblage can manage to produce norms, policies and strategies which present some degree of cohesion, depends on the extent to which the hegemony of certain social forces is successfully elaborated in the state and the legal system, and manages to secure a social majority for its (active or passive) support. (Hegemony refers to the capacity of a social force to successfully represent its long-term interest as that of society as a whole, and hence to exercise intellectual and political leadership: Jessop 2002a: 6; Gramsci 1998: 57–58, 181–182; Showstack-Sassoon 1987: 111.) Social hegemony would tend to give direction to policies and strategies criss-crossing the various branches, agencies and departments of the state (Jessop 1990: 210–211; 2012: 53, 57–61; Poulantzas 1978: 136–139). Thus, the successful coupling of the state- and the law-form can be seen as symptomatic of a successfully elaborated hegemony. Similarly, increased gravity of the legal system, and systematic recurrence of the state to law as a means of government, indicates a stable hegemonic configuration; while the weakening of the legal framework and the substitution of law by other means of government indicates weak and unstable hegemony.

By setting out the definition of politics, the strategic-relational approach which sees the state and law as social relations, the inter-relation between law and the state, and the notions of the state- and the law-form as key areas of analysis, this chapter has unwrapped the theoretical framework of this book. As it lacks a specific subject, it must stop here. The analysis commences in Chapter 3, addressing the actuality of social dynamics, the law-form and the state-form in the US on the eve of 9/11.

3 11 September 2001: a social, political and legal charting

This chapter maps the social, political and legal situation at the time of the 9/11 attacks. It sets the law-form, the state-form, their associated accumulation regime and their crisis on the eve of 9/11.

The state-form: post-national, workfare regime

General outline

The last quarter of the twentieth century was marked by a deep crisis of a social settlement forged to sustain a model of accumulation based on high demand for commodities. In this settlement, a national corporatist state would arbitrate between organised labour and capital, promote abroad the interests of its national capitalist class, constitute a major source of demand through public sector contracts and infrastructure projects, and undertake the provision of services crucial for the reproduction of capital. This settlement largely resulted from the relative empowerment of subaltern social forces (especially labour and women) and it, in turn, tended to solidify their advance: The combined effect of publicly provided welfare, health, education and the commitment of the state to provide work for everyone who wanted it, resulted in an inclusive sense of citizenship, and to an increased share in the national wealth – and a declining share for capital. By the mid-1970s, this settlement faced overlapping, political and economic crisis. These crises converged on its associated state-form, the Keynesian welfare national state (KWNS). Its dismantling began (in the UK and US) in the early 1980s, and eventually crystallised into a transition to a new state-from, to a Schumpeterian workfare post-national regime (SWPR). The transition implicated the whole range of social relations of the previous settlement, and is marked by the abandonment of Keynesian and welfare policies and the adoption of directly pro-capital ones. To elaborate on this, it is useful to briefly present each of the form's key aspects.

The term 'Schumpeterian' refers to an accumulation mode based on supply-side intervention in open economies, where perpetual innovation is intended to strengthen economic competitiveness. There is a shift in the organisation and relations of production away from the capital-intensive, semi-skilled Fordist model, towards one based on flexibility and constant innovation in the organisation of production, its sources, products and markets. Education and research and development are introduced at the heart of the production process, resulting to an organisation of production known as the 'knowledge-based economy' (Jessop 2002a: 119–132, 250–254; 2002b: 204). This entails the subjugation of expanded areas of socio-political activity (education, health, public services, security and administration) to the logic of accumulation; and to a conceptualisation of social relations in economic terms and market calculi. The subjugation of knowledge by capital also entails the proletarianisation of large segments of the middle class: in terms of remuneration and control over their work, the 'professionals' increasingly became mere knowledge-workers (Liodakis 2010: 88–91).

The shift of focus from demand to the supply side of the economic process led to a re-conceptualisation of labour and the worker. *Workfare* is a strategy guided by the perception of the (social) wage as a cost of production rather than a source of demand. It involves persistent downward pressure on wages, and the transformation of social security into a factory for the perpetual training of the workforce to suit employers' demands. Work ceases to be a right guaranteed by the state; it becomes an obligation whose fulfilment is the personal responsibility of the individual. This means that, access to – increasingly scarce and meagre – social security becomes restricted and conditional. Benefits are not seen as a citizen's right, but as handouts to those choosing to be needy, and a burden to everyone else. Welfare provision is increasingly outsourced to the private sector and marketised. Access to social security is thus conditioned upon the demonstrated, unconditional, eagerness to work. These trends combine to construct the 'flexible' worker. Temporary, part-time, under perpetual re-skilling, scantly protected by law, badly remunerated and often uninsured, the precarious worker constitutes the par excellence subjectivity of the new social arrangement (Jessop 2002a: 141–171, 250–254; 2002b: 204; see also Crouch 2004: 36, 66–67, 90; Mackleavy 2010).

The spatial matrix of the state is also redefined. The national scale loses its position as the predominant site of economic and political strategy, while the scales below (local, regional) and above (international, global) increase their importance as sites for accumulation, planning and policy-making. The *post-national* element refers to the tendency to develop accumulation strategies at sub-national and supranational level, and to do so not only through the national government, but also through public-private partnerships pertinent to each level (Jessop 2002a: 172–215, 250–254; 2002b: 204, 206).

Finally, *regime* refers to a new institutional configuration, which involves not only state apparatuses operating through hierarchical command, but also a variety of public-private bodies, comprising governmental entities, representatives of capital sectors and select entities from civil society. In this inter-scalar, networked configuration of *governance*, the national state is the overall director and facilitator: it enables and encourages the leasing out of authority, initiative and responsibility to public-private mechanisms, and provides them with strategic orientation, arbitration and know-how. In other words, the state is diffused into a trans-scalar governance regime, towards which it assumes the function of *metagovernance* (Jessop 2002a: 228–246, 250–254; 2002b: 204, 207).

SWPR in the US, neo-liberalism and finance

The above is a nutshell version of Jessop's account of the SWPR, which is probably the most comprehensive account of the state-form at the end of the twentieth century. It describes the institutionality of the state and its spatial matrix, and shows the shaping of a new state-from as the outcome of social dynamics, and as a strategic factor in their re-shaping. With further elaboration, it can account for the state-from on the eve of 9/11.

To begin with, Jessop's is a general account, informed by developments in a variety of countries in either side of the northern Atlantic. A more specific look at the configuration of the SWPR in the US would complement the picture of its state-form.

Starting with spatiality and scales, federalism meant that sub-national scales were long developed as sites of strategy and policy, and the same was the case with public-private partnerships in policy production. Nonetheless, the sub-national scales (city, region, inter-region) became increasingly independent in developing economic strategies, especially during the 1990s. These strategies were increasingly elaborated and implemented by governance mechanisms, and were often oriented towards innovation, in search of competitive advantage (Best 2000: 460–461; Hooghe and Marks 2003: 233–241; Wallance 2000: 225, 231–238, 245). At the supra-national scale, the federal government was a driving force towards 'international governance' regimes and their principal beneficiary – advancing US-based corporate interests, and the hegemonic role of the US in the international scene (Jones 2002: 238–242; Strange 2002: 201).

While local governance strategies bore clear workfarist elements, and international governance was directly linked to deterioration of labour's condition, a directly workfarist tendency was emphatic between 1980 and 2000. It comprised stagnant or declining wages, a drastic increase of inequality, and the withering of social security. The income of the top 1 per cent of the population rose by 75 per cent, while for the 'bottom' 80 per cent by 25 per cent, thus reversing a 30-year trend towards income equality. The average top-managerial income in 2000 was 531 times that of the average worker, compared to 42:1 in 1980. Regarding wealth accumulation, in 2000 the top 1 per cent claimed 38 per cent of total household wealth, up from 21 per cent in 1979, while the poorest 40 per cent lost 76 per cent of its accumulated wealth. Consequently, savings rates plummeted and consumer debt and personal bankruptcies rose, largely due to rising health care costs. The reorganisation of the labour market resulted in a third of the workforce becoming low-paid, uninsured, temporary workers. Welfare was hollowed out through reductions in access, coverage and level of compensation, and the 1996 Personal Responsibility and Work Opportunity Act legislated workfarism (with bipartisan consensus), and caused mass-exodus from welfare rolls (Collins and Yeskel 2005: 17–20, 40, 43, 53, 92, 109–110, 118; CRS 2004d; Crouch 2004: 11; Hacker 2004; Wolff 2000). Welfare dependency is seen as a personal failing, leading to the stigmatisation of claimants, their reduction to second-class citizens, and their increased penalisation (Brown 2006; Mackleavy 2010; Wacquant 2009).

Therefore, the US was much better suited institutionally to economic governance on sub-national levels than most European states. It was also unique in its capacity to shape the structures of political economy within which other actors (states, corporations and bureaucracies) would operate, in trans-national and global scales; and was amply exercising this 'structural power' throughout the world (Barrow 2005; Palan et al. 1996: 121–139; Strange 1987: 565). Lastly, workfarism was far more advanced in the US than in most European countries.

The transition to the SWPR in the US is interwoven with neoliberal ideology and political economy. Neoliberalism emphasises the exchange- over the use-value of products and practices, and seeks to subject all social activities and relations to the logic and calculus of accumulation. Its Chicago School variation propagates a full withdrawal of state power from regulating market (including labour-market) activity, coupled with increased state involvement in subjugating all realms of social activity (family life, welfare, education, health, leisure) to the logic of accumulation, and in safeguarding it through force. Neoliberalism entails deregulation of markets, privatisation, internationalisation, mushrooming of market-proxies in the public sector, reduced direct taxation, and shifts in social policy towards workfarism and precariousness (Jessop 2010).

Apart from these supplementary points, some adjustments to Jessop's general account are also needed in order to describe the US state-form. I start from the 'Schumpeterian' component. While the emphasis on innovation and the cult of 'competitiveness' are undeniable, their connotations – namely, the predominance of production over circulation in the circuit of capital, and the dominance of productive capital (the sectors associated with the knowledge-based economy) amongst capitalist fractions – are debatable. Since its very start, the transition to the SWPR was related to, and driven by, *financial* capital, and came as a strategic response to the overaccumulation crisis of the 1970s. The SWPR form is a reconfiguration of the state to provide a good fit to strategic planning particularly tailored to the needs of finance. Breaking the national shell is primarily suited to financial interests, and so is the proliferation and strengthening of governance mechanisms, especially in supra-national scales. The relentless innovation said to be the driving force of the economy could equally refer to financial products. In addition, workfarism is ideally suited to financial interests, where wealth is produced in a relatively closed circuit and does not need a mass base of consumers. Moreover, finance-driven growth does not need an ample workforce, a condition which expanded to all sectors of the economy through the introduction of information and communication technology (ICT). Hence the phenomenon of jobless growth, and the decline of *capital's* need for the welfare state (health, education, material infrastructures) (Brenner 2009: 3; Gruppe Krisis 1999: §13; Trenkle 2008). The outcome was an astounding augmentation of the financial volume of the economy, and a dwarfing of industry's share: in the US, the financial sector accounted for half of corporate profits, while 97 per cent of transnational transactions were speculative (Fine 2010: 164; Lapavitsas 2009; Liodakis 2010: 22, 39–45; Nitzan and Bichler 2009b; Trenkle 2008).

In this manner, the predominance of the production of immaterials in capital accumulation, foreseen by Guy Debord (1967) as a trend leading to the full capitalisation of social relations and practices, is accomplished. The hegemony of finance is displayed in, and abated by, its ability to steer production to its ends. The dominant industrial sector of the 1990s (ICT) and its key products (computers, software, mobile phones), where best suited to enhance the connectivity, expansion and coordination of financial operations (Harvey 2005: 157–159).

Moreover, the temporality of financial transactions – measured in milliseconds – caused a drastic acceleration of social life, resulting to marked increase in stress and anxiety. This acceleration also implicated the state-form. The capacity for quick-fire policy became increasingly necessary for managing an economy dominated by the hyper-velocity of financial capital. It caused the empowerment of the Executive in relation to the other state branches, the acceleration of decision-making processes throughout state agencies, and the increased importance for policy-making of parallel networks which circumvent the official state. The 'temporal sovereignty' of the state was weakened, and its capacity for longer-term planning was undermined (Jessop 2008: 189–198; 2009: 149–158; Scheuerman 2000; 2004).

Finally, neoliberal strategies, while beneficial to capital in relation to labour, are especially privileging the financial moment of capital over its other forms. The disengaging of capitalist activity from social relations and institutional orders which neoliberal strategies bring about, enhances especially the profitability of the most mobile, free-floating, rapid-turnover capital which does not need to be valorised in specific times and places. Financial capital is differentially privileged by neoliberal strategies and structures in relation to other forms of capital, and often at their expense (Jessop 2010). In short, the rise of neoliberalism and the SWPR state-form it brought about, are driven by, and result in, the *dominance of financial capital* among capital forms, and upon social relations, institutions, practices and meanings.

The predominance of finance is connected to economic crisis. It emerges as a result of the 1970s' overaccumulation crisis which left capital without significant investment outlets, as profitability was low across industrial sectors. Accumulation within the financial circuit helped ameliorate this situation. Yet, the increased reliance on finance also resulted in recurring financial crises, the frequency and intensity of which have intensified since the relaxation of state controls and restrictions in the late 1970s and early 1980s (Brenner 2009: 1–11; Harvey 2003: 145–161; Jappe 2009; Norfield 2012: 113; Rogoff and Reinhard 2008; Trenkle 2008).

A last observation is necessary, regarding the relative importance of the components of the SWPR form. The four trends are of *unequal* value, for state strategy, and for social dynamics. In their finance-led, neoliberal configuration, all four facilitate intensified exploitation and inequality. The 'Schumpeterian' trend of constant innovation signifies the proletarianisation of the highly skilled, scientific and academic sections of the labour force, bringing the 'new middle class' under intensive *and* expanded exploitation. The post-national trend enhances the capacity of inter- and trans-national capital to manoeuvre, and puts pressure on the other classes, who are less mobile and largely rooted in the national scale. This results in the notorious 'race to the bottom' regarding work conditions, relations and (social) wages. And the regime trend, the proliferation of governance mechanisms, institutionalises the exclusion of popular voices from economic, social and political decision-making, and shields the political process from democratic channels of influence, control and accountability. Thus, in the SWPR state-form, the 'W' – workfare – is the crucial trend; the other three are strategies configured for its support (see Aronowitz 2002: 282; Tsoukalas 2002: 224, 230–233).

Post-national workfare regime: phase II of authoritarian statism

The post-national workfare regime pertains to the 'authoritarian statism' (AS) state-form. It constitutes a transformation of AS, a reconfiguration of that broader specification of the state-form, and a new phase thereof.

Authoritarian Statism phase I: crisis of the welfare national state

Authoritarian Statism is a term coined by Nicos Poulantzas in the late 1970s to account for emerging changes in the structure and function of the welfare national state, and intended to counter its crisis. The overall direction of this shift is towards 'intensified state control over every sphere of socio-economic life *combined with* radical decline of the institutions of political democracy and with draconian and multiform curtailment of so-called "formal" liberties'. AS is a normal form of capitalist state, which, nonetheless, incorporates, combines and renders permanent, several authoritarian features (Poulantzas 1978: 203–204, 209, original emphasis).

It originates in the KWNS and the role of the state in the reproduction of capital and of the labour force. The expanded state presence in the economy meant that economic crises could metastasise into political ones, and vice versa. The eruption of an actual crisis depends on social antagonism, and its acquiring an intensity which cannot be accommodated by existing institutional arrangements (Poulantzas 1976b: 294–302). AS is the evolution of the KWNS form when such crisis did occur. In fact, Poulantzas considers it as a state-form configured for dealing with *crisis as a permanent feature* of social arrangements in the late phase of monopoly capitalism (Poulantzas 1976b: 319–320; 1978: 204–207).

The main features of AS include the *transfer of power from the Legislature to the Executive* and its concentration at the upper summits of the latter, so that governing functions are monopolised by the Presidency or the Cabinet. The decline of the Legislature is partly responsible for the *erosion of a stable, abstract and universal legal framework*, and the proliferation of *ad-* and *post-hoc* legislation and prerogative powers. With the decline of parliaments, political strategy and decision-making increasingly occurs in a hidden *parallel network of power* consisting of multiple forums that criss-cross state branches and agencies, and bypass formal channels of representation in the state.

While blatantly anti-democratic, these trends were mainly developed to permit the state the scope and velocity to react to an evolving, unpredictable and devastating economic crisis. They combine with others which are focused on the political exclusion of the population, and attempt to quench the political crisis. Thus, *the role of political parties is reversed*: from platforms where members could suggest and even impose policy choices on the leadership, they become conveyer belts relaying the leaders' decisions to the members. This reversal is coupled by the *rise of the mass media*, which become the predominant ideological mechanism. Substituting the declining Legislature and parties, *the administration is inflated* and it becomes the central site of policy determination and social antagonism. This bureaucratisation of politics entails a *change of legitimacy* of the state, which now occurs on a techno-scientific basis, to the expense of 'general interest' notions.

Finally, while the transition to AS is effectuated under the leadership of the economic apparatus of the state, it also *hardens coercion*. In the context of 'draconian and multiform curtailment of so-called "formal" liberties', policing starts with the 'mentality' (the presumed intention) of the individual, and 'control is shifted from the criminal act to the crime inducing-situation, from the pathological case to the pathogenic surroundings', introducing pre-emption as a distinct policing strategy. A 'veritable arsenal' – legal, martial, and administrative – is established to prevent the rise of popular struggles, which remains 'hidden in reserve', and is mobilised only against acute antagonistic expressions (Poulantzas 1976b: 321–322; 1978: 186, 210, 217–241; see also Jessop 1985: 285–287; 2011: 48–51).

It is absurd to conceptualise AS without (some of) these key features. Yet, I treat them as historically specific symptoms, providing important but variable indications regarding the state-form. Their variation may not entail a change *of* form, but a change *in* form, i.e. a change within the compounds of AS. The *defining feature* of AS is increased state presence in social activity, combined with exclusion of the population from political participation and control, inasmuch as this occurs within the formal shell of the bourgeois republic (Poulantzas 1978: 238).

While intended to counter the crisis, AS also accentuates crisis elements. In comparison to a plural party system, the 'parallel network' and the administration are rigid frameworks for the representation of (different and often mutually opposed) capitalist interests within the state, thereby making intra-capital ruptures more likely. Moreover, the direct relations between state and capital undermine the state's claim to express the 'general interest' of the entire population. 'Thus the rise of authoritarian statism involves a paradox. While it clearly strengthens state power at the expense of liberal representative democracy, it also weakens its capacities to secure bourgeois hegemony' (Jessop 2011: 52; Poulantzas 1978: 241–247).

Authoritarian Statism phase II: post-national workfare regime

While AS emerged in an attempt to conserve the crisis-ridden national welfare state, it survived the latter and through adequate adaptation, was reconfigured into the post-national workfare regime. We can speak of AS because its core characteristic (intensified state control over social life; curtailment of popular political participation) is present and accentuated in the new state-form. Nonetheless, in the US the latter was forged through neoliberal political and ideological hegemony, and bore acute 'anti-state' features. Its discursive framework emphasised a curbing of the (national) state, to permit the self-determination of the (global) market.

While the state's economic function was not cancelled, it underwent important changes. The state gradually retreated from its welfare provider and entrepreneurial roles. It focused its activity to coordinating the (largely transnational) private economy; aligning social and political institutions and relations with the demands of capital valorisation and reproduction; and (de)regulating national and trans-national production, commerce and finance. This 'weakening' of the state involved augmented state activity, and its mechanisms and modalities were reshaped to correspond to the new functions. Its new role can be summarised as one of metagovernance, where the state assumes the governance of governance mechanisms. In its context, the state is crucial in instituting the market as self-regulating, autonomous and determinant social practice, and in providing it strategic direction and coordination (Belandis 2004: 68; Cox 2004; Jessop 2002a: 216–246; 2010; Panitch 1994; Wood 2003). This role involves concentration of power in the finance department and the central bank, which are the main bases of transnational capital in the national context and increasingly operate on a technocratic basis, away from parliamentary control (Wissel 2011: 225).

Moreover, the state's role as strategic coordinator of a prolific fauna of governance mechanisms entails a decline of its 'statist' organisation along hierarchical lines of command and control. The (meta) governance mechanisms are well suited to exclude popular participation from the determination of economic and social policy. From local committees to trans-national directorates, governance signifies a dramatic proliferation of the 'parallel network of power' and an inflation of its importance. Furthermore, the clear lines of command and control pertinent to hierarchy were also lines of accountability, something lost in the endless entanglement among governance mechanisms (Davies 2011: 59–61; Santos 2005). Thus, the crucial AS tendency, the exclusion of the population from politics, is strengthened in the context of the SWPR form. The most direct trend towards popular exclusion in the previous phase – the reversal of the party function – is now coupled with the exclusion of labour input in economic policy. Through the dismantling of corporatist structures, reorganisation of work relations and sustained direct attacks, trade unions are weakened and cease to be a 'social partner'.

Further, the rights-based notion of the 'citizen' is eclipsed, and state-population relations are conceptualised along managerial lines as relations between providers and consumers (Ball et al. 2010). Like in the previous phase, the change in governmental structures, concepts and modalities is driven by, and co-evolves with, the state's role vis à vis the economy.

The exclusion of the population from political influence means that the state's only interlocutor is organised capital – and hence the possibility of sustained workfarist attacks. This arrangement is crisis-prone. It weakens the state's claim to represent the interest of the entire society, and impedes its ability to engage in long-term strategic planning on behalf of capital. State strategies are exposed to frictions and challenges, both by subaltern forces and by capital fractions. The

SWPR is a form weak in hegemony, unstable and crisis-prone, as we would expect of an AS form.

To guard against political crisis, a drastic expansion and intensification of coercion occurred (Garland 2002: 193–196). Replacing the welfare net, an ever-expanding penal one is cast, that takes huge sections of the (sub) proletariat out of 'dependency' and into prison. This penal dragnet comprises surveillance and profiling of the potentially dangerous segments of the population, and intolerance to even minor offending. It constitutes the dispossessed, socially devalued (and, in the US, mainly black) segments of society, as permanently excluded from economic activity: a surplus population dealt with by force (Monahan 2010: 97–99; Wacquant 1999; 2009). At the same time, violence becomes the preferred means of dealing with collective political action. The quintessential democratic condition, the right to assembly, is subjected to restricting measures, on the grounds of protecting economic and social life. Demonstrations are often prohibited and repressed with increasing intensity (Belandis 2004: 213; Klein 2002). Lastly, policing is also undertaken by governance mechanisms: local governance platforms mushroom and they directly involve private sector entities in developing policing targets, methods and strategies (Garland 2002: 170–173).

In sum, we can distinguish two phases of AS: the first was geared to safeguard the welfare national state; the second towards the imposition of a post-national workfare regime. While the operational mode, tactics and institutional outfit differ significantly across the two phases, the essential AS trend – popular exclusion from politics – is maintained and intensified.

The law-form: *lex mercatoria*

The overarching tendency of the law-form from the 1980s onwards is the relative withdrawal of the state from legislation, adjudication and enforcement. This is expressed in a retreat of state-law from regulating economic affairs, a relative decline of public law and constitutionalism, and restriction of popular access to justice. These trends cause significant shifts in the logic of law, and to the outlook and institutional gravity of the legal system.

Starting with economic relations, there is deregulation of working relations, which is key in producing a 'flexible' workforce, and strips working people from legal protections and from the capacity to negotiate collectively their employment conditions. Employees are increasingly contracted individually into deals dictated by employers, remuneration is determined by the employer (so that the wage resembles a tip), and dismissal is dictated, without further ado, by the 'needs' of the enterprise.

At the same time there is heavy restructuring and significant reduction in funding for programmes (e.g. Legal Services, Legal Aid) facilitating popular access to justice. This is a key tactical move in the curtailing of the welfare state, as it helps galvanise the exclusion from welfare entitlements and labour protections by withdrawing the institutional means to challenge it. Instead, welfare provision is subject to a peculiar regime of contractual 'agreements', which would be unrecognisable in contract law: their terms, including sanctions, are completely arbitrary; they are dictated exclusively by one of the parties involved (the provider); and are coercive in character, since the other party (the claimant) has to agree or lose their lifeline. This legal regime intensifies class divisions. It also affects citizenship, which becomes fragmentary, financialised, punitive, and its obligations are piled only on the citizen (Daniels and Martin 2009; DiMatteo 2010; Green 1999; Handler 2004: 48–54, 58–59, 76–78; Sommerlad 2004; 2008; White 1999).

Beyond the national envelopment, there is a mushrooming of post-national mechanisms of legal governance, in areas like human rights, security and risk mitigation. Transnational governance of these areas is organised through the development of positive law frameworks. While termed 'constitutionalisation', this legal order lacks the democratic considerations, legitimacy and subjectivity which are essential to a constitutional order (Dobner 2010; Loughlin 2010). Rather, it antagonises the latter, as its norms tend to colonise national-constitutional frameworks (Krisch 2010: 3–9). The substitution of (national-democratic) *constitutions* by (transnational-positivist) *constitutionalisation* implies a shift in legal logic. Its principle-based orientation to an holistic institution of society in terms of the 'common good', gives way to outcome-based effectiveness, which renders law instrumental to the smooth functioning of the social practices it seeks to regulate, accommodate and facilitate. Its legitimacy lies not in popular input and accessibility, but in its capacity to help 'deliver the goods' in the areas in which it applies (Krisch 2010: 16–17, 21; von Bogdandy et al. 2008: 1379).

The tendencies towards transnationalisation, instrumentalism and de-regulation are most pronounced in the regulation of capital entities and their activity. Here the overarching tendency is the withdrawal of public law elements from commercial and company law, which are increasingly conceptualised in terms of private law, especially contract (Sugarman 2000: 75, 111). Essentially, the new regulatory regime provides for the (self-)regulation and even (self-)-institution of the market.

The advent of the contract form and self-regulation is associated with the need of capital entities for a type of regulation which transgresses the limitations of national law. This is typically attributed, without explaining much, to 'globalisation'. It can better be understood as a coefficient in a broad realignment of economic activity, which involves the shape and role of law. Economic activity has broken the envelopment of the national scale as it shifts from vertical integration to a networked, disperse outlook, captured in practices of subletting, just-in-time production, licensing, franchise, joint ventures and the frantic production and circulation of financial commodities. To support this shift, a normative form is needed which can operate throughout sub- and supra-national scales. Hence, large corporations increasingly arrange their relations to their peers, their workers and their host countries and localities through contracts bearing loose or no connection to contract law, and are arbitrated by extra-judicial adjudication bodies. In its purest form (especially in regulating transnational relations between big capital entities), these trends materialise into *Lex Mercatoria*, a regime self-legislated and self-adjudicated by its participants.

As law produced by its users, *Lex Mercatoria* shares the self-constitutive element of contract and its trans-scalar operational ability. Furthermore, it comprises a regime of arbitration which is anti-formalistic in character. Its basic norms derive from the shared 'commercial ethic' of its users, and are vague and open-ended. Its rulings are discretionary, ad hoc and secret, while access to it is restricted to transnational capital (Cutler 1995; 2003: 237; Dezalay and Garth 1996; Scheuerman 1999; 2001; 2004: 170–172; Scott 2004). True to its roots in the middle ages, *Lex Mercatoria* represents the *diametrical opposite of the rule of law*. Being the most advanced expression of the trends dominating the broader legal configuration, *Lex Mercatoria* will give its name to the law-form. (I use – capitalised – *Lex Mercatoria* to refer to the self-regulation regime for transnational capital, and *lex mercatoria* – without capitals – to refer the broader law-form.)

Alongside its transnational reach, the main appeal of *Lex Mercatoria* for capital entities is its capacity to resolve disputes much faster than formal processes of national or international law. Paradoxically, due to its success in attracting a large number of important disputants, *Lex Mercatoria* is becoming somewhat systematised. It is increasingly standardised in terms of rules and principles, adjudicated by specialised professional lawyers, procedures become increasingly ritualised, verdicts are accompanied by express opinions, decisions become precedent-based, etc (Berger 1999; Michaels 2007; Weiler 2001). *Lex Mercatoria* shreds a good part of the flexibility which made it attractive to market players at the first place, in order to respond to their need for predictability and universality. It seems that, at the very moment it eclipses formal law from intra-capital disputes, *Lex Mercatoria* itself becomes formalised.

The key traits encapsulated in *Lex Mercatoria* – the increased gravitas of the contractual form, of speed, and of instrumental logic – are also prominent in legal practices and relations beyond its confines. Thus, contractual logic comes to apply to, and enables the, commodification of spheres of social activity situated outside commercial logic. This is the case with resources and services previously regarded as public (health, education, transportation, water distribution, etc); archived information (personal databases); and the outcomes of research and knowledge (patterns, intellectual property, communal knowledge) (DiMatteo 2010).

The emphasis on speed affects state-law and the legal system, as law struggles to catch up with the temporalities of an increasingly accelerated economy. The 'motorisation' of law dates back to the 1930s, and is associated with the increased, direct involvement of the state in managing the economy (Scheuerman 2004: 105–117). In the current round of legal acceleration, the speed of economic processes threatens to render law obsolete (Santos 1993). There is marked decline of both formal and substantive regulation, as the norms they produce are stillborn, immediately outpaced by economic developments. This results in vague regulation, weak in both its normativity and its implementation. Accordingly, economic management largely becomes the Executive's own affair, especially as the Executive is the sole interlocutor of capital in transnational economic governance, which lays beyond the reach of the (national) Judiciary and Legislature. In important ways, the Executive *de facto* assumes law-making capacity, to the detriment of the other two branches.

This regime of legal governance not only permits capital to escape legal control and sanctions, it also renders it unaccountable for the impact of its activities upon society: 'externalities' such as the mental well being and family relations of labourers, the environment, or morals, are irrelevant to a legal regime which operates on commercial logic, and do not enter its remit (Carbonneau 1990; Cutler 2003: 195–197, 220, 233; Scheuerman 1999; 2001; Sugarman 2000: 101–108). With the subjugation of law to the economy, and the loss of its distinct logic, comes the undermining of its capacity to institutionalise social conflict, and to provide a long-term framework for social and economic planning (Kapstein 1994).

The enlistment of law at the service of market forces also affects the legal profession. While a few, select lawyers are involved in designing the legal architecture for a transnational capitalist class, the subjugation of law to the market changes the structure of big law firms. Working conditions become 'flexible' and extremely stressful, long hours prevail, and client-lawyer relations are led by the paying party, compromising legal ethics and the capacity of lawyers to determine their work. Lawyering in areas indifferent to corporate profitability is severely devalued: badly paid, insecure and subject to strenuous pressures by state exigencies and market competition. In a word, lawyers become proletarianised (Abel 1989; Hanlon 1997; Sommerlad 2002).

At the heart of the developments described above is the intolerance of capital's current *modus operandi* towards formal and substantive law (Picciotto 1992; Scheuerman 2001; 2004: 151–175). There is a mismatch between the law-form and the accumulation mode, forcing the reconfiguration of the former. The resulting law-form is a departure: from the rule of law, to the deal of merchants: *lex mercatoria*.

The last major trend in the law-form is the rapid ascendance of a human rights (HR) agenda, as relevant demands of popular movements and organisations took high priority in the practice of states and international organisations. This was highlighted in the creation of the International Criminal Court (and the special Courts on Rwanda and Yugoslavia which preceded it); the military interventions by the UN and NATO in Africa and the Balkans; the appearance of Universal Jurisdiction; and the expansion of the European Union, which was conditioned on the HR record of prospective members and the adjustment of their national law. The logic, philosophy and discourse of HR introduce a sweeping universality in the application of law. Furthermore, as 'species-rights' (i.e. universal and unalienable endowments of all individual members of the human race), HR transcend notions of rights and entitlement deriving from citizenship. They introduce a disjunction between legal subjectivity and political status, and thus, the potential for a cosmopolitan transgression of nation-based juridico-political categories.

The universalising impetus of HR fits uneasily with the tendency towards particularisation of legal rules, their differential implementation, and plurality of legal structures, characteristic of the *lex mercatoria* form. Still, in other respects, HR complements the latter. It contributes to the operative and institutional trans-nationalisation of the legal process, and to the decline of citizenship-based identifications in the construction of legal subjectivities.

Moreover, the dominant content inscribed in HR is also compatible with the general tendency of the law-form. Human rights comprise mainly negative rights (Miéville 2008: 102). Absent from the mainstream human rights' agenda are notions of political empowerment of the population, and notions of substantive social equality beyond the nominal level of non-discrimination. Notably, this constitutes a reversal of the dynamic developed in relation to citizenship rights in the post-war period. Moreover, special emphasis is placed on the 'human rights' of big capital subjectified as a legal person, which often reduces HR to a subterfuge for the imposition of neoliberal relations upon societies, a move frequently accompanied by brutal repression, which wrecks havoc on the population's human rights (Baxi 2006; Douzinas 2013). This is not surprising: if all law is, ultimately, overdetermined by the balance of power among social forces (a balance which the law, at the same time, helps define), then even more so is the case for the (legally underdeveloped) notion of human rights. The strategic hijacking of its agenda by big capital is symptomatic of its relevant empowerment over other social forces. Lastly, due to perceiving the state as a subject with 'its own' power, will and interests, HR is focused on the targeting of the physical perpetrators of HR violations. Yet, as the state is not an autonomous subject with its own will and interests, but a particularly mediated expression of wills and interests of social forces, the question must be asked: on whose behalf is a state acting when engaging in systematic HR violations? Human rights advocacy tends to isolate the phenomenon of massive violations, and to obfuscate its relation to specific economic and political strategies of specific social forces (Klein 2007: 118–121, 211; Marks 2008; Poulantzas 1976c: 281–285).

Lastly, HR exceeded the status of a legal imperative and came to be considered as the final destination of politics (Castoriadis 2012: 60), another 'end of history'. In this manner, it managed both to restrict the horizon of politics, and to conceal it under a juridicial (but essentially moral) veil.

Lex mercatoria and post-national, workfare regime

The law-form on 9/11 was marked by the withdrawal of state-law. This meant different things for different people. For citizens, it meant restricted access to justice, and weakened rights; for workers, it meant precarious working relations; for big capital, a private regulation regime. The retreat of legal mediation means that social arrangements are determined by force. Legal self-governance is driven by, and beneficial to, the fastest and more itinerant social forces: capital over labour and national states; transnational capital over national; finance over industry (Gessner 1998; Scheuerman 1999; 2001). As national judiciaries and legislatures are kept at arm's length from economic regulation, they are essentially charged with managing the *effects* of economic activity over society. They manage situations caused by processes beyond their reach. This leads to a key question regarding the law-form: does the withdrawal of state-law constitute a transition to 'law without the state' (Teubner 1997; Krisch 2010: 5)?

Even as state-law and assorted logics decline, a 'state-less law' hypothesis should be approached with caution. Even in the most de-statalised area of law the state is heavily involved, along with capital and specialised professional bodies, in drawing its legal framework. Here, the US assumes the leading role, so much so that US commercial practices and custom dominate the drawing of *Lex Mercatoria* (Cutler 2003: 234–235; Santos 1995: 292–293). It is, indeed, the state which actively privileges soft-law regulation of international and national trade, precludes its courts from dealing with trade disputes, and underwrites the binding, enforceable, character of private arbitration mechanisms (Cutler 2003: 225–226, 237–238). In short, while driven by capital, the process of de-statalisation of law is largely authored by the state. Interestingly, the state-less *Lex Mercatoria* gradually assumes state-law characteristics to procure some measure of stability and predictability. In fact, the rise of a parallel, private legal order is not a change of 'ownership' of the law (from state/public to capital/private), but a strategic withdrawal of the state which drains selected areas of legal practice from political considerations (Michaels 2007).

Furthermore, the national state is heavily involved in processes of commodification and privatisation, and a key contributor in their codification into contractual terms. Governance through public-private partnerships highlights the state as the main generator of the private contract form, throughout the different scales of political, social and economic activity – from town councils to the World Trade Organization (WTO) (Amstutz et al. 2007). In formal and quasi-formal fora of transnational governance (e.g. WTO, G8, G20) national Executives undertake the strategic management of the self-managed economy. The 'regulation of self-regulation' is a key state function in relation to the economy and its effects on society (Cassese 1998; Teubner 1983; 1985). So, the state is a key author of the decline of its law: it is heavily involved (through instigating, coordinating, selectively incorporating or simply differing to legal trends) in shaping the law-form.

More importantly, *the state is also changing*. The discussion of their respective forms shows a *co-evolution of law and state*. Law is significantly trans-nationalised, accelerated, and is produced and distributed by mechanisms of legal governance. Its norms lose their formal, systematic and conceptually hierarchical character, and increasingly become rhizomes of flexible rules and open-ended principles. The logic of market efficiency predominates that of public interest, access to justice is restricted, lawyers become proletarianised, and key areas of social activity are regulated according to the dictates of capital.

Thus, the law-form presents pronounced 'workfarist', 'post-national' and 'regime' features. Therefore, we are *not* witnessing a divorce between law and state. The pluralist 'law without a state' thesis is premised on viewing law and society as continually evolving systems, while negating this capacity from the state, which seems castigated to an eternal (westfalian) form. This is symptomatic of understanding the state as a juridical subject, rather than as a relation pertinent to social dynamics.

The ascendance of human rights is an aspect of the law-form which does not seem to fit the general contour of the state-form, and even contradicts the most authoritarian coercive trends in the latter. Still, there is scope for confluence and strategic co-option. The notion of rights postulates the existence of a state and a society, their constitution as separate entities, and an arrangement between the two, where effective social power is exclusive to the state, but its exercise is subject to certain codifications and limitations. Thus, without describing it fully, rights present strong affinity with liberal forms of the capitalist state. As the prefix 'human' postulates a biological, pre-political being as the subject of rights, the reach of the political regime described by rights becomes global (Douzinas 2013). Thus, the advance of HR augments the capacity of (certain) states to project power at an international level. This projection is often geared towards political restructuring which would transform the states receiving intervention into a structure similar to, and compatible with, the intervening states: into 'juridico-democracies' and/or into capitalist states (Esmeir 2007; Klein 2007: 326–359; Whyte 2010). Thus, the shift of emphasis from citizenship rights to HR is compatible with the post-national element of the state-form. Similarly, their promotion through multi-scalar configuration of formal and informal organisations (ranging from the UN, through national states and international alliances, to non-governmental organisations (NGOs) and social movements) shows their ascendance as compatible (and simultaneous) with that of governance regimes.

In sum, instead of a fabled rupture between law and state, there is co-evolution of their logic, institutional shape, scope and orientation. What passes for 'stateless law' is in fact the legal expression of a post-national, workfarist regime of meta-governance. This convergence is not surprising. The law-form is *a constitutive part of the state-form*; and the relative coincidence of their general movement is due to their shared nature as creations of the same configuration of social forces and strategies.

Economic crisis, political stalemate, and the 9/11 breakthrough

On the eve of 9/11, the SWPR state-form, and associated social and economic arrangements, were challenged by both the population and capital. Under fire from 'below' and from 'above', the neoliberal social, economic and political arrangements were in crisis.

From below, neoliberal strategies were attacked by a popular movement. Appearing, as out of nowhere, in Amsterdam (1997), it came to prominence in Seattle (1999), and passing through Prague, Gothenburg, and Genoa (2000–2001), it posed a clear challenge to neoliberal strategies and institutions. While traditional forms of popular organisation (unions, Euro-Left and Green parties) were important components, the movement gained much of its bulk, and most of its character, from the participation of Anarchist, Autonomous, Leftist, and Feminist political organisations, and numerous NGOs. The movement remained largely outside institutional party and union politics, its main field of public operation was the streets. While it had no strict unity of purpose, all participating tendencies converged in their opposition to the neoliberal advance and rejected the strategies of dominant capital and trans-national governance consortia. Furthermore, it was a movement in a state of flux, as constant osmosis between its elements led it to increasing radicalisation. Having repeatedly caused the cancellation of transnational policy-making forums, it was disrupting the 'logistics' of neoliberal strategic coordination and metagovernance.

Importantly, neither the affected transnational consortia nor national states attempted to engage in dialogue with this social opposition, or to incorporate, co-opt and institutionalise it. Showing the rigid nature of the SWPR state-form and its incapacity to accommodate popular opposition, its only response was an overkill of repression. The movement made its most massive and aggressive stance in Genoa, six weeks before 9/11. It was the last major global political event before the Al Qaeda attacks. There, following a week of extraordinary police brutality culminating with the police killing the young anarchist Carlo Giuliani, a march of half a million people branded the conferring G8 leaders 'assassins'. Rather than a mere problem of legitimacy ('democratic deficit') of transnational governance, this was political crisis in full swing, defined by a sudden politicisation of large parts of the population, and their mobilisation against neoliberal socio-political strategies and institutions (Day 2005; Della Porta 2006; Graeber 2002; Klein 2002: 3–40; 2007: 279–280; Notes from Nowhere 2003).

Conversely, from above, the accumulation strategy which gave SWPR its distinctive characteristics was running out of steam. The wave of mergers which drove capital accumulation for some 15 years was exhausted and, due to the astronomic debt it bequeathed to the capital market, the shadow of a global crash came to replace economic euphoria. Share values collapsed, investment slowed, and demand for goods was reduced. Financial crisis was spreading from the periphery to the core countries, the 'new economy' bubble was bursting, creative accounting was exposed, deflation reared its head, and neoliberal ideology was increasingly challenged within capitalist circles (Brenner 2009: 27–30; Chesnais 2001; Nitzan and Bichler 2004a: 320; 2004b: 5; Vergopoulos 2002: 180). In the US in particular, Wall Street lost over US$6.4 trillion – equivalent to 66 per cent of gross domestic product – during 2001, the NASDAQ lost 70 per cent of its value, and 1.4 million jobs were lost between January and September 2001 (Vergopoulos 2002: 51, 61, 200). The sense of a systemic crisis engulfed capitalists (Nitzan and Bichler 2009c: 47–49) and top economic personnel: the Director of the Federal Reserve, Alan Greenspan, was admitting a 'high degree of uncertainty', and World Bank economist, Joseph Stiglitz, was openly drawing parallels with the 1929 crash (cited respectively in Noctiummes and Page 2000; Brecher 2003). Attempted adjustments failed to either reverse the situation or stifle the criticism (Panitch 2000).

In March 2001, the US entered recession. While analysts agree that this was due to the exhaustion of the economic circle (see Vergopoulos 2002: 203), the approach advanced by Jonathan Nitzan and Shimshon Bichler permits a fuller understanding of the conjuncture and should be briefly discussed here. For them, 'accumulation' in absolute terms does not make sense. As a concept, and as a practice, accumulation is *differential*: each capitalist entity – each firm, corporation and sector of capital – tries to accumulate faster than the others. The target is to beat the average rate of accumulation. This relies on the ability of each entity to *shape the socio-political environment* in a manner which advances its accumulation needs and hinders that of the others. Whether capital entities achieve differential accumulation depends upon (and indicates) their intricate involvement in government, law, ideology, international relations, mass-persuasion, etc. Through them, they can define and impose a favourable accumulation regime. *Accumulation regime* refers to the social, legal, political and economic conditions within which accumulation takes place, and includes the *accumulation mode*, which refers to the specific model of economic practice which drives accumulation. Successful differential accumulation is proportionate to the capacity of capitalist entities to determine the rules of the game. This means that the *foremost object of accumulation is power*, the capacity to institute society.

Its differential character gives accumulation an intrinsically antagonistic, political character. In this context, talking of 'capital as a whole' is not helpful: the social environment best suited to the accumulation of different sectors may be drastically different (e.g. finance vs forestry); within each sector there is conflict between small and big, national and transnational segments, with possibly conflicting interests regarding taxation, labour relations, tariffs, etc; and within each of these segments there is also competition among different companies. The key player in the accumulation process is 'dominant capital', i.e. the entities (companies, conglomerations, coalitions, calculated at about 0.01 per cent of US capitalist enterprises) which can shape the environment of accumulation. In turn, different fractions of dominant capital may have different preferences regarding the optimal social environment for their differential accumulation (Nitzan and Bichler 2004a: 256, 270–272; 2006: 27–32; 2009a: 125–166, 305–333, 383–397).

During the course of the twentieth century, the US economy was alternatively dominated by one of two accumulation modes, which became increasingly well-defined and alternated almost automatically. The first mode is based on *breadth*. It rests on the expansion of economic entities' size, achieved by green-field investment or through mergers and acquisitions, with mergers gradually becoming the more important tactic. The other, intensive rather than expansive, is based on *depth*. It involves the expansion of earnings per employee, achieved by cutting production costs, and stagflation (inflation combined with slow growth or recession) (Nitzan and Bichler 2004a: 272–274; 2006: 35–36; 2009a: 334–397). These two modes of accumulation are sustained by opposing accumulation regimes. Breadth necessitates an environment of stability, economic optimism and cheap money. It is historically associated with tight monetary policy, reduced government expenditure, loose state control over the economy, and market deregulation. Depth can only advance its major tactic – stagflation – in an environment of perceived crisis. It is associated with protectionist measures and expanded state expenditure mainly oriented to contracts and subsidies.

On the eve of 9/11 the breadth phase driven by, and beneficial to, an *ad hoc* coalition organised around finance and the information technology sector, was exhausted. A well-established (since the 1970s crisis) rival coalition of the arms and energy sectors (A&E) saw an opportunity to impose its preferred depth accumulation mode, based on perceptions of scarcity (especially regarding oil, the universal good), and imminent crisis. Such a shift in accumulation mode was the only clear way to avoid the approaching crash. Still, dominant capital and its political representatives were hesitant, because a depth-based accumulation mode is extremely crisis-prone. Stagflation can easily spiral out of control. And, as it is wildly detrimental to the interests of working people and cannibalises small and medium capital, it intensifies the conditions for large scale, multifaceted social crisis (Nitzan and Bichler 2004b: 198–273; 2004a: 39; 2006: 279–284; 2009a: 370–382).

This approach to political economy presents strong compatibility with a strategic-relational approach to law and the state, inasmuch as it helps understand the economy as a field of social dynamics, rather than one of technique and science. Furthermore, it shows political power as inherent in the very constitution of capital, not as an external 'intervention'. In addition, the importance of the state and law in the organisation of (and alternation between) accumulation regimes highlights them as terrains of social struggle, and as strategic agents which define and privilege the interests of some forces over others. Its main shortcoming is that, having shown that the capacity to accumulate is (depended upon) political power, it ignores the question of the interrelations among the two processes and their mechanisms, and pays no attention to how accumulation modes are 'translated' into political action and accumulation regimes. Thus, politics and economy, market and state, are collapsed into the singular notion of 'power', irrespective of their different forms, functions and logics. This, possibly, results from conceptualising accumulation as a tango for two: state and capital. The fractions of dominant capital are the only active social forces, and the state becomes their affair. Hence, the alteration between accumulation modes becomes mechanical.

The notion of the *power bloc* helps overcome this automatism, and discuss political and economic dynamics in their interrelation. It refers to the field of social dynamics, and describes an evolving, often contradictory, strategic alliance of dominant social forces. Its unity is determined by the force which assumes the leadership of the alliance. The bloc aims to determine state strategy, and is organised in the state, with state actors crucial in shaping the common strategy of its fractions and in organising popular support for this strategy. In turn, power bloc strategies give state policy its general lines of orientation, and reshape the institutional structure of the state (Buckel 2011: 157; Demirović 2011: 265–266; Jessop 1982: 166; Poulantzas 1973: 296, 299; 1978: 127–139).

The dual crisis on the eve of 9/11 was combined with a shift in the power bloc as, in the 2000 election, the A&E sector installed its agents in the White House. This heralded a shift in the accumulation mode, from breadth to depth. Yet, there was a moment of indeterminacy in policy orientation. Dominant capital contemplated the dilemma between a crash with unpredictable consequences, and an accumulation mode which would severely undermine its hegemonic capacity, precisely when, under pressure from below, it could not afford such a thing.

The attacks cut the knot. Under a determined state leadership, closely aligned to A&E, 9/11 forged a topsy-turvy alliance of capital sectors under A&E dominance, setting the US to depth mode. Crucially, 9/11 offered a platform for legitimacy and support to an acutely anti-popular mode of accumulation – thus staving off some of its crisis-tendencies. The perception of an omnipresent, imminent threat, coupled with the explosion of militant patriotism, were the building blocks of popular support for a new era of 'homeland security' – shorthand for a new accumulation regime, and new law- and state-forms.

4 Heralding a new politics: the *war on terror* discourse

In all likelihood, 9/11 is *the* most written about subject in the twenty-first century. This makes easy to forget that 11 September 2001 was marked by a *lack* of words. Perhaps the ocean of words, produced by journalists, politicians, international relations' experts, political scientists, psychologists, sacerdotes, sociologists, artists, security experts, philosophers, aiming to make sense of the events, is commensurate with, and results from, the void in comprehension registered on that day.

Every society constitutes a cognitive closure: it organises its understanding of the social and natural world, and ascribes meaning to the events occurring therein. Nothing can make sense (or even exist) if it is not introduced to society's cognitive world and endowed with meaning – nothing but a *catastrophe* in the full sense of the word (Castoriadis 1989c: 365). 9/11 was a catastrophe, a moment when something burst into a social world unable to comprehend it, thus disrupting its meaning-making processes and categories. In the weeks after 9/11, 70 per cent of the US population was reported to have suffered depression as a result of the attacks, 48 per cent reported 'lack of focus', and 33 per cent suffered insomnia. Seventy per cent said to have cried, and 87 per cent stated the attacks were 'the most tragic news event' in their lifetime (Gallup 2001c; Pew 2001a).

The first eloquent attempt to fill in this traumatic void of meaning was undertaken by President Bush. He produced an organised and increasingly comprehensive discourse which endowed the events with meaning. He explained the events to the citizenry and, in doing so, he provided the framework for understanding 9/11, the world, and the role of the US in it. Exploiting, as it were, the paralysing aporia of the population before the event, the presidential discourse provided a narrative which reset the US political significations *tout court*.

Here, I examine this new narrative – the 'war on terror' discourse – to decipher the key representations regarding political subjectivities, their qualities and roles, and their interrelations – especially those between the state and the population. To do so, I examine exclusively the discourse of the President, which was systematically reproduced by the entire administration. The President is the most inclusive and authoritative voice in politics, and claims symbolic links to the population unparalleled by any other actor. The President is heavily invested ideologically, and ascribed to a multitude of roles. Apart from being the top manager of the Federal government and Head of State, he also is the personification of the political system, and a symbol of national unity, 'outside' and 'above' political antagonisms. Vis à vis the nation, he represents a unifying, benevolent and protective force (Barger 1984; Cronin 1977; Easton and Hess 1962; 1969; Greenstein 1965; Hetherington and Nelson 2003). Thus, for a study aiming to decipher the representation of state-population relations (especially at a time of ordeal), the discourse of the President-father is the obvious choice. Highlighting both the traumatic aporia and the President's exceptional status, is the fact that the 'rally round the flag' effect after 9/11 was *not* caused by the events as such, nor by their saturated coverage in the media, but by the Presidential addresses to the nation – especially those on 11 and 20 September (Schubert et al. 2002).

My study focuses on only the first four presidential addresses to the nation: the President's radio addresses on 11 and 15 September; his remarks after a meeting with the National Security Council on 12 September; and his address to the Joint Session of Congress and the American people on 20 September. This choice is dictated by the purpose of the study. If the main interest is on the relations between the state and the population, the presidential texts selected need to be addressed to the nation with large, rather than specific sub-groupings. Furthermore, as these are the very first public addresses, they are the ones which fill in the void of comprehension for the population, and build up the war on terror discourse. And, with the fourth address, all elements of the war on terror discourse are present, developed and coherently articulated – so the study can stop there. Of these four truth-telling monologues, the last – the televised Joint Session address – is the most important. It combined the elements introduced by the other three addresses, to produce the definite version of war on terror discourse. It was the polished outcome of, often conflicting, input from various power centres in the administration (Max 2001), and had a triumphant reception in Congress. The Joint address was expressing the general lines of state strategy.

Given the political orientation of my study, I (loosely) employ a Critical Discourse Analysis (CDA) approach in this examination, especially the strand developed by Norman Fairclough. CDA conceptualises discourse as a social practice, existing within given social order(s) – relations, institutions and structures – which it simultaneously affects. Discourse is *socially constituted*, as it is largely shaped within and by social orders; and it is *socially constituting*, as it contributes to their constitution, maintenance, alteration or abolition (Fairclough 1992: 63–65; Fairclough et al. 2001). As social orders are characterised by unequal relations of power, each discursive artefact is located within a complex, mediated, dynamic of power relations (Fairclough 1992: 67). CDA provides a framework for the study of discourse in relation to ideology, politics and power (Fairclough 1995: 1; Wodak 2001: 3). Here, I conceptualise the presidential discourse as utilising a meaning-less moment to launch a *strategic ideological intervention* aiming to impose *a new meaning on politics*: its main actors, their respective qualities and roles, and the relations among them.

The enemy, the US, and *we*: political subjects and relations in the war on terror discourse

We: the nation

The first words the US population heard from the President after the attacks were:

> Today, our fellow citizens, our way of life, our very freedom came under attack
> (US President 2001a: §1)

This is the core meaning of the 9/11 events; all understanding of the situation takes place within this context. We note that the description of what came under attack soars upwards from the tangible-specific 'fellow citizens' to the vague-abstract 'way of life' and 'freedom', without any explanation of how 9/11 constitutes an attack 'our way of life' or 'our freedom', what these notions mean or how can abstract entities be attacked. 'Freedom' constitutes the existential core of the 'we' subject.

This move to abstraction is based upon shared, deep understandings of the population: it is common sense that 'America' is 'freedom'. This does not need explanation, but it provides the platform on which further elaboration of meaning takes place. The movement from tangible-specific people to abstract national essence is reproduced throughout the first radio address:

> The victims were … secretaries, businessmen and women, military and federal workers; moms and dads, friends and neighbours.
> (US President 2001a: §1)

> America was targeted for attack because we're the brightest beacon for freedom and opportunity in the world.
> (US President 2001a: §4)

And, it is repeated and finally elaborated, in the Joint Session address:

> They hate what we see right here in this chamber – a democratically elected government. […] They hate our freedoms – our freedom of religion, our freedom of speech, our freedom to vote and assemble and disagree with each other.
> (US President 2001d: §24)

> America is successful because of the hard work, and creativity, and enterprise of our people.
> (US President 2001d: §43)

At first instance the 'we' subject emerges as a list of specific entities (secretaries, businessmen, etc) unified under their common denomination as 'victims'. Quickly and irreversibly, these entities are merged into the universal 'we' of America. The latter is identified with a host of abstract qualities that constitute its essence, producing a 'chain of equivalence' (Laclau and Mouffe 1975) which culminates in the political and economic system. The 'we' subject is identified along the equivalent terms of: America – freedom – democracy – opportunity – hard work – enterprise. It is this universalised, highly abstract, subject which is victimised and targeted by the attacks on its tangible, living components. Importantly, the 'we' subject is targeted (and hated) because of its very essence. This portrays the adversary's activities as existentially threatening, and deprives them of any causality and rationality. The sole reason for the attacks is the enemy's envy and existential hatred. Against it, 'we' stands in perfect unison in order to defend the qualities it embodies:

> [...] all Americans from every walk of life unite in our resolve for justice and peace [...] to defend freedom and all that is good and just in our world.
> (US President 2001a: §12)

While more abstract qualities (justice, peace, good) are added to the chain of equivalence, the important point here is the unity displayed by the subject. Inner differentiations are briefly acknowledged only to be rapidly dismissed into a seamless unity mandated by the common undertaking. This is expressed in extraordinary manner in the following statement:

> I am engaged in extensive sessions with members of my National Security Council, as we plan a comprehensive assault on terrorism [...]
> (US President 2001c: §1)

> We are planning a broad and sustained campaign to secure our country and eradicate the evil of terrorism. And we are determined to see this conflict through. Americans of every faith and background are committed to this goal.
> (US President 2001c: § 3)

At first instance, the 'we' is *planning*. This exclusive 'we' refers to the President and 'his' National Security Council. Then, the 'we' is *determined*. It is harder to decipher what this 'we' refers to: it might be the President and his Council, or the nation. Lastly, a third, inclusive 'we' (Americans of every faith and background) is *committed*. It is important to note that while 'commitment' is common for the entire nation, 'planning' is reserved for the higher echelons of the leadership, indicating some functional differentiation between sub-entities of the 'we'. What is astonishing in this statement is that it transverses the distance between the Executive summits to the lowlands of society within three sentences. Unity is a matter of course, a natural condition. The differentiated functions are precisely that: different roles undertaken in the context of a common mobilisation. This is discursively carried through by a slippage on the use of the 'we' pronoun: from *exclusive* referring to the author, expressing 'I + power' (Inigo-Mora 2004: 34); through *ambivalent*, attempting to assimilate the 'people' with the government (Fairclough 1989: 180); to *inclusive*, implying the President's right to speak on behalf of the people, thus assuming both authority and communality (Inigo-Mora 2004: 44; Fairclough 1989: 180–181).

The unity of the subject is so tight that in most presidential utterances it is impossible to identify which 'we' he is referring to. They range from dazzling transitions among different sub-entities:

> Now we honor those who died, and prepare to respond to these attacks on our nation. I will not settle for a token act. Our response must be sweeping, sustained and effective. We have much to do, and much to ask of the American people.
>
> (US President 2001c: §6)

to perfect absorption into the national-inclusive 'we':

> The United States of America will use all our resources to conquer this enemy.
>
> (US President 2001b: §4)

> Tonight we are a country awakened to danger and called to defend freedom. Our grief has turned to anger, and anger to resolution. Whether we bring our enemies to justice, or bring justice to our enemies, justice will be done.
>
> (US President 2001d: §5)

These statements also convey a conception of justice. Justice is completely dissociated from law and judicial institutions, and is apportioned by force, by the Executive. The defendant is merely prey – there is no defence and no explanations. The meaning of the word justice has shifted. From a truth-finding process involving excavation of facts guided by reason, it becomes an issue of divine right. *Justice becomes a purely moral category – its legal aspect is vanished.*

Described as a process involving everyone ('all our recourses'), initiated by 'awakening' and 'calling', passing through escalating 'grief-anger-resolve', to inevitably conclude to 'justice', the distribution of justice is an effort of biblical proportions. By implication, the subject that undertakes it is close to omnipotence. The 'we' subject is elevated to divine status:

> But this country will define our times, not be defined by them. […] this will not be an age of terror; this will be an age of liberty, here and across the world. Great harm has been done to us. We have suffered great loss. And in our grief and anger we have found our mission and our moment.
>
> (US President 2001d: §50–51)

The 'we' is a subject on a messianic mission. And it is supremely powerful: It can predict the future with absolute certainty, using the strongest modality in English language, because it is defining the future. The question is which among the alternating, merging entities that comprise 'we' possesses these abilities.

Before addressing this question, it is necessary to examine the discursive construction of the 'other', and its relation to the 'we' subject.

The enemy

Parallel to the construction of the 'we' subject runs that of the terrorist-other. The two subjects are alien to one another, but maintain a nucleus of similarity.

We have already seen the overarching significance of the terrorist-other: he seeks to destroy 'our very' essence. This is not just any alien or adversary, but an existential Enemy. The war on terror discourse script pertains to the concept of the 'political' as defined by Carl Schmitt. If anything, the presidential discourse will over-egg the existential pudding by overlaying it with notions of justice and morality:

> This enemy hides in shadows, and has no regard for human life. This is an enemy who preys on innocent and unsuspecting people, then runs for cover. But it won't be able to run for cover forever. This is an enemy that tries to hide. But it won't be able to hide forever. This is an enemy that thinks its harbors are safe. But they won't be safe forever.
> (US President 2001b: §3)

> There are thousands of these terrorists in more than 60 countries [...] sent to hide in countries around the world to plot evil and destruction.
> (US President 2001d: §15)

So, the Enemy is brutal, murderous, but also a coward (hides in shadows, runs for cover). This stresses the vitality of the threat, and expresses moral condemnation of the Enemy's practices. The Enemy is dehumanised – a move that Schmitt considered likely to result in its inhuman treatment (Schmitt 1996: 36, 54, 66). It is brought to close resemblance to a spiteful, coward animal – a hyena, perhaps (on the metaphor enemy = animal in political discourse, see Charteris-Black 2005: 181–184).

Crucially, we are informed that the enemy 'plots'. Certainly, the 'we' also designs before it acts – but it never 'plots', it 'plans'. The otherness of the enemy is conveyed by shifts in wording that describe identical functions in morally contrasting manner. And, in terms of policy, this little word – plot – maybe the most important of the entire discourse: it provides the first glimpse of a titanic realignment of law enforcement towards pre-emption:

> Al Qaeda is to terror what the mafia is to crime. But its goal is not making money; its goal is remaking the world – and imposing its radical beliefs on people everywhere.
> (US President 2001d: §13)

> The terrorists practice a fringe form of Islamic extremism that has been rejected by Muslim scholars and the vast majority of Muslim clerics – a fringe movement that perverts the peaceful teachings of Islam.
>
> (US President 2001d: §14)

The main problem with the Enemy is its 'radicality'. 'Remaking the world', and promoting a set of 'beliefs everywhere' are confessed objectives of US policy. Yet, while the US promotes 'freedom and democracy', the Enemy imposes 'radical' worldviews. There is thus certain compatibility between the US and the Enemy, and the critical distance between the two is provided by the vague but powerful proverb 'radical' (Sowińska 2012: 18).

Moreover, there is an obvious attempt to isolate the Enemy from its social environment. Not only the Enemy does not represent Islam, it constitutes a perversion thereof:

> Afghanistan's people have been brutalized – many are starving [...]. Women are not allowed to attend school. You can be jailed for owning a television. Religion can be practiced only as their leaders dictate. A man can be jailed in Afghanistan if his beard is not long enough.
>
> (US President 2001d: §18)

> [The Taliban regime] is not only repressing its own people, it is threatening people everywhere by sponsoring and sheltering and supplying terrorists. By aiding and abetting murder, the Taliban regime is committing murder.
>
> (US President 2001d: §19)

> [...] commit evil in the name of Allah blaspheme the name of Allah. The terrorists are traitors to their own faith, trying, in effect, to hijack Islam itself. [...] Our enemy is a radical network of terrorists, and every government that supports them.
>
> (US President 2001d: §22)

The enemy is not only a distorter, but a tyrant. In Afghanistan we witness the Enemy's handwriting, and it conveys an utmost degree of alienation. This is consequence of the Enemy's extreme disjunction from the Muslim world and the Afghan people. The radical division of the 'them' camp between a passive, pathetic and repressed general population, and an unscrupulous, murderous and blasphemous leadership, is crucial in delimiting the Enemy, and stands in stark contrast with the unconditional unity of the 'we' camp.

Yet, the determining characteristic of the Enemy lies beyond cognition, or description (Robin 2004: 159); it is pure essence:

> [...] evil, the very worst of human nature.
>
> (US President 2001a: §5)

This is the very first presidential reference to the Enemy, on the evening of 9/11. It is the headline under which all descriptions of the Enemy occur. The existential alienation that cancels the possibility of cognition recurs throughout the discourse:

> [The terrorists are] enemies of freedom.
>
> (US President 2001d: §11)

> These terrorists kill not merely to end lives, but to disrupt and end a way of life.
>
> (US President 2001d: §26)

Existential contrast cannot be stressed more forcefully: the target of the Enemy is the nature of our collective being, not just our bodies, but our essence. Finally:

> They are the heirs of all the murderous ideologies of the 20th century. By sacrificing human life to serve their radical visions [...] they follow in the path of fascism, and Nazism, and totalitarianism. And they will follow that path all the way, to where it ends: in history's unmarked grave of discarded lies.
>
> (US President 2001d: §27)

This is how the US intends to relate with the Enemy: not only total destruction, but historical annihilation. This statement sets the two protagonists in a course of total war, and predicts its outcome in the strongest categorical mode of the English language as a future fact. The 'we' makes an astonishing claim to power: not to predict, but to guarantee and command developments regarding past, present and future.

War on terror: a relation

The subjectivities set up by the war on terror discourse develop fully only through their engagement with each other. Their interrelation completes each subjectivity, and provides the discourse with strategic force. Still, these subjectivities are not genuinely dynamic entities but primordial ones, and their fundamental qualities determine the type of their relation. Unsurprisingly, the relation is one of conflict:

> This battle will take time and resolve. But make no mistake about it: we will win.
>
> (US President 2001b: §5)

> This will be a different kind of conflict against a different kind of enemy.
>
> (US President 2001c: §1)

> This is a conflict without battlefields or beachheads, a conflict with opponents who believe they are invisible. Yet, they are mistaken. [...] Victory against terrorism will not take place in a single battle, but in a series of decisive actions against terrorist organizations and those who harbor and support them.
>
> (US President 2001c: §2)

> [...] a lengthy campaign, unlike any other we have ever seen. It may include dramatic strikes, visible on TV, and covert operations, secret even in success.
>
> (US President 2001d: §30)

The relation between 'us' and the Enemy is exclusively martial. What is stressed in every statement is that the war-relation will be prolonged. Its characteristics derive from the nature of the two protagonists. First, as the Enemy consists of 'terrorists' and 'supporters', both entities are equally caught in the US targeting: *decisive actions against terrorist organisations and those who harbour and support them*. They will include two wars, and the rise of guilt by association in US law (Chapter 5).

Second, the secretive nature of the Enemy provokes a secretive response by the US: *covert operations, secret even in success*. The effort of the US government is cast into 'spectacular secrecy': institutional secrecy is openly advertised (Bratich 2006).

Third, the flux nature of the Enemy dictates that the terrain of warfare can potentially envelop every spatial and social site.

Thus, hardly a week after the attacks, the President had effectively described and justified the key elements of homeland security: justice delivered by force, guilt by association (including targeting of terrorist-friendly countries), pre-eminence of intelligence cloak-and-dagger *modus operandi*, and expansion of security to cover all social activity.

Once again, the omnipotent nature of the 'we' permits the President to utter his predictions on the outcome of the conflict in the most categorical style. It assigns the presidential discourse as fixed in an epistemic modality regarding the future. As opposed to the *deontic* modality (e.g. 'ought', 'should') which relates to persuasion-deliberation and permits for democratic decision making, the *epistemic* modality ('will') declares absolute knowledge of future-truth, and cancels democracy to advance government by experts (Dunmire 2005: 483–484). This recasting of the republic in terms of techno-military statism is, arguably, the most encompassing political trend of homeland security.

Underlining the existential character of the struggle, the ultimate target of the effort is the destruction of every hostile entity:

> Our war on terror begins with Al Qaeda, but it does not end there. It will not end until every terrorist group of global reach has been found, stopped and defeated.
>
> (US President 2001d: §23)

This is so, because:

> [...] it can threaten the stability of legitimate governments. And you know what – we're not going to allow it.
>
> (US President 2001d: §37)

So, among a host of vague and general justifications for the conflict, based on the Enemy's representation, this statement adds a tangible reason: the protection of international political order as sanctified by the US. The Enemy as a political antagonist seems to be the reason for the conflict.

This was an odd statement in the context of war on terror discourse, where rational explanations are rare. On the contrary, the dominant strategy is to portray conflict as a (natural) consequence of the protagonists' respective natures. The relation is properly joined only when it is saturated by existentiality:

> [E]vil, despicable acts of terror [...] intended to frighten our nation into chaos and retreat. But they have failed [...] Terrorist attacks can shake the foundations of our biggest buildings, but they cannot touch the foundation of America. These acts shattered steel, but they cannot dent the steel of American resolve.
> (US President 2001a: §1–3)

and:

> [...] night fell on a different world, a world where freedom itself is under attack.
> (US President 2001d: §11)

Most clearly:

> This will be a monumental struggle of good versus evil. But good will prevail.
> (US President 2001b: §6)

> Freedom and fear are at war.
> (US President 2001d: §51)

> Either you are with us, or you are with the terrorists.
> (US President 2001d: §30)

These statements portray a relation of existential confrontation. They do so by reducing the two protagonists to pure elemental form (good-evil), establishing chains of equivalence where 'US-freedom-good' combats 'Enemy-fear-evil'. Political reality becomes Manichean. It comprises two enemy camps, with no neutral entities, no room for negotiation and no bridges in between. This is encapsulated in the either/or form of the last statement, which constitutes a declaration of tremendous political force: full, unconditional support to the national effort or castigation to the sphere of evil. Worse than a direct threat of annihilation to those who do not actively support the administration's efforts, this statement constitutes a forceful, absolute closure of the political horizon. The relation between total confrontation and total subordination is expressed here:

> [...] the only way to defeat terrorism as a threat to our way of life is to stop it, eliminate it, and destroy it where it grows.
> (US President 2001d: §33)

The President's way is not 'one', 'a good', or even 'the best' way. It is *'the only way'*. The ultimate *telos* of the struggle is a fitting culmination of the discursive set up:

> The advance of human freedom [...] now depends on us.
> (US President 2001d: §51)

> The course of this conflict is not known, yet its outcome is certain. Freedom and fear, justice and cruelty, have always been at war, and we know that God is not neutral between them.
> (US President 2001d: §55)

In full paranoid style (Hofstadter 1965), the US emerges as the Chosen subject, and it is on a mission. US actions are God's actions, the US is a by-grace-of-God republic. Thus, politics is not just cancelled due to the existentiality of the struggle. It is reduced to a predetermined course to destiny. It is *not a human affair at all*.

A different 'we': the state vs the population

While the existential struggle commands the seamless unity of the Nation, it also dictates some differentiation among distinguishable sub-entities of the 'we' subject. There is a state-entity undertaking expanded activity. At its summit, the President plans, oversees, and directs the entire effort:

> I implemented our government's emergency response plans. Our military is powerful, and it's prepared.
> (US President 2001a: §6)

Yet, the President does more. As we have already seen, it is he who explains the situation and its stakes, portrays the two protagonists, defines their relation and raises the unified 'we' subject to divine status. Moreover, he defines the functions pertinent to each of the 'we' sub-entities. He determines the activity of the state-entity and requests the population-entity to act in certain ways. The two entities are brought together in their allocated functions:

> Many will be involved in this effort, from FBI agents to intelligence operatives to the reservists we have called to active duty. All deserve our thanks, and all have our prayers. And tonight, [...] I have a message for our military: Be ready. I've called the Armed Forces to alert, and there is a reason. The hour is coming when America will act, and you will make us proud.
> (US President 2001d: §34)

This statement designates action as a state monopoly. Within the state, action is the preserve of the Executive. And, within the Executive, the security mechanism – police, intelligence and military – are the most active and valued entities. By contrast, Congress is deprived of political initiative. Its purpose is to showcase national unity (TV coverage on the evening of 9/11 of Republican and Democrat members singing 'God Bless America' in unison), and to provide the funds for the effort (US President 2001d: §7). Congress is effectively a privileged spectator of the mobilisation. For its part, the population-entity is proud, grateful and dependent on the state. Much more than a technical differentiation of functions, the discourse designates a relation between the state and the population. This relation was defined on day one:

> Our first priority is to get help to those who have been injured, and to take every precaution to protect our citizens at home and around the world from further attacks.
>
> (US President 2001a: §7)

Or, more clearly:

> Those in authority should take appropriate precautions to protect our citizens.
> (US President 2001b: §6)

This protected citizenry has its role set out:

> We have seen the unfurling of flags, the lighting of candles, the giving of blood, the saying of prayers.
> (US President 2001d: §3)

> [...] amazing spirit of sacrifice and patriotism and defiance. I met with rescuers who have worked past exhaustion, who cheered for our country and the great cause we have entered.
> (US President 2001c: §4)

> American people at their very best everywhere in America. Citizens have come together to pray, to give blood, to fly our country's flag.
> (US President 2001c: §8)

These statements appear to be reports on facts. Yet, the positive evaluation of the reported behaviours constitutes them as covert imperatives ('hortatory reports') (Fairclough 2003: 96). They describe not so much what the population actually does, but what it should do: nurse the victims; pray; fly the flag; and display patriotic spirit. Another set of requests is more explicit:

> I ask you to live your lives, and hug your children. [...] to be calm and resolute.
> (US President 2001d: §38)

> I ask for your patience, with the delays and inconveniences that may accompany tighter security; and for your patience in what will be a long struggle.
> (US President 2001d: §42)

> I ask your continued participation and confidence in the American economy.
> (US President 2001d: §43)

> [...] continue praying for the victims of terror and their families, for those in uniform, and for our great country.
> (US President 2001d: §44)

Resilience, patience and trust in the government – the political role reserved for the population is thoroughly passive. While the unified 'we' enters the 'long struggle', the population sub-entity is requested to lick its wounds, pray excessively, wait until it is over and, above all, to 'cheer for our country and the great cause we have entered'. Essentially, the political position of the US population is identical with that of the Afghan population: they are both spectators and victims of history – of history made by their (legitimate or tyrannical) leaders, according to their pre-determination by their respective, contrasting natures. As the structure of the leaders-led relation is identical in both camps, their difference lies solely on the contrasting character of the leading entities: the Afghans are a passive, victimised population, oppressed by a 'brutal regime'. The Americans are an (equally passive) population which is nonetheless unified with its 'democratic government' into a single subjectivity.

Therefore, while the unitary 'we' enters an existential mobilisation whose aim is nothing less than settling the fate of the human race, the population-we is restricted to the sidelines. This is because the unitary 'we' has never entered anything. All activity was determined, initiated and undertaken by the state, with the population reduced to expressions of blind faith.

The meaning of homeland security

Within just ten days after 9/11, the presidential discourse had outlined the key features of homeland security, without detail, but with astonishing clarity, thus indicating that homeland security was a comprehensive political project. The key formulation has been the construction of the Enemy and its relation to the US. Political reality is represented as a closed, exclusive relation between two principal subjects; and these subjects are structurally identical but substantially opposite, like a picture and its negative. They both embody pure essences: 'freedom-good' or 'fear-evil'. This relation of symmetrical opposition justifies the adoption and pre-eminence of specific modalities of power by the 'we' subject. As the Enemy is secretive ('lurks in the shadows') secret intelligence is key; as the Enemy can be anyone, anywhere, surveillance of all places, relations and activities is necessary; as the Enemy 'plots', pre-emption is paramount; as the Enemy depends on third-party support, war against 'harbouring' states is justified, and so is the legal equation of 'material support' with terrorism. And, as the Enemy is 'evil', justice is already pronounced.

Against the existential threat of the Enemy, the 'we' unites, and marches on to battle. A Schmittian conception of the political as *polemos* – existential warfare

– is obvious. If anything, presidential discourse exceeds it: first by investing the 'we' and 'Enemy' subjectivities with opposing, primordial, moral significations (good – evil) thus justifying, potentially, the inhuman treatment of the Enemy; and, second, by vesting the 'we' subject with divine power and apocalyptic force, enabling it to guarantee the outcome of cosmo-historical events.

The friend-enemy set up, and the omnipotence and unity of the 'we' subject, form a discursive strategy which conceals the impotence ascribed to the population in homeland security politics. While the unified 'we' is omnipotent, the population-entity is bereft of any capacity to initiate, determine, control or influence action. Action is monopolised by the state-entity and, within the latter, it is the special preserve of the Executive's security mechanism. The population is reduced to passive matter, whose maximum (permissible) input in politics is to cheerlead the efforts of the Executive. It participates in the omnipotence of the 'we' only through identification with the state. The inflation of the unitary 'we' power is in fact *the inflation of the power of the state vis à vis the population*. The moment that the 'we' subject is represented as a perfect people-leadership unity, is precisely the moment when the power-relation between these two entities becomes most unequal (Robin 2004: 23).

Therefore, war on terror discourse outlines the fundamental political relations of homeland security. It implies a move towards concentration of power at the security apparatus, and relative marginalisation of the Legislature, the Judiciary, and the non-security components of the Executive. Most importantly, it indicates a relapse of the state-population relationship to one of obedience in exchange for protection (Hobbes 2008). In the context of lethal threat and existential battle, failure to comply with the role designated for the population – by questioning, disagreeing or protesting the policies of the government – will result in banishment from the safety of the 'we', and association with the Enemy.

Politics is not only placed beyond the reach of the population but, strictly speaking, does not exist. Neither of the two protagonists practices it. The Enemy does what it does ('fear', 'cruelty') only because it is compelled by its essence ('evil'). Surprisingly, even the omnipotent state subject is about to re-make the world not in accordance to its will, but in affirmation of its nature ('freedom', 'good') and to the duty and destiny allocated to it by an extra-social, supernatural power (Sowińska 2012: 17). The homeland security regime is an order of heteronomy, founded in the concealment of the social character of politics.

The war on terror discourse: one nation, one issue, one narrative

The president goes on (and on ...)

The political representations of the war on terror discourse (a Manichean conception of the world; the reduction of politics to *polemos*; the apotheosis of the armed mechanisms of the state; the pre-eminence of the Executive; the radical power-differential between state and population, and its concealment; and the concealment of political logic and agency) constitute a narrative that dominated US political discourse in the first years of the twenty-first century. Far from being restricted to the early post-9/11 period, war on terror discourse was the only language which President Bush would speak. Over a third of his presidential addresses were dedicated to some aspect of security policy, and pertained to the war on terror discourse. For instance, in July 2005, the point of an address commenting on the London attacks was that:

> The terrorists cannot shake our will. America and its allies will act decisively, because we know that the future of civilization is at stake in this struggle, and we know that the cause of freedom will prevail.
> (US President 2005)

While war on terror discourse dominates security-related statements, it is not restricted to security issues. Addressing the nation on 20 October 2001 from Shanghai, where he was attending a meeting of the Pacific Realm Nations, the President recasts the war on terror narrative to discuss trade issues. First, he expands the 'we' subject to the international realm, so that it incorporates the Pacific Realm Nations (Australia, Canada, China, Japan and Russia). These are included in the 'we' camp due to their quality as 'friends', 'allies' and 'trade partners' of the US, and by this token constitute 'civilized nations'. A synonymy occurs, identifying 'trading partner' with 'civilised' (US President 2001e: §1–2). The civilised world is united in facing a common threat: 'if we do not stand again terrorism now, every civilised nation will at some point be its target' (US President 2001e: §6). And the action they undertake is two-pronged: destroying the Enemy's network 'wherever it is found', while 'building an enduring prosperity that promises more opportunity and better lives for all the world people'. A one-on-one juxtaposition is made between envy-resentment-anger, and growth-trade-democracy (US President 2001e: §6). In other words, neoliberal economic policy is a *component* in an overarching security strategy. Then, again, what the Enemy seeks to destroy, and this strategy seeks to secure, is a specific organisation of the economy. After all, 'the terrorists attacked the World Trade Centre'. They did so, because they understand 'that trade brings freedom and hope' – and we 'advance world trade, because we know that trade can conquer poverty and despair' (US President 2001e: §9). The address establishes extraordinary hyponimies, synonimies and chains of equivalence, between we, the civilised word, trade, growth, democracy, the World Trade Center, prosperity, freedom, opportunities, better lives, openness, success; *versus*: evil, terrorism, terrorist network, evil at heart, envious, resentful, angry, hateful, fear trade. Trade is identified as the source of all that is good, and hating trade is associated with evil.

The Shanghai address blended homeland security and neoliberal economics, incorporated economic affairs into the war on terror narrative, and thus expanded the remit of war on terror discourse to issues far beyond its initial specification. Four years later, the message remained unaltered: 'These barbaric attacks occurred as world leaders gathered in Scotland for the G8 summit. While terrorists were killing innocent men and women in London, leaders at the G8 were discussing how free nations can combat poverty and HIV/AIDS, create a cleaner environment, and improve the lives of people everywhere' (US President 2005: §2). The 'dialectic' whereas terrorism targets trade, which, in turn is a key resource in combating terrorism became a permanent fixture on addresses with an international economy thematic (e.g. US President 2006).

The new status of the economy as a key component (target and weapon) in a security effort, rather than an end in itself, is also conveyed in relation to the national economy: 'the terrorist attacks [...] hit our economy hard' (US President 2001g); 'we fight a war at home, and part of the war we fight is to make sure that our economy continues to grow' (US President 2001f). To the extent that economic policy keeps an autonomous status, it ranks third in the list of political priorities, behind National Security (the international side of counterterrorism) and Homeland Security (its domestic side) (US President 2002b). The economy is not only outranked by security, but also conditioned by it. Thus, the President boasts both his public sector expenditure reductions *and* the generous increases for defence and homeland security. The expenditures which will not be tolerated are those that have 'nothing to do with a national emergency' – for example funding for public housing (US President 2002d). In short: 'Congress must control its enormous appetite for excessive spending so we can meet our national priorities' (US President 2002c).

Moreover, the modalities of war on terror discourse define the meaning of economic activity. First, economic issues become a matter of outmost *urgency*. They are often addressed in martial terms, and Congress is constantly harassed to act quickly (US President 2001h; 2001i; 2002a; 2002b). In terms of temporality, the President treats Congress as part of the Executive, effectively bullying it to 'fast politics' (Scheuerman 2004: 19–27).

Second, the President conceptualises the behaviour of economic actors in *moral* terms, addressing it as ethical/unethical, right/wrong (US President 2002b; 2002c). Economic behaviour is seen as neither an economic nor a legal matter, but as an expression of the good-evil dichotomy.

Third, the national unity displayed in the security effort, is also the cornerstone for the grandeur of the national economy: '[the terrorists] don't understand the entrepreneurial spirit of our country. They don't understand the spirit of the working men and women of America [...] [T]he bases for economic growth are very strong. The entrepreneurial spirit is really strong in America' (US President 2001f); 'we're the most productive people in the world' (US President 2002b). The synagonistic unity among different classes implies, in more pragmatic terms, that policies which favour capital will also favour labour. Simply: the tax cuts 'will create jobs'. Divisive policy is assumed away in a framework of national unity which gains its force and conviction from the counterterrorism battlefield.

This metastasis of war on terror discourse is not limited to economic issues. On 5 November 2003, the President announces that:

> America stands for liberty, for the pursuit of happiness, and for the unalienable right of life. And the most basic duty of government is to defend the life

of the innocent [...] We are asked to honor our own standards, announced on the day of our founding in the Declaration of Independence [...] This right to life cannot be granted or denied by government, because ... it comes from the Creator of Life [...] This is the generous and merciful spirit of our country at its best.

(US President 2003)

The President summons all the national totems not in order to set the nation on a do-or-die mission, but to witness his signing of an Act banning partial-birth abortion – or, in presidential phrasing, guaranteeing the 'rights of the unborn' (US President 2003). The war on terror narrative features even its mini-enemy: 'no lawyer's brief can make [the facts] seem otherwise'. Still, much more than 'facts', what we see here is the full significance of war on terror discourse: the monopolisation of truth and morality granting the President divine power, which he employs to impose policy and – when necessary – thrash the opposition, in a spirit of national unity.

... and everyone else follows

Far from being the President's own preserve, the war on terror narrative, adjusted to personal idiosyncrasy and area of competence, reverberated through the administration and political personnel of all persuasions and calibres (Croft 2006).

The Attorney General develops the presidential theme of the camouflaged Enemy, and places him in our midst. The Enemy 'infiltrates our communities' and exploits 'America's freedom as a weapon against us'. Terrorists are trained to use the freedom of the press to 'stalk and kill their victims' and, when captured, they exploit the judicial process to pass operational information to terrorists outside and to 'concoct stories of torture' to embarrass the authorities. As the Enemy exploits our essence (freedom) as a weapon against us, unauthorised invocations of freedom are considered hostile acts:

> [T]o those who scare peace-loving people with phantoms of lost liberty, my message is this: Your tactics only aid terrorists – for they erode our national unity and diminish our resolve. They give ammunition to America's enemies, and pause to America's friends. They encourage people of good will to remain silent in the face of evil.
>
> (US Attorney General 2001)

In other words, the only entity of the 'we' subject permitted to summon the national essence is the state. When the population attempts to do so, it is siding with the Enemy. This peculiar distinction crystallises with time. Attempting to justify the investigative powers it was granted by counterterrorism law, the Department of Justice (DOJ) divides the population into innocent and guilty:

> We're not going after the average American [...] We're only going after the bad guys [...] If you're not a terrorist or a spy, you have nothing to worry

about [...] [the DOJ] goes to great lengths to protect the privacy of every American unless you happen to be a foreign spy or member of a terrorist organisation [...] The average American has nothing to fear.
(ACLU 2003e: 7, citing DOJ Spokesman Michael Corallo)

Since the 'innocent' Joe Averages have nothing to worry about, it follows that whoever 'worries' and raises concerns about police powers is guilty, somewhat 'terrorist'. Thus, the narrative of watertight national unity shows its flip side: those who do not comply belong to the Enemy camp. Indeed: you are either with us or you are (with the) terrorists.

Beyond political personnel, the US media have been loudspeakers for war on terror discourse. They changed their areas of coverage, and adopted a 'patriotic' tone so that it would correspond better to the post-9/11 'reality' (Missouri School of Journalism 2002: 13–15). They promptly obliged to the administration's ordinance to embargo terrorist communiqués (Chang 2002: 129–131). And were rife with organisational and self-censorship, so that nothing put 'out there' would possibly undermine the national effort (Reese and Lewis 2009: 791; Robin 2004: 169). The outcome was a grand scale rehashing of the war on terror narrative. The world was cast in good vs. evil terms, ignoring its political, economic and historical dimensions. The predominant relation was combat between two, internally unified and mutually alien, blocs (Leurs 2007: 55). International relations were framed in military terms (Papacharissi and Oliveira 2008: 68–69). Complex and contingent processes were bulldozed into a simplistic narrative of heroism (Reese and Lewis 2009), and events were dramatised and addressed as singular, isolated episodes, without socio-historical perspective (Papacharissi and Oliveira 2008: 65–67).

The affinity of the media to war on terror discourse was not surprising. The recipe of high drama, simple storyline, and clear-cut us/them, good/evil distinctions was first formulated as a broadcasting strategy for audience maximisation (Leurs 2007: 47). This elective affinity helped war on terror discourse to become a thunderous hit for the mass culture industry. The themes of war on terror discourse were picked up and reproduced in countless variations in TV dramas, country songs, church (tele-) ceremonies, film, pulp fiction, poetry, etc (Croft 2006). Apart from the commercial success of war on terror discourse, its adoption by the spectacle industry indicates an alignment of capital (especially the IT sector) with the homeland security project. In any case, the war on terror narrative became part of the national 'common sense'.

While the war on terror discourse marked the Bush administration from beginning to end, it did not survive it. Personal idiosyncrasy, a shift of tone with regards to security and, more importantly, radically rearranged priorities, meant that the Obama presidency never engaged in war on terror discourse. Characteristically, while over a third of Bush's addresses were security-related, the corresponding figure for Obama is one-eighth.

When Obama does address security, he displays a certain resemblance to his predecessor. Justice remains a question of might, and there is categorical commitment to the outcome of future events, implying the omnipotence of the speaking subject: '[…] those who attack our people will find no escape from justice. We will not waver in their pursuit. And we will never allow anyone to shake the resolve of the United States of America' (US President 2012d: §6). The discursive tactic to isolate the Enemy from its cultural milieu is also decipherable: 'There is no religion that condones the targeting of innocent men and women […] for every angry mob, there are millions that yearn for freedom and dignity, and hope […]' (US President 2012d: § 8, 11). And, more importantly, the security apparatus (intelligence, law enforcement, first responders and the military) are the most valued entities of the 'we' subject (US President 2010b; 2010c; 2011a; 2011b; 2012c; 2012d).

Still, these resemblances appear in a completely different discursive landscape. To begin with, the Enemy has lost its elemental character. There is no Manichean division, and words like 'terror' or 'evil' are extremely rare in Obama's security-related addresses. The Enemy has shrunk in proportion and become identifiable (Al Qaeda) and manageable (US President 2011a). Similarly, the struggle loses its existential streak and becomes rather technical, a matter of strategic and operational improvements (US President 2010a: §8; 2011a: §5). Finally, Obama emphasises the need to discover why terrorists attack the US, implying that they may be motivated by a reason other than their evil nature (US President 2013).

In this context, the 'we' subject has become unrecognisable. Transcendental references to 'freedom' and 'democracy' become rare (Sowińska 2012: 14–15); and the archetype of the Avenging Angel is replaced by that of the Sacred Family. '[W]e must come together to ensure that every American has the chance to work for a decent living, own their own home, send their kids to college, and secure a decent retirement' (US President 2011b: §10; see also 2012a: §7–8); 'we are one American family' (US President 2012c: §9). This domestication of the 'we' effectuates a reduction of the power-deferential between the population and the state, whose key role is to serve and care for the former (US President 2010a: §6).

The 'we' subject has undergone this change to align with a completely new mission: 'nation building here at home' (US President 2011a: §9). This consists of 'rebuilding America' (US President 2011b: §8) as 'a country where everyone gets a fair shot, everyone gets their fair share', instead of prioritising 'tax cuts for millionaires while cutting the kinds of investments that built a strong middle class' (US President 2012a: §7, 10) – class cleavages crack the image of national unity. Even the endless praise for war veterans and their sacrifices is geared towards building the case of a competent, deserving nation: 'Because no one who fights for this country should have to fight for a job or a roof over their head when they come home […] Today's veterans have the skills, the discipline to help this country come back stronger than before' (US President 2012a: §13; 2012b: §6, 8). In short, even when addressing security issues, Obama is in fact *discussing the economy*, using security as a leverage to promote his economic policy. Regarding the representation of political priorities, this reverses war on terror discourse and its subjection of economy to security.

So, did they like it?

The war on terror discourse was a runaway success with the public, at least in the early post-9/11 period (roughly 12 months from the attacks) when the public had no resources to contradict the presidential narrative. To begin with, the audiences for the early addresses were vast: up to 99 per cent of the public were following the news closely, while the Joint address was watched by 88 per cent – the highest news event audience ever. Of those who watched it, 87 per cent evaluated it positively, and the President's already stratospheric post-9/11 popularity rose by four percentage points to 90 per cent – the highest ever recorded (Gallup 2001b; 2001c; Pew 2001a). So, when the President was setting out the new meaning of politics, the population was listening and approving overwhelmingly. The public continued to listen and approve over the course of the next year (Gallup 2002b; 2002d; 2002f; Pew 2002a; 2002c).

More than listening and agreeing, the population fully subscribed, often in minute detail, to the presidential representations of the Enemy (Gallup Unknown Date; 2001g; 2002e); the nature of the struggle (Gallup 2001f; 2001h; 2002a; Pew 2001b; 2002b); and, most importantly, its own role in the effort. The 'actions taken by Americans as a result' of the attacks, consist of 82 per cent of the population displaying the national flag and 74 per cent praying 'more than usual' (Gallup 2003e). The population accepts its designated role as cheerleader of state activity, as spectator of politics. They also started to work harder and with more zeal, proving patriotism to be a powerful (and cheap) managerial weapon: 'never before, perhaps, has work been imbued with such significance. Less than a week after the terrorist attacks on September 11, President Bush urged Americans to "go back to work." Since then, *resuming one's routine has become an act of defiance, an expression of patriotism* and, as a practical matter, America's best hope for averting a severe economic downturn' (Gallup 2001i; 2002c; 2002g).

This condition of a government willing to lead and a population willing to be led was disrupted by the Iraq war, marking a second phase in popular attitudes towards counterterrorism (September 2002 to May 2003). While popular majority still aligns with the President, whose interventions can sway up to 5 per cent of public opinion, this period sees the rise of considerable disagreement with counterterrorism policy, which solidifies between 30 and 35 per cent (Gallup 2003a; 2003b; 2003c; 2003d; 2003f; 2004; 2005d; 2005f; 2005h). Since the presidential declaration of the Iraq war being over (in May 2003) and until the end of its days, the Bush administration was fighting a defensive battle to galvanise consensus to counterterrorism. The President still carried some convincing power, but it was limited, restricted mainly to Republican supporters, and waning.

A side-note could help appreciate this percentage game of counterterrorism consensus. When, in 2005, with his approval ratings on the rise, the President declared his first priority to be social security reform (i.e. privatisation), and the relevant propaganda was set in motion, the effect on popular perceptions was nil. When the administration upped the tone of its argument (declaring social security 'in crisis', and the issue to be an 'emergency'), it *lost* support (Gallup 2005c). It seems that when the population has direct experience, everyday knowledge and tangible interest in an issue, the manipulative capacity of the government is limited. This is a most important lesson regarding counterterrorism policy: it is *beyond the involvement, control, knowledge, and even apprehension of the population*.

The meaning vested on 9/11 stirred the political agenda to this, inaccessible by the population, realm. On the eve of 9/11, the most important issues for the public were education (61 per cent regarding it 'extremely important'), prescription drugs for the elderly (49 per cent), the patient's bill of rights (39 per cent), social security/Medicare (37 per cent) and the economy (34 per cent). Three weeks after 9/11, the priorities were turned upside-down: terrorism (70 per cent) tops the list, followed by military and defence issues (57 per cent), the economy (54 per cent) and foreign affairs (52 per cent). The population was reflecting the presidential agenda (national security – homeland security – economy). It thus prescribed to its own exclusion from politics, and signalled a *shift in the legitimation of state authority*, from the provision of welfare, to that of security. The security protocol stabilised with time, and was finally (but not fully) reversed by the onslaught of the economic crisis (Gallup 2001d; 2001e; 2003i; 2005g; 2012).

Confirming the deep shift in popular political attitudes, about ten years after 9/11, and despite the reversal in political priorities, almost a third of the population feels personally threatened by terrorism, and tends to support hard security measures (Huddy and Feldman 2011). A final expression of the deep impact of war on terror discourse is reflected on the nation's most trusted institutions. The relevant index moves with glacier speed, yet, in the wake of 9/11, the approval ratings for the military – which was already topping the list – skyrocketed: they rose by 13 percentage points (66 per cent to 79 per cent) between 2001 and 2002, to eventually peak at 82 per cent in 2003. Despite the current shift in priorities, the 9/11 boost has not been neutralised. Similarly, the police saw its approval ratings stabilising higher than in the pre-9/11 years. Finally, the percentage of those who regard themselves 'extremely patriotic' received a formidable boost. It cut across the cleavages of race, ideology or party affiliation, and is still growing (Gallup 2003g; 2003h; 2005a; 2005b; 2005e; 2010; 2013).

The vacuum of meaning caused by the 9/11 attacks was filled in by an extraordinarily successful political discourse, which radically reset political representations regarding the power-modalities of the state, the state-population relation and roles, intra-state relations, the legitimation of state authority, and a popular cult of statism and patriotism. The end result was the subscription of the population to a political project set to repress and marginalise it. This project, loosely decipherable in presidential discourse, is labelled *homeland security*.

5 A blueprint of power: legislating counterterrorism

Moving on from political discourse and its impact on popular representations, this chapter discerns the key features of US counterterrorism law. The first section discusses the legislative process, especially the passing of the Uniting and Strengthening America by Providing Appropriate Tools Required to Intercept and Obstruct Terrorism (USA PATRIOT) Act of 2001 (Patriot Act). The next three sections focus on the investigatory powers the law grants the security mechanism, and on how they redraw its spatiotemporal matrix and stir its modalities towards intelligence. The next two sections examine the legal dynamics between 'exceptional' powers and their normalisation, focusing especially on the penal regime exemplified by Guantanamo. The penultimate section discusses 'domestic terrorism', the crime at the centre of homeland security policy. The last section examines how the law empowers the state to deal with economic matters: the controls on financial transactions suspected to involve terrorist organisations; the protection of the entities comprising the US economic infrastructure; and, beyond the frame of counterterrorism, the legal prescriptions for dealing with the post-2008 economic crisis.

This examination is premised on an understanding of law as a formally distinct, but inherently social and political practice (Chapter 2). The discussion of legislation is geared towards the assessment of the broader juridical and political organisation.

Patriot(s) in Congress

In its 342 pages, the Patriot Act effectuates changes to more than 15 statutes, ranging from electronic surveillance to immigration control, from money laundering to compensation for terrorism victims.

Attorney General John Ashcroft submitted the first Patriot Act draft just one week after the attacks, and demanded that Congress enacted it within seven days. The administration pressed Congress members for its quick passage, effectively blackmailing legislators to consent or have the blood of future victims on their hands. Final drafts were prepared in closed meetings involving administration officials and the Senate and House leaders. The Bill was never subject to a Senate committee debate or mark up; the House heard no testimony from the

Bill's opponents; and amendments proposed by the House Subcommittee on the Constitution were ignored. The Bill was formally introduced in the Senate on 5 October 2001 and was passed six days later. A brief debate revealed that senators had not read or understood it. It was then introduced and enacted in the House on the same day (12 October) under a procedure barring amendments. Representatives had no time to read the Bill, and based their vote on summaries (ACLU 2003f: 5; Chang 2002: 43; Cole and Dempsey 2002: 151; EFF 2001). The vote was 98:1 in the Senate, and 356:66 in the House of Representatives. The President signed it into law on 26 October 2001.

This haste also meant that a Bill introduced to 'protect the American people from further attacks', was enacted *before* any assessment was made of the vulnerabilities and failures which led to 9/11, or of the Act's relevance for preventing similar events. The 9/11 Commission, comprising Congress members from both parties, was formed more than a year after 9/11 (compared with a similar investigative commission on Pearl Harbour, which was established three weeks after that attack). Its budget was US$3 million (compared with about US$80 million provided for the Columbia space shuttle disaster inquiry) (Leone 2003). Yet, not knowing what the Bill was supposed to rectify did not mean that the government was flying blind: most of the changes introduced by the Act were part of a long-standing Federal Bureau of Investigation (FBI) wish-list, and some had been previously rejected by Congress.

This brief account of the legislating process raises questions regarding the comparative tempo of the Legislature and the Executive, and their respective access to the knowledge which would inform the drafting of counterterrorism measures. I address these issues in Chapter 6; in this chapter, I only question the prominent explanation for the irregularities in legislating the Patriot Act, as it distorts our understanding of who makes counterterrorism law.

The predominant explanation of the Patriot Act's legislating process pits Congress against the Bush administration. There is a power-hungry administration, keen on amassing powers, which has a clear view of its objectives (the FBI's 'wish-list' of investigative powers). To achieve these objectives, the administration bullied Congress (by invoking of patriotism, and casting anathemas) to vote for the measures put before it. Faced with life-threatening emergency, Congress's commitment to upholding the rule of law was countered by its urge to protect the people. It managed to curtail a lot of the excesses put forward by the administration, but ultimately succumbed to it (Chang 2002: 13–15; Lawyers' Committee for Human Rights 2002: 7–8; Roach 2011: 161–162, 174–176).

This is certainly a very didactic explanation. But it cannot withstand scrutiny. First, the majorities in both houses were overwhelming. Such a consensus is extremely rare, and contradicts the notion of a forced, torn or succumbing Legislature. Moreover, Congress had all the (symbolic, legal and procedural) means necessary to resist Executive pressures and infringements, but made no protestation about the legislating process or the content of the provisions.

Second, the Patriot Act was not the only counterterrorism Bill. Between 2002 and 2007, there was a flurry of homeland security legislation, with six major Acts and numerous piecemeal amendments brought before Congress. In every case there was proper and full deliberation, both in the informal club of Congress barons and administration chiefs, and in the formal structure of Committees and Assemblies. The time lapse from the attacks meant that the Legislature was no longer 'under the influence' of acute emergency. Yet, this sober Congress passed almost every proposal put before it, and with comfortable majorities. What was put before it was a further expansion and intensification of the Patriot Act's provisions and a legal framework which deregulated policing even further. The Homeland Security Act (HSA) was debated in Congress from July to November 2002, and passed with a House majority of 299:121. In February 2006, Congress had the opportunity to repeal 16 expiring Patriot Act sections. It chose to take nothing back: the Patriot Improvement and Reauthorization Act (PIRA) made permanent 14 out of 16 expiring sections. The other two were renewed until 31 December 2009, and consequently, until 15 June 2015. In December 2011, Congress voted for military detention of US citizens as part of the National Defense Authorisation Act (NDAA). And in July 2013 it chose to not curtail the National Security Agency's (NSA's) surveillance of US communications. Thus, counterterrorism law is not the product of an Executive (or a Republican) coup. It is part of a *state strategy*, a strategy which involves *both branches and both parties in unison, and consolidates over time*.

Foreign Intelligence Surveillance Act (FISA) expansion – total intelligence?

Probably the most important achievement of counterterrorism legislation is the redrawing the matrix of police investigations. The relative provisions are clustered in the Patriot Act, and the powers they grant are upgraded and expanded, mainly by the 2003 Intelligence Enhancement Act, and the 2006 PIRA. They are represented as tearing down the 'wall' that used to prevent communication between intelligence agents and criminal prosecutors. This unification is much more than a technical adjustment, and the provisions do much more than 'bridging' two compartments. In their combined force, they effectuate a radical reconfiguration of policing structures and modalities; of the temporal and spatial framework of policing; and of its targets. To appreciate the Patriot Act's impact on investigations, we need to start with the pre-Patriot Act framework.

Enter FISA

Since the late 1970s, two separate legal frameworks regulate the conduct of domestic investigations and surveillance. The main one was provided by the US Code, Title III. It regulated surveillance in *criminal investigations*, conducted by *law enforcement personnel*, with a view to *legal prosecution*. In Title III process, the government (DOJ) would request the judge within whose jurisdiction the surveillance would occur, to issue a warrant. The petition was based on 'reasonable suspicion' or 'probable cause' to believe that the targets were involved in criminal activity. The warrant specified the person, places and methods of surveillance.

The second framework was provided by FISA. FISA was enacted in 1978, to ameliorate the total ban on domestic surveillance which Congress had imposed earlier, after Cointelpro and similar works by Hoover's FBI had surfaced. The ban soon felt like a leash too tight, given the country's cold war circumstances. The compromise was FISA, an Act allowing intelligence operations in US soil, but only against foreign spies. The purpose of FISA surveillance was counter-intelligence. FISA investigations had no criminal prosecution objective, and people could be targeted regardless of whether they were suspected of criminal activity. FISA regulated surveillance regarding *foreign intelligence investigations*, carried out by *intelligence personnel*, for the purpose of *intelligence collection on the* activity of '*foreign powers*' or '*agents of foreign powers*'.

A FISA investigation was an arrangement between two bodies, the DOJ and the Foreign Intelligence Surveillance Court (FISC). This court comprised seven judges, and the only party with access to it was DOJ. All dealings and decisions of the FISC were secret, and subject to appeal and review by the FISA Court of Review, another secret court which sat for the first time in 2002. To initiate an investigation, the DOJ would submit to the FISC an application approved by the Attorney General. The application should establish 'probable cause' to believe that the target was a foreign power or an agent thereof, and that foreign intelligence acquisition would be *the* purpose of the surveillance. Through a wholly secret process, the FISC would approve the requested authority, usually within 24 hours. Approval was guaranteed: in FISA's first 20 years, the FISC rejected two in about 10,000 applications (Colangelo Unknown Date; Henderson 2003; Poole 2000).

Re-enter FISA – a significant rephrasing

The Patriot Act radically rearranged this dual framework by augmenting the government's investigative powers and releasing them from judicial control in relation to both Title III and FISA processes. It also introduced FISA process into criminal investigations. This is probably the most important thing the Patriot Act did. It provides the policing mechanism an alternative avenue to investigate and prosecute when levels of suspicion are too weak to satisfy criminal investigation criteria. It subjects the population to a deregulated process of surveillance and prosecution. It also unleashed a shock-wave which engulfed the structure, operational mode and culture of the policing mechanism; and it redefined the role of the Judiciary.

The Patriot Act introduces FISA into criminal investigations by enhancing the collaboration between intelligence and law enforcement mechanisms, and by enabling the participation of law enforcement personnel in the application for FISA warrants. It does so by amending the grounds for FISA investigation: before the Patriot Act the DOJ needed to claim that gathering foreign intelligence was '*the purpose*' of the investigation for which it was seeking FISC authorisation.

Section 218 amended this to '*a significant purpose*'. It thus opens the way for law enforcement to employ FISA, and makes the findings of FISA investigations valid in criminal prosecution (CRS 2001: 14–15). Since foreign intelligence must only be 'a significant' purpose of the investigation; and since the meaning of the word 'significant' is not defined or elaborated in the legislation, federal officials can use FISA in order to collect evidence for criminal prosecution, as long as they certify that some foreign intelligence purpose is served (US Senate 2003b: 5–6). The 2004 Intelligence Reform and Terrorism Prevention Act amplified the scope of FISA and further removed it from its original counterespionage purpose. Its 'lone wolf' amendment (§6001a) allows FISA investigations to be initiated against solo acts – individuals who are not thought to have any connection to a foreign power or terrorist network, insofar they are not US persons and are suspected of terrorist activity (CRS 2011a: 5–7). Furthermore, in sections 203, 901 and 905, the Patriot Act instructs the Central Intelligence Agency (CIA) Director to establish priorities and requirements for FISA use and, in tandem with the Attorney General, to develop a set of secret guidelines ensuring the two-way flow of information between law enforcement and intelligence agencies (CRS 2001: 5–6, 53–54; Paye 2007: 47–48).

Granting FISA to law enforcement use, gearing it towards criminal prosecution, and breaking its envelopment so that it no longer applies only to spies, signals the cancellation of its legal specificity, and incorporates its procedures in mainstream law. It also renders Title III redundant: when unable to meet its requirements, the police are granted an avenue to bypass it by using the much lower FISA thresholds (US Foreign Intelligence Surveillance Court 2002). Finally, the incorporation of FISA into the framework of normal, routine, policing, indicates *a merging of the two distinct policing functions and modalities* – intelligence and law enforcement – within and across federal agencies.

Blanket investigations

The Patriot Act not only introduced FISA to everyday policing, it also drastically expanded its powers. Section 215 permits even lower-grade FBI officials (Assistant Special Agents) to apply for access to records or any 'tangible object', as part of an investigation to 'keep the United States safe from terrorism' (CRS 2001: 11; 2011a: 9–13).[1] What constitutes an 'investigation' is defined by the police. Indeed, DOJ loosened the relevant definition, so that §215 powers apply even to preliminary investigations (Donohue 2008: 234–235).

Before the Patriot Act, the government could force, under FISA authority, certain types of business to disclose their client records: courier, accommodation, vehicle rental and storage facilities (CRS 2011a: 10). Section 215 expands record-access under FISA to every interaction kept on record, plus 'other tangible

---

1 This section originally included a 'gag order' prohibiting the party whose assistance was sought from disclosure. The 2005 PIRA introduced a process of appealing the gag to FISC (CRS 2011a: 11–12).

things'. The government gains full access to the records of citizens' activities, at the time when 'computerisation' results in the recording of virtually the totality of social interaction. In practical terms, this means that the FBI can access, for example: personal belongings (books, letters or computer hardware, i.e.' tangible things') directly from one's home; lists of people who visited a particular website or borrowed a particular book from a library; medical and psychiatric records; membership lists of political organisations; genetic information, bank records and financial transactions; purchases by debit and credit cards; email and mobile phone communications. As in all FISA investigations, the government's activity is secret and exempt from review (ACLU 2002b; 2003e: 6; 2003i: 4–6).

The scope of this power threatens to undermine any notion of the right to privacy (e.g. ACLU 2003a; Chang 2002: 46–61; Etzioni 2004: 43–77; Sullivan 2003). Equally important is the question of its target. In its original form, FISA did not require that its targets were suspected of illegal activity. Now, as the Patriot Act lifted the 'foreign intelligence' requirement, and the lone wolf amendment cancelled the requirement of the target's relation to any 'power' or organisation, FISA can be employed to investigate people suspected of nothing at all. In its applications to the FISC, the government has to certify that the investigation involves some foreign intelligence or terrorism element; but it does not need to show that the targets are themselves suspected of espionage, terrorism or other criminal activity (ACLU 2003i: 4–5; Rutherford Institute 2003). While this is the case for all FISA provisions amended by the Patriot Act, §215 seems to take a further leap: *it does not demand a target at all.* It permits the FBI to conduct open-ended investigations, using its record-obtaining power without naming specific individuals as targets. Relevant FISC orders may encompass entire collections of data, related to any number of individuals, thus permitting the investigative authorities to sweep up entire databases indiscriminately (ACLU 2002b; 2003e: 6; Center for Democracy and Technology 2003: 2; US House of Representatives 2003a: 19; US Foreign Intelligence Surveillance Court 2013).

The Act also amended Title III investigations, replicating the deregulation of counterespionage powers and their expansion to cover the entire population. It relaxed the requirements for issuing National Security Letters (NSLs), the FBI's self-issued subpoenas. Whereas, previously, agents' requests had to provide specific facts establishing their target as (an agent of) a foreign power, and could only be authorised by a Deputy Assistant Director (or higher), §505 permits anyone with a rank of Special Agent in charge of a field office to issue NSLs. Moreover, NSLs need only to be *relevant* to an authorised investigation to protect against international terrorism or clandestine intelligence activities. Lastly, the type of third party required to comply with NSLs also expands, as Internet Service Providers (ISPs) are added to financial institutions as main NSL recipients. The ISP category includes not only internet providers, but also providers of internet services (e.g. email), and providers of internet access (e.g. cafes, schools, libraries). The 2004 Intelligence Reform Act further brought under NSL authority: travel agencies; car, airplane and boat sellers; pawnbrokers; dealers in jewellery, precious stones and metals; telegraph companies; casinos; and the US Postal Service.

The Patriot Act accompanied the NSL provisions with a gag order, prohibiting the recipients from disclosing the fact, but did not specify a penalty. PIRA fixed this, by providing for a five-year sentence (Donohue 2008: 236–241).

The Patriot Act expands NSL authority, enabling once again the FBI to make blanket searches, collecting entire databases of information without targeting specific, suspect individuals (US House of Representatives 2003a: 17). It should be repeated that NSLs are self-issued subpoenas, produced by FBI agents without any external overview or review. They allow the FBI to bypass courts completely. The expansion of NSL authority signifies a commensurate expansion of Executive power to conduct investigations unilaterally (US House of Representatives 2003a: 19; US Senate 2003b: 7, 30).

Finally, the 2002 HSA made all-encompassing, unilateral surveillance an obligation for the newly founded Department of Homeland Security (DHS). Section 201(d) charges the DHS Undersecretary for Information Analysis and Infrastructure Protection to collect and analyse intelligence and any 'other information [deriving] from [...] private sector entities', and to establish and use an 'information technology infrastructure, including datamining and other analytical tools' to collect, analyse and disseminate information. Thus, the pooling of infinite volumes of information, potentially covering all social transactions by every single individual on US soil (and beyond); the development of capacity to analyse this information; and the sharing of the resulting intelligence with the entire federal policing mechanism, are not just Executive *powers* anymore. They are its *duty*.

Finally, shortly after 9/11 the President authorised the NSA to monitor communications (phone calls and emails) of terrorist suspects, even if one end of said communications was situated in the US. When, in 2005, the investigation was revealed, and the administration defended its legality on the basis of the 2001 congressional Authorisation for the Use of Military Force (AUMF). Given the scope of the operation (said to involve thousands of US residents and citizens), the political furore it raised, and its precarious legal authority, Congress passed the 2008 Protect America Act, granting the Director of National Intelligence and the Attorney General powers to authorise this type of warrantless surveillance. Initially temporary, these powers were rendered permanent by subsequent amendments in 2008, rendering the practice perfectly legal (Cole and Lederman 2006; Kris 2007: 231; Roach 2011: 184–186).

Counterterrorism law establishes a strong trend to totalise the scope of surveillance, and make it exclusive to the Executive. As the law provides several separate avenues to this end; the Executive is prepared to overstep its legal authorities to undertake such operations; and Congress is eager to clean up the legal mess they leave behind, it is safe to conclude that *the move towards unlimited surveillance is of capital importance, and undertaken by the state apparatus in unison*: it is a key state strategy.

Roving surveillance, secret searches

The move towards expanding and deregulating investigations does not refer only to their scope and targeting, but also involves their space and time. The relevant

Patriot Act provisions are clustered around two themes: roving surveillance and secret searches.

Roving surveillance refers to the capacity of investigative authorities to use a warrant beyond the jurisdiction for which it was issued. The Patriot Act (§§206, 213, 214, 216, 219, 220) provides that (Title III and FISA) electronic surveillance can occur under a single court authorisation. Rather than being limited to the location, telephone and internet lines, and the apparatuses they were issued for, surveillance warrants are valid nationally and even internationally, where 'local law' permits. The surveillance techniques in question include both intercepting communications' traffic (pen register, trap-and-trace), and intercepting communications' content (wire-tapping) (CRS 2001: 7; 2011a: 7–9). The same mode of surveillance comes to apply to physical searches: a single warrant authorises the search of a person's property and dwellings anywhere in the US, and beyond (CRS 2001: 15–16).

The obvious purpose of roving surveillance is to avoid applying for a new warrant every time the people under investigation change their mobile phone or internet providers. A marked feature of these provisions, whether for electronic surveillance or physical search, is their lack of legal standards. The warrants' scope means the issuing court has no power to oversee investigations. They are practically blank, and law enforcement agents fill in the places to be searched. There are hardly any requirements for obtaining a roving warrant: the FBI does not need to show probable cause or reasonable suspicion of criminal activity. It only has to certify that the warrant relates to an ongoing criminal investigation and the judge has no grounds to reject the request (US House of Representatives 2003a: 17).

Regarding physical searches, the Patriot Act couples their roving mode with permissions for (indefinite) delay of notification that a search has taken place. Such delays were permitted only if real-time notification would pose a threat to life or physical safety, lead to destruction of evidence or risk the fleeing of the suspect. The Patriot Act (§§213, 219) adds a fourth reason: that notification may have 'any adverse impact' on the 'government's interests'. The evaluation of what the 'government's interests' are, and whether a timely announcement would imperil them, is left to the agents themselves: the notification delay applies not only to the target of the investigation, but also to the courts. And its length is merely specified as 'a reasonable period' (US House of Representatives 2003a: 17; US Senate 2003b: 24). Thus, the Act cancels the investigatory 'knock and announce' etiquette, an elemental condition for privacy that claims its origins in the Magna Carta (Rutherford Institute 2003: 3).

While these provisions enhance governmental capacity to investigate crime, they also diminish the role of the Judiciary in investigations, which are monopolised by the Executive. Another effect is that roving warrants tend to unify US territory into a single jurisdiction; and secret searches tend to neutralise the physicality of 'personal' space, making it directly accessible to the state. Further amendments to FISA display indirect spatial characteristics: the 2007 Protect America Act and the 2008 Foreign Intelligence Surveillance Amendments Act gradually lift the protections afforded by FISA to communications within US territory, making them subject to completely warrantless surveillance, as communications outside the US have always been (Kris 2007: 28–40). *Ergo*, NSA surveillance of all electronic communications in the US (Chapter 7).

The examination of the investigation process has identified several key trends introduced by counterterrorism legislation which lay down a marker regarding the law-form. It would be useful, before we proceed to other areas of counterterrorism law, to pause and consider them.

Revolution in policing: the mechanism, its space, time and target

An obvious general tendency of counterterrorism provisions is the increased authority for the Federal Executive to act unilaterally in the context of criminal investigations. Judicial control over the investigation process is severely limited – FISA procedures and 'roving' warrants render its participation rather ornamental, and NSLs dispose of it altogether. Thus counterterrorism law emancipates the Executive from judicial control, and settles the issue of the 'dual patronage' of the police by the Executive and the Judiciary (Neocleous 2000: 106), to the benefit of the former.

The sidelining of the Judiciary is *per se* a crucial reconfiguration of state power and of the power balance between state branches. It is further associated with a reconfiguration of the operational modalities of the state, especially regarding its *speed*. The homogenisation of the social *space* of policing, brought about by the shattering of jurisdictional limits and houses' walls by roving warrants and secret searches, is tightly related to the reconfiguration of policing *time*. By homogenising space for the police apparatus, the roving surveillance provisions diminish the time needed for intervention, as they make redundant the application for new warrants each time an investigation shifts its attention on the map. Spatial provisions are also temporal, and can be grouped together with the Patriot Act, §207, which extends the duration of FISA surveillance from 45 to 90 days for physical search orders, and from 90 to 120 days (and, through consequent renewals, up to a year) for electronic surveillance and physical search orders (CRS 2001: 7–8).

The concern with speed highlights a conflict between the logic of the Executive – that of timely intervention and effectiveness – and that of the Judiciary, concerned with the adherence to the law and procedural fairness. By sidelining the Judiciary, counterterrorism law settles this conundrum by making legal standards and fairness conditional (at best) to investigatory effectiveness. The banishment of the Judiciary and its logic from police work is the means to a time-compression of operations. To achieve acceleration, counterterrorism law has *revolutionised the ideological, institutional, spatial and temporal matrix of policing*.

The apparatus which undertakes this enhanced, fast policing is itself significantly altered. By introducing FISA into the framework of criminal investigations, the Patriot Act initiates an amalgamation of the two distinct categories of policing, intelligence and law enforcement, and of their respective mechanisms. It also stirs the operation and logic of policing towards pre-emption. Counterterrorism law remodels the policing apparatus into a unified entity, with singular logic and purpose, compatibility of operation techniques, undisrupted flow of information, common directives, etc.

The unification of the police mechanism which the Patriot Act initiated at the federal level, is accomplished by HSA with regards to the sub-national scale. Title V provides for the guidance and coordination of first responders by the federal state. It mandates federal supervision, funding and coordination of local police and emergency personnel, thus expanding federal control over local law enforcement. Local personnel comprise 11 million employees (compared to 11,000 FBI agents). Given the vast scope of investigative powers, their implementation depends on roping in sub-national police personnel. HSA effectively brings state and local personnel under federal control, creating a unified police body. In addition, it provides a single, central point of control: the DHS. The overall tendency is to unify the coercive apparatus both horizontally (law enforcement–intelligence) and vertically (federal–sub-national), and to bring it under central, political control. This centralisation consists not in direct command, but in control over priorities, directions, practices and results. The police mechanism is restructured as a constant network, characterised by operational autonomy at the basis combined with centralised control at the top.

The strategic objective of this, legally codified, realignment of policing is the *drastic expansion of the state's coercive power over the population*. This is pronounced in the blanket character of surveillance, and in the stirring of policing towards pre-emption. But it is also the goal towards which all the trends of counterterrorism law converge: from emancipating the police from judicial overview; to concentrating control of state and local police personnel at federal level. In line with the discursive construction of the Enemy as being potentially anyone/anywhere, the scope of surveillance seeks to encompass all: all social interaction, by all individuals. The totality of social activity is the ultimate target of surveillance. Thus, the unified police mechanism, operating in a uniform space, is set to police an homogenised target: all of us.

The *ratchet effect* in law: FISA, aliens, material support

There is one more insight offered by the Patriot Act's amendment of FISA, one referring to legislating tactics. The objective of FISA in its original inception was to provide the federal Executive a platform for operative discretion: secretive, low-standard and bereft of oversight and review processes. This platform was meant to be used strictly for investigating persons suspected of spying on behalf of a foreign state – a tiny category, suspended in a political grey zone. The virtual extinction of its target (the Red saboteur and spy) caused neither repealing or restriction of FISA powers. On the contrary, the Patriot Act rediscovered this sleeping beauty, and expanded its scope so that it can now serve as the framework to investigate anyone on US soil, provided that some 'foreign intelligence' element is present in a terrorism or common crime inquiry. While the scope of initial FISA powers expands to potentially envelop the totality of the US population, its intensity increases with regards to politically exceptional categories towards which the state can negotiate its obligations for due process and legal protection. As the rule for the marginal category (spy) becomes the rule for everyone, a new, harsher rule is introduced for the marginal category ('alien'): the 'lone wolf' amendment disengages FISA from any requirement that its target is associated with any 'power' of any description, as long as this target is not a US person. For want of a better term, I use 'ratchet effect' to mean the legislating tactic (or pattern) involving the expansive movement *from the niche to the majority, accompanied by intensification of the treatment of the niche* – in reserve (or preparation) for a new wave of expansion.

This margin-mainstream-margin movement is illustrated in the material support clauses and the 'alien-US person' differentials which drive them forward. In 1996, following the Oklahoma City bombing, Congress passed the Anti-Terrorism and Effective Death Penalty Act. Its section 323 criminalised the provision of 'material support' for specific acts of international terrorism, applicable to non-US persons only. It defined material support to include the provision of anything ranging from 'lethal substances' to 'lodging', and from 'weapons' to 'transportation', also adding 'other physical assets' for good measure.

Building on this, the Patriot Act (§411) expanded the definition of 'terrorist organisation' to include whatever the Secretary of State identifies as having provided, *inter alia*, material support for terrorist acts. In other words, providers of material support are now designated as terrorists *per se* – any distinction between primary and secondary relation to the crime is abolished. The presidential designation of the Enemy as 'terrorists and those who *harbour* them' is, thus, codified in law. Material support is augmented to apply to political and social groups 'whose public endorsement of terrorist activities undermines our efforts to reduce or eliminate terrorism' (CRS 2001: 34). Material support comes to include verbal support to terrorism (implicating free speech), while it has the particularity of being a crime not only by association but also by designation: the provisions are to be enacted or not at the discretion of the Secretary of State and the Attorney General (Cole 2003: 64–65). Having strengthened the guilt by association principle regarding 'aliens', the Patriot Act expands it to apply to the mainstream US population: material support features among the federal terrorism crimes which comprise the newly founded criminal category of domestic terrorism.

The constant expansion and intensification of the material support category signifies that the state is not so much concerned with red-handed terrorism, but uses it as a leverage to produce new crimes of affiliation, and then increasingly targets the latter. This indicates that the state seeks to include the largest possible multitude in the scope of penalisation (Ericson 2007: 48). If in any conceivable case terrorism would be practiced by an insignificant number of individuals, crimes of association can be stretched however widely the authorities choose. Moreover, while terrorism is a politically informed activity which involves criminal practice, material support is socio-politically informed activity *only*. Criminalising material support means criminalising political conviction and social bonds of solidarity as such, regardless of employed means.

Finally, it is not only the trees (specific measures) that pertain to the ratchet tactic; so does the forest. The very construction of 'terrorism' as a crime – a crime referring to acts already covered by criminal law – aims at introducing rules and practices which depart from the established framework of criminal law. Counterterrorism legislation introduces an exception into the framework of penal justice, and this exception is irreversible: counterterrorism powers are not repealed after the specific emergency that triggered them has passed. Once special powers are exercised, 'the *idea* of using them is no longer extraordinary' (Donohue 2009: 374, original emphasis). They are used against organised and even common crime, and become incorporated in the normal criminal justice framework. In addition, as previous exceptional powers have become routine, new terrorist incidents result in their intensification in a new 'exceptional' counterterrorism framework, which again gradually becomes the norm (Donohue 2009: 372–379; Paye 2007: 223; see also Cole 2003: 85–153).

The Guantanamo treatment: *ius regis*

While flattening the citizen-alien legal distinction, counterterrorism legislation simultaneously re-introduces it by devising an astonishing legal arsenal against 'aliens'. The Patriot Act permits the Attorney General to detain foreign terrorist suspects for an indefinite period, on the sole basis he has 'reasonable grounds to believe' that a non-citizen endangers national security (CRS 2001: 35; Lawyers' Committee for Human Rights 2002). But the real leap forward came in the form of the presidential Military Order on the 'Detention, Treatment, and Trial of Certain Non-Citizens in the War Against Terrorism'. Issued on 13 November 2001, it draws its authority from the AUMF – a joint resolution of both houses of Congress, passed (almost unanimously) three days after the attacks, and authorising the President 'to use all necessary and appropriate force against those nations, organizations, or persons he determines planned, authorised, committed, or aided the terrorist attacks that occurred on September 11, 2001, or harboured such organizations or persons'. On this basis, the Military Order provides the treatment to which 'certain' non-citizens are subjected.

Subject to this treatment is any non-citizen regarding whom *the President determines* there is reason to believe: is or was member of Al Qaeda; has engaged, aided or conspired to actual or planned acts of international terrorism, aiming to *effect adversely the US, its citizens, its foreign relations and its economic interests*; or anyone who has knowingly harboured such persons. Non-citizen detainees thus designated are placed under the exclusive authority of the Defense Secretary. The latter determines the appropriate location for the detention, in or outside US territory, and the appropriate conditions for it.

Such detainees are tried by military commissions for which it is not 'practicable to apply [...] the principles of law and the rules of evidence generally recognised in the trial of criminal cases'. But they can apply all penalties permitted by law, including life imprisonment and death. The Defense Secretary issues orders and regulations for the appointment of military commissions and the rules for their conduct, including pre-trial, trial, and post-trial procedures. These Commissions are *not* Military Tribunals. While Tribunals are pre-established bodies with defined powers, military commissions are set *ad hoc* by the Secretary to judge each separate case (Agamben 2005: 3; Steyn 2003: 12). Their institution violates the principle of the *natural judge* which dictates that defendants have the right to be tried by a court legally instituted before the commission of the crime, not one conjured to try their specific case (Belandis 2004: 272). The Secretary also determines what evidence is admitted, the defendant's access to it, and the conduct of the trial's proceedings. The record of the trial, including sentencing, is submitted to the President or the Defense Secretary, who can uphold the Commission's verdict or order a new trial. The Order clarifies that the military commissions have exclusive jurisdiction in such cases, and that the defendant cannot appeal.

If the new 'normality' introduced by the Patriot Act constitutes a severe upsetting of a liberal law-form delimited by the rule of law, the new 'exception' described in the Military Order completely thrashes it. *Habeas corpus* is cancelled, and so is every single requirement of fair trial. The Judiciary is thrown out of the process, which is taken over by *ad hoc* Executive bodies. Indeed, the Guantanamo treatment constitutes *a parallel legal regime*, devised at its every step by executive *fiat*. The only element of the legal process still remaining is punishment – even then, the President can overrule the sentence. This is essentially a pre-bourgeois regime, where law is the Right of the King – *ius regis*. The liberty, life, dignity and well being of the individual are caught in a mechanism of punishment which invents itself in the process. From beginning to end, its sole basis is presidential determination; the individual is at the complete disposal of the *rex*. The Military Order draws justification from the present situation of 'extraordinary emergency'. But it is also the President who determines that such emergency exists.

Reacting to the 2004 Supreme Court decision in *Rasul v Bush* (542 US 466; 124 S. Ct. 2686) which affirmed US courts' jurisdiction over non-citizens held in Guantanamo, Congress passed the 2005 Detainee Treatment Act, stripping courts of *habeas corpus* jurisdiction. In the same year, *Hamdi v Rumsfeld* (542 US 507) upheld the presidential authority over detention of enemy combatants, but introduced some due process standards. The administration sought to clarify procedures. It acknowledged detainees should receive notice of the reasons for their detention, and granted them some opportunity to respond. But evidence could remain secret and undisclosed to the defendant, there would be a presumption in favour of the government, rules of evidence would not apply, and trials would be conducted by military commissions (Donohue 2008: 83–88; Paye 2007: 61–64; Roach 2011: 200–203). The 2006 Military Commissions Act (MCA) (§948a) defined the term 'unlawful enemy combatant' as anyone who has engaged in hostilities against the US, *or provided material support* thereto, and is not a member of a force belonging to a state. The determination of the prisoner's status is left to presidentially appointed military commissions (§948d). MCA upheld the trial and sentencing procedures provided by the Military Order. It explicitly denied enemy combatants *habeas corpus*, and clarified that the Geneva conventions do not constitute a basis for such petitions (Donohue 2008: 88–89; Paye 2007: 64–71). In doing so, MCA discredits not only the US courts, but also international law as a possible competitor of the President, whom it constitutes as the only source of law.

In 2008 (*Boumediene v Bush*; 128 S. Ct. 2229), the Supreme Court challenged the constitutionality of the MCA *habeas corpus* provisions. Subsequently, Congress passed the 2009 MCA (2010 NDAA, Title XVIII). It introduced a modicum of due process (permitting the defendant some access to expert witnesses and evidence, but at a lower standard than in federal courts); it installed review of the continuation of detention by the District of Columbia US Court of Appeals; and did not explicitly prohibit (or allow) *habeas corpus* review (CRS 2010; Mariner 2009). Finally, in Executive Order 13567 ('Periodic Review of Individuals Detained at Guantanamo Bay Naval Station Pursuant to the Authorization for Use of Military Force') issued in March 2011, President Obama explicitly recognised the detainees' right to *habeas corpus*; authorised the participation of non-military Executive officials in status-review procedures; and allowed the detainees access to private council. Still, the Executive Order upheld the use of secret evidence, and the government's capacity to unlimited detention (Roach 2011: 210). These comings and goings between the Supreme Court, Congress and the White House can be seen as pitched battles through which the Court strives to introduce legal standards in the Guantanamo treatment. Yet, neither the Supreme Court decisions nor congressional Acts challenge the capacity of the Executive to detain *ad infinitum* and punish in full discretion those charged with the peculiar offence of being 'enemy combatants'. They, therefore, fine-tune and *legalise* the unregulated, parallel system of justice which the Executive has conjured up and owns, incorporating it from the margins to into the main body of US law (Paye 2007: 54–57; Roach 2011: 207–211).

While the Guantanamo treatment would only be imposed on an arithmetically tiny and politically marginal category, it is disproportionally important, as it describes the maximum power the state can legally exercise. And the dissection of the ratchet tactic dictates caution: the special treatment reserved for the few may be expanded to apply to all. Indeed, while the Military Order and all legislation enacted since (including the 2009 MCA) apply only to 'aliens', already since 2002 there is a certain (discursive and legal) slippage, bringing the term 'enemy combatant' to refer to US citizens, as highlighted in the *Hamdi v Rumsfeld* and *Padilla* cases (Roach 2011: 192–194, 201–203). Even though the latter are to be tried by proper courts, the terms of their detention (including its duration, location, interrogation practices, etc) are subject to the determination of the Defense Secretary. Finally, the 2012 NDAA allows the President to indefinitely detain or try by military commission anyone captured on US soil whom the President determines to be an 'unprotected enemy belligerent'. This term replaces the 'unlawful enemy combatant' and refers to operatives of Al Qaeda or of 'associated forces', engaged in 'hostilities' against the US, and to those providing 'substantial support' thereof, *irrespective of citizenship* (CRS 2012a: 15–18). President Obama's commitment to 'not authorise the indefinite military detention without trial of American citizens' (CRS 2012a: 2) signifies that he *does* have such powers, and that future presidents (or the current one, 'in an emergency') can activate them – 'the *idea* of using them is no longer extraordinary'. Thus, NDAA introduces indefinite military detention without charge or trial into law for the first time in US history (ACLU 2012a). Moreover, in abstracting 'enemy belligerents' engaged in 'hostilities' from the battlefield and allowing their capture anywhere in the world (ACLU 2012a), NDAA effectuates another flattening of the operative space of the coercive apparatus.

The objective behind the detention subtitle of NDAA was to define the presidential powers granted by the 2001 AUMF, as subsequent interpretations by the courts and the Executive have left them in a confused state. Its effect is to verify and expand them. In doing so, it subtracts them from the emergency context of the AUMF and codifies them in the mainstream body of US law. Thus, while the Guantanamo *camp* is hollowed out, the Guantanamo *treatment* becomes universalised – and *ius regis* legalised.

Finally, *ius regis* is being intensified in relation to its initial targets. The Obama administration is circumventing detention, interrogation and trial processes altogether, and restricts the treatment to punishment. The presidentially authorised assassinations (usually, but not exclusively, by unmanned aircraft) are a cheaper and less troublesome means of neutralising enemy combatants. They occur through the Guantanamo procedure: an intelligence-based presidential designation of select individuals is followed by 'trial' by the Executive (the President and his National Security Council), and the decision is executed by the CIA or the military (Cobain 2013).

We have seen that counterterrorism law introduces novel investigatory and penal regimes, redefines policing, recalibrates the balance of power among state institutions, runs havoc with the rule of law, and augments state power over the population. But what is this 'terrorism' the law seeks to counter?

Terrorism defined: crime, politics, punishment

The legal definition of 'terrorism' is the heart of counterterrorism legislation and policy: it describes what relevant law and state activity proposes to counter. The Patriot Act, section 802 modifies the pre-existing definition of international terrorism (18 USC 2331) to create the crime of *domestic terrorism*. It refers to activities which:

(A) Involve acts dangerous to human life that are a violation of the criminal laws of the US or of any State;
(B) Appear to be intended:
　(I) to intimidate or coerce a civilian population;
　(II) to influence the policy of a government by mass destruction, assassination, or kidnapping; and
(C) Occur primarily within the territorial jurisdiction of the US.

The first condition stipulated by this definition (§802-A) is that, for an activity to be considered terrorism, it must: 'Involve acts dangerous to human life that *are a violation of the criminal laws* of the US [...]'. Therefore, it provides against activities already covered by established law. It begs the question, why *outlaw something that is already illegal?* In any case, clause A sets a necessary, but not a sufficient condition in defining terrorism.

The condition which specifies terrorism as such is in the second clause (§802-B). The activity in question must: '*Appear to be intended*: to intimidate or coerce a civilian population', and/or to 'influence the policy of a government by mass destruction', etc. Hence, it is not the action as such that constitutes terrorism, but the actor's *apparent intention*. Terrorism is a criminal category defined not by objective deed. It is defined subjectively by the intention 'behind' the act, and that, not as it is expressed by the actor, but as interpreted by the prosecuting authorities (Manitakis 2003: 18–19; Paye 2007: 222; Sarafianos and Tsaitouridis 2003: 191). Thus terrorism is a (doubly) subjective category, signifying a substantial re-orientation of criminal justice.

The definition proceeds to outline what kind of intentions constitutes terrorism. First (§802-Bi), is the intention to 'intimidate or coerce' the population. 'Intimidation' is a broad concept which does not help specify the type of intention. The Act is also silent regarding what the population should not be 'coerced' into doing. This would indeed be hard, given that the legal system does not recognise any power of the population to develop or implement collective decisions. This capacity is exclusive to the state. Similarly, the concept of 'civilian population' is left unexplained. It can apply to anything ranging from the entire US population, to associations, however circumstantial, of two or more people. In all, sub-section 802-Bi provides a matrix that is nebulous, elastic and, hence, short of legal certainty. Second (§802-Bii), is the intention to 'influence' the 'policy of a government' through certain, illegal, means. The Act does not elaborate either on what 'policy', or on what type of 'government' must be protected. As it does not specify any conceivable conditions under which it may be justifiable to influence the government or its policies, it follows that influencing any policy decision, made by any government, constitutes terrorism. Therefore, what transforms common crime into terrorism is the *actor's perceived intention to influence (any) state activity*. Terrorism is the aggravated illegal activity which state officials interpret as being motivated against governmental policy and institutional normality.

In defining the crime at the heart of counterterrorism, the Act also describes what is to be protected. This is nothing less than the 'social order': the policy of the government plus the 'peace' of the population. The relations, structures, institutions and practices which prevail in society at the present moment are elevated to the status of a self-referent legal good, to be protected by force. This indicates a rigid social organisation, closed and averse to change. Nevertheless, the institutions, structures, practices, etc of a society are bound to change. What the Act does is to designate *the state as the only legitimate source of social change*. Moreover, notions like governmental policy and social order cannot be considered as objective, factual goods; they are abstract, ideological constructs. Its appointment as guardian of abstract concepts, leads penal justice to derailment (Sarafianos and Tsaitouridis 2003: 196, 200). In specific terms, 'social order' in a capitalist society is related to the maintenance of capitalist rule. The demand for order is directed against 'those who challenge the order of capital and the state: in a class society the content of the word "Order" always indicates repression' (Barthes 1982, cited in Neocleous 2000). Thus, the definition of terrorism makes apparent that the intentions of both the terrorist *and the legislator* are thoroughly political; and, through their shadow-play in the legal text, they outline a new political reality.

Once the political motivation becomes 'apparent' crime x is no longer x. It is terrorism, i.e. it subscribes to a qualitatively different, aggravated status, subjecting its suspect to special investigatory techniques, juridical procedures and penal treatment. Section 808 supplements the general definition of terrorism with a list of 38 'federal crimes of terrorism' (CRS 2001: 49–50). These include arson, kidnapping, possession and use of biological and chemical weapons, assault against federal high office holders, intimidation, conspiracy to destroy property of a foreign government, malicious mischief against US government property, injury to buildings or property, violence against mass transportation systems, destruction of property of an energy utility, cyber crime and material support.

Sections 803, 810, 811 and 814 increase the penalties for these crimes. Penalties range from 20 years to life, regardless of whether the act is committed or conspired (CRS 2001: 46–47, 50–52). In 2003, the Pretrial Detention and Lifetime Supervision Act, and the Terrorist Penalties Enhancement Act provided for lifelong supervision of ex-convicts of non-violent terrorism crimes which caused 'severe financial damage', and applied the death penalty to all terrorist crimes (including material support) if death results from the act, and to terrorism generally defined. In addition, the Pretrial Detention and Lifetime Supervision Act (§2602) shifts the burden of proof for pre-trial release to the defendant. This reverses the presumption of innocence principle, thus turning western legal culture on its head (Manoledakis 2003: 41).

The list of 'federal terrorist crimes' exceeds the general principle of danger to human life which the general definition prescribes as a necessary condition for terrorism. They include virtually every federal crime, and refer mostly to *protection of property rather than life* (Belandis 2004: 280–281).

Next to the legal definition of domestic terrorism, Executive agencies use their own, operative ones. These are important for they determine the conduct of investigations, and the training of police personnel. For the FBI, terrorism is defined as:

> the unlawful use of force or violence against persons or property to intimidate or coerce a government, the civilian population, or any segment thereof, in the furtherance of political or social objectives.
>
> (US Department of Justice 1988)

Here we meet again the themes of the Patriot Act definition: the unlawfulness of the act, the intimidation-coercion of the government and/or the population, and the emphasis on the protection of property and life. The notable differences are that: (a) a general reference to 'violence', whether it is directed *against persons or property*, replaces the 'dangerous to human life' requirement in the Patriot Act; and

(b) political motivation is *explicitly* identified as the crucial factor which transforms common crime to terrorism.

Finally, counterterrorism law also targets popular politics *directly*. PIRA criminalises insubordination to the police practice of arbitrarily designating 'off-limits' areas. Section 602 makes it a federal crime to enter or remain in a restricted area during an event of 'national significance'. This term remains undefined, and is to be determined by the Secret Service on an *ad hoc* basis. This authority of the Secret Service is upheld in the 2011 Federal Restricted Buildings and Grounds Improvement Act. The latter also reinstates that public protest in the proximity of people under Secret Service protection, and the disruption of governmental and official business, constitute federal offences, and facilitates their punishment. Enacted in March 2012, it is likely that this Act was indented to counter the Occupy movement (ACLU 2012b). It makes a mockery of the 'right' to assembly, reducing it to a police-issued permission.

We are starting to decipher what counterterrorism law seeks to protect. Some further indications are provided by legislation with economic content, both within and beyond the homeland security context.

Terrorism, capital, crisis

Financial counterterrorism

Counterterrorism legislation sets out a model for combating financial crime. Its key elements are the strengthening of state powers over financial institutions and transactions; the monopolisation of said powers by the Executive; and the adoption of an intelligence over a law enforcement approach to crime-fighting, involving capacities for blanket surveillance, emphasis on guilt by association, and a reversal of the burden of proof.

The marching orders to this direction were issued by the President just days after 9/11. Executive Order 13224, issued on 23 September 2001, draws its authority from the 1977 *International Emergency Economic Powers Act*. It orders the confiscation of all property from a list of non-US persons who, the Secretary of State determined, pose a risk to the citizens, the national security, the foreign policy, or the economic interests of the US. Special mention was made of Osama Bin Laden and Al Qaeda (who were already sanctioned), their associated groups and their supporters. The Order expanded asset-blocking to foreign institutions and persons the Treasury Secretary had determined were acting on behalf of, assisting or providing financial or material support to those listed by the State Department; and to anyone who the Treasury determines is somehow associated with those in the list (Donohue 2008: 166). The targeting of association constitutes an entry-point for state power into the interconnected space of flows that is financial transactions. The expanse of this power is determined exclusively by top Executive personnel.

Congressional contribution deepened these trends. The Patriot Act, Title III was dedicated to finance (especially money laundering, whether or not connected to terrorism), and moves in the familiar direction of intensifying state power and concentrating it in the Executive. But it also codifies a peculiar regime of regulation of the financial sector on counterterrorism grounds. Setting off where the Executive Order stopped, the Patriot Act (§106) authorised the President to confiscate any property, subject to US jurisdiction, of any foreign person, organisation or country the President determines has authorised, planned, aided or engaged in armed hostilities with the US. The Executive's reach expands beyond US jurisdiction, as §311 authorised the Secretary of Treasury to place restrictions on foreign institutions or types of account, if he determines they pose a 'primary money-laundering concern' to the US. Moreover, the Patriot Act expands the list of offences which can lead to asset seizure, to include foreign crimes, corruption, extraditable offences, firearms and customs offences, computer offences, cash smuggling, etc. Individuals are granted a review procedure, albeit with the burden of proof reversed; and courts can consider otherwise inadmissible evidence, when they find that compliance with the Federal Rules of Evidence could jeopardise national security (Donohue 2008: 161, 163).

Finally, the Patriot Act (§§318, 326, 352, 365, 373) required financial institutions (banks, mutual funds, credit unions, brokers, etc) to record the accurate name of each of their customers, their date of birth, and their Social Security and passport numbers, and to keep these records for five years. It also required all financial institutions (including casinos, credit card system operators, and money service businesses) and other businesses (e.g. insurance companies, investment advisers, commodity trading advisers, dealers in jewellery, precious stones and metals, travel agents, car dealers, estate agents) to incorporate programmes against money laundering in their operations. It further required any person receiving over US$10,000 in cash to file a Suspicious Activity Report, and the filing of all currency transactions by non-financial businesses. While these measures aim at flagging up suspicion of criminal activity and create a paper trail to help potential investigations, the Patriot Act also provided for blanket surveillance of financial transactions. Section 314 obligates financial institutions to conduct searches on any person, entity, account or region specified by the Treasury, and to report suspected money laundering to law enforcement.

Thus, counterterrorist law replicates with regards to the economy the operational mode of criminal investigations: expanded, often disproportionate powers, with a tendency to engulf the totality of relevant activity in their targeting, and yielded unilaterally by the Executive. Indeed, if regarding criminal investigations and prosecutions the Judiciary is crippled, financial measures ignore it altogether. Surprising here is the sudden introduction of some kind of control over financial transactions, as it goes against the dominant current of deregulation of that sector's operations. Financial flows are conceptualised as potentially criminal, providing the coercive apparatus a foothold for controlling them. This indicates a possible shift in the law-form, involving its modalities; and in the state-form, regarding which state mechanisms are predominant. It is too early for such an assessment. Instead, let us consider how counterterrorism helps redefine state-capital relations more broadly.

State-capital collusion on homeland security

The 2003 HSA set up the institutional architecture of the DHS. Comparable in importance was its treatment of the 'critical infrastructure' category. The destruction of critical infrastructure would imply disruption of economic and governmental activity, destruction of property, loss of life, and could undermine public order. Therefore, critical infrastructure condenses the abstract objects of security (private property, government policy, public peace, social order) into a tangible object-for-protection. In fact, along with top state managers, it is the only specified object for protection (see US Department of Homeland Security 2006).

Nonetheless, HSA does not define critical infrastructure. It leaves its designation to the discretion of the President and the DHS Secretary. They are authorised to select and introduce in this category any state-owned or private premises (factories, offices, land). The designation signifies a special regime of protection. Namely, the information disclosed (even orally) by the owner of critical infrastructure about its condition is protected, and even partial disclosure thereof is prohibited (to that effect, HSA also exempts DHS employees from the Whistleblowers Protection Act). Moreover, the owner is automatically under impunity, even if infrastructure vulnerabilities result from criminal negligence. In addition, the law does not require either the owner or the DHS to rectify any vulnerabilities (§§212–215). Thus the 'critical infrastructure' designation allows capital entities (e.g. chemical, medical, armaments, energy and agriculture industries) to avoid publicity and prosecution for the threat they may be posing to their personnel and the neighbouring population, without being required to do anything to ameliorate such threats.

In a similar vein, §835 allows the DHS Secretary to award security contracts to private entities at will, even on the basis of considerations irrelevant to security – for example the bidder's threat to move jobs abroad if not awarded the contract (Talanian 2003). Likewise, §871 enables the DHS Secretary to establish Advisory Committees consisting of top DHS personnel and private sector representatives, and to keep policy-making decisions therein secret.

Thus, under the pretence of security, counterterrorism law delineates new state-capital relations. While insulating the state from popular pressures, homeland security institutionalises its influence by capital.

Countering financial crisis

Finally, from a security crisis, we move to a 'securitisation' one. Facing a full-blown meltdown of the financial sector, Congress passed the *Emergency Economic Stabilisation Act* (EESA) on 3 October 2008. Deliberation was brief, driven by crisis-panic, and backed by political blackmail: 'if we don't do this, we may not have an economy on Monday' (Federal Reserve Chairman Bernanke addressing Congress members on 18 September 2008, cited in Samples 2010: 7). In short, congressional procedures went into Patriot Act mode. Another procedural similarity is that discussion was not informed by an assessment on the causes and aggravating factors of the crisis, or a strategy on how to overcome it. Once again, Congress did not know what it was trying to redeem through legislation, but voted whatever the Executive put before it.

Section 101 authorised the Treasury Secretary to 'establish the Troubled Asset Relief Program [TARP]' in order to purchase 'troubled assets' from any financial institution established or regulated by federal or state law. These assets comprised 'residential or commercial mortgages', related securities, and 'any other financial instrument that the Secretary [...] determines the purchase of which is necessary to promote financial market stability' (CRS 2009a: 3, 6–7; Samples 2010: 3–4). Thus, the law left the definition of 'troubled asset' and, up to a point that of 'financial institution', to the Secretary (CRS 2012b: 1). The potential scope of the programme was vast, and the Secretary was granted full discretion to shape it and utilise its resources (US House of Representatives 2008b: 53). The Treasury's licence was further enhanced by the lack of purpose and guidance in EESA. The latter sets numerous, broad and potentially conflicting priorities for the TARP, and fails to rank them (promoting financial market stability; protecting home values, college funds, retirement accounts and savings; preserving home ownership; promoting jobs and economic growth; maximising returns to the taxpayer; minimising national debt; stabilising communities, counties and cities; maximising efficiency; avoiding discrimination; preventing unjust enrichment of financial institutions, etc: EESA, §§2, 101(e), 103).

The lack of definition and priorities in the EESA effectively granted the Treasury Secretary carte-blanche in implementing the TARP (Samples 2010: 4–5; US House of Representatives 2008b: 41–42, 54). This was compounded by exempting his actions from judicial review, and by the absence of oversight. EESA (§§104, 116, 121, 125) created three mechanisms to oversee the TARP. Two of them were Executive entities, while the Congressional one lacked any authority, and was ignored by the Treasury (CRS 2009a: 4; Samples 2010: 5, 10, 17–19; US House of Representatives 2008b: 9, 17, 64, 79).

Left unrestrained, the Treasury produced 12 different programmes under the TARP aegis, some tailored to specific companies. It also shifted its main leverage under the TARP from buying toxic debt from troubled institutions, to injecting capital to healthy ones through stock purchase. This major shift came only ten days after EESA was enacted. The only consultation or notification to Congress was an out-of-hours telephone call from the Treasury to the chairman of the House Committee on Financial Services (CRS 2009a: 8; 2012b: 2; US House of Representatives 2008b: 14–15, 23, 30, 79). The targeted bailout of two financial corporations (Citigroup, Bank of America); an insurance company (AIG); and two car manufacturers and their assorted financial institutions (General Motors-GMAC, Chrysler-Chrysler Financial Services) was an *ad hoc* action, stemming from the same broad authorisation.

Nothing in the legislation precluded the Treasury from setting up the Public Private Partnership Investment Programme, and let private investors decide TARP acquisitions; or the Legacy Securities Programme, which exposed public money to risk while letting most gains to the private sector (CRS 2009b: 12–13).

Neither was there a statute preventing the hiring of financial entities to advise the Treasury on the allocation of TARP funds. The Treasury hired a Goldman Sachs subsidiary (Ennis Knupp) for that role, and declined to inform Congress on its remit or its reward (US House of Representatives 2008b: 35–36).

As the Treasury effectively handed over the running of TARP to the financial sector, it showed a marked disregard towards mortgage holders facing foreclosure. It ignored and resisted Congress's calls to help out struggling borrowers. It allocated a modest US$45 billion to housing support, of which only US$4 billion got disbursed – compared with (fully disbursed) US$250 billion for banks or another US$68 billion for AIG (CRS 2012b: 4; Samples 2010: 14–16; US House of Representatives 2008b: 10, 27–28)

The same latitude which EESA allowed the Treasury, the latter granted to the financial institutions receiving TARP money. The stocks which the Treasury bought were strictly non-voting. Even in AIG, which after the bailout was 80 per cent government-owned, the Treasury did not exercise any directive capacity (CRS 2009a: 7; 2012b: 8). Moreover, the TARP did not impose any regulatory adjustment upon financial institutions. It did not even impose any conditions upon their use of bailout money. Financial institutions could do what they wanted with it, and did not have to tell anyone how they spent it. Recipients did not inform the Treasury of their use of TARP money, neither was the latter monitoring its use (US House of Representatives 2008b: 2, 8–9, 13, 31, 36, 47–48, 93). Most recipients either hoarded the money, or used it to finance mergers and buy assets abroad. In any case, they did not lend it to businesses (as Congress and the Treasury were hoping), resulting in prolonged stagnation of the US economy *after* the financial sector had recapitalised (US House of Representatives 2008b: 12, 14–15, 31, 52).

By authorising the Secretary to set up the TARP as he saw fit, Congress effectively authorised an Executive entity to legislate. Yet, Congress has no capacity to delegate its duties. Thus, the TARP raises important constitutional issues, which should have been examined by the Judiciary – but were not (Samples 2010: 1–3).

From its viewpoint, the Executive demanded the broad, open-ended powers which EESA granted, on a perceived need for speed and flexibility in responding to unpredictable situations, mirroring again the justification for broad investigatory powers in counterterrorism law.

It must be noted that the TARP is not the primary vehicle for managing the crisis or bailing out the financial sector. The Federal Reserve spent about ten times the amount of TARP money for the same purpose and away from any regulation or overview. The reason the Executive went through the motions with Congress in order to be granted powers it was already using, was that it sought to incorporate emergency powers into law, thus legitimising its actions *tout court* (Samples 2010: 2; US House of Representatives 2008b: 31, 54).

The examination of EESA and the TARP shows that *the legal mode devised for dealing with terrorism is employed to deal with economic matters*. The empowerment of, and license to, the Executive; the eclipse of the Legislature and the Judiciary; the acceleration of congressional procedures; and the prevailing justifications, are all replicating the counterterrorism model. Moreover, the institutionalisation of special relations between the Executive and select capital entities in the TARP is similar to that set out in HSA, albeit with the Treasury, rather than the DHS, in charge. The urge to legislate and normalise these powers across different areas of social activity indicates that they comprise a preferred mode for the exercise of power. And the willingness of both Congress and the Judiciary to accommodate this model indicates that this mode is not an Executive (or a one-party) policy, but a state strategy. In any case, both the security- and the economy-related legislation raise important questions regarding the law-form and the state-form.

6 Counterterrorism legislation and the law-form

Ius regis – elements of a new law-form

In their totality, the main trends which counterterrorism law brings about signal a departure from the previous law-form, and outline a new one.

Undoubtedly, there are strong similarities and continuities between some key elements of the *lex mercatoria* form and certain dominant trends in counterterrorism legislation. The first continuity is the decline of the Judiciary's role in the distribution of justice. While *lex mercatoria* involved a circumvention of its powers by shrinking its jurisdiction, counterterrorism law diminishes its participation in, and overview of, the criminal investigation process. This means that, even if the Judiciary's role in adjudicating crime remains formally intact, its banishment from the investigation, and the Executive's monopoly over facts and evidence, *de facto* undermines its importance in adjudication.

A second continuity, related to the decline of the Judiciary, is the increasingly discretional and *ad hoc* character of legislation. While in the context of *lex mercatoria* specific categories of legal person could determine the rules governing their interactions and relations almost at will, counterterrorism law grants Executive agencies broad licence to determine, in a case-specific manner, the penal categories and subjectivities they target, the means through which they persecute and prosecute crime, and whether they do so at all. The targeting of the potentiality, rather than actuality, of crime, and the stirring of policing to intelligence, underlay this trend. They imply broad latitude for the Executive to determine both the temporalities and the objects of the investigation. Thus, the real subject of (perpetual) investigation is the (actual or potential) behaviours, mentalities and dispositions of the population. Amongst all this, the presumption of innocence which is fundamental to criminal law resembles a relic from a legal civilisation which is long gone.

The above trends find their fullest expression in the creation of a parallel penal regime for specific categories of the population. Here, any similarity with *lex mercatoria* and its parallel legal system is strictly formal. The two regimes are diametrically opposed regarding their substantive content (more on this below). The continuity between the forms is abstract, and lies in their tendency to create exceptions to the general jurisdiction, and subject certain categories of subjects and relations to para-legal regimes of governance and adjudication.

Equally important is the strong continuity between the undercurrents which inform these features – the trends behind the trends. The need for speed which was determinant of *lex mercatoria* is crucial in establishing the key legal features of counterterrorism. It accelerates the legislating process, so that it can occur without open deliberation or debate; and it dictates both the eclipse of the Judiciary and the broad licence to the Executive. Similarly, it is a main justification for the parallel penal regime: people are subjected to it to effectuate their quick removal from the operational field; and their treatment is justified by the need for speedy extraction of vital information, as testified in 'ticking-bomb' scenarios and similar securitarian fantasies.

All this implies a fundamental reconfiguration of the logic of law. Rather: the logic of procedural fairness and fact-based, dispassionate administration of justice according to already-existing norms that is specific to, and specifies the legal system, gives way to an instrumental conception of law, not so much committed to the distribution of justice, but employed to achieve certain outcomes in a most efficient way. The instrumentalisation of law was already crucial in shaping the *lex mercatoria* form, where law is but a toolbox at the service of actors concerned with economic effectiveness. In counterterrorism, instrumentalisation enters the realm of criminal (hence public) law. Here, the desired outcome is saving 'innocent lives', and law's effectiveness consists in minimising limitations on the means the state can use, the time to employ them, and the people against whom it can use them. Adherence to legal procedure becomes an optional course, followed or ignored according to its ability to ensure operational success (Roach 2011: 234, 235). The effectiveness principle is the one that encompasses (or even dictates) virtually all trends identified in both the *lex mercatoria* and counterterrorism law (including acceleration), and is, in this sense, the strongest continuity which transgresses the previous law-form and the new one that counterterrorism seems to outline. (It is also a reminder of how easily a utilitarian calculus can ultimately lead to the impoverishment of law as a distinct field of social practice with a unique contribution therein.)

Despite strong continuity in these key trends, counterterrorism legislation is not merely a progression of the *lex mercatoria* law-form. To begin by stating the obvious, its principal point of application is security, not the economy, and its core is firmly situated in criminal law, rather than trade or contract law. This makes a comparison between *lex mercatoria* and counterterrorism law seem like one between apples and oranges. Still, the law-form is an analytical notion referring to the overall configuration of legal norms, structures and relations in a specific socio-historical context. This, in turn, implies that developments in each different area of law – and the very demarcation of such areas – is not *necessarily* random or self-propelled, but can be an expression of broader political projects and strategies, and hence can possibly result in relative coordination or compatibility between developments in different legal areas. Law, and every single piece of legislation, is a codification of state- and social dynamics. In this framework, the comparison between *lex mercatoria* and counterterrorism not only makes sense, but already indicates possible shifts in the law-form: its centre of gravity has moved from trade to criminal law, reflecting a shift in political emphasis from economy to security. (By 'centre of gravity' I mean the area of law where most activity and 'innovation' is taking place, but also the one that has greater social impact, and can possibly influence developments in other areas.)

A major rift with the previous state of affairs caused by counterterrorism law is the sudden re-introduction of state-law into social life. The tendency to withdraw state regulation over social matters is reversed. The state is back in control, and law is re-statalised. Moreover, counterterrorism law is firmly anchored in the national scale. Regarding the sub-national scales, it indicates (especially in HSA) a subjection of regional and local matters to central, federal control, circumscribing the autonomy of sub-national government (Chapter 8). As for the supra-national scale, it merely features as an extension of national jurisdiction wherever 'local law permits'. The international, transnational or global scales constitute spaces of detour for a law whose subject and object are situated in national territory.

Lastly, counterterrorism law brings a resounding defeat of HR. In a spectacular reversal, HR retreats, from being a state-endorsed ideology, to a rearguard defence against a massive assault on rights and liberties (Gearty 2006: 102–109, 123–139).

The shift in law's centre of gravity, its re-statalisation and re-nationalisation, and the recoiling of human rights constitute reversals of main *lex mercatoria* trends, indicating that counterterrorism brings forth a new law-form. The emergent law-form does not cancel the twin predominant conditions of *lex mercatoria*: it does not reverse the deregulation (or self-regulation) of transnational capital; and it does not provide any legal security to the population in their capacity as workers or as citizens. The new form does not disrupt existing trends in given areas of law. It mainly emerges by introducing opposite trends (e.g. nationalisation, statalisation) in other areas.

When counterterrorism law addresses economic relations, it provides a flexible framework for capital, with velocity and effectiveness inbuilt as key objectives, in alignment with dominant *lex mercatoria* tendencies. Yet, the capacity of specific capital entities to enter this privileged regime depends entirely on the state. By holding the keys to Shangri-la, the state can, potentially, dictate terms and conditions to capital, and determine the formation of the power bloc. And it can do so, not only through general strategic stirring in metagovernance terms, but also through direct, case-specific, arbitrary selection. As the legal framework devised to manage the economic crisis shows, this model, forged in the context of homeland security, is replicated in relation to economic policy.

Finally, both law-forms developed parallel legal regimes: the *Lex Mercatoria* (here in capitals, as a specific mode of regulating transnational economic activity), and the 'Guantanamo treatment' – the penal regime reserved for those the President designates as 'unlawful enemy combatants'. Apart from being beside the legal system, these two regimes have nothing in common. *Lex Mercatoria* applies to certain types of economic activity, it is determined by its own subjects according to their needs and interests, and it is marked by the absence of over-determination by state or public power. The Guantanamo treatment, on the contrary, pertains to the field of security. Its subjects are totally excluded from determining its character. Their treatment is something which is *happening to* them, they are subjected to it in the fullest sense of the word. It is determined by the President (or the Defense Secretary, acting as his surrogate) in full discretion – without plan, principle, order or norm. This constitutes a complete negation of the rule of law, i.e. to the distribution of justice according to *a priori*, general and public rules (and courts). Here, the law is the rule of the president-king. The parallel regime may not be the most central, or even the most important, element of the new law-form. But it brings together its main trends (the decline of the rule of law, the eclipse of the judiciary, the apotheosis of penalisation, the disappearance of human rights, the emphasis on intelligence and pre-emption, the logic of effectiveness, and the monopolisation of power by the Executive) in their most acute and unmediated – their 'purest' – expression. Hence, it can give the whole law-form its name: the right of the king, *ius regis*.

The ascendance of the *ius regis* form signals the recasting of state-population relations in penal, rather than economic, terms. They are reconfigured on a criminal law model. This entails a relocation of the centre of ideological and political authority, from the citizenry to the state (Paye 2007: 225–226). It also entails a shift in juridico-political subjectivities: the rational, calculative, free-choice, Benthamite individual is replaced by a threatening, always potentially dangerous one, whose motivations and rationale are opaque, incomprehensible and delirious. From a society of individuals modelled on the ideal-type of the entrepreneur, we pass to a society of suspects – of criminals in potential.

The replication of legal modalities forged in a security context, to the realm of economic policy, signifies that the new law-form is capable of adapting and expanding; that *ius regis* is not a 'single-issue' model restricted to one area of political activity, but a potentially durable and generalisable form.

Finally, we note that in the context of both the *lex mercatoria* and the *ius regis* forms, the key relation between the state and the population (economy; security) is where their respective parallel legal regime springs up (*Lex Mercatoria*; Guantanamo treatment). Even as these two para-legal regimes pull in opposite directions – if *Lex Mercatoria* is 'law without the state', then the Guantanamo treatment is 'the state without law' – they describe a common, deep tendency: *the importance of law as an expression of state power and as an organisation of social relations is declining*. As law recedes from mediating social relations, the latter increasingly become determined by force. In the case of *Lex Mercatoria*, these are force-relations between equals, resulting in a regime of self-regulation; while contractual arrangements between entities of different might (poor country vs big corporation; welfare recipient vs provider) do not even bother to conceal the force differential that underpins them. In addition, in the Guantanamo treatment, the state-population relation ceases to be based on (legally mediated and defined) *power*, and relapses to one of *force*. We suddenly contemplate the hubristic sense of justice, where 'right, in the human sense, is only in question between equals in might, while the strong do what their force allows them, and the weak submit and accept it' (Thucydides 2011: §89).

State of exception?

Granting the Executive sweeping, discretionary powers seems to be the typical, even routine, response of north-American and European legislatures in times of crisis, i.e. when the reproduction of the social order is perceived to be under threat. The speed and unpredictability of these situations calls for urgent responses, a task which the unified, non-deliberative, rapid-fire Executive is best suited to undertake. While this pattern is the canon regarding crises of 'national security' (caused by external or internal Enemies), William Scheuerman has shown that it is also replicated in the context of industrial dispute and economic crisis. Throughout the twentieth century, Congress had been vesting the Executive with emergency powers which ossified but were never repealed (Scheuerman 2000; 2004: 107–116). In the twenty-first century, both homeland security and economic emergency legislation display emergency features in abundance. Unsurprisingly, no one seems in a hurry to repeal the new economic powers; and the homeland security ones are now well-established and constantly intensifying. Major crises of some kind seemed to come thick and fast in the first few years of the twenty-first century, triggering emergency powers addressing different aspects of social life. In addition, these powers tend to settle and become part of legal and social normality. Thus, things resemble a Schmittian model of a sovereign who unifies the people, acts in the situation of emergency according to no rule but its own decision, and this decision sets the new norm (Papacharalambous 2009: 38–44, 49; Schmitt 1985; 1988; 2004).

Indeed, the ostracism of the judiciary from investigations, the enveloping of the entire population in a surveillance dragnet, the dissociation of surveillance from suspicion of criminal activity, the pre-emptive orientation of policing, the authorisation of the Executive to pick the targets and devise the means of prosecution (and economic policy), the dissociation of the punitive sentence from the illegal act, the presumption of guilt, the emphasis on guilt by association, the conjuring of a parallel regime of detention and adjudication monopolised by the Executive, the highly subjective-interpretative nature of the central crime in counterterrorism law – every single feature of counterterrorism legislation – contributes to a devastation of the rule of law, inasmuch as with the latter we refer to a system of public, general, universal rules, set *a priori* and delimiting (defining and limiting) the exercise of state power.

In Schmitt, the exception indicates the emergence of an (internal or external) Enemy. It triggers the exception, and constitutes politics in its real sense ('the Political') as a friend vs foe distinction. The relationship between the two is one of mutual existential negation, of struggle to the death (Schmitt 1996). While enmity constitutes real politics, the real Enemy is the Partisan. This is the irregular, criminal, fighter, who fights by all means available. By disrespecting the rules and customs of warfare, the Partisan brings forth real war. In doing so, she exempts herself from the legal (and moral) order: the Partisan 'knows and accepts that he is an enemy outside of right, law, and honour [...] The modern partisan expects neither law, nor mercy from the enemy. He has moved away from the conventional enmity of controlled and bracketed war, and into the realm of another, real enmity, which intensifies through terror and counter-terror until it ends in extermination' (Schmitt 2007: 30, 11). Finally, while traditionally the Partisan is a telluric and defensive fighter, socialist revolutionary warfare results in a new partisan type, one who is cosmopolitan and aggressive.

Independently of Schmitt, and without subscription to a decisionist framework, contemporary jurist Günther Jakobs draws from classic liberal thought, to claim the *de facto* existence of a parallel penal code which deals with the Enemy. The criminality of the Citizen does not negate the judicial order. Hence, the criminal-citizen is a legal person, and therefore treated with all the due process and guarantees of criminal justice, in a rule of law context.

On the contrary, the crime of the Enemy may not be breaking the law directly, but it undermines the judicial order. Thus, its perpetrator does not pertain to the latter. The Enemy is not a legal person, and her treatment is not geared towards correction but towards neutralisation. The state is obliged to employ all means necessary to annihilate the danger she represents. The paradigm for this treatment is not the rule of law, but the 'right of state', and its criterion is not adherence to legal principles, but effectiveness in neutralising the threat, even before it materialises. This special treatment is triggered by the failure of individuals to appear to be lawful. The latter is essential for law to really exist and affect social behaviour: people must know that other people are adhering to it. The state is responsible for guaranteeing lawfulness, and needs to monitor the population, locate apparently or potentially lawless individuals, and pre-emptively detain them for as long as it takes to ensure that they do not threaten the judicial order. As for who this Enemy is, Jakobs draws from Hobbes and Kant, who respectively designate 'high treason' and anomic behaviour as crimes which undermine the social order. On this basis, he names the terrorist as the modern Enemy, but also criminal organisations, gangs (and sheer membership in such groupings suffices, regardless of the actual commission of a crime) and people with compulsory criminality can be brought into the foil (Jakobs 2003; 2011).

Regardless of their validity, what makes the juridical constellations of Schmitt and Jakobs interesting is their eerie resonance with counterterrorism law – the enhanced investigatory regime for terrorism suspects, the increased penalisation of terrorist convicts, the exemption from law of enemy combatants, the criminalisation of antagonistic politics. The key trends of counterterrorism law are a good fit to authoritarian jurisprudence, classic and contemporary, and are perhaps consciously utilised as foundation for the post-9/11 legal architecture.

Still, if we are to subscribe to the exception dogma, we must be aware of certain caveats. To begin with, the above elements were not foreign to the legal order predating 9/11. They were already present, and in some cases increasingly entrenched, in the legal system, and were mainly regulating the relations between the coercive state apparatus and 'special' categories of the population: the spy, the alien, the 'international terrorist', the gangster. We can argue that the norm for the exceptional category becomes the norm for all. But this hardly means that we are witnessing the phantasmagoric force of the sovereign decision which shutters the existing social normativity and casts it anew. What we see is more akin to a pullover of a legal blanket to cover more (or all) parts of the social body; or, as already explained, a ratchet effect.

Furthermore, while the Bush administration represented the 9/11 events as a genuine moment of existential emergency (an assumption unchallenged by political and legal personnel and intellectuals), its actions testify marked reluctance to be seen 'acting decisively' in the Schmittian sense. No part of the Constitution was for a single day suspended or circumvented, and Congress was immediately drafted in to fine-tune and legislate overwhelming (and largely arbitrary) powers for the Executive. The result was the open-ended AUMF and the Patriot Act's 300-odd pages of meticulous amendments to pre-existing legislation. In these terms, the entire body of counterterrorism law produced in the wake of 9/11 is precisely a juridical and political denial of decisionism. It seeks to draw draconian, discretionary power *from* law, and inscribe it *into* law. Even the most excessive practices undertaken by the Bush and Obama administrations (e.g. extrajudicial assassinations) are defended in (however dubious) legal terms. Even the emblematic exceptional case (Guantanamo) is marked by the paradox of the absence of law being compensated for by a maze of extra-, quasi- and pseudo-legal regulations; and, in repeated triangulations among the three branches, it is increasingly being normalised. Therefore, the invocation of emergency does not result in a sovereign decisionist onslaught, but in a kind of compulsion-ism, where the Executive is, allegedly, *forced* to act and its action is immediately codified, procedurised and, ultimately, legalised. Thus, the exception is domesticated, the decision is negated and the responsibility it bears is dissolved (Johns 2005).

Along these lines, the reaction of leading American constitutional scholars is telling. Oren Gross (2003) calls for a clear re-instatement of the exception and its radical separation form the constitutional framework, in order to rectify their present creeping amalgamation. Contrary to Gross's 'separationist' or extra-legal approach, Bruce Ackerman (2004; 2006) suggests the absorption of the exception into the Constitution, and its taming through clear, demanding procedures for congressional authorisation of emergency powers to the Executive.

The above indicate that an exception-normality model may be rather simplistic. Moreover, these concepts seem somewhat rusty, if not outright useless. Inasmuch as the centrality of the sovereign decision in Schmitt casts politics as law-creating, draws attention to the violence which underpins law, and reminds of a certain arbitrariness in the foundations of social institution, it is a welcome counterpoint to liberal jurisprudence which systematically tries to disengage law from the state and politics and conceal its ultimate foundation and reliance on force. But problems abound with Schmitt's understanding of politics. His construct of the sovereign as the organic expression of 'the people' (a pre-political, eternal entity) in its entirety is highly idealistic (indeed, mythological). While upholding the nature of politics as an antagonistic process, his concept of the political (in fact, of the polemical) as a friend-foe distinction, constitutes a radical impoverishment of politics, collapsing its intricacies, complexities, mediations, expanse and depth into a singular, all-constituting act and relation. Inherent in this construction is an essentialism, an urge to identify the eternal source of social phenomena.

Schmitt's essentialism and his impoverishment of politics are inherited by Giorgio Agamben, the political and legal philosopher whose work attempts to produce a left-wing critique of post-9/11 counterterrorism policy and law as a permanent state of exception (Agamben 2005).

Agamben's juridico-political ontology is also marked by the eminence of the exception, and its primacy over the norm. The exception is not only an ever-present possibility, but the constitutive act of normality – the moment of open-ended war which results in the establishment of social organisation. In the contemporary mode of power, the exception becomes the norm. The foundation of the political on the opposing elements of law and pure violence is overcome. Political power is unfettered by law, and becomes sheer violence. Individuals are stripped of their juridico-political mediations vis à vis power and are reduced to 'bare life' (Agamben 1998; 2005).

The claim that the foundation of power is the capacity for unlimited violence is a salutary counterpoint to the liberal mystification of the rule of law as a force-less realm. But it is equally mystificatory, and its analytical value for specific developments in specific societies is limited. This is due, first, to the abstract and historically selective, character of Agamben's treatise; second, because it construes a general theory of power, with all the analytical bulldosing that such endeavour entails; and, third, because, as general theories go, it is particularly flat-footed, and its main categories are flawed.

In an idiosyncratic historical inspection of the state of emergency, Agamben misses the dual movement of expanding what constitutes an exception and of intensifying exceptional powers, which are consequently incorporated into law. Exceptional powers are already integral to the rule of law; and, the latter constantly expands by re-covering its exceptions and externalities – thus rendering the duality between the exception and normality problematic (Neocleous 2006a: 194–201; Scheuerman 2000). In fact, normality, and its limits, defines the exception: Agamben's exception presupposes the existence of a normal-legal framework (Johns 2005: 625; Schmitt 1988: 13) which is, by definition, deposed of the violence of the exception. While in Schmitt the conception of *liberal* jurisprudence as force-less and therefore defence-less against revolutionary violence was an inspired subterfuge for advocating dictatorial rule, in Agamben, Schmitt's conceptually and historically specific schema becomes transcendental and loses any – even polemical – value.

This juxtaposition between (an essentially anomic) politics and (a presently irrelevant) law reproduces the liberal-positivist occultation of law's political character. It ignores the nature of law as a (political) codification of violence – as an organisation of the terrain, objects and modalities of violence (Neocleous 2006b; Poulantzas 1978: 76–77, 91–92). It also conceptualises political power as, exclusively, force. Its organisational, institutive and meaning-making aspects are mere accessories (or cover-ups) to its real essence. The essence of power is eternal, a natural fact, susceptible to unimportant variation in time and space.

This quest for the essence of power represses a set of questions crucial not only for the understanding of specific socio-historical conjunctures, but also for the normality-exception conundrum. To begin with, it is difficult to interrogate the reasons for, and the processes through which, the sovereign switches to exceptional mode. How, and why, is the decision *of* the exception (logically prior to the decision *in* the exception) taken? Second, it is clear from Agamben's own selection of constitutional texts that the substantive content of the exception varies. In Roman times the state of exception entailed the arming of the citizenry by the Senate, in homeland security it signifies the immobilisation of the population through quarantine. What is the value of a concept used to describe two opposite realities? Third, can indeed sovereign power strip the individual of all socio-political mediations and significations? Is 'bare life' possible? And, fourth, why does the bearer of powers most awesome use them only occasionally? In other words, why does an omnipotent sovereign tolerate any kind of normality, for any length of time (Colatrella 2011)?

These problems are symptoms of an institutional fetischisation of the state and law, which ignores their relations to society in favour of an analytics of pure power. A more nuanced attempt to understand the relationship between the state and law as *social* phenomena is needed for understanding either one. This cannot be done within Agamben's framework, as the social is absent from his analysis (Huysmans 2008: 174–176). In fact, *the constitutive fallacy* in Agamben's thesis is the juxtaposition between an anthropomorphic 'sovereign' acting by its own will and for its own accord, and an atomised 'individual', abstracted from social meanings, bonds and relations (Whyte 2010: 148). Abstracted from social dynamics, structures and practices, the law, the state and the individual are *pseudo-entities*, and their interrelations in 'normal' or 'exceptional' modes are a caricature. In trying to uproot the liberal mystification of a rule of law situated outside and against state power, Agamben replaces (or couples) it with a primordial, a-historical mystification: the exception as the secret essence, 'the hidden structure', of power.

A serious attempt to demystification would start from a conception of the law and the state as social creatures, and conceptualise both the rule of law and the state of exception as different codifications of social power within the legal framework (and therefore, already, within that of the state). This helps lift the liberal mystification of the rule of law as a force-less mode of rule, and Agamben's essentialism of power and fetishism of the state. Along these lines, it is precisely the state's role as main producer, overviewer and guarantor of law which renders it capable to negotiate, circumvent, amend, overwhelm or abolish it. In addition, the historically specific extent to which it can do any of these varies according to the configuration of social dynamics and their inscription in the institutional framework of the state. Thus, whether the 'sovereign' will declare a state of exception; in the context of what emergency it will do so; the content, intensity and duration of the exceptional moment; and its success – pending on the support, tolerance or resistance by the population – all depends on social forces and the manner in which they are represented in the state. As for normality, rather than being the exception's poor relation, it is the stable configuration of social forces, and the framework for its reproduction and for its orderly change.

Thus, we return to the question of forms. I hope that this discussion has helped clarify that the *ius regis* law-form is not an exceptional law-form, but a normal one, deriving from partial realignments, intensifications and reversals of the previous form. And, in a broader discussion of social power, it pointed to the analytical poverty of the normality-exception binary. This brings us to the state-form.

A shift in the state-from?

Almost 30 years before Agamben presented the permanent exception thesis, Poulantzas conceptualised authoritarian statism as a state-form developing to enable the state to cope with permanent crisis. The phraseology of the two authors appears similar, but only superficially. Rather than referring to a general-abstract state of exception, Poulantzas (1976b) devised a detailed typology of crises (economic, ideological, political, crisis of the state, etc), and noted that the increasing role of the state in managing the economy meant that a crisis erupting in one area was likely to metastasise to other areas and other types of crisis (e.g. an economic crisis turning to political crisis and vice versa). In any case, crises occur as a result of acute social antagonism – they are not merely technical phenomena, nor can they be conjured by the state at will. In fact, far from being an omnipotent subjectivity, the state has no power of 'its own'; it is a social relation, and its power derives from the differential in the balance among social forces.

Its susceptibility to socio-historical specificity, and its emphasis on the social nature of the phenomena and developments under examination, makes Poulantzas's analytical framework much more relevant to the analysis of homeland security than Agamben's. In its context, we can use the new law-form to provide some indications regarding the state-form. This is possible not only because law provides an abstract framework for the exercise of state power, and can therefore testify on the character of the state (Belandis 2004: 58), but, more directly, because *the law-form is a constitutive component of the state-from*.

The overarching characteristic of *ius regis* – the proliferation of emergency elements and their incorporation into the mainstream body of law – indicates that we are in the realm of AS, which is the state-form characterised by, precisely, the incorporation of authoritarian elements in to the democratic institutional shell. Still, AS has already undergone two different configurations, two phases (Chapter 3). It is worth asking whether homeland security constitutes a third. I will therefore trace continuities and possible ruptures between the previous AS phases and the indications which *ius regis* provides for the present state-form.

The preference of unlimited Executive authority displayed by both counterterrorism and economic emergency law is premised on deeply seated conceptions deriving from classic liberal political philosophy. Even if they were valid in their era (the eighteenth century), they are seriously distorting the contemporary reality of political institutions. The first premise is that the Executive is best suited to act in an emergency, because it comprises a single, unitary actor, prompt to non-deliberate, quick-fire action. On the contrary, in contemporary states, the Executive is a maze of directorates, departments and agencies, whose unitary action is not a given, but a possibility secured through excessive deliberation (and intrigue, plots, and circumventions). The Executive is not necessarily faster than any other branch; hence its perception as the ideal actor in an emergency stands on shaky ground. The second premise is that 9/11 constituted a genuine attack to the 'body politic', which needed to employ quick-fire action to defend itself from an existential threat. On the contrary, 9/11 did not pose a serious threat to the existence or the social order of the US, and the state could enjoy the advantages of sober and thorough deliberation in planning its reaction (Scheuerman 2002).

Knowledge differentials further tip the balance of power in favour of the Executive. In legislating the Patriot Act and EESA, Congress had no detailed knowledge of the crises' specific features, or of their causes. All knowledge of the facts surrounding 9/11 derived from the Executive's intelligence agencies. Similarly, the official narrative of the financial crisis was provided by the Federal Reserve and the Treasury. Executive pre-eminence is underpinned not only by the fabled speed of the Executive, but also from its superior knowledge. It results in a situation where the entities primarily responsible for the crisis dictate the measures to overcome it.

The need for speed not only privileges the Executive, it also impacts Congress. The legislating process is accelerated – especially in the cases of the Patriot Act and EESA, the cornerstone Acts for dealing with each crisis. Still, this did not entail a cancelling of deliberation. Deliberation *did* occur, albeit not on the Congress floor, but behind closed doors among a restricted club of members. Effectively, in terms of rhythm and procedure, the Legislature operated as a special committee of the Executive. Rather than being subordinated to the Executive in a state of emergency, the Legislature *as such* did not appear in the legislating process.

If the decline of the Legislature indicates a deepening of key tendencies of previous AS configurations, the trend towards forceful coercion signifies their hardening. The surveillance dragnet and the penal overkill which played peripheral, supportive roles in the previous AS phase, targeting social outcasts and negators of the neoliberal order, now occupies the political centre stage (Brown and Gray 2007). Surveillance is universal, and coercion defines state-population relations. This is not restricted to legal provisions: in activities ranging from pre-emptive warfare to accentuated police presence in the city, and from the thrashing of demonstrations, to targeted assassinations, the state is parading an excess of violence.

Similarly, the political character of the crime at the heart of counterterrorism, signifies increased criminalisation of popular political activity. This presents an interesting continuum. In the context of the first AS phase (the crisis of KWNS) the structure and functions of political parties was reversed, to preclude rank-and-file members from determining policy. In the second phase (SWPR), labour representation was banished from policy-making processes. Now, popular political expression is stifled even 'outside' the state, in the streets. By contrast, the participation of capital in policy-making becomes increasingly institutionalised, as homeland security law makes the parallel network of state-capital governance an acknowledged component of the official state.

Nevertheless, the tight state-capital relations are now *determined by the state*: specific sectors and enterprises can enter the state only if they are selected by the Executive. This means increased capacity of the state to determine the outlook of the power bloc. Here, homeland security law gives unlimited discretion to the Executive to select whatever capital entities it sees fit, and EESA upholds this discretion, but also legislates the return of finance into the power bloc: it institutionalises the colonisation of the Treasury by its agents; it sets the state as the key lender to the financial sector, introducing a collusion of interests; and, by granting entities receiving federal money full discretion as to how they use it, it allows a new wave of financial sector mergers, so that entities 'too big to fail' become even bigger.

The statalisation of economic policy signals a significant reversal of the previous form. The setting up of the homeland security regime occurred under the aegis of the coercive state apparatus, signifying its predominance among state mechanisms – a rare occurrence in the context of a capitalist state. The anomaly did not last long. As homeland security became established and normalised, and as the economic crisis erupted, the economic apparatus is back in the driving seat, and inherits the power modalities introduced by homeland security.

Moreover, the logic of homeland security entailed a marked re-nationalisation of state activity and strategic planning. This nation-centrism persists in the current context of economic crisis. While the dominant logic guiding and unifying state activity is once again 'economic', its horizon is not a 'glocalised' one as it was in the SWPR form, but one rooted in, and referent to, the *national* economy.

Finally, the decline of law's importance as a medium for social organisation and governance signifies, from the viewpoint of the state-form, a weakness of the state in regulating social developments in a prospective, orderly manner. The constant reliance to discretion, *ad hoc* legal measures, and para-legal orders means that the state is constantly overwhelmed by social dynamics. This, in turn, highlights the *brittleness* of the state-form.

The developments in the state-form cannot be affirmed or fully assessed only through the legal 'blueprint'. This requires a study of the (re)organisation and practice of state institutions. But before that, I evaluate the political impact of the legislation, focusing on its implementation and the resistance to it.

7 The Act and the state: implementation, friction, resistance

This chapter discusses the reaction of entities within the state to counterterrorism legislation. It identifies trends in the implementation of the law and associated points of friction, and highlights connections between state dynamics and the broader field of social antagonism.

Executive

A major point of convergence among DOJ officials (including then Attorney General Ashcroft and FBI Director Mueller) is in praise of the merger of law enforcement with intelligence (US House of Representatives 2003a: 8–9; US Senate 2002b: 4; 2002c: 4–5; 2003b: 2–3). The Patriot Act's provisions for information sharing between intelligence and law enforcement agencies (especially §203) are used routinely (US Department of Justice 2003a: 20–29). Based on the 'significant' FISA amendment (§218), the DOJ uses FISA to conduct law enforcement investigations oriented to criminal prosecution, substituting Title III with the wider powers and lower legal standards of FISA (US Senate 2002b: 4, 42). The DOJ created a unit dedicated to standardising FISA procedures and training law enforcement personnel; and the FISC members were increased from seven to nine, to make the Court more available (US Senate 2003a: 16).

To be sure, the DOJ uses FISA frantically. FISA applications have increased ten-fold since 9/11 (Roach 2011: 177; see also EPIC Unknown Date), and investigations are often initiated by the DOJ before FISC authorisation is requested (US Department of Justice 2002: 4–5; 2003a: 17). FISA powers are involved in about a quarter of terrorism cases brought before the courts (CLS 2011: 13). They mainly relate to electronic surveillance, including multiple instances of roving surveillance (49 times to mid-2005), obtained in cases where investigations would not comply with Title III standards (Moran 2005: 341; US Department of Justice 2002: 3). Physical searches are not rare either: secret searches (§213) were used 153 times to July 2005. To April 2003, they resulted in 248 extensions of delayed notice. As they apply to all federal crimes, they are being used mainly against drugs and common crime: up to mid-2005 only 12 per cent of the 153 delayed notification search warrants were related to terrorism investigations (Donohue 2008: 235; US Department of Justice 2003a: 7–11; 2004). As for the notorious access-all-records provision (§215), it seems that DOJ started using it only in mid-2004. Between then and the end of 2005, it was used 162 times (21 FISC authorisations of §215 orders, and 141 authorisations to use §215 in combination with other powers). The total number of individuals targeted remains secret, and so is the type of records requested, but there seems to be emphasis on university and library records (US Department of Justice 2007: 17–36, 45–46). Still, due to its capacity for blanket surveillance, talk of numbers or targets makes little sense. Its crowning achievement (of those that we know of) is that it provides the legal authority for the NSA's PRISM and X-Keyscore programmes, which monitor virtually *all* telecommunications that have at least one end on US soil (Greenwald 2013a; 2013b).

Even if conveyed through sporadic and heavily redacted data, the picture is rather clear: *the merging between law enforcement and intelligence is happening*. The legislative request was fully adhered by the policing mechanism, which in operative terms increasingly resembles an intelligence agency. Apart from the operational mode, the policing mechanism and its space are also merged and homogenised, in accord with the legislation. This is encapsulated in the FISC's authorisation for generalised §215 surveillance: the relevant request was submitted to the Court by the FBI (Justice), but the warrant authorises the NSA (Defense) to carry out surveillance (US Foreign Intelligence Surveillance Court 2013) – indicating that the blurring of boundaries between agencies and Departments, both military and civilian, and domestic and foreign, is advanced.

If anything, FISA investigations resemble orderly operations when compared to NSLs. Since 2003 (when data became available) the FBI has issued between 40,000 and 56,000 NSLs annually, compared to 8,500 in 2000. Their use has become routine in the context of preliminary investigations and during the 'threat assessment' stage, well before a criminal investigation has commenced. The Bush administration failed to offer a single example where their use was instrumental in interrupting terrorist activity. There is no statutory limit on how much information can be gathered or how many people can be implicated by an NSL. When, in late 2003, the FBI requested Las Vegas hotels and airlines to disclose customer records for the last week of December, an estimated 270,000 people were implicated. A 2007 Inspector General's audit found serious procedural violations regarding the issuing, use, and recording in up to a quarter of NSLs it reviewed (ACLU 2009: 12, 16; Donohue 2008: 237–242; US Senate 2011a).

Lastly, under the requirements of the Patriot Act, §§356 and 357, the submission of Suspicious Activity Reports (SARs) by financial institutions to the FBI and the Treasury skyrocketed from under 200,000 in 2000 to over 1.2 million in 2007 (ACLU 2009: 12). This caused a drag on the operations of financial institutions, which were forced to create specialised departments to deal with SARs.

The way FISA, NSLs and SARs are used verifies another trend: *blanket investigations are becoming a regular feature of police practice*. This trend is further evident in the context of surveillance of political activity.

The coercive mechanism has interpreted correctly the character of the terrorism crime and, accordingly, focuses on policing popular attempts to 'influence the policy' of the government. In March 2002, Attorney General Ashcroft eliminated the (internal to the FBI) wall between prosecution and intelligence operations (US Attorney General 2002a). His Guidelines to FBI agents (the Bureau's internal law[1]) direct them to target political activity. They urge agents to monitor spaces open to the public (including political meetings and rallies, religious sermons and the internet), and to use almost the entire intelligence arsenal, including infiltration, to obtain information which may relate to criminal activity. Agents are directed to employ said methods even before the preliminary investigation stage – i.e. to conduct *fishing expeditions*. The Guidelines make it hard to terminate such expeditions: the agents conducting one can only finalise it when they are certain no criminal activity will occur. Moreover, the FBI is required to maintain a database with the fruits of all these expeditions, which is shared with other federal agencies as well as state and local law enforcement. Agents are specifically directed to monitor demonstrations involving groups on which there is 'reasonable indication' that they may 'aim to engage in activities involving force or violence', or commit any federal terrorism crime or activity covered by the general definition of terrorism.[2] The FBI claims that it tries to identify 'anarchists and extremist elements' and that it does not monitor 'law-abiding' protesters. Despite this acute democratic sensitivity, the FBI has been targeting liberal, systemic organisations like the American Civil Liberties Union (ACLU), People for the Ethical Treatment of Animals or Greenpeace (Donohue 2008: 249–250; US Attorney General 2002b).

Dividing the population into law-abiding citizens and terrorist sympathisers, and bluntly associating popular political opposition with terrorism, is a mainstay of DOJ counterterrorism effort. 'If you're not a terrorist or a spy, you have nothing to worry about'. The DOJ 'goes to great lengths to protect the privacy of every American unless you happen to be a foreign spy or member of a terrorist organisation' (DOJ Spokesman Mark Corallo, cited in ACLU 2003e: 7). Since the DOJ only persecutes spies and terrorists, it follows that it is the act of investigating that determines guilt. And, since the innocent 'have nothing to fear', anyone expressing 'worries' about counterterrorism is *de facto* suspicious. This is a valid interpretation of the terrorism crime. Expressing concern about counterterrorism can be interpreted as an attempt to influence governmental policy through undue means. Social opposition is a borderline case of terrorism.

From its part, the DHS created (in 2007) the Extremism and Radicalization Branch, a unit designed to monitor 'all forms of extremist activity'. It was mainly

---

1 There is no legal statute guiding the FBI's internal practices; this is done by the Attorney General's Guidelines, which are normally approved by Congress. For the first time in history Congress was ignored in the introduction of the 2002 Guidelines.
2 An FBI bulletin elaborates what kind of activity agents must target and report to the Joint Terrorism Task Force: internet-based recruitment, fund-raising and coordination efforts by 'activists'; activist 'training camps'; passive resistance (sit-ins), since it disrupts traffic, creates a 'climate of disorder' and possibly intimidates people from attending the protest; demonstrators' 'self-defence methods', like dressing in layers and wearing gas masks; the use of cameras, tape recorders, etc: these are 'intimidation techniques' used to document 'potential cases of police brutality' (US Federal Bureau of Investigation 2003).

dedicated to infiltrating anarchist and deep ecology groups and monitoring their open source material, even when the groups were said to adopt 'a no-harm doctrine [...] claiming to ensure the safety of humans, animals, and the environment' and were only suspected of potential cyber-attacks. Such attacks in the past involved deleting user accounts, spamming a corporation's inbox, 'and other types of e-mail assaults intended to force business to exhaust resources' (US Department of Homeland Security 2009a). While a long way from the 'threat to life' requirement, the inclusion of these groups and practices high in the DHS agenda is perfectly compatible with a 'counterterrorism' policy focused on the protection of property rather than life. The unit was terminated in 2009, after pressures by right-wing politicians and organisations upset that right-wing 'extremism' was also monitored (US Department of Homeland Security 2009b). Still, the targeting of anarchist, green, and black radical groups on the basis of their conviction (not action) remains an entrenched DHS policy (US Department of Homeland Security 2011b).

Police practice confirms two key trends deciphered from the legislation. First, intelligence and law enforcement agencies and operations are amalgamated. Rather: *law enforcement is steered towards intelligence*, something witnessed in the collapse of the three, previously distinct, stages of a criminal investigation (threat assessment, preliminary investigation, full investigation) so that the rules of a full investigation apply even to 'threat assessment' operations. This results in blanket surveillance, fishing expeditions, disappearance of judicial control and the presumption of guilt. This, in turn, is the outcome of the pre-emptive character policing has acquired – an implicit principle in the legislation, dictated by the secretive, camouflaged and omni-present nature of the Enemy in war on terror discourse, and forcing policing to assess and manage the innate criminal potentiality of the social body. And, second, the coercive mechanism understands that terrorism is a political crime and, therefore, within its total intelligence spectrum, it *primarily targets the (potential) crime of antagonistic popular politics*.

These methods are not devoid of success. Pre-emptive targeting and the policing of (alleged) criminal potentiality, has resulted in a lack of major ideologically and politically motivated crimes in the US for over a decade. Until September 2010 almost a thousand cases had been brought before the courts, 688 of them concluded. Of them, 87 per cent led to convictions. Still, the sentences passed seem surprisingly lenient: they average about 5.5 years (CLS 2010). This may be symptomatic of law enforcement intervening early, resulting in weaker evidence and a reliance on extracting guilty pleas from the defendants in return for a reduced sentence – a consequence of intelligence-led, pre-emptive targeting. Also, under the Bush administration, the DOJ was systematically stretching what it defined as terrorism-related cases (Chesney 2007; Roach 2011: 216–217). Especially in the early days, counterterrorism law was used almost exclusively against common crime, and even misdemeanours, often to tragic-comic effect (ACLU 2004a: 5; US DOJ 2003a: 20–29; US Senate 2002c: 4–5; 2003b: 16). According to the Transactional Records Access Clearinghouse at Syracuse University, until late 2003, out of 616 defendants convicted in 'terrorism' cases, only 236 were sentenced to prison terms, with an average sentence of two months.

While, with time, genuine counterterrorism success has accumulated (leading to today's 5.5 years average sentence), it is not certain that investigations have become more targeted. On the contrary: even the DOJ finds the vast majority of international terrorism cases referred to it by the FBI are unfit for prosecution. Between 2003 and 2006, it was rejecting 70 to 87 per cent of these cases. The cases which the FBI refers to the DOJ are a tiny fraction of the terrorism investigations it initiates. Still, the findings of all these investigations are kept on record and shared across policing agencies (ACLU 2009: 13). Under the Obama administration, the FBI increasingly relies on sting operations, in an attempt to assure some counterterrorism relevance and improve the evidential basis of prosecutions. In addition, prosecutions came to rely heavily on material support charges. Such charges were used in almost 70 per cent of court cases between 2008 and 2011, an almost seven-fold increase compared to the 2001–2007 period (CLS 2011: 18–20). Finally, it seems that political targeting is also becoming more focused. The harassment of the liberal Left has ceased, and police attention targets exclusively the anti-state and anti-capital Left (Erdely 2012; Potter 2012a–d).

Finally, a devastating assessment of the relevance of counterterrorism law to fighting terrorism can be deduced from a statement made by the then FBI Director, Robert Mueller. Summing how the 9/11 hijackers worked, he stated that they entered the US legally; contacted no known terrorist sympathiser; committed no crimes; left no paper trail; had no computers or laptops; used payphones and telephone cards; and withdrew money in small amounts (US Senate 2002a: 3). All post-9/11 counterterrorism measures would have been irrelevant to the actual case.

Counterterrorism law has little to do with terrorism. As it subjects every individual and activity to a draconian regime of surveillance, 'counterterrorism successes' occur as *collateral gain*:

> The contemporary model of penal policy introduces even the non-deviant into institutions of policing and coercion, construing thus the 'average citizen' as an 'internal enemy'. The economico-political sub-layer of this perception is the galloping concentration of wealth into tiny groups of the population, who in turn see everyone else as a potential enemy […] The main characteristic of this new system is that its function focuses on controlling the majority, while countering criminal activity is a welcomed collateral gain.
> (Paraskevopoulos 2004: 42, author's translation)

Congress

In the period after 9/11, Congress was reduced to a single-issue institution, producing exclusively counterterrorism measures. More than 450 of them were considered in the first four months after the attacks, virtually representing the totality (97 per cent) of congressional output (Donohue 2009: 382). Building the homeland security state dominated the congressional agenda over the next two years, with recurring waves in 2005 and 2009, when expiring measures were due

Table 7.1 Proposals for amending the Patriot Act

Title	Provisions	Chamber; sponsorship	Date
Freedom to Read Protection Act	Adds standards and overview to §215 for libraries and bookstores	House; Independent	6 March 2003
Library and Bookseller Protection Act	Exempts libraries and bookstores from §215 provisions; and libraries from §505	Senate; Democrat	23 May 2003
Surveillance Oversight and Disclosure Act	Enables oversight of the FISA process	House; Democrat	11 June 2003
Reasonable Notice and Search Act	Introduces Judicial and Congress overview of §213	Senate; Democrat	11 June 2003
Library, Bookseller and Personal Records Privacy Act	Introduces legal standards and overview for §§215, 505	Senate; Democrat	21 July 2003
Protecting the Rights of Individuals Act	Same as previous; plus limitations on §215 and on pen/trap provisions	House; bilateral	31 July 2003
Benjamin Franklin True Patriot Act	Repeals many of the surveillance powers of §§213, 216, 215, 505	House; bilateral	24 September 2003
Patriot Oversight Restoration Act	Introduces oversight for the entire Patriot Act; adds provisions to the sunset list	Senate; bilateral	1 October 2003
Security and Freedom Enhanced (SAFE) Act	Brings FISA under pre-Patriot Act standards; limitations on roving wiretaps and secret searches; exempts libraries from NSLs	Senate; bilateral	2 October 2003
Security and Freedom Ensured Act	Limits Executive powers relating to: secret searches, record access and roving wiretaps; amends the definition of 'domestic terrorism'; adds provisions to the sunset list	House; Republican	21 October 2003

for renewal. While the overall effect of this production was the creation, maintenance and hardening of homeland security, here I focus on Congress's work in 2003. That year saw the rare occurrence of attempts to restrict (or even reverse) some powers. Between March and October, ten bills were presented to Congress, targeting a range of Patriot Act provisions, and suggesting amendments thereof (Table 7.1).

The first thing worth noting is timing. The first Bill was presented by the odd independent Representative. Two months of complete inaction followed, and then the Democrats set up a cottage industry of amendments. And, from July onwards, the amending Bills become bipartisan. Second, proposals became bolder. The first two target only one section (§215), and only in relation to libraries, i.e. one among thousands of potential points of application. The next four proposals are still very narrow in their targeting, while the final four aim to amend a wide range of the Patriot Act sections, by subjecting them to congressional review and judicial control.

The stance of Congress is perplexing. For over 18 months it had not displayed the slightest concern with counterterrorism legislation. Then, suddenly, a shower of increasingly bold proposals broke out, involving members of both parties. It lasted six months, and disappeared without trace until late 2005, when Congress considered renewing the Patriot Act's sunset clauses.

It is hard to explain this mood by focusing only on Congress. To understand it, we need to look further. By the time Congress started proposing amendments, the monolithic war on terrorism consensus was disrupted, and popular opposition had recoiled along two issues: Iraq, and counterterrorism law – the first massive and intense, the second persistent in time. When Congress started considering amendments, a popular undertaking against the legislation, the *resolutions movement* was already spreading throughout the country (Chapter 12). Congress members were responding to it. The first, isolated amendment attempt was made when the resolutions movement was making its presence felt; by the time the bulk of proposals appeared in Congress, the resolutions had become a mass movement; and when the movement started to decelerate, the storm of congressional amendments ceased. Moreover, there is a certain (partial) coincidence between the provisions respectively challenged by the resolutions and the congressional proposals. Congress focuses disproportionately on one provision (§215), and almost exclusively in relation to libraries; the librarians were a driving force of popular resistance.

Counterterrorism law effectuates two moves. The primary one, referring to social dynamics, is to augment the powers of the state over the population. The secondary one, referring to state dynamics, is to bring these powers under the control of the Executive. All Bills and amendments brought in Congress sought to (partially) reverse the secondary move, leaving the primary one intact. They sought to introduce overview and legal standards in the provisions, but not to repeal them. They aimed at sharing state powers among the branches, without ameliorating their force in relation to the population. Implicit here is the claim that congressional and judicial participation in repressing the population constitutes the desired system of checks and balances, which guarantees democracy and personal freedom.

It is therefore difficult to speak of congressional resistance to counterterrorism policy. First, because Congress was only trying to claw back its share in the powers it had so generously granted to the Executive. Second, because regulated repression is better than arbitrary, but it is still repression. And, third, because all the amendments were easily defeated. Indeed, they were moribund, the members who introduced them knew they did not stand a chance. They also knew that they were riding a rising wave of popular discomfort with counterterrorism, and that their gesture would reinforce popular resistance. In short, they were pulling the seams in the war on terrorism consensus further apart. If their motivation was personal conviction, it took a long time coming. If it was electoral survival, it is hard to explain why amendments ceased on the eve of election year 2004. If, instead, the Representatives were doing what most of their colleagues in capitalist democracies do, i.e. express in political-institutional terms the interest of capital sectors, then we have an indication that in 2003 some capital fractions were starting to feel uneasy with counterterrorism – especially as the Iraq invasion would secure the long-term pre-eminence of A&E. Thus, the sudden rash of amendments may be interpreted as a symptom of possible struggle in the power bloc. The reaction of the courts presents certain similarities.

The courts

The dramatic re-drawing of the legal framework effectuated by counterterrorism law activated conservation reflexes in the Judiciary.

The first reaction came in December 2003, when two federal courts (California 9th Circuit; N. York 2nd Circuit Court of Appeals) declared unlawful the mass detentions carried out by the administration in the wake of 9/11. The rulings invoked the separation of powers and due legal process, but did not challenge the validity of counterterrorism legal provisions. This occurred in January 2004, when a federal court in Los Angeles declared unconstitutional one of the Patriot Act's material support provisions (providing 'expert advice and assistance' to terrorists) (Scarry 2004: 19). Since then, Court decisions challenging the validity of legislation and the legality of governmental practices have proliferated, culminating in the battles between the Supreme Court and the other two branches on the issue of *habeas corpus* for enemy combatants (Chapter 5).

However, it is hard to make the case for 'judiciary resistance'. The general motif of courts' dynamics is that for every decision against counterterrorism measures, there is another, at a higher level, which vindicates the government. For instance, in 2007, a lower court found that the President's authorisation of the NSA monitoring of telecommunications of citizens was violating the first and fourth amendments. The decision was unceremoniously overturned, not on substantive grounds, but on the procedural finding that the plaintiff (ACLU) lacked standing and could not establish a claim to actual injury (Roach 2011: 185). Another example of courts ducking substantive responsibility by sticking to legal procedure is the case of Jose Padilla, a US citizen, arrested in 2002 in a Chicago airport. A presidential order designated him an enemy combatant, and he was detained incommunicado and subjected to extreme interrogation techniques under military custody in South Carolina. In 2004, the Supreme Court dismissed his *habeas corpus* claim on the basis that, by litigating in a New York court rather than a South Carolina one, he had brought his case before the wrong forum (Roach 2011: 192).

Moreover, Federal courts tend to show deference to the Executive when the latter invokes reasons of national security. In 2006, District courts considered two similar cases of alleged torture resulting from extraordinary rendition (*Arar v Ashcroft*; *Khaled el-Masri v George Tenet et al.*). In both cases they dismissed the lawsuits, reasoning that a trial would reveal features of US security agencies' *modus operandi*, and could therefore compromise their activity (Donohue 2008: 111).

As for the Supreme Court decisions upholding *habeas corpus* for enemy combatants (noted in Chapter 5), they permit the Executive ample space to manoeuvre, and they incorporate a para-legal regime of detention and adjudication into the legal framework. As a commentator noticed after the first (*Hamdi*, June 2004) Supreme Court decision, '[a] few more victories like this, and we will all be eating prison gruel' (Norton 2004).

A case which brings together these three tendencies – the normalisation of the Guantanamo treatment (and its expansion to citizens), the reversal of lower courts' decisions by higher courts, and judicial deference to the Executive on national security matters – is that of Yaser Hamdi. A US citizen, captured in Afghanistan, he was held by the military in Virginia. While lower courts expressed concern about the quality of the government's evidence against him, the Fourth Circuit deferred to the government on national security grounds, and in 2004 a Supreme Court majority opined that his detention was authorised by AUMF (Roach 2011: 194).

Surprisingly, the first and, to date, most unequivocal challenge to the legal framework came from the FISA secret court. In May 2002, the FISC publicised its unanimous opinion rejecting the DOJ's interpretation of the Patriot Act, §218 and the subsequent Attorney General's guidelines authorising law enforcement personnel to initiate and conduct FISA investigations as long as some foreign intelligence interest was involved (US Department of Justice 2002: 4–5). The FISC argued (correctly) that such practice was effectively cancelling the particularity of FISA as a framework covering an especially designated area of operations; it expressed fears that the DOJ was intending to use FISA to initiate investigations which would not comply with Title III requirements; and refused to co-operate with the DOJ under these conditions, proposing its own interpretation of §218 as a basis for continuing co-operation (Donohue 2008: 233; US Foreign Intelligence Surveillance Court 2002). The DOJ appealed the decision, claiming (also correctly) that the intention of the 'significant purpose' amendment in §218 was precisely to eliminate the wall between intelligence and law enforcement agencies (US Senate 2002b: 4). For the first time in history, the three-judge FISA Court of Review was summoned. It reversed the FISC's decision, finding that FISA could be used in common crime investigations and that the Patriot Act amendment meant that the primary purpose of a FISA investigation could be criminal prosecution (Donohue 2008: 233).

Even if reversed by a higher court, the FISC's decision has been the most forceful challenge to counterterrorism law by a court, and it targeted the provision at the heart of the reconfiguration of policing. It was an utterly surprising development, first because a hitherto perfectly compliant court mutinied; and, second, because a secret court decided to publicise its opinion, hence turning it into a political matter. Apparently, the FISC had submitted its opinion to the DOJ two months before its publication. The judges were convinced to go public by a small group of Senators in the Judiciary Committee. This indicates that fairly early in the homeland security project, some top state personnel were seeking ways to constrain it.

The complex and ambivalent stance of the Judiciary is a reminder that the three state branches cannot be treated as integral, solid blocs. They are internally divided and horizontally linked. To the extent that (fractions of) the Judiciary poses any challenge at all, this is mainly directed not against the augmentation of state powers over the population, but against the Executive's capacity to wield them unilaterally. Much like the Legislature, it is preoccupied with the *normalisation and legalisation of augmented powers*. This point is particularly pertinent given the tendency of the liberal Left to treat the participation of the courts and Congress in coercion as a panacea.

Resistance in the perimeter of the state: the constitutional left

Since the launch of homeland security, organisations of civil libertarian lawyers have been the most persistent source of resistance, and have made important contributions in organising forms of broader, popular resistance. Such organisations include the Electronic Frontier Foundation, the Centre for Democracy and Technology (CDT), the Centre for Constitutional Rights, the Electronic Privacy Information Centre, and, most importantly, the ACLU. These are left-liberal organisations, concerned with defending the political rights encoded in the Constitution. Their advocacy is geared towards promoting an inclusive form of citizenship and protecting democratic institutions. They defend key morphological characteristics of liberal-democratic polity: the rule of law, individual rights (including privacy, property and due process), a pluralist civil society, representative government, etc. Given that these arrangements are encoded in the Constitution, they present their advocacy as defending constitutional order and freedoms (Scheingold and Sarat 2004: 15–17, 102–103, 107–112).

Discussing these organisations in a chapter considering reactions to counterterrorism law from within the state seems odd. It is informed by a conceptualisation of lawyers as state personnel, in the sense that their professional activity tends to reproduce the state relation. They participate in statist ideology, hence they rarely question the division of political labour between rulers and ruled. They are prone to maintain the continuity of the state apparatus as they largely share statal notions of the common good, and are consequently suspicious of self-organisation and rank and file initiatives which refuse to enter the strategic terrain of the state (Boukalas 2013; Poulantzas 1978: 154–158; Jessop 2008: 123–124; McEvoy 2007: 421–424). From thereon, whether they are officially state employees is only a matter of juridical definition.

Due to their particular positioning vis à vis the state, these organisations play an important political role. They can penetrate the legal hieroglyphs and explain the substantive content of law to popular audiences. They are routinely present in the courts, and are interlocutors in Congress, often invited as witnesses in its hearings. Among them, the ACLU is a public membership organisation which popularises law, draws strategies in relation to it, and seeks to engage the public in them – it is an all-out political player. Given the bipartisan support to homeland security, it is not exaggerated to claim that the ACLU is the 'party' of opposition to it. In short, due to their peculiar positioning in relation to the state, liberal lawyers' organisations can channel their positions 'upwards' towards the state summits, and 'outwards' towards the population. Hence, it is hard to overstate the importance of their reaction to counterterrorism law.

Civil-libertarian lawyers target a range of legal provisions. Especially the new investigative regime (the 'significant' FISA amendment, secret searches, FISA wiretaps, and NSLs) comes under persistent fire, along with provisions on immigrants, and the definition of domestic terrorism. Still, they most persistently target the notorious access-all-records provision (Patriot Act, §215), and Guantanamo. The democratic goods seen as being imperilled by counterterrorism are free speech and, most importantly, privacy.

In their public discourse (books, articles, brochures, press releases), lawyers address these provisions in long paratheses, where each provision and its interpretation is added to the previous, until a specific theme (e.g. surveillance vs privacy) is exhausted. Then the next theme is similarly added – and so on. Often, they combine these paratheses with flashbacks in US history: the cancellation of the right to civic trial during the Civil War; the crackdown on anarchists and the deportation of Emma Goldman in 1917–1920; communist witch-hunts in the 1930s; concentration camps for Japanese-Americans in the Second World War; McCarthyism and Hoover's crackdown on leftists; the crackdown on Vietnam protests and the Black movement in the 1960s (Brinkley 2003; ACLU 2002a). The paratheses serve to highlight the broadness and intensity of the attack on liberties pursued by the Bush administration; the flashbacks convey the feeling that all historical nightmares are revived at once.

While this is the case in the texts destined for public consumption, when the lawyers address state actors things are different (e.g. Nadine Strossen (ACLU President) and Jim Dempsey (CDT), cited in US Senate 2003c). The polemical and alarmist tone is dropped, replaced by sober, cautious discourse. Also, the hierarchy of democratic freedoms is adjusted, so that due process and checks and balances top the list: the right of judicial review of Executive authority is recognised as 'the most basic liberty of all' (ACLU 2001: 4). And, even in relation to powers they recognise as highly undemocratic (e.g. domestic terrorism definition, Guantanamo treatment, secret searches, access-all-records), their objective is not to repeal, but to endow them some legal standards: 'we are not saying repeal it. We're saying amend it slightly' (Strossen, cited in US Senate 2003c: 37–38).

This contrast between the lawyers' official and popular discourse is a matter of tone rather than substance. A careful reading of the popular-consumption texts shows that the heart of the problem is always the lack of judicial controls – seen as 'legal chains' which keep governmental powers on the leash (ACLU 2003a: 1, 16). Much like the courts or Congress, the lawyers' strategy is to normalise the augmented state powers by sharing them among state branches.

As to what is to be protected, things are unequivocal: the American people are to be alert and protect their constitutional freedoms. Even the disruption of 'the most basic liberty of all' (juridical review) is problematic only because it erodes the Constitution (ACLU 2001: 50).

Selecting the Constitution as the ultimate stake defines the character of civil-libertarian resistance, and this causes a number of problems and limitations. First, constitutionalism frames their critique in a self-referential context which often fringes on the paradoxical: we must exercise our constitutionally protected rights in order to protest against measures which infringe on constitutional freedoms (Chang 2002: 135–137). The Constitution is not a weapon which helps the resisting population justify its protest, but an absolute, for-itself totem, to be protected for its own sake.

Second, constitutionalism also implies that *only* constitutionally protected social activity is worth defending. When civil-libertarians refer to popular political expression, it is always conditioned as 'legitimate protest', 'peaceful dissent' or some combination of these terms (ACLU-New York 2003). The relation between these two terms is also important: it means that, if a protest(er) is to be 'legitimate', she must be 'peaceful'. This is not remote from the legal definition of domestic terrorism.

Third, while the Constitution is to be secured by the nation as a whole, its legal-technical nature dictates that a caste of master-technicians is given the protagonist role: 'The decision whether this nation will uphold the Bill of Rights or acquiesce in its surrender will ultimately fall to the judiciary' (Chang 2002: 136). The fetishisation of the Constitution proves to be undemocratic, calling for the determination of society not by the people, but by (legal) experts.

Fourth, constitutionalism is the platform for a particular ('left') patriotism, complete with mythical figures (the Framers). These guardians of the Nation had predicted Bush-style Executive infringements, devised safeguards against them, and stored them in the Constitution (Schulhofer 2003: 79). The Constitution is the heart of the Nation and the jewel in its crown. The ACLU refers to '[…] the free and robust debate that made our way of life the envy of nations […]' (ACLU 2003h: 18). Its president displays its patriotic credentials ('[w]e pledged on that day to support President Bush in the battle against terror […]'); and re-articulates American nationalism: 'Put aside our popular culture which changes by the day, and our material success which is now vulnerable to the vicissitudes of the global economy – strip away all that is truly superficial. What is left that distinguishes us if not our constitutional values? These values […] are the very source of strength as a nation and the bulwark of our democracy' (US Senate 2003c/Strossen Testimony). The Left weaves its own national mythology, in juxtaposition to that of the Right. It subscribes fully to the homeland security narrative: the 9/11 attacks targeted the nation; they represent a novel form of threat; against it, we must devise coercive measures for our self-protection (Strossen and Edgar 2004). Thus the debate is narrowed to 'how far' can counterterrorism measures go without imperilling our national-constitutional essence.

Unchallenged in defining the terrain of the battle, the administration had already won. Liberal resistance could only negotiate the terms of surrender: 'striking a balance between safety and freedom'. In quasi-Benthamite terms, it demanded a security vs liberty calculus: '[…] does this measure really maximise national security with minimal cost to civil liberties? That's the substantial test'

(Strossen, cited in US Senate 2003c: 9; see also Cole and Dempsey 2002: 178–181). As for how can completely abstract, ideological volumes, be compared, the answer depends on judicial authorisation. Civil-libertarians are in the awkward position of having to articulate opposition to a governmental practice stemming from premises they wholly accept. The coup-de-grace is their declaration that freedom is valuable only insofar as it enhances national security: 'this narrowing of discussion is harmful *not* because diversity or dissent is good in the abstract but because the views that are being exiled or marginalised are *critical to our collective security* and advancement' (Robin 2003: 50, emphasis added).

In this manner, civil-libertarians took on the administration in its preferred terrain: patriotism. By raising the Law-Constitution-Liberty patriotic platform against the administration's Might-Combat-Destiny one, they transformed this formerly monopolised terrain into an ideological battle-zone. Yet, they conceded to the administration the decisive advantage: defining the meaning of events and the strategic orientation of the nation. Thus they remained restricted to negotiating minor points, like the fabled balance between liberty and security, identified with judicial overview of coercion. Therefore, their contribution restricts the horizons of popular resistance within a legalistic-statist framework. This results from their subscription to legal-statist ideology. A closer, critical look at this ideology is needed, as it informs the main form of resistance to homeland security.

Civil-libertarians conceptualise liberty as the key value safeguarded in the Constitution. But what exactly is this liberty? Liberal political philosophy provides a negative definition of liberty as a space – the individual's 'private domain of action' – where others (individuals, collectives or the state) cannot intervene without permission. This private domain comprises the institution of private property, freedom of association and contract, and freedom of choosing employment. Maintaining the private sphere requires the imposition of limits which preclude the majority from producing statutes which violate it. Legislating takes place within a framework which cannot be touched by legislation, and sets limits which legislatures cannot cross. This framework is the Constitution (Tomlinson 1990: 17–18). The Constitution's role is to restrict the operational scope of 'majority rule', so that the individual's liberty is safeguarded. This liberty consists in 'stability of possession, of transference by consent, and of the performance of promises'. The liberty safeguarded in the Constitution is property, exchange, and contract (Hayek 1960: 158; Tomlinson 1990: 32). Clearer still: 'Law, liberty and property are an inseparable trinity' (Hayek 1979: 107). The Constitution is the defensive bulwark securing capital rule from the risk raised by parliamentarism.

The right to ownership is the root of all liberal rights. Far from being confrontational to 'liberty', security is its foundation – the securing of capital's private economic sphere and property from possible incursions by the dispossessed or by a state that has fallen into their hands. '[S]ecurity is the supreme concept of bourgeois society', and civil society 'is the security project by excellence' (Neocleous 2000: 61; see also Foucault 2008: 63–67). In short, the antithesis (and the need for 'balance') between security and liberty is an analytical and conceptual absurdity.

Constitutionalism entails the sanctification of the ideological premises inscribed in the constitutional form and in the constitutional text. Regarding form, the constitutional order is one of heterenomy. While the Constitution recognises the people as the sole source of social institution (replacing divinity or other extra-social sources), constitutionalism sets the Constitution as precisely such an extra-social source which determines social organisation and is untouchable by society. Thus, the significance of the constitutional form is that social organisation is set once and for all, and is beyond the reach of living people. Moreover, in the constitutional form a historically specific political arrangement is expressed in an (eternal) legal text, implying the separation of law and politics, and the association of the former with orderly, neutral regulation of social affairs, opposed to the violent, willed, political ordering. The civil-libertarian demand for legalising, rather than repealing, state powers, results from their incapacity to conceptualise law as political praxis, and as a particular codification of force, domination and oppression (Neocleous 2000: 107–109; 2006b: 16–18).

In terms of constitutional content, the civil-libertarian strategy aims at galvanising the separation of powers, and the 'checks and balances' it entails. Here, constitutionalism precludes civil-libertarians from understanding the contemporary character of the state, and from drawing an effective strategy in relation to it. They failed to question whether 9/11 constituted a genuine emergency, i.e. an existential threat to US statehood or its social order; and left unchallenged the axiom that the Executive is best suited to act on an emergency (Chapter 6). They also took the constitutional separation of powers too literally. The separation of powers does not guarantee that each branch constitutes an autonomous bloc, or that they will be in mutual antagonism, balancing each other out. On the contrary, both inter-branch synergy and intra-branch conflict are possible, and we have seen how the Legislature and the Judiciary are internally divided, and establish horizontal links with each other. The failure of civil-libertarians to grapple with these realities was caused by ideological closure, and resulted in anaemic resistance.

Finally, even if the desired effect of inter-branch 'checks and balances' is achieved, the stubborn fact of repression may remain. If repression is legal, regulated, limited and controlled by opposing forces in the state, it does not mean that it is cancelled, nor does this constitute political freedom. The fascination with checks and balances, and the faith that they, somehow, make power disappear is rooted in a legal ideology which obscures the social nature of the state. Relations between the branches are important because they constitute channels through which social dynamics are selectively guided in the state and influence the direction of its powers. If dissent within each branch is sporadic and anaemic, this means that popular opposition is weak, or that the state-form does not permit its channelling into the state. If popular politics are weak or excluded, then inter-branch conflict indicates intra-capital frictions, rather than a democratic 'balance'.

The fundamental distortion guiding the constitutional Left is the perception of law as opposed to the state, and as predominant to it. Law is not a negation of state violence, but a specific organisation of it. It poses limits to the exercise of repression, and it gives permissions to popular expressions of resistance (Poulantzas 1978: 91–92; Neocleous 2006b: 4). Yet, by the same token, it limits resistance, dictating what expressions thereof are acceptable. This not only brings illegitimate forms of resistance face to face with state violence, it also annihilates them symbolically as criminal, 'anti-social' behaviours. Hence, civil-libertarians defend 'legitimate' and 'peaceful' protesters only.

Moreover, the state is predominant over law, and not vice versa. Legal gaps, blanks and loopholes; straightforward violations; state practices not covered by law; the provision in every legal code for its own cancellation in exceptional circumstances; and the fact that the state creates and modifies law, should not leave much doubt about this (Poulantzas 1978: 84–85). To assert the state's primacy over law is to assert the primacy of social dynamics over its state-mediated legal crystallisation. Civil liberties are legal crystallisations of popular victories in social struggle. Their protection and expansion depends on the proliferation of social struggles: struggles which refer directly to law and make it their stake, but also struggles which defy it and expand in practice what is permissible.

Counterterrorism legislation is a key feature of a galloping, excessively coercive, authoritarian statism, in the context of a capitalist attack against the population. If the Left does not devise a strategy aiming to reverse this trend, the skirmishes over legislation are insignificant. Popular questioning of the need for security, its objectives, the prerogative of the state to provide it, and the demand for popular participation in the outlining of security policy (and every policy), are much more likely to reverse the legal trends, precisely because they go beyond counterterrorism law, and address its root causes.

Civil libertarians were unable to move the Left, or the broader population, in a similar direction. Their arguments are ultimately based on national mythology. In creating their own blend of nationalism they perpetuate the tradition of the US Left as the only one among its western counterparts which has never attempted to confront nationalism (Laliotou 2005: 155–156; see also Bratsis 2003: 127). Like all blends of nationalism, the Constitution-based one is an order of heteronomy. It implies that the people who live in the US today, their needs, aspirations, desires and will, are trivialities. Their only legitimate contribution is to defend their constitutional liberties. And they must do so, not because they like these liberties, but because they are integral to the national spirit. The people do not have a choice (or liberty); they have a patriotic duty (ACLU 2009: 8–9, 30). Essentially, the presidential nationalist narrative is faithfully reproduced.

Hiding the political nature of the confrontation under nationalistic mystification has grave implications for the Left. Insofar as its purpose is the emancipation of society and not mere re-arrangement of the conditions of subordination, its first duty is to de-mystify the social world. The living social being and her aspirations should be the focal point of its politics, replacing the endless rehash of the (naval-gazing) question *who are we?* with the open and creative *how do we want to live?* Instead, the civil-libertarian strategy perpetuates and reinforces every fundamental political myth of capitalist rule, and narrows the horizon of what is politically thinkable.

8 Department of homeland security and police restructuring

Creating the realm

The term 'homeland' made an inconspicuous appearance in 1995, in a report by the Senate Committee on the Armed Forces (US Senate 1995). It soon provided the adjectival complement for 'homeland defence' and 'homeland protection'. 'Homeland security' was coined by the Pentagon to describe recovery and crisis management efforts on the wake of an attack on US soil (Beresford 2004: 1–6). Throughout its variations, the 'homeland' motif signified an attempt to reverse the cuts in military spending during the 1990s, and to relaunch a civil defence ideology for a post-cold war era (Beresford 2004: 9). Considerations with the 'homeland' remained politically marginal and restricted to state bureaucracy (including nominally independent defence behemoths, like RAND). By contrast, since 9/11, homeland security has become a top political priority, a distinct institutional mechanism, and a powerful popular ideology.

The institutionalisation of homeland security begins on 20 September 2001, with the creation of the Office of Homeland Security (OHS) in the White House. Its elaboration as a political project starts with the issuing of the *National Strategy for Homeland Security*. The *Strategy* begins with the President saluting the nation and explaining the nature of the Enemy: a 'new and changing threat' which 'takes many forms, has many places to hide and is often invisible' and 'seeks to exploit our vulnerabilities because of the freedoms we hold dear'. The President designates homeland security as *the* top priority of the state, which 'has no more important mission than protecting the homeland from future terrorist attacks'. He hails the *Strategy* as a first attempt to define this mission, and to 'rally our entire society' to overcome the terrorist challenge. From the get go, homeland security is designed as a pan-social effort. Importantly, from the very start, homeland security is seen not only as a reaction to a crisis, but as constituting a new normality: 'as a result of this Strategy, fire-fighters will be better equipped to fight fires, police officers better armed to fight crime, business better able to protect their data and information systems [...] While protecting against the rare event, [homeland security technologies] should enhance the commonplace' (US Office of Homeland Security 2002a: 3, 53).

Regarding the features of the Enemy, the *Strategy* emphasises one in particular:

opportunism. Terrorists shy away from attacking what they perceive as well-defended targets, and concentrate on less protected ones. To inform their planning, they exploit public information on vulnerability, even by 'monitor[ing] our media' (US Office of Homeland Security 2002a: 7–8). Their 'opportunism' justifies augmented governmental secrecy, as well as 'visible' and 'aggressive' police presence in public space.

The Republican administration was not undertaking the homeland security endeavour by itself. The Democratic Party was fully supportive of the project. This is manifest in its stance on the threat that surveillance could pose for civil liberties, which colludes with that of the administration, and ignores popular concerns: 'Innovative information technologies can make a substantial contribution to the war on terror by providing the government with new tools to identify potential terrorists. In addition, there exists significant amounts of information in the private sector that, when accessed by the government under proper guidelines and safeguards, can strengthen the war on terror by identifying terrorists and saving lives'. Its celebration of total intelligence is informed by the nature of the Enemy: 'Al Qaida continues to seek ways to kill our citizens, destroy property and infrastructure, disrupt our economy, and demoralise our nation. Our enemies are opportunistic, and will remain fixated on identifying and exploiting our weaknesses. We must remain vigilant in bolstering our homeland defences' (US House of Representatives 2004a: 2, 14). The Democrats subscribe the homeland security project, down to the minute detail of the war on terror discourse.

The *Strategy* provides its own definition of terrorism as any 'premeditated, unlawful act dangerous to human life or public welfare that is intended to intimidate or coerce civilian populations or governments'. Along with kidnappings, hijackings, etc, the definition also specifies as terrorism crimes cyber attacks and 'any number of other forms of malicious violence' (US Office of Homeland Security 2002a: 2). It therefore preserves the key feature of the legal definition of terrorism as a crime resides on the actor's political intent, while its specification as 'unlawful' designates the act as already outlawed, and tends to exempt the state's lawful violence. The inclusion of 'any number of other forms of malicious violence' broadens the definition to the point of absurdity, and it introduces moral judgement as a key feature. It is increasingly obvious that terrorism is a term devoid of theoretical or scientific value; its purpose is strictly polemical. It is attached as a moral stigma, to devalue actors, actions and political convictions and objectives, independently from the employment of criminal (or 'violent') means for their promotion, and to galvanise the unity of the population with the state in its struggle against them (Abrahms 2012: 383; Sanguinetti 1978).

The *Strategy* emphasises the pan-social nature of the endeavour. Defending the homeland is a new 'mission' which requires 'coordinated and focused effort from our entire society [...] based on the principles of shared responsibility and partnership with Congress, state and local governments, the private sector, and the American people. The *National Strategy for Homeland Security* belongs and applies to the Nation as a whole' (US Office of Homeland Security 2002a: 1–2). It defines the nation's 'long struggle' to protect the homeland. The effort is endless, for 'some level of terrorist threat [is] a permanent condition'. It is also a managerial endeavour, resulting from cost-benefit calculi between security, expenditure, and 'the infringements on individual liberty that [risk] mitigation entails'. The balance 'must be determined by politically accountable leaders exercising sound, considered judgement informed by top-notch scientists' (US Office of Homeland Security 2002a: 3). The pan-social effort is determined exclusively by the state. It seems that state monopoly over politics is deeply entrenched in every facet of homeland security.

The priorities of the homeland security effort are: (a) to prevent terrorist attacks in the US; (b) to reduce vulnerability to terrorism; and (c) to minimise damage and recover from attacks that do occur. The three priorities designate homeland security as a pre-emption project. To carry out this mission and ensure the unity of purpose of its components, the DHS was introduced (US Office of Homeland Security 2002a: vii–xiii).

The top priority, preventing terrorist attacks, indicates expansion of intelligence capabilities, in order to 'detect terrorist activity before it manifests itself in an attack'. The *Strategy* envisions the enhancement of the FBI's analytic ability; the building of new capacity in the DHS Division of Information Analysis and Infrastructure Protection (IAIP); and the implementation of the Homeland Security Advisory System, a medium for communicating the threat-level to the population (Chapter 10). It champions data mining and blanket surveillance, justified by the Enemy's tendency to camouflage amongst 'innocent civilians' (US Office of Homeland Security 2002a: 9–10, 15, 26–27).

The second priority, reducing vulnerability to terrorism, refers almost exclusively to protecting 'critical infrastructure', by assessing the vulnerability of relevant assets, coordinating efforts with state and local forces, and 'unifying' the effort in the DHS. Given the range of eligible assets and the Enemy's 'opportunism', a drastic augmentation of security measures and police presence is essential. In contrast to the first priority which employs invisible means of surveillance, the second relies on the pronounced presence of security personnel. Homeland security turns pre-emption into *the* dominant mode of policing.

The DHS was envisioned as the centre of the homeland security effort. It was designed to unify and streamline the federal mechanism and its operations by integrating 22 federal entities with relevant remits; and to develop and coordinate relations with sub-national governments, the private sector and the broader population. This combined effort is geared towards protecting 'critical infrastructure', which is of national importance, but locally situated, and mostly privately owned (US Office of Homeland Security 2002a: 12, 29–34, 48).

Lastly, the *Strategy* prescribes for the DHS a model of working relations. The DHS 'must have the advantage of modern management techniques [and] 21st century approaches' to personnel and procurement policies, and 'authority to enhance operational effectiveness as needed'. Considering that the DHS is the largest federal employer domestically, the *Strategy* promotes flexibility as a recipe for the entire public sector (US Office of Homeland Security 2002a: 4, 44–49).

Between them, the design of the legislation, the vision of the *Strategy*, and the materiality and perfomativity of the DHS construct a new realm of political activity: homeland security. As a concept, and as an operation, homeland security may involve anything: from financial donations, to research in biology; from flood recovery, to background checks on airline passengers. In the context of the recent economic crisis, it has come to include 'economic security', which may comprise anything from customs collection, to fighting copyright piracy, to funding arctic expeditions (Napolitano 2012: 17–18). Homeland security is constituted by a molecular transformation of all social activities: they are perceived and treated as inherently suspicious and thus as a police matter. Homeland security signifies that *security becomes the single currency into which all social activities are abstracted*. Homeland security is the arrival of the 'police state'; not in its traditional form of coercive state intervention upon society, but as transubstantiation of all social relations into the total meta-relation of policing (Caudle 2009; Donohue 2012: 1705–1751).

The DHS is a key actor and the defining entity of the new fund realm. Here, I examine the Department's structure and operations, and its relations with other entities in the homeland security effort: federal security agencies, sub-national governments, the private sector, and its employees.

The DHS structure

The Homeland Security Act, which officially established the DHS, was enacted on 25 November 2002. The Department became fully operational on 1 March 2003, and all transfers of agencies to it were complete by 30 September 2003 (US DHS/OIG 2003a: 3). Its establishment was the greatest restructure of the Executive branch since the unification of military forces into the Defense Department after the Second World War. The DHS represents a similar reorganisation of the security mechanism. Until then, counterterrorism responsibilities were divided among multiple federal entities, whose operations were loosely orchestrated by a leading agency, usually situated in the DOJ (Cmar 2002: 457). In the DHS, counterterrorism functions are consolidated in a single federal entity, a development closely related with the construction of 'homeland security' as a distinct field of political practice.

The reorganisation was publicly promoted as a response to the nature of the Enemy: 'The changing nature of the threats facing America requires a new government structure to protect against invisible enemies that can strike with a wide variety of weapons [...] America needs a single, unified security structure that will improve protection against today's threats and be flexible enough to help meet the unknown threats of the future' (US President 2002e).

The Department comprises 22 agencies. Their integration is said to produce greater efficiency. After two years of adjustment, the DHS acquired a settled form (US DHS/OIG 2003a: 3; 2003b: 1, 12). It comprises four major Directorates (Border and Transportation Security; Emergency Preparedness and Response; Science and Technology; and Information Analysis and Infrastructure Protection (IAIP)), and two stand-alone agencies, the Coast Guard and the Secret Service

Table 8.1 DHS components and their function

Directorate	Main agencies	Purpose
Border and Transportation Security	Customs and border protection; immigration and customs enforcement; Transportation Security Administration	Secure borders and transportation systems; enforce immigration laws
Emergency Preparedness and Response	Federal Emergency Management Agency	Shield from catastrophic events by organising, implementing and over-seeing federal preparedness and response strategy
Science and Technology	Office of National Laboratories; Homeland Security Laboratories; Homeland Security Advanced Research Projects Agency	Homeland security research and development; science and technology resources for police; battling 'catastrophic terrorism'
Information Analysis and Infrastructure Protection	Homeland Security Operations Centre; IAIP offices	Perpetual vulnerability assessment; dissemination of information to federal, state, local, private, international partners; critical infrastructure protection
Stand-alone Agencies	Coast Guard; Secret Service	Entry denial and deportation of illegal immigrants; border protection; protection of leaders

Source: DHS: *Department Sub-components and Agencies*, http://www.dhs.gov/dhspublic/display?theme=13; last accessed, 2 June 2007 (page now defunct). For an up-to-date, detailed overview of the DHS structure, see http://www.dhs.gov/department-components; last accessed, 31 October 2013.

(Table 8.1). This basic template has been tinkered with, added to and fine-tuned. Importantly, several policy and management entities have been added to this structure (e.g. Office of Policy; Directorate for Management); a Law Enforcement Training Centre was created; while the IAIP's intelligence component has become a separate Office of Intelligence and Analysis.

The DHS is the largest government agency in the US (the Department of Defense excepted), employing over 200,000 people. Its operations are multifarious and their volume impressive. Daily operations typically involve: screening 1.5 million airline passengers; inspecting 57,000 trucks and shipping containers; making 266 arrests and 24 drug seizures; seizing an average US$715,652 in currency, US$23,083 in arms and ammunition and US$467,118 in merchandise; apprehending 2,617 people crossing illegally into the US; reviewing 2,200 intelligence reports; issuing information bulletins to 18,000 recipients; training 3,500 federal officers from 75 different agencies; deploying 108 patrol aircraft; operating 238 remote video surveillance systems; watching over 8,000 federal facilities, ports, power plants, tunnels and bridges; deploying 1,200 dog teams; making 5,479 pre-departure seizures of prohibited agricultural items (Brzezinski 2004; US DHS 2003g).

Since its inception, a main worry for the DHS was its ability to consolidate the

22 legacy agencies, and the variety of functions they perform, into a singular unit and a comprehensive mission (US DHS/OIG 2003b). Despite attempts in this direction (e.g. the introduction of a 'policy shop' in the Undersecretary of Policy Office in 2005), ten years into its life the DHS is still unable to consolidate, both institutionally and operationally. Its policy focus remains blur, strategic leadership is weak and coordination inadequate (Allen 2012; Baker 2012; US Department of Homeland Security Secretary 2009: 10; US Government Accountability Office 2012b). It seems that, ten years on, the DHS is failing its 'existential' mission to establish itself as a single, coherent, unit.

Perfect security and its unloved child: the DHS in the federal sector

The early years of the DHS (roughly up to 2005) were marked by astonishing dysfunction. Security weaknesses in its cyber-structure meant that DHS was for over a year unable to receive classified data, making it irrelevant to information sharing and intelligence co-operation (CRS 2005h: 34–36). There was no single authority in charge of one of its most well-funded missions, the protection from biochemical and nuclear attacks (Larsen 2005; US House of Representatives 2004a: 4–12); and no one was in charge of critical infrastructure protection (Brzezinski 2004; US DHS/OIG 2003a: 32; US House of Representatives 2004a: 12, 16–17). In addition, land borders were seriously understaffed, while the Transportation Security Administration was failing in even basic passenger screenings (US House of Representatives 2004a: 5–7).

This perception of failure (and the intense criticism which accompanied it) is partly due to the increased political importance of homeland security. Characteristically, the only criticism that the Democrats waged against security policy was that the 'administration is not moving fast enough, and is not taking strong enough action' to effectively secure the homeland (US House of Representatives 2004a: 2). Their full subscription to the homeland security project, and its elevation to top political imperative, resulted in 'perfect security' becoming 'the only acceptable standard' (Harvey 2007: 301).

It seems that their absorption into the DHS hindered, rather than enhanced the operation of the legacy agencies, initially at least. This is partly because the DHS was not meant to be. The administration was reluctant to create it. The President was suspicious of 'big government' and hostile to the relevant expenditure, and would have preferred the operational control that a White House Office of Homeland Security would have offered. The creation of the new super-department was propagated by the Democrats, and the administration had to give in, unable to oppose such a spectacular counterterrorism measure (Brzezinski 2004: 2; Progressive Policy Institute 2003: 25). The DHS was a Democrats' concept that the Bush administration was forced to foster. Being unwanted, it was forced to spend much of its early life in a warehouse in a DC residential area, well apart from the federal buildings downtown; its offices were scattered at impromptu housing, and until 2011 it was struggling to consolidate its headquarters at a single, functional centre (Brzezinski 2004: 1–2; Napolitano 2010). Its status among Executive personnel was extremely low: Secret Service staff almost mutinied against their incorporation into the DHS; agents in the FBI cyber-security division refused to be transferred; and the DHS intelligence office only attracted a fraction of the necessary personnel, as it was considered second grade to those of the FBI or the CIA. In 2003, 15 senior intelligence experts rejected the DHS's offer to head its analysis unit. The Department still suffers rapid turnover in top management positions, which deprives it from operational stability and continuity (Brzezinski 2004: 4; Progressive Policy Institute 2003: 25–26; US Government Accountability Office 2012c: 7).

Until 2008, the DHS budget was modest, starting from c. US$31 billion in the 2003 financial year, to c. US$42.5 billion in the 2007 financial year. The only sector which significantly bucked the austerity trend was protection from nuclear and bio-chemical attacks (DHS 'Budget in Brief', 2003–2006). Put in perspective, the DHS's entire budget for the 2006 financial year was half of the February 2005 supplemental appropriation (one of many) for the Iraq war (CRS 2005h: 50–52). Possibly because the DHS was a Democrat conception, the Obama administration has been more generous: the DHS budget rose to c. US$57 billion in the 2012 financial year, to suffer its first cutback in the 2013 financial year, as the urge to discipline public finances finally caught up (DHS 'Budget in Brief', 2007–2012). If bio-security was the privileged area for the Bush administration, Obama's favourite is cyber-security, possibly indicating adjustments in the power bloc.

The single, most decisive blow to the DHS was the early decision to not include the FBI's Counterterrorism Division in the Department, against all managerial common sense. This established the DHS as an inferior unit among federal Executive components (Brzezinski 2004: 4; Progressive Policy Institute 2003: 25–26). It was the opening salvo in an intra-Executive battle, in which the newly founded DHS was in disadvantage, losing important components to the DOJ (Donohue 2008: 159). Within weeks from the IAIP's assignation to integrate and analyse all-source information on terrorist threats to the US interior, the President established the Terrorist Threat Integration Centre (TTIC), which has the same mandate but is led by the CIA and the FBI (CRS 2004b: 19; 2005e: 4). The Pentagon also moved to establish its presence in domestic affairs: it set up an Assistant Secretariat for Homeland Defense, created programmes for the collaboration of military intelligence and civilian law enforcement, reinvigorated the National Guard, and asserted the President's authority to deploy combat forces domestically, to 'intercept and defeat threats' (US Department of Defense 2005: 27). In short, the Pentagon and the DOJ sought to, and were successful in, occupying the newfound realm, elbowing out the newcomer. Thus, the department created in order to concentrate and unify the homeland security effort ended up controlling just half of the homeland security budget and operations (Ellman et al. 2012: 3). The department designed to coordinate the federal security mechanism, needs, in turn, to have its activities coordinated, in a federal structure as byzantine as it was before its inception.

In the White House, the Homeland Security Council (HSC) – the, mainly DHS-comprised, key adviser to the President on homeland security issues – was severely understaffed, to the point of failing to develop a core strategy or to implement policy. Its importance was limited in comparison to the – mainly Pentagon and CIA-comprised – National Security Council. At the heart of the state, the HSC was a second-class citizen (Locher 2009; Ridge 2009; Wormuth 2009). In May 2009, President Obama merged the respective staffs of the two Councils, while keeping their top echelons separate. Given the power differential between the two, this possibly signals the swallowing up of homeland security as a distinct structure, and its digestion into the remit of national security (Ridge 2009; Wormuth 2009). The merging of the two structures signifies the unification of security into an uninterrupted, planetary continuum, which is total in scope regarding the people, activities and phenomena in its remit (Locher 2009). Such an endeavour will endlessly throw up the need for more and higher levels of integration and coordination. It seems that the DHS was nothing but a first step down that path.

DHS vs lesser governments

The DHS is the main federal instrument for orchestrating and directing the security-related activity of sub-national governments. It assumes the overall direction of homeland security policy, disseminates it to sub-national governments through the state-based Homeland Security Offices, distributes federal security funding and grants to sub-national governments, and is the traffic centre for intelligence and counterterrorism information flows to, from, and among sub-national entities.

The allocation of funds is still in search of a method. The Patriot Act stipulated that each state would receive 0.75 per cent of the overall fund allocation, and a fully discretionary allocation of the rest of the relevant budget. It thus locked almost half the available money in an equal share between states and territories, favouring smaller states. Until 2004, the most populated states (California, Texas, New York, Florida) were receiving homeland security funding equal to US$6 per capita, while states with low population (Wyoming, North Dakota, Vermont) were receiving six times as much (CRS 2005i: 6). The DHS moved to alleviate the situation, imposing allocation of the discretionary half of the funds according to population numbers. This did not make a significant change to the final distribution, and, in 2006, Congress attempted to put fund distribution on a risk-assessment basis, without ever repealing the 0.75 rule (Gilliard-Matthews and Schneider 2010). Congress sought to prioritise funding applications based on terrorism threat to: agriculture; food, banking and chemical industries; the defence industrial base; emergency services; energy; government facilities; postal, shipping, public health, health care, information technology, transportation and telecommunication systems; water; dams; commercial facilities; national monuments and icons. Each of those would be considered against the following types of threat: biological, nuclear, radiological, incendiary, chemical, explosive, suicide-bombing and cyber. Also weighing in were the historical precedent of attacks at a locality, the designation of parts or the whole of a state as under high alert by the Homeland Security Advisory System, or 'any other factor determined by the DHS Secretary' (*Faster and Smarter Funding for First Responders Act* 2005; CRS 2005i: 7–9). The sheer scope of an undefined 'mission' lead Congress to comical efforts to cross-tabulate a multitude of priorities before giving up and letting the Secretary decide. Exasperating this difficulty is the pre-emptive emphasis in security operations, the targeting of the 'plotting' phase, which can occur anywhere, away from the likely sites of attack.

However distributed, the funding for sub-national security is scarce (Progressive Policy Institute 2003: 13; US House of Representatives 2004a: 14). The total DHS allocation for sub-national governments fell from US$5.5 billion in the 2005 financial year, to US$3.1 billion in the 2006 financial year (CRS 2005i; 2005j; 2006). It was also the area most severely hit by fiscal discipline, thus ending up with US$1.3 billion in the 2012 financial year (Caudle 2011: 13; US Department of Homeland Security 2012). This austerity, combined with the counterterrorism exigencies, results in the straining of law enforcement, health, and fire services to the point that they cannot fulfil their mission (Benjamin 2012; CRS 2005i: 2–6; US Senate 2003a: 42–59).

Despite limited resources, and an initial lack of strategy, the DHS is making significant headway in imposing operational unity across the different levels of government. It is estimated that approximately one-third of police departments throughout the country have expanded their operation to include, and prioritise, intelligence collection, threat and vulnerability assessment of infrastructure, and emergency planning and response (Morreale and Lambert 2009: 13). This indicates that state and local mechanisms are executing federally determined functions, in a federal agenda. The most advanced points of this unification of the police mechanism are the 'fusion centres'.

Over 70 in number, and employing over 800,000 officers, fusion centres are hubs of integrated intelligence. They are DHS-led, but mainly staffed by sub-national personnel. They pull together at local level the combined intelligence of federal and sub-national governments and private businesses. They are users of, and contributors to, a combination of vast pools of personal and relational data, almost none of which has any relevance to terrorism. Fusion centres are *not* counterterrorism units. Given that any kind of 'suspect' behaviour can be preparatory for terrorism, they systematically employ an all-crimes/all-hazards approach (Monahan and Palmer 2011: 618–619, 624–626; Sena 2012: 5). Regarding intelligence collection, their main target is the political activity of the population, which they systemically treat as criminal threat (Brooks 2011: 17–22; Monahan and Palmer 2011: 628–629). Despite the almost complete lack of counterterrorism effectiveness and persistent coordination problems (Monahan and Palmer 2011: 621–623), fusion centres are positively evaluated by both the DHS and sub-national governments, because they make the federal-local traffic of intelligence more two-way than it had previously been, and engage sub-national personnel more creatively (Brooks 2011; Cillufo 2012: 7; Lanier 2011; Sena 2012).

Older, more established platforms for federal-local amalgamation are the Joint Terrorism Task Forces (JTTF). These are best understood as intelligence-led, trans-governmental police departments. They comprise local, DHS and FBI personnel, under the leadership of the FBI Headquarters (Chapter 9). Effectively, JTTFs are vehicles for subjecting the personnel of sub-national government to federal control (Herman 2008b: 86; Waxman 2009: 389). Each JTTF operates on the basis of an (often secret) 'Memorandum of Understanding' between the FBI and the state or local Executive. This causes a shift in the balance of powers at sub-national level, depriving sub-national legislatures of control over their police apparatus (Herman 2008b: 78–80). It also raises the question of whose law applies. Frictions arise when federal agents request their sub-national counterparts to violate state law, and can even, occasionally, lead a local authority to pull out from the JTTF (Herman 2008a: 8; 2008b: 80, 83; Waxman 2009: 394–395). The subjection of sub-national personnel to federal control compromises the 'anti-commandeering' doctrine. Set by the Supreme Court (*Printz v United States*) in 1997, it prohibits the federal government to commandeer state or local officials to 'administer or enforce a federal regulatory programme' (Althouse 2008: 27; see also Herman 2008b: 86). Homeland security is seen as a reversal of the courts' tendency during the 1990s to limit federal power over the states (Herman 2008a: 2–3, 6–7; Althouse 2008: 42).

DHS and the private sector: critical infrastructure and homeland security economy

Critical infrastructure

The question of critical infrastructure (CI) is central to the study of homeland security. First, because it introduces the private sector into the effort, thus expanding it beyond the confines of the official state. Second, because its protection is the most important DHS function. In fact, CI is the main object for protection of the entire homeland security effort.

In its official definition in the 2002 HSA, 'critical infrastructure' comprises:

> systems and assets, whether physical or virtual, so vital to the United States that the incapacity or destruction of such systems and assets would have a debilitating impact on security, national economic security, national public health or safety, or any combination of those matters.
>
> (P.L.107–297, Sec.2 (4)) (CRS 2004c: 7)

Practically, CI is specified through recurrent lists issued by the DHS or the President. The latest Directive (US President 2013) includes 16 sectors: chemical, commercial facilities, communications, critical manufacturing, dams, defence industrial base, emergency services, energy, financial services, food and agriculture, government facilities, health care and public health, information technology, nuclear reactors, transportation systems, and water systems. It is estimated that CI is 90 per cent privately owned (NIAC 2008: 3).

The DHS is charged to identify and protect the assets that comprise CI. In conjuncture with sub-national governments, it has to list the protected items, and perpetually re-evaluate these lists. It has to assess the vulnerability of each asset, and cross-tabulate it with the risk of an attack. The DHS's access to information on assets' vulnerability depends on voluntary disclosure by their owners. The threat information derives from intelligence gathered and perpetually reviewed by DHS and sub-national agents. Lastly, the DHS has to suggest measures for each asset's protection, which, for the owners, are voluntary.

To complement the weak definition of CI, terms like 'vulnerability', 'threat', 'risk', 'catastrophic', etc were used to guide DHS planning. But, they too are not defined, and are used casually and often interchangeably (CRS 2004b: 3). As a result, the designation process was incongruous. State Homeland Security Advisers identified 33,000 facilities as critical infrastructure. The IAIP examined its files, and determined that 1,700 of them were 'attractive' terrorist targets (CRS 2004b: 13). How the initial (33,000 items) selection was made is unclear. The information disclosed by the owners, which forms the basis of all further assessments, is believed to be often inaccurate and inadequate. No guidelines were provided to the state Homeland Security Advisers who made the initial assessment, and in some cases they were not contacted at all. Their reports do not include any methodological remarks. The initial list included derelict and demolished assets, had mislocated some facilities, and missed others which the industry acknowledged as 'obvious'. It is also unclear how the IAIP filtered the initial 33,000 facilities to 1,700 (CRS 2004b: 20–21; 2004c: 13; Siperco 2006).

The federal procedure appears perfectly reasonable compared to what occurred at state level. States are required to designate, with the help of federal experts, the facilities which are crucial to their security and economic life, and to compile them into lists, which would form the basis for funding allocation by the DHS. Thus, Iowa, for example, included casinos, family farms, landing pads, the Danish Windmill Museum and a vast Wildlife Refuge area; it omitted most skyscrapers, courthouses or banking centres. Mississippi included miniature golf courses and dirt bike tracks (Dalmer 2005). When, based on local assessments, the DHS produced a draft national list (National Assets Database, 2006), it included a popcorn factory in Pennsylvania, the Groundhog Zoo, a kangaroo conservation centre, and a beach 'at the end of the street'. It did not include the Statue of Liberty or the Empire State Building (Arkin 2006; US DHS/OIG 2006: 5, 11–12).

The DHS approach to CI protection appears somewhat random. The situation would be rectified by the production of a threat-vulnerability assessment. Six years behind schedule, the DHS managed to produce a Plan to develop a Strategy to enable the production of such assessment (Progressive Policy Institute 2003: 11; US House of Representatives 2004a: 9–10). The National Infrastructure Protection Plan informs that a national Inventory of Key Assets does exist. It is called IDW (no explanation provided), it is constantly being re-assessed, and is classified. It says nothing regarding the criteria for the assessment, except that IDW 'includes assets, systems, and networks that are nationally significant and those that may not be significant on a national level but are, nonetheless, important to State, local, or regional [CI] protection, incident management, and response and recovery efforts' (CRS 2005g: 2–4; US Department of Homeland Security 2009c: 29). The risk assessment is said to be done using the formula $R = f(C, V, T)$, where T = threat, V = vulnerability, and C = consequence. 'Consequence' includes not only public health and safety, economic and governance impacts, but also 'psychological' ones (US Department of Homeland Security 2009c: 32). This meticulous vagueness is replicated in the sector-specific Protection Plans the DHS produced for each of the 16 CI sectors.

The inability to produce a definite method for CI protection is puzzling, given that protecting infrastructure (or at least developing a methodology for doing so), is not that difficult. After the 1995 Oklahoma bombing, the Interagency Security Committee (ISC) took only two months to assess the vulnerability of all 491,465 federal buildings and produce security guidelines for each facility type. In another two years, the ISC had produced security standards for the construction of new federal buildings (CRS 2005g: 1–2).

Being perplexed by the DHS's incapacity to respond to one of its most important missions, means that we have misunderstood the nature of the endeavour. CI protection is not only about securitising important facilities. CI is *private* property. The designation of specific assets as CI entails the inclusion of the owning entity into a privileged regime of secrecy regarding the state of their facilities, and amnesty from relevant legal liability. This occurs automatically, even if the entities in question decide to do nothing to securitise their assets. Deciding to take action entails a significant cost to their operation – but public funding is also available to help them out. Thus, CI protection becomes a cost-benefit calculus for private entities, to be negotiated with the federal state (Hayes and Ebinger 2011). Indeed, early disagreements between the DHS and owners were reportedly impeding progress (CRS 2005h: 47).

At least as important as the $R = f(C, V, T)$ formula in determining CI is the National Infrastructure Advisory Council (NIAC). This is a public-private, parallel to the IAIP, body which advises the President through the DHS Secretary. It consists of up to 30 members, appointed by the President. Its current line-up comprises three public sector officials (two of them police), and 17 business representatives, from airlines, energy, agro, security, transportation, construction, chemicals, IT, and finance, who participate in the Council as representatives of their companies (US Department of Homeland Security Unknown Date I).

The effort of protecting CI is one of forming a power bloc. It devises a platform for *direct policy determination by capital*, a platform which is acknowledged by, but runs parallel to, the official state. This privileged positioning of capital depends entirely on the state – or, rather, the Executive. The inclusion of capital entities in the top-secret CI Inventory, and in the policy-defining NIAC depends entirely on the discretion of the DHS Secretary and the President. Capital can determine policy directly, but only capital *selected* by the Executive can do so. Thus, the meticulous open-endedness of CI designation and the absurdity of early attempts, indicates that the Executive would keep its options open, while capital entities were jostling for position. And the recent calm on the CI front indicates that the bloc is relatively settled (for early indications, see NIAC 2008). In this process of state-capital osmosis, the Executive is the gatekeeper. It also holds the wild card of being the sole proprietor of the totality of available knowledge regarding the ways of the Enemy and the features of each specific threat. This gives it a negotiating advantage vis à vis each specific capital *and* capital as a whole.

Finally, CI protection brings forth an element of class antagonism lurking behind security concerns. While seeking to safeguard capital, CI protection ignores the threat that neglected infrastructure poses for workers and the neighbouring communities. It also conceptualises the worker as a potential, possibly the main, threat to the infrastructure. Thus, CI personnel have to undergo thorough and perpetual checks to assess their lawfulness; and the key threats that, along with terrorism, CI protection seeks to neutralise are sabotage, workplace violence, and theft (Asgary 2009).

Homeland security economy

Since its initiation, DHS spends about a third of its budget on the acquisition of products and services from the private sector, an allocation fluctuating between US$14 and US$18 billion dollars between 2005 and 2011 (Ellman et al. 2012: 7; some observers put the figure higher, at 40 per cent: Skinner 2012: 6). This money helped create a new breed of enterprise or, at least, a new lobbying specialisation. Since the inception of DHS, Washington saw a five-fold increase in 'counterterror' lobbyists, and companies tried to vest even manifestly irrelevant interests under the guise of homeland security (Dalmer 2005: 3).

The allocation of the DHS's contracts displays certain trends. First, throughout the years, the DHS allocates over two-thirds of contract money to services, and only one-third to industry. In the services side, the main recipients are private security and IT firms, while the allocation to industry mainly ends up in IT, the classic 'defence' industry, and chemical-pharmaceuticals (Ellman et al. 2012: 8–9; US Department of Homeland Security Unknown Date II). The latter sector was virtually the sole appropriator of the DHS's meagre research and development allocation, in the quest for protection against bio-chemical, radiological and nuclear attacks – a threat which was played up in public, while considered incredible in internal communiqués (CRS 2005f: 2–3, 10; 2005h: 1, 48). This indicates an Executive preference to the pharma-chemical sector. The shrinking of the DHS research and development budget (from 8 to 2 per cent of its total budget between 2006 and 2011) signals its fall from grace, and leaves IT as the Department's undisputed favourite. The small and decreasing research and development budget also shows the DHS as a rather 'executant' department, second rate to Defense, which dedicates up to 20 per cent to research and development (Ellman et al. 2012: 8).

Since the scattergun acquisition of US$30 billion worth of items ranging from airport screeners to anti-hacker software in 2002, federal expenditure on homeland security has had a deep impact on the economy. That initial acquisition of miscellanea provided a silver lining to the IT sector after its collapse in 2000, and a sense of hope to a debt-ridden and panicked market (Chapter 3). Since then, the abundance of public money has caused existing industries to re-orient operations towards homeland security, it has encouraged a mushrooming of start-ups, and made an impact (initially at least) on universities' research agenda. The sectors seeking a slice of the pie range from IT to armaments, and from pharmaceuticals to finance; the merchandise they parade includes explosive-detention systems, smallpox drugs and vaccines, vehicle identifiers, mini-cannons, facial recognition systems, protective fabrics, data-profiling technologies, biometric photography, and detectors of anthrax, hazardous cargo and fake visas (Koerner 2002). Mirroring the homeland security realm's existence as a new meaning given to pre-existing relations, the homeland security economy is a compilation of old stuff in novel branding.

The homeland security 'sector' was a success. Major speculative organisations (Merrill Lynch, Forbes) saw it as a motor of growth for the entire economy. This was due to the sheer volume of federal money thrown at it. The DHS has been spending between US$31 and US$53 billion every year (with an exceptional US$76 billion in 2006), and awarded over 115,000 contracts in the 22 months to August 2006 (Ellman et al. 2012; Klein 2007: 13). The Department of Health & Human Services and the DOJ also make significant contributions, and the Pentagon matches all of them combined, spending up to US$60 billion on new security technologies. At the pick of the homeland security economy, in 2006, federal handouts were estimated at US$150 billion, IT stocks were performing at almost double the average rate of accumulation, while security and defence stocks were beating the average by 4:1 (Harvey 2007: 288). Despite belying its early promise to overcome its dependency on public money and become a major commercial player, the homeland security 'sector' remains relatively unscathed by the discipline imposed on public spending. Relevant allocations by the DHS fluctuate between US$43 and US$53 billion in the crisis years (2008–2011), making it a relatively safe haven in a devastated economy.

However, the homeland security economy remains flux and unstable, not least thanks to the DHS. Unlike the Pentagon and its well-defined procedures, and strategic objectives, which determine its allocations to established fiefdoms, DHS allocations are a free for all. The DHS distributes funds to the private sector apparently at random. It lacks a medium-to-long term strategic view, a plan, criteria or specifications, and lacks oversight mechanisms. Awards take place without a competitive process, on a selective, discretionary basis, resulting in extremely wasteful contracts, with ill-defined requirements and without performance measures. This earned DHS the reputation of being the most wasteful federal Department (US House of Representatives 2006; Skinner 2012).

Yet, this randomness and wastefulness is what gives the homeland security economy its dynamism. Rather than a fault or a miscalculation, it seems to be a tactic of the federal state. To begin with, the DHS was established on this basis: the *Strategy* envisioned it as infinitely 'flexible' in its dealings with its private partners, and HSA gave the Secretary carte-blanche to award contracts.

In short, the DHS is a Department 'open for business'. Indeed, a tacit but central mission of the new Department is to selectively allocate public funds to the private sector (Klein 2007: 298–306). Behind security concerns, it is easy to decipher a platform for creating a power bloc, with the federal Executive as the undisputed host and gatekeeper. The continuing chaos in procurement and contract awards signifies inability to reach a stable intra-capitalist arrangement and forge a solid power bloc – an inability that is exasperated by the highly discretionary and dictatorial (rather than de-personified and regularised) character of the power bloc formation process.

The only certainty about the power bloc formed on the homeland security platform, is that it will be *national*. Due to the nature of homeland security, foreign interests (including trans- and international concerns) are excluded. Characteristically, out of 40 or so prime contractors to the DHS, only one is not US-based: BAE Systems, the UK-based defence behemoth, which is majority-owned by US capital.

Finally, the long-term reproduction of the homeland security economy refers to the training of relevant personnel, and largely passes through the higher education system. The homeland security research and development allocations by the DHS, the Department of Defense, the Department of Health & Human Services, and the DOJ, have bucked two trends. The first is the de-Americanisation of scientific personnel. Numbers of scientifically educated US citizens were declining sharply, while US universities increasingly awarded science degrees to 'foreign born' students (US Department of Homeland Security/Office of Science and Technology Unknown Date). The other was the government-imposed austerity on education, with declining budgets, curtailment of university funds, and drastic reduction in student grants (Pear and Janofsky 2005). Through its Homeland Security University Fellowships, and the establishment of 12 Centres of Excellence which fund universities (selected by the Secretary) for conducting security-related research, the DHS created an oasis of affluence into a desert of scarcity, and set an agenda for future research and production (US Department of Homeland Security Unknown Date III). Access to relevant research and funding is classified and restricted to US citizens only, ensuring that not only the ownership, but also the workforce of the homeland security economy will be national. The free-flowing, cosmopolitan aspects of the 'knowledge-based' economy are reversed as the homeland security mega-factory is nourished, just like its war sibling, on national soil.

The pattern is the same for the future blue-collar homeland security workers. Generalised scarcity combined with a single area of relative affluence stirred Community Colleges to become training grounds for police, fire-fighting, emergency, and nursing personnel. With some exaggeration, we can claim that the dispossessed youth is effectively restricted to one viable (and legal) choice to earn a living: soldier or cop. Thus, those most devastated by the prolonged capitalist attack are scheduled to become the bodyguards of their oppressors. Needless to say, they will be badly paid and devoid of rights.

Working relations in the DHS: public sector managerial despotism

The notion of 'flexibility' permeates the DHS's working relations. The sensitivity of its operations justifies expansive managerial latitude and the cancelling of collective bargaining (Barr 2005a; 2005b; CRS 2005c). Based on a clause (US Code V, §7103b) which authorises the President to exclude from collective bargaining agencies whose primary function is intelligence, investigative or national security work, the DHS operates its own regime of working relations, exempt from the legal framework regulating federal sector employment. Employees become subject to Regulations issued by the Secretary and the Office of Personnel Director (CRS 2005b). They are under special status, determined unilaterally by their boss: changes in the Regulations do not need to pass through Congress like those in the US Code. The main differences between the general framework provided by the Code (Title V) and DHS Regulations are highlighted below.

Arbitration between federal employees and employers is undertaken by the independent Federal Labour Relations Authority (FLRA); in the DHS it is done by a council of three officials, appointed by the Secretary, the Homeland Security Labour Relations Board (HSLRB). The HSLRB is responsible for resolving issues related to the scope of bargaining, and for resolving complaints of unfair labour practices. It can assume jurisdiction over any matter concerning DHS employees which has been submitted to the FLRA, if it determines that the matter affects homeland security. The HSLRB has monopoly over 'internal affairs' and its decisions are not subject to appeal (CRS 2005b: 4–5). Thus, oversight of working conditions is sealed from the outside, and employees must swear secrecy oaths regarding most aspects of their work.

Regarding *management rights*, the Code recognises the authority to hire, assign, direct, lay off and retain employees in the agency, and to suspend, remove, reduce in grade or pay, or take disciplinary action against employees. DHS Regulations add the ability to determine the technology, methods and means of performing work; the ability to assign and deploy employees to meet operational demand; and the ability to take *any other actions* necessary to carry out the Department's mission (CRS 2005b: 6; added emphasis).

Regarding the creation of *unions*, the Code enables the FLRA to determine the appropriateness of any proposed unit on the basis of whether it is likely to promote 'effective dealings' and 'efficiency of the operations of the agency involved'. The Code does not permit national security employees to participate in 'units'. The Regulations also prohibit 'professional and other employees' from doing so (CRS 2005b: 7–8).

The Code defines as *'unfair labour practice'* the enforcement of any rule or regulation in conflict with a pre-established collective bargaining agreement. In the Regulations there is 'no similar provision' (CRS 2005b: 11).

Regarding the *protection of syndicalist action*, the Code clarifies that any personal view, argument, opinion, or publicity related to a representational election encouraging employers to exercise their right to vote, *shall* not constitute unfair labour practice. The Regulations replace this 'shall' with a 'may' (CRS 2005b: 12).

According to the Regulations (there in no similar provision in the Code), the management need not bargain, confer or consult over a change to a condition of employment (CRS 2005b: 13).

While the Code already favours the employer, the Regulations subject working relations to the employer's command. Conditions of employment in the DHS are determined not by law, but by the whim of the 'manager', which is in turn dictated by the urge for effectiveness. Apart from highlighting the authoritarian nature of managerialism as unaccountable, arbitrary power, the Guidelines introduce workfarist conditions at the heart of the public sector. The ratchet effect is, again, at play: a special framework initially reserved for a particular category of workers (those working in 'national security') is expanded to apply to the single largest workforce in the US. Once established in the largest domestic Department in the US, it is likely that workfarism will expand to the entire public sector.

Managerial flexibility is also imprinted in the Department's hierarchical and pay structures – termed 'classification' and 'pay adjustments' respectively.

The basic unit of labour organisation in the DHS is the *cluster*, a grouping of personnel according to the nature of their work. Clusters can be further divided into sub-clusters according to specialisation. Within each cluster the personnel is divided into four ranks, called bands: entry-developmental; full performance; senior expert; and supervisory. The Secretary can add or eliminate bands within the clusters at will. Unions are banned from bargaining issues related to labour classification (CRS 2005b: 3, 17–18).

Each cluster has an annual payment budget, determined by mission requirements, labour market conditions, available funds, etc. It is distributed differentially among the bands, differing by at least 8 per cent from one band to the next. Within each band, each worker is paid according to personal performance. There are three performance denominations: 'unacceptable', 'fully successful' and 'above fully successful'. Employees rated 'unacceptable' receive their band's minimum payment, while higher rated ones receive extras. Ratings are done by the supervisor, but the Personnel Office Director and the Secretary can shift employees' denomination at will. Payments are not subject to collective bargaining (CRS 2005b: 3, 22, 28, 33, 37, 46, 48, 55, 59–60, 62). Essentially, the DHS transports to the public sector the private sector's model of labour organisation, characterised by the fragmentation of the workforce and the dependency of the isolated worker on the manager.

Rather than enhancing effectiveness, this regime of work seems to undermine it. The DHS suffers serious 'human resource' malfunctions: increased personnel turnover, understaffing, and impositions of overtime in most agencies. Annual surveys show DHS personnel persistently ranking at the bottom of the federal sector in terms of job satisfaction, and topping the list of those wanting to quit. Dissatisfaction unites the fragmented workforce, as it runs across the different 'bands' and 'clusters' (Emerson 2012; Stier 2012; US Government Accountability Office 2012a; US House of Representatives 2004a: 16)

The invocation of 'effectiveness' was a pretext for introducing workfarism in the public sector, thus subjecting to it a large number of workers that had hitherto escaped it. Initiating the race to the bottom, the administration envisions the DHS model as the new paradigm for public sector labour: the human resource regulations which 'dramatically affect DHS employees […] could serve as a model for the whole federal government' (US Department of Homeland Security/Office of Inspector General 2004: 48–49).

DHS and the state-form

The examination of the new Department, and the broader political adjustments around it, strengthens the indications that the legislation and the law-form provided about the state-form.

To begin with, it confirms that the coercive apparatus became the predominant state mechanism. Not only its newfound logic (of stopping crime before it occurs) and operational mode became predominant, forcing the instrumentalisation of law, as we see in Chapters 5 and 6, but it also became a key *economic* player and constitutes a main platform for power bloc formation, situated on the most dynamic area of the economy. It power-pedals production, picks national champions and plants advanced detachments inside the Treasury (e.g. Office of Terrorism and Financial Intelligence; Foreign Terrorist Asset Tracking Centre, financial Action Task Force) (Clunan 2006; Heng and McDonagh 2008; Kimmitt 2007). The discretion the Executive enjoys in handing money to private capital results in the Executive's ability to chose its interlocutors at will, therefore gaining full control over the process of power bloc formation. This constitutes a new *statalisation* of governance, albeit not one based on legal or administrative rules. It occurs exclusively in private-public forums, parallel to the official state. These impromptu 'partnerships' are granted institutional recognition and protection, and are acknowledged as *the* decision-making bodies. Thus, capital is granted political authority, but only Executive-selected capital enjoys the privilege. In last century's terms, governance is now statalised.

The economic role of the coercive apparatus is not only statist, but also national. Both the governing capital of the parallel networks and the workers of the homeland security economy are strictly picked from a national pool. This indicates a shift in the scale and horizon of economic organisation and policy, and creates an excellent platform for economic protectionism (Clunan 2006: 558; Heng and McDonagh 2008: 595). The Schumpeterian tactic is also renegotiated. The new model maintains elements of innovation, but it is driven by, and dependent on, state subsidies.

Crucially, while the predominance of the coercive apparatus among state mechanisms has been reversed since the advent of the economic crisis and the change of guard in the White House, the above modalities remain predominant in the state-form.

The economic activity of the DHS is not its only function which displays these trends. The re-assertion of the national as the predominant scale of political organisation and activity is clearly seen in the restructuring of the coercive mechanism. The subjugation of sub-national personnel and resources to federal direction and control reverses the previous form's tendency towards greater autonomy of state and regional governments.

The DHS creates a vast, unified police mechanism, characterised by diversity and multiplicity at ground level, tailored to local realities and knowledge, and extreme concentration at the top. Both the outlay and the size of the mechanism are essential for implementing the expansive powers granted by the legislation.

In turn, the pyramid structure of the police mechanism signifies the return of statism as a mode of governance (Caudle 2011), and this in an area (law enforcement) where this has never been the case before. While formal lines of command are absent, the DHS and the FBI set the targets, strategies, structures, operational modes and, largely, the budgets of sub-national police forces. Governance is absorbed into a resurgent statism.

Thus, state power goes through several rounds of concentration. Within sub-national governments, power is concentrated at the Executive, as federal-state arrangements overlook local legislatures. Furthermore, power is concentrated from the sub-national to the federal level. Within the latter, it is captured by the federal Executive, as the other two branches have no say in the running of the police, especially in this trans-scalar context. The only level where power is not (yet?) concentrated is within the federal Executive, as acute competition seems to repeatedly throw up the need for new consolidation at an ever-higher level.

Finally, in stark contrast to the privileged treatment of capital and the institutionalisation of its participation in policy-making, the DHS story affirms the persistence of *workfarism*. This is so because the workers in the protected infrastructure are conceptualised as potential terrorists, and workplace resistance is associated with terrorism. Moreover, the workers in the security mechanism are devalued, fragmented, deprived of rights and subject to the whims of the management – and their proletarianisation is meant as a model for the entire public sector.

Thus, the reversal of the key tendencies of the previous form (trans-nationalisation vs nationalisation; governance vs statism; innovation vs state-subsidies) does not affect the key trend: workfare. On the contrary, the advancement of these tendencies serves to reinforce it. It thus seems plausible that workfare was not just a part of the mixture of the previous form, but its defining tendency; and that, now, the entire reconfiguration of the state-form is occurring in order to entrench and advance workfare.

9 Total intelligence, intelligence-led policing, 'totalitarian' state?

The discussion of the DHS highlights important changes in the structure of the policing apparatus, and implies concomitant shifts in the state-form. But it says little regarding the police *modus operandi*. As indicated by the legislation, the latter is marked by a sudden turn towards pre-emption, involving the reshaping of the police mechanism into an intelligence unit, and the expansion of the scope of intelligence. These trends are traced here, in the operational redirection of the FBI and in the restructure of the intelligence mechanism.

America's new intelligence agency: the FBI

Immediately after 9/11, the FBI announced a shift in its priorities, from crime prosecution to terrorism prevention. This shift signifies the predominance of intelligence as a *modus operandi*, an occurrence which, in turn, involves an organisational overhaul.

A major feature of this reorganisation was the upgrading of the FBI's intelligence units, and their integration into a single programme, by consolidating the intelligence programmes of four FBI Divisions (Counterterrorism, Counterintelligence, Criminal and Cyber). The unified programme came under direct control of the FBI Headquarters, and is managed by a single official in the new position of Executive Assistant Director for Intelligence (EAD-I). Moreover, a new Intelligence Office was created, to control the FBI's hitherto fragmented intelligence elements. It develops the FBI intelligence strategy and carrier paths for analysts, and ensures that intelligence is appropriately shared within the FBI and with other federal agencies. Thus, intelligence operations in the FBI are centralised, and the autonomy of its 56 Field Offices is curtailed. Lastly, a Field Office Intelligence Group was created in each Field Office, comprising intelligence analysts, who largely conduct tactical analysis; special agents, who collect information; and report officers, responsible for disseminating raw intelligence in the FBI and to other federal agencies (CRS 2004a: 5–7; Ragavan 2005). The process culminated with the consolidation of the FBI's pre-emptive components (Intelligence, Counterintelligence, Counterterrorism and Weapons of Mass Destruction) into a single, predominant agency, the FBI's National Security Branch (Blair and Leiter 2010: 6)

This restructuring corresponds to changes in operational priorities. Counterterrorism, counterintelligence and cybercrime are now the FBI's top three priorities, displacing law enforcement (Ragavan 2005: 6).

Thus, the FBI's disparate intelligence activities were consolidated horizontally (across Divisions) and vertically (across levels of command) into a distinct, comprehensive structure. The visibility of this structure helps the Bureau to strengthen and augment its intelligence operations. Congress authorised repeated increases of the FBI appropriation. It doubled between 2001 and 2007, reached its peak (US$8.3 billion) in 2011, and remained above US$8 billion in the next two years. Much of this money was dedicated to hiring intelligence analysts, three distinct intelligence career paths were created, and existing personnel were reassigned from drugs, white collar and violent crime to counterterrorism. Ten years after 9/11, the number of Intelligence Analysts had tripled (to over 3,000), and that of 'collector' agents doubled (approaching 5,000). Moreover, half the Bureau's 285 Special Agents were post-9/11 recruits and therefore steeped in the new intelligence culture, and trained in counter-intelligence and counterterrorism (CRS 2004a: 8–9; Mueller 2011: 6–7; Ragavan 2005; US President 2002f).

In its attempt to streamline its operations as an intelligence agency, the FBI adopted the CIA's 'intelligence circle' model. It also intensified its collaboration with the Agency, as both their operational field and the nature of their activity increasingly converge, with the CIA augmenting its domestic presence and the FBI becoming an all-out intelligence agency. Thus, the two Directors produced a memorandum of understanding to better streamline their agencies' operation in the US and abroad (CRS 2004a: 8–9; Ragavan 2005).

The reshaping of the FBI is an ongoing saga. It faced frictions with CIA stations caused by the FBI's expansion abroad, and serious problems and delays to its IT architecture (CRS 2004a: 9–13). These IT problems were still persisting ten years after 9/11, as the FBI was unable to consolidate and take full advantage of its various databases. The rise to prominence of cyber-security in the homeland security realm caught the Bureau unprepared, both in terms of expertise and of organisational structure (US Senate 2011b: 231, 245).

More importantly, the transformation had to overcome the persistent treatment of intelligence personnel as mere auxiliaries to their law enforcement colleagues. This was symptomatic of the FBI's 'historically neglected and weak' intelligence function, particularly in the area of strategic analysis (CRS 2004a: 4), and of the clash in rationale between intelligence and law enforcement. Law enforcement and intelligence demand operational modes, skills and incentives which are antithetical to one another. Police officials are oriented towards arrest and conviction, their operational style is impatient with long-term surveillance, they prefer an early arrest and interrogation to secure a confession, and are reluctant to share intelligence. By contrast, intelligence officials want as little attention as possible on their operations, follow their targets for long periods, are prone to share the intelligence they collect, do not care about making arrests or delivering tangible outcomes, and often operate beyond the law (Odom 2005; Treverton 2009: 125–127).

Thus, the re-invention of the FBI involved the monumental task of upturning the institutionalised ways in which the personnel work and understand their work – what is commonly termed 'culture', a culture that in the FBI is set like concrete (Ragavan 2005). The 'cultural' issue was essentially one of pre-emption vs reaction, of strategic intelligence (intelligence for itself) vs tactical intelligence (intelligence for prosecution). The reactive approach of targeting suspects of committed crimes was entrenched in the operation and attitude of FBI personnel. Intelligence analysis in the FBI had been 'tactical', i.e. auxiliary to criminal investigation. Strategic intelligence was unheard of, and not valued by the directing personnel who, furthermore, were unversed in national security affairs (CRS 2004a: 11–13; US Senate 2006: 56, 76–80).

The clash between the political urge for a paradigm shift, spearheaded by the formidable Robert Mueller, the FBI's longest serving Director since Edgar Hoover, and the personnel's incorrigibly law enforcement mindset and their lack of understanding of pre-emptive ways, was bloody (Associated Press 2005; Johnston 2005). The Counterterrorism Director was replaced four times between 2001 and 2007; five people took turns in leading the information technology section in 2002–2003; and the Trilogy IT system had ten different project managers who redrafted its contract 36 times (Ragavan 2005). Lower down the hierarchy, nearly one-third of the FBI intelligence analyst posts remained unfulfilled in 2004, mostly due to rapid turnover. Personnel hired for analysis had to spend much of their time on 'escort, trash and phone duty', being second-class citizens to their gun-carrying colleagues (Progressive Policy Institute 2003: 9). The resistance was so fierce that senior Congress members and DOJ officials doubted whether the FBI would ever overcome its reactive, law enforcement character (Eggen and Pincus 2005; Odom 2005). Still, the perseverance of the pre-emption cadre, mobilised by unremitting political will, overcame inertia and resistance, to deliver a new intelligence agency: the FBI.

The FBI intelligence operation expands at sub-national level through the JTTFs. These predate 9/11, but have been multiplying since, to exceed 100 nationwide. They comprise a balanced mixture of local and federal personnel, with the latter assuming directive functions. Their overall operation is directed by the National Joint Terrorism Task Force, situated at the FBI Headquarters. They are trans-governmental entities, whose law enforcement work is intelligence-led. The centralisation of control in federal hands has estranged local personnel. State and local police directors complain that, while nominally a joint effort, JTTFs mainly comprise one-way information traffic – from local to federal – due to FBI unwillingness to share information with them (CRS 2004a: 20–21; IACP 2005; Lanier 2011: 4; Mueller 2011: 7, 10). In effect, the pre-eminence of intelligence has caused a division of labour: the (mainly federal) components possessing intelligence assume a directive role over those (mainly sub-national) who do not (Morreale and Lambert 2009; Ratcliffe 2008: 99–101).

Despite its inadequacies and the difficulties it still faces, the FBI restructuring signals a departure of policing from the *status quo ante*. It is a key part of the irreversible, political impetus towards merging intelligence and law enforcement under the prominence of intelligence. It is part of the same move described in the Patriot Act's recasting of FISA. While the FBI restructuring exemplifies the stirring of policing towards pre-emption, the emphasis on intelligence also brought an overhaul of the traditional intelligence mechanism.

The new intelligence apparatus: centrally controlled – but by whom?

The restructuring of the intelligence mechanism was spurred by the trauma of 9/11 and the failures which let it happen. It was aiming to address the lack of communication and coordination among intelligence entities. It opted for the consolidation of intelligence agencies and functions under a single point of authority.

For an effort aiming at coordination, the restructuring of intelligence started rather haphazardly. In December 2002, the Pentagon introduced the Joint Regional Information Exchange System, a structure that enables information sharing between sub-national governments and the Defense Intelligence Agency (DIA). A year later the DHS used this structure to create the Homeland Security Information Network (HSIN), which connects the DHS Operations Centre with all states, the National Guard, local police and the private sector (CRS 2005a: 2–3, 6). Additionally, initiated in late 2002, the Anti-terrorism Information Exchange of the Regional Information Sharing System is the counterterrorism branch of an international network, covering law enforcement agencies and private sector entities in the US, Australia, Canada and England (CRS 2005a: 10–11). Lastly, the CIA, the FBI, and the Departments of Defense, State, Justice and Homeland Security participate in the Terrorist Threat Integration Centre (TTIC), which assimilates and analyses domestic and foreign information. In doing so, the TTIC largely replicated the functions of the DHS's IAIP Directorate (CRS 2004e: 9). It was in turn undermined by clashes over leadership between the CIA and the FBI. The battle between the two was joined in the foreign front by the Pentagon's DIA. Thus, up to 2004, the integration effort kept spawning new programmes, entities and conflicts which threatened to paralyse the mechanism and prevent it from executing even the simplest of tasks (like the integration of the 12 federal terrorist watch-lists, made impossible by agencies' reluctance to share their lists with antagonists: Democratic Members of the House Select Committee on Homeland Security 2004: 8–10).

Moved by the recommendations of the 9/11 Commission and the intelligence failure leading to the Iraq war, Congress stepped in to install some order. The 2004 Intelligence Reform and Terrorism Prevention Act (IRTPA) introduced the Director of National Intelligence (DNI) and the associated Office (ODNI) as stand-alone federal entities. The DNI was envisioned as the overlord of the intelligence mechanism. Appointed by the President, the Director would be the sole overviewer of the entire intelligence landscape, the principal adviser to the President and the National and Homeland Security Councils, and the most authoritative person in determining intelligence strategy and overviewing policy (Gannon 2011: 2; Blair and Leiter 2010: 6; US White House/Office of Press

Secretary 2004). In introducing the DNI, Congress was determined to 'strengthen the centre of the Intelligence Community' (Hayden 2011: 1). In this manner, it attempted to reverse the decades-long movement towards a centrifugal model, where agencies popped-up according to the needs of military, diplomatic and police missions (Gannon 2011: 2).

In tandem with the DNI, IRTPA also (re)introduced the National Counterterrorism Centre (NCTC). It was pre-empted in doing so by Executive Order 13355 issued a few months earlier (27 August 2004). Both Congress and the President envisioned the NCTC as the orchestrator of intelligence functions. It was meant to serve as the primary analysis and integration hub for all federal counterterrorism intelligence; to conduct strategic operational planning for counterterrorism activities, by 'integrating all instruments of national power, including diplomatic, financial, military, intelligence, homeland security, and law enforcement activities' within and among agencies; to assign operational responsibilities to departments and agencies; to establish a shared 'knowledge bank on known and suspected terrorists, groups, strategies, goals, capabilities and networks; to establish information systems and architecture; and to disseminate terrorism information to the President and the Vice President' (Blair and Leiter 2010: 7; CRS 2005e: 5, 15; US Senate 2011b: 218).

Already, some jurisdictional issues arise between the DNI and the Director of the NCTC. IRTPA divided the latter's reporting duties, so that the NCTC Director would report to the DNI for intelligence and budget issues, but directly to the President for non-intelligence counterterrorism issues. This double reporting duty of the NCTC Director complicates relations with the DNI. It fails to clarify the hierarchy between them, and undermines the DNI role as principal adviser to the President (CRS 2004e: 6–8).

Much more ferocious were the clashes between the newcomers and the established players. While the creation of the DNI Office was still pending, Pentagon created the post of Defense Undersecretary for Intelligence. The particulars of the role were unclear, but the new office signalled a centralised approach to military intelligence, especially regarding acquisitions and budget allocation. It was also a message of hostility to the DNI. At the same time, the then Secretary of Defense, Donald Rumsfeld, mobilised support in Congress, and successfully introduced into IRTPA, §1018, which deprived the DNI from budgetary control over entities belonging to established Departments (Blair 2011: 20; CRS 2005e: 16–19, 22–23; 2011c: 10; Harman 2011: 2; Hayden 2011: 2). In this manner, the Pentagon secured effective control over its eight intelligence agencies. But it also neutralised the DNI's budgetary authority (and with it much of his power), as almost every agency was situated in a federal Department. All except one. The CIA.

The CIA allocation was at the hands of the DNI and, moreover, the latter threatened to dethrone it from its privileged position in the intelligence 'community'. To begin with, the DNI replaced the CIA Director as a principal political actor. The latter, in his capacity as Director of Central Intelligence (DCI) had overview of intelligence operations, and was the President's primary adviser on relevant matters, a function that now passed to the DNI. The latter also replaced the DCI in the President's National Security Council hearings, where the DCI had a place for over 60 years (Burger 2005; CRS 2011c: 21).

Moreover, the CIA's responsibility for integrating and analysing all-source intelligence passed to the NCTC, threatening to reduce the CIA to a mere collection unit, responsible for organising clandestine networks (Blair 2011: 12; De Young 2006). Even at this level, the CIA suffered considerably. The presidential appointment of Porter Goss in 2004, seems to have come with a brief to clear the decks. During his 18-month tenure, he clashed with most senior officers, resulting in 20 of the Agency's more coveted spots being vacated. He oversaw a mass exodus of field veterans, amounting to the loss of 'centuries of experience', resulting in the CIA fielding the most inexperienced team of agents in its history (Robinson and Whitelaw 2006).

Apart from its devaluation, the introduction of the new entities also undermined the CIA operationally. Most of the 300 NCTC employees derive from the CIA's Counterterrorism Centre, which has also dispatched staff to the FBI, the DHS and the DNI Office, and was therefore drained of experienced personnel (Pincus 2005).

The lack of experienced personnel, aggravated by the high demand for intelligence, resulted in mass outsourcing of operations to start-ups headed by high-rank intelligence veterans. These private companies appropriate roughly 70 per cent of the yearly (non-military) intelligence budget, i.e. over US$40 billion annually. Their operatives cost the government double the amount they would if they were hired by the public sector on a permanent basis. These contracted intelligence workers are, in some cases, granted by the FBI a licence to kill (Monahan and Palmer 2011: 618; Amey 2011). Even in the NSA, which seems to emerge as the dominant agency, an estimated 70 per cent (70,000) employees are contracted (MacAskill et al. 2013). This caused some institutional soul-searching by the neoliberal state about what its core functions are, and whether they can be leased to the private sector (Dickinson 2012; US Federal Register 2011). Apart from oiling the homeland security economy, mass outsourcing introduces precarious working relations at the heart of the state. Over a quarter of intelligence personnel are temporary, contractually hired workers (Allen 2011; Amey 2011; Lowenthal 2011). With the exception of those working for the Pentagon, these workers are subject to the performance-based, pay-band system pioneered by the DHS (CRS 2011c: 24). Lastly, given that their next contract depends on it, private intelligence companies are systemically motivated to produce intelligence which suits the objectives of their clients in the state (Klein 2007: 305).

The main beneficiary of intelligence restructuring is the Pentagon. Its intelligence operations were drastically strengthened, and it was also established as a major player in the *domestic* field. The Northern Command inaugurated two intelligence-gathering centres, the Counterintelligence Field Activity was introduced with the mandate to collect and analyse information from police, military and intelligence sources, the NSA and the DIA began monitoring all domestic telephone and internet traffic, and the Geo-spatial Intelligence Agency mapped 133

US cities, acquiring the capacity to identify the occupants of every house, their nationality and political affiliation (Donohue 2008: 184, 246–247; Roach 2011: 196). The trend is set to continue, as top intelligence officials see the Pentagon's presence in domestic intelligence as necessary and unproblematic (Blair 2011: 9–11).

Thus far, the big picture shows the Pentagon to be the winner of the restructure, while the new entities mainly feed off a reduction in the CIA's size, capacity and importance. This was the situation during the Bush administration. Under Obama, signals are rather mixed. On the one hand, Obama has appointed three CIA Directors (and two interim ones) between 2009 and 2013, something that does not bode well for the stability of the Agency. On the other hand, the President has ignored the DNI's recommendations for these appointments, an obvious snub to the latter and a sign that, with presidential support, the CIA is regaining its independence from the DNI. Moreover, the CIA is said to be systematically undercutting DNI authority, either by seeking overall leadership in specific operations, or by ignoring the DNI and acting independently. Importantly, the CIA resisted the DNI's jurisdiction over its station chiefs and supervision over covert operations. In the clashes that ensued, the President decided in favour of the Agency (Blair 2011: 12, 18).

There is a sense that the CIA is clawing its own back, and that this is done to the detriment of the DNI. The latter, already circumvented by the Pentagon and delicately balanced against the NCTC, seems to be losing its overlord status, and to be increasingly reduced to a reviewing and advising role (Hayden 2011; Harman 2011). In its struggle to cope, the DNI Office has developed a chaotic structure, with 16 National Mission Managers overviewing an equal number of intelligence missions, while being largely ignored by the agencies they are supposedly supervising (Blair 2011: 2–3). Thus, the entity meant to unify the mechanism is simply replicating the diversity of the mechanism within its frame. The new entities are also undermined by instability at the top. Both the NCTC and the DNI office have consumed five Directors each since their inception in 2005 (US Senate 2011b: 216).

The attempts to centralise the apparatus have only managed to add new components therein. The centralising entities introduce complication and rivalry, thus reproducing the need for centralisation. Still, the failure of the centralising entities does not signify failure of integration and coordination at operational level. On the contrary, platforms like the Interagency Threat Assessment and Coordination Group in the NCTC; the influx of new agents and analysts versed in the culture of information-sharing; and the construction of intelligence-sharing electronic platforms (like the Library of National Intelligence which hosts all finished intelligence pieces of all agencies, or Intellipedia, a user-amendable source for evolving intelligence), have resulted in unprecedented levels of inter-agency co-operation (Blair and Leiter 2010: 4–7; Olsen 2011: 8).

Finally, the failure of centralising entities *does not mean that the mechanism is not being centralised.* The FBI and the NCTC Directors, and the DHS Secretary, promptly identify John Brennan, the Deputy National Security Adviser directly accountable to the President (only), as the principal coordinator and supervisor of counterterrorism and homeland security efforts, and as the principal intelligence adviser (Harman 2011; US Senate 2011b: 220–221). Thus, there is a centre in intelligence, but not where Congress indented it to be: it is in the White House. This means that Congress has no supervisory access over the strategic and operational epicentre of counterterrorist intelligence (CRS 2004e: 12; US Senate 2011b: 247–248). It also means that, at the moment when intelligence becomes a crucial political premium, as basis for both decision-making and justification of state power, it is brought under the direct, exclusive control of the President.

Total intelligence: everyone, everything, everywhere, for no particular reason

While the above describe the effort – and struggle – to impose intelligence as the dominant mode of policing, and to restructure the relevant mechanism, it says nothing about what this mechanism does, or how. What are the methods, scope and targets of intelligence?

The bloating of the apparatus is reflected in its budgets. Estimated total spending on intelligence has more than doubled since 9/11, from US$26.7 billion in 1998, to US$55 billion in 2011. This refers to national security intelligence only, and excludes military intelligence that amounts to, approximately, another US$25 billion per year (CRS 2011c: 9).

All the (structural) developments discussed above, and all those (functional trends) whose discussion follows, comprise a paradigm shift, a radical reconceptualisation of intelligence, its methods, use, value, purpose and mechanism. This shift corresponds to the prominent position of counterterrorism among intelligence priorities, and among state priorities in general. The overarching trend is the establishment of pre-emption as the defining principle of structures and practices, and this constitutes a departure from the previous (cold war) organisation of intelligence under the deterrence imperative.

Supposedly dictated by the change in the nature of the Enemy, intelligence operations are redefined. As the Enemy is not territorially bounded, but operates in multiple sights both outside and within US territory, intelligence operations must take place everywhere in the world. This includes, emphatically, the US itself, in contrast to the cold war situation when domestic operations were (allegedly) scarce, and intelligence was focused primarily in a few countries. This reconfiguration is not just spatial, but also organisational. Mirroring the shift in the Enemy's nature from 'state' to 'network', the scattered intelligence operations are interconnected, communicate with one another, and adjust their course accordingly, thus generating the need for a centre conducting their coordination (Treverton 2009: 21–30, 81–82, 104–133).

The most crucial departure concerns the nature of the targeted people and activities. The cold war intelligence machinery was set up to monitor a defined range of easily identifiable people situated in specific hierarchical structures, and activities which were relatively standardised and easy to interpret. On the contrary, anyone can be (or become) a terrorist, and the activity building up to a terrorist hit can comprise virtually anything, as each attack is unique in character and does not easily fit into discernable patterns. Thus, all activities, or their combinations, can be possible harbingers of a terrorist attack, and therefore of interest to intelligence (Treverton 2009: 26, 107, 139–163). The ideal condition, therefore, is the *constant surveillance of all people and all activity*. In short, intelligence must become *total*.

The key move to this direction is what David Lyon terms *integrated surveillance* (Lyon 2003: 88–108). Ever since the New Deal, the coercive and the welfare mechanisms of the state collect, classify, aggregate and retain information on almost all individuals inhabiting the US. Since the early 1990s, as an ever-increasing amount of interactions became electronically mediated, the private sector became the leader in data collection, aggregation and retention, driven by its need to optimise marketing techniques and to discipline its workforce. However, public sector data were strictly compartmentalised, according to agency and use; private sector data were safeguarded or commercialised; and dissemination of both sectors' data was restricted by law. Since 9/11 all data, from all different sources, is fused and directly accessible to the coercive mechanism of the state – a move eloquently described in counterterrorism legislation (Chapter 5).

The exemplary programme along these lines is the Pentagon's Terrorism (initially *Total*) Information Awareness System (TIA). Operated by the Defense Advanced Research Projects Agency (DARPA), it would be a 'programme of programmes', aggregating data from *all* transaction records into a 'centralised, grand database'. These would be analysed to establish patterns of 'low-intensity/low-density' criminal or terrorist activity (EPIC 2003; 2005; Moran 2005: 345). While Congress stopped funding for the programme, the tendency to total surveillance continues unabated.

The TIA model is constantly replicated, metastasising from one programme and agency to the next. Thus, the Pentagon introduced TALON, an all-source aggregation database which would evaluate threats to military personnel; and the DHS developed ADVICE (Analysis, Dissemination, Visualisation, Insight and Semantic Enhancement), an IT system which would collect information from a vast array of sources (including blog and email content, corporate information, news stories, etc) and cross-reference it against intelligence and law enforcement records. According to its manager 'the key is not to identify terrorists [...] but to identify critical patterns in data that illumine their motives and intentions' – a declaration much in tune to the nature of terrorism as defined in the Patriot Act: a crime residing on motives and intentions. This is done through 'understanding the relationships among people, organisations, places and things [by] using social behaviour analysis and other techniques'. Like TIA, these programmes were officially discontinued as the Bush administration was drawing to a close. Concerns were raised about ADVICE infringements on privacy, while TALON had developed a speciality in targeting political groups. Nevertheless, these programmes still continue: TALON is absorbed in FBI databases, while ADVICE was nothing but a complex software programme; the DHS continues the same lines of data aggregation and analysis through (better and cheaper) software acquired in the market (Anderson 2007; Clayton 2006; US Department of Homeland Security/ Privacy Office 2007; Donohue 2008: 245–246). In addition, in 2013, the existence of NSA's PRISM and X-Keystroke programmes was revealed. PRISM is based on FISA, §215 ('access-all-records') orders to major telecom providers (Google, Facebook, Apple, Verizon, etc) to submit to the NSA the transactional records of *all* communications with at least one end in the US. The Senator responsible for the 'significant' FISA amendment claims that PRISM had been running for up to seven years to 2013 (Feinstein, cited in Wheeler 2013). Thus, the NSA has real-time access to an estimated 20 billion transactions per day, which it stores and analyses to decipher patterns regarding 'a wide variety of threats' (DNI James Clapper, cited in Hopkins 2013; see also Greenwald 2013a; MacAskill et al. 2013). Similarly, X-Keystroke is a programme enabling the monitoring and storing of all internet use (Greenwald 2013b). In short, TIA is alive and well: it is a fixture in the political landscape because total intelligence is a state strategy – with only casual relation to terrorism.

The entrenchment – and permanence – of the total approach is exemplified in the dominant analysis method: pattern revelation. The pools of personal and transactional data are vast and rapidly growing. The problem is not collection or aggregation, but analysis: how to locate significant information and 'situations of interest' in enormous pools of recorded activities and interactions pestered with noise. As a consequence, emphasis is given to the development of algorithms able to connect scattered pieces of information and thus reveal patterns that will enable the forestalling of terrorist attacks (RAND 2004: 11; Unknown Date: 15; SRI International 2004: 1; Treverton 2009: 148).

The analytical techniques and the political implications of this approach are discussed in Chapter 10. Here, I merely note that this type of algorithmic analysis is pertinent to open-ended, multi-variable, speculative investigations, rather than ones focused on specific situations, hypotheses or persons (Treverton 2009: 139–140). Indeed, the data under analysis exceeds greatly traditional police and secret agency footwork; it comprises the totality of data available to governmental agencies, and much of those collected by private entities. Surveillance extends, potentially, to the totality of transactions by the totality of individuals (Mattelart 2010: 144; Monahan and Palmer 2011: 630; Nunn 2005).

This full-spectrum intelligence pays special attention to the internal enemy. In perfect alignment with the Patriot Act definition, the DOJ associates all kinds of 'anti-government' subversives (ranging from Black Bloc anarchists to fascist hit-squads, and from deep ecology activists to the Ku Klux Klan) with terrorism, and seeks to educate its newly acquired state and local intelligence helpers in combating them (US Department of Justice 2009). The DHS collects strategic intelligence on subversive political action (US Department of Homeland Security 2009a; 2009b), and the amorphous notion of 'domestic extremism', thus far seemingly limited to jihad-type indoctrination, emerges as a key reference for the intelligence mechanism.

Intelligence-led policing

The stirring of policing towards intelligence, and the total character of the latter, outline a new conceptual and operational paradigm for policing, one we may conventionally call 'intelligence-led policing' (Ratcliffe 2008). To describe it, and assess its relative novelty, a comparison with late twentieth century (post-1968) policing models would be useful.

In his pioneering work, Stanley Cohen (1985) showed how the alternative to incarceration – 'communitarian' – penal approaches developed in the 1960s became increasingly formal, professional and bureaucratic, to finally merge with the 'hard' penal apparatus in the early 1970s. Moreover, the coercive potential of (state and non-state) sites of socialisation, like the school, the family or the neighbourhood, was enhanced and systematised, drawing these institutions to the penal constellation. The incorporation of the 'soft' mechanism and the co-option of non-penal institutions resulted in an expansion of penalisation to behaviours and individuals that were previously beyond its interests. Harmless deviance became targeted, causing the doubling of individuals subjected to penal treatment between 1965 and 1985. At the same time, prevention was defined as part of the policing mission, and the likelihood of deviance was sufficient to bring the individual to the attentions of the coercive mechanism. This pre-emptive approach was left to the 'soft' mechanism, which related the 'likelihood' or 'high risk' of deviation to factors like 'deprived background', 'risk of unemployment, homelessness, and family break-up', or 'lack of work skills'. The result was that an estimated 45 per cent of those captured in the penal net had done nothing illegal. Finally, Cohen implies a second turning point, located circa 1982 and the vast prison building programmes. It signals a course of reversal, away from the 'soft' approach and back to 'hard' penalisation ('back to justice'), and involves the participation of private capital in the 'hard' mechanism.

Cohen's criminological account resonates with some key accounts of that period in political theory. For Foucault, the expanded, pre-emptive policing model would be a manifestation of the logic inherent in liberal rule ('biopolitics'), a mode of power whose considerations exceed the legal-illegal duality, and envelop broader behavioural trends, like industry-idleness, decency-indecency, healthiness, cleanliness, etc (Chapter 10). In the context of biopolitical power, the question asked by criminal law – *What have you done?* – is replaced by another: *Who are you?* (Foucault 2007: 319–323; 2008: 34). For Poulantzas, the policing model is concerned not with the criminal act but with the crime-inducing mentality and pathogenic social environment, and 'dangerousness' is a feature of the new authoritarian statism (AS), a state-form developing to combat the crisis of the Keynesian welfare state (Poulantzas 1976b: 322; 1980: 410; 1978: 186–187; see also Oppenheimer and Canning 1979). Similarly, Stuart Hall interpreted the advent of pre-emptive policing as a response to acute crisis, and underlined its class and racial bias (Hall et al. 1978: 181–273; Hall 1980). Indeed, we can see both turning points identified by Cohen as hallmarks in a periodisation of social struggle. The first (c. 1972), marks a defensive realignment of the capitalist state against the 1960s popular offensive;

the second (c. 1982), is part of the counteroffensive of capital and the break with Keynesian and welfare policy.

David Garland's (2002) account of policing starts where Cohen's broke off, and stops just before 9/11. Since the early 1980s, 'hard' coercion has been expanding and intensifying: the volume of the penal system is augmented, and there is much greater use of (prolonged) incarceration (see also Wacquant 1999; 2009). The preventive functions previously monopolised by the 'soft' apparatus are now undertaken by the police. There is increased emphasis on 'order-maintaining' or 'quality of life' policing, i.e. the targeting of incivilities and misdemeanours (Garland 2002: 168–169). The official coercive apparatus is larger than ever, and it is complemented by rapidly growing private security enterprises and organised security activity by communities and commercial organisations. This 'third sector' apparatus consists of crime-preventing organisations, public-private partnerships, community policing groups, multi-agency forums, local authority panels, working groups and action committees, linked to one another and to the formal police (Garland 2002: 124–125, 170, 173). This network is determined by private interests, and alters the logic of policing. From pursuing-punishing individuals, its focus shifts to reducing the 'supply' of criminal events, by minimising vulnerability and enhancing situational controls (Garland 2002: 171). The state seeks to organise and align the activities of this coercive network. The policing agenda, and legislation, is determined directly by political personnel in conjunction with private interests, in a tandem between newly conceived 'community demands', and the promptness of governmental centres to 'satisfy' them, bypassing police and justice professionals (Garland 2002: 172). Thus, the 'integral' coercive apparatus described by Cohen, is replaced by a joint governance enterprise, where policing concerns are elaborated in state-capital forums.

Pre-emption is also pioneered by this mechanism. Yet, it differs from the 1970s model. Governance-style pre-emption does not focus on identifying the dangerous individual and preventing the criminal act. It only seeks to *secure property*, and elevates this to primary policing mission. 'Potential offenders are numerous and by no means always recognisable. By contrast, we do at least know what property to protect and where it is' (Walker 1986, cited in Garland 2002: 129). Crime is a normal, common place and inevitable aspect of life. It is seen as a routine, calculable risk. It is a matter of utility, reducible to supply-demand and cost-benefit calculi. It is conceptualised prospectively and in aggregate, so that risks can be calculated and averted by adequate preventive measures (Garland 2002: 128, 130). Thus, managerialism dominates the logic of policing. The costs of crime, prevention, punishment and policing are calculated and their comparative figures inform policy choices. This model derives from capital sectors which have to consider crime in their circle of business (insurance, private security, large commercial enterprise) (Garland 2002: 189).

Alongside this neoliberal approach, a neo-conservative one is also on the rise. The criminology of 'the dangerous other', an anti-modern ideology which pictures crime in melodramatic tones: as a catastrophe, warfare, and assault on the social body and its moral fibre (Garland 2002: 184, 191). These two conceptualisations share some fundamental premises. First, they both naturalise crime. Whether it results from rational choice or from natural wickedness, there is nothing to be asked or explained about it. Second, they both see the interest of the offender as fundamentally opposed to, and irreconcilable with, that of society, hence even misdemeanours are disproportionately targetted (Garland 2002: 181–182; Wacquant 2009: 252–269, 290–292).

The new mode of policing is part of the workfare regime, and pertinent to class warfare. Its targets are the declining middle class, the working class and the sub-proletariat, which are conceived as a social risk or as the internal enemy. The shifts in policing are part of the substitution of the welfare state with a penal regime. Whether moralistic and neo-conservative, or value-free and managerial, the fortified, expanded, policing machinery is the strong arm of neoliberal politics: 'control is re-emphasised in every area of social life – with the singular and startling exception of the economy, from whose deregulated domain most of today's major risks routinely emerge' (Garland 2002: 195–196; Wacquant 2009: 3–13, 20, 243, 299, 307–311). In short, '"[w]orkfare" and "prisonfare" are two integral components of the neoliberal Leviathan' (Wacquant 2009: xviii)

The policing model of homeland security magnifies some key features of the pre-9/11 one, and disrupts some others. Starting with its target, the property under protection ('critical infrastructure') is elevated to the status of a superior social good. At the same time, the criminal (now terrorist) is not just a risk or even a miasma, but an all-out existential Enemy. This intensification of the police-criminal relation into enmity triggers a qualitative shift that shakes the coercive apparatus and, at the same time, elevates its importance among state mechanisms. For the first time, pre-emption becomes *the* main priority of policing, and intelligence its dominant modality. And, it does not target just the 'dangerous' few, but envelopes the entire society. This pre-emptive police apparatus is pyramid-like in structure: expanded at the base, and concentrated at a singular point at the top. It is also politicised: it is controlled by a closed political directorate, and its main target is popular political activity. Finally, intelligence-led policing is 'mission-driven', guided and judged by its efficiency in achieving outcomes, not by its adherence to law (Morreale and Lambert 2009: 6; Ratcliffe 2008: 48, 56–57, 68–75, 164, 172, 177, 224).

Intelligence and the state: totalitarianism or authoritarian statism?

The discussion of policing confirms the indications offered by counterterrorism legislation: the subjection of the entire society to constant surveillance is a strategic political priority.

Under the pre-emption imperative, intelligence becomes a central function of the state. Its disengagement from suspect persons and activities (already expressed in legislation) results in its ubiquity. As the threat it is targeting is, mainly, potential (today's law-abiding citizen *may* become tomorrow's terrorist), intelligence is not only omnipresent, but also perpetual. In the words of pre-emption's philosopher-king (and former Defense Secretary) Donald Rumsfeld, 'the absence of evidence is not necessarily the evidence of absence' (cited in Treverton 2009: 39–40). Uttered in reference to Iraq's weapons of mass destruction, this aphorism encapsulates the new pre-emptive police logic, and informs the FBI's monitoring of political groups. It mandates the constant policing of everything, in case some threat springs up somewhere. What constitutes a threat is determined by top state managers. In addition, it further galvanises the reversal of the burden of proof: everyone is guilty of their own potentiality.

The apparatus that would undertake such a herculean task is under construction. It recombines the existing loose, decentralised, assemblage of continuous surveillance, into a mechanism that has no exterior, and is consolidated, appropriated and directed by the state (Lyon 2003: 31–32; Haggerty and Ericson 2000). Of equal importance with its appropriation by the state is the concentration of control *within* the state, so that the whole mechanism comes under a single point of control. Rather than public property and concern, the intelligence megamachine is of personal use to the President. Thus, the formerly chaotic mechanism acquires 'unity of purpose': the purpose of its political directorate. And, unlike its welfare state counterpart, the workfarist surveillance ensemble only has a punitive purpose.

Intelligence-led policing is a realisation of '[t]he police dreams that one look at the gigantic map on the office wall should suffice at any given moment to establish who is related to whom and in what degree of intimacy' (Arendt 1973: 435). While Arendt considers this dystopic snapshot to be specific to 'totalitarian' rule, there is no need to be melodramatic about homeland security. Foucault and, later, Neocleous have shown that this 'dream' is inherent to liberal rule. Security is the par-excellence project of the liberal conception of government, and it is geared towards the fullest possible knowledge of society (Foucault 2008: 63–67; Neocleous 2000: 117). Moreover, the notion of totalitarianism is problematic. 'Totalitarian' analyses essentialise the formal separation of powers and the private ownership of ideological mechanisms and, on this basis, juxtapose a capitalist-pluralist type of state to a fascist-totalitarian one. Thus, they obfuscate that both of these are forms of capitalist state – with dictatorial forms resulting from acute political crises that cannot be accommodated in the context of pluralist-democratic forms (Poulantzas 1974: 313–315).

Since it is the *form* of the capitalist *type* of state we are discussing, homeland security is very much of the AS mould: direct state (here: police) interference in every sphere of social life is combined with centralisation of the direction and control of a vast policing enterprise.

A side-note to the discussion of the state-form comes from the comparison between the two most recent intelligence models: cold war deterrence and homeland security pre-emption. Even if it comes from a RAND Director (Treverton 2009), the juxtaposition between a cold war paradigm and a counterterrorism one, is simplistic. The soviet Enemy was never confined into specific national-territorial space(s), its intelligence mechanism was hardly more coordinated than that of the US in the Kennedy era, its covert operations no more predictable that the Bay of Pigs. And the notion that the domestic field and the enemy within were of no interest to US intelligence is an insult to the memory of J. Edgar Hoover and Senator McCarthy. Their juxtaposition serves to construe the Enemy as the mirror image of the US state: transnational, and directed by governance networks rather than statist hierarchical command. As Carl Schmitt cryptically wrote, 'the Enemy defines me' (Schmitt 2007: 85n), albeit it is always 'me' that perceives (and construes) the Enemy. This 'existential' line of inquiry would have the US fighting a mirror image of itself in the war on terrorism. What makes it somewhat interesting is that the construction of the Enemy lags behind the present configuration of the 'self', and contributes to its altering. The war is waged against transnational governance networks at the very moment that the US state-form becomes more national and more state-like – the centralisation of intelligence is further evidence to that. Thus, continuing with the pseudo-existential metaphor, in the war on terrorism the US is fighting against its former 'self'; and it is through this fight that its 'self' is changing.

10 The political significance of intelligence: government by experts[1]

Informed by the discussion of intelligence, its apparatus and its scope, this chapter examines what this intelligence does – its overall function as a political technology. It examines intelligence as a mode of government, as a justification of state authority and as a basis for state-population relations. Drawing from modern and ancient political philosophy, it argues that the advent of intelligence signifies an oligarchic, anti-democratic political relation.

This assessment is based on a discussion of the Homeland Security Advisory System (HSAS or the System). A homeland security icon, the now defunct colour-coded threat warning system, offers a rare glimpse in the workings of intelligence. This glimpse is, necessarily, partial and incomplete – after all, we are dealing with state secrets. Yet, it remains comprehensive, in the sense that it offers an overview of intelligence in all its stages – collection, analysis and implementation. Importantly, given that it was designed for popular consumption, the System also informs on how the population (is meant to) react to intelligence and, therefore, on the ways in which intelligence defines its relation to the state.

The intelligence oracle in action

The Homeland Security Advisory System

The HSAS would condense at any given moment all available knowledge on the terrorist threat in a colour-coded chart, with every colour representing a level of threat-intensity and corresponding to a set of measures. Widely advertised and accessible, it was a loud visualisation of an invisible threat.

The System was introduced on 11 March 2002 by a Presidential Directive. A year later, it was taken over by the DHS. It was administered by the IAIP Undersecretary, and the Secretary was ultimately responsible for changing the threat level. The measures it prescribed were mandatory for the federal government and recommended for sub-national governments, the private sector, and the public (CRS 2005d; US House of Representatives 2004b: 6, 40, 100).

---

1 This chapter is an amended version of my article, 'Government by Experts: Counterterrorism Intelligence and Democratic Retreat'. *Critical Studies on Terrorism* 5 (2): 277–296, 2012.

There were five levels of threat-intensity. In the *Low/Green* condition, federal agencies should be undertaking personnel training, and systematise and finetune their security and response plans and equipment. To this, the *Guarded/Blue* condition added prescriptions regarding checks of the emergency agencies' communications network.

In the *Elevated/Yellow* condition, declared when the country was under 'significant risk' of an attack, federal agencies should increase the surveillance of possible target points, coordinate emergency plans with neighbourhood jurisdictions, and adjust them to the precise characteristics of the threat. This is the lowest level HSAS ever reached. In its context, increased, targeted, police surveillance and patrolling became permanent.

In a *High/Orange* condition, federal agencies were additionally required to: (a) coordinate security efforts with state/local law enforcement, the National Guard and other Armed Forces organisations; (b) increase security at public events, and consider moving or cancelling them; and (c) restrict access to facilities under threat to essential personnel only. Thus, at this level the federal government subjected the resources of sub-national governments to its command; activated the military in US territory; and claimed authority to move or cancel congregations.

The *Severe/Red* condition entailed full mobilisation of resources and coordination of activities to meet critical emergency needs. It also prescribed constant monitoring, redirection, or constraining of transportation systems, and the closing down of public and government facilities (US Department of Homeland Security Unknown Date IV). 'Red' represented the maximum force that the coercive apparatus would exercise upon the overall population, culminating in full quarantine, where all movement is suspended, and public space monopolised by the security forces.

Telling as they are regarding police modalities, these prescriptions remain an exercise on paper. I now turn to situations actually occurring under Orange alert.

Orange alert – the System in action

During the System's lifetime, the threat level moved from Yellow to Orange five times nationwide (10–24 September 2002; 7–27 February 2003; 17 March–16 April 2003; 20–30 May 2003; 21 December 2003–9 January 2004), once for specified locations in the North-East (1 August–10 November 2004), once for mass-transit systems (7 July–12 August 2005), and once for airplane flights (10 August 2006–31 April 2011). The threat level only rose to red once, between 10 and 13 August 2006, in relation to incoming UK flights.

The efforts of agencies in all government levels during Orange alerts produced an extraordinary variety of security measures: schools rearranged their security plans, underwent drills and cancelled field trips; business persons cancelled conferences; the military patrolled air space; protest marches were banned; flights from Europe were cancelled and draconian security measures upon foreign airlines were imposed; local law enforcement increased their patrolling and security checks and prepared for bio-chemical incidents; surveillance and security measures around landmark sites were heightened, security in tiny villages was reinforced, the National Guard and other military units were mobilised (CRS 2005d; DiGrazia 2003; Herszenhorn 2003; Leigh Brown 2003; Lichtblau 2003; 2004; Shenon 2003a; US House of Representatives 2004b: 20). Orange alerts dominated the media, provided an opportunity to air new ideas about public spending in homeland security, and helped in the testing of controversial security measures (Shenon 2003b). During Orange alerts, share values nose-dived, and presidential approval ratings soared (Schneier 2006: 236; Willer 2004). DHS officials and security experts stressed that the decision to raise the threat level had significant economic, physical and psychological impacts. The exact cost of an Orange alert remains unknown, as costs to sub-national governments have not been estimated. It was estimated to at US$1 billion per week for the federal government, and a similar total expenditure by sub-national ones. This was only the direct cost, discounting, for example, effects on tourism or the aviation industry (US House of Representatives 2004b: 3, 61; 2004c: 6, 95; CRS 2005d).

The last nationwide alert (21 December 2003–9 January 2004), billed as the 'greatest danger since 9/11', coincided with the Christmas holidays. While 'tight security controls' were a country-wide reality, in New York citizens went 'about their business' while police were searching packages and cars for explosives. During the New Year's eve celebration in Times Square, 'helicopters swept the sky' and clusters of police officers stood guard on street corners (Lee 2004; Tavernise 2004; Walkin 2003). The pronounced presence of the armed forces during a period of swarming social activity can be seen as an exercise in military occupation of a metropolis, in an era when urban operations are a strategic priority for the Pentagon (Packer 2006; Press 1999; Warren 2004).

An Orange alert had multiple, significant effects on social activity. Therefore, the question of how the decision to change the alert level was reached becomes pressing.

The decision-taking process and 'pattern revelation'

The DHS Secretary described the decision to raise the threat level as a 'difficult and complex' one; DHS and embedded experts are a little more forthcoming. Intelligence agencies (the FBI, the CIA, the DIA, the Drug Enforcement Agency and the TTIC) are perpetually gathering, analysing and reviewing information on potential terrorist activity. Their analyses are forwarded to the Homeland Security Information Centre, which reduces the hundreds of incoming reports to about ten significant ones per day. These are reviewed by the Homeland Security Council, which makes recommendations to the DHS Secretary, who accordingly decides whether to raise the alert level. Once the decision was made, the DHS communicated it to sub-national governments, the private sector and the public, using different channels for each. Constant reviewing of intelligence would determine whether identified threats remained active and, accordingly whether the threat level should be lowered (US Senate 2003a: 24; US House of Representatives 2004b: 10, 25, 40, 43–44; CRS 2005d: 2–4).

Thus, the decision-taking process resembles a spiral of information filtering, breaking at a decisive moment at the top, then spiralling downwards again. What spirals upwards is *knowledge*, while what spirals downwards is *command*.

The process is one of perpetual analysis. As we see in Chapter 9, the abundance of stored and incoming information makes the identification of meaningful elements therein extremely difficult. To solve the problem of identifying patterns in vast pools of transactional data, three different tactics have been developed. The first is to find matches in the data for known patterns of interest. The second, based on the idea that by identifying the things that do not fit the norm we can discover their true nature, is to find anomalies when data violates known patterns. The third is to discover new patterns, and can take two forms: (a) social network analysis, which analyses the types and frequencies of interactions among people to discern who are acting as groups in pursuit of common goals; and (b) data mining, which aims to discover new patterns among indicators of events of interest (SRI International 2004: 1–2). Analysis occurs in an elaborate automated framework, combining things like a 'synthesiser' which helps identify possible patterns, an 'analyser' which picks up and juxtaposes relevant information, and a 'decision tool' which interacts with decision makers and helps them to determine the steps to be taken. It is effectuated by 'complicated algorithms', while 'automated relationship agents' look for relations between new and existing 'dots' (RAND 2004: 12–14).

The first approach – finding matches for known patterns – is exemplified in a SRI International operational system called Link Analysis Workbench (LAW). LAW helps analysts to define and match patterns in relational data. It is able to assess matches to patterns by handling data of more than 10 million relations. While some of the known patterns may have been defined by data mining, the majority will have been constructed directly by experts on the field of interest (SRI International 2004: 2, 11, 38–39).

The second approach – finding patterns where the pattern is violated – is exemplified in RAND's Atypical Signal Analysis and Processing (ASAP). ASAP is based on an alternative schema of 'connecting the dots', where the analyst first determines the norm, and then scans for signals which significantly deviate from the norm. ASAP draws information from governmental and private sector databases into a structured pool. Therein, a set of algorithmic agents evaluate dozens of vast data-fields simultaneously looking for out-of-the-ordinary signals, while 'automated relationship agents' identify relations between new and existing 'dots'. Once the dots are linked, 'hypothesis agents' produce and test possible interpretations. The results are prioritised, and high priority ones are forwarded to the analysts, who decide whether to take further action. Unlike 'pattern matching', this approach does not weed out signals which do not fit the pattern but, by searching for irregular behaviour, allows the detection of previously uncharted patterns (RAND Unknown Date: 16–25).

The third approach – data mining – involves the use of data analysis tools to discover previously unknown patterns and relationships in large data sets. Such analytical tools include statistical models, mathematical algorithms and machine-learning methods – i.e. algorithms which improve their performance automatically through 'experience'. Data mining applications use various parameters to examine data: association (one event is connected to another), sequence or path analysis (one event leads to another), classification (identification of new patterns), and forecasting (prediction of future activity based on pattern discovery). Compared to other data analysis applications (structured queries, statistical analysis), data mining represents a difference in kind rather than degree, due to its blanket nature. While other methods seek to verify of falsify certain hypotheses, data mining utilises a discovery approach in which algorithms are used to examine several multidimensional data relationships simultaneously (CRS 2004f: 2–4).

Some observations are pertinent here. First, the initial problem was one of intelligence overload. While numerous complex, automated solutions are suggested, the most obvious one – reducing the amount of data – remains inconceivable, indicating that the state is in a total surveillance orbit. Indeed, relational databases are growing rapidly, and elaborated machinery is set to unearth the modalities and affections of social life ('patterns'). Large scale data mining combined with pattern revelation is the main focus in developing intelligence technologies (Treverton 2009: 163).

Second, by its nature, algorithmic analysis is open-ended and speculative, designed to complement extended surveillance that would, potentially, envelop the totality of the population in the totality of its activities (Chapter 9).

Third, analysis consists in treating said transactions as suspicious: they may be meaning something other that they seem to, and may form assemblages ('patterns') and realise their unwanted potential. These approaches are based on the belief that, in the accumulated 'vast sea of data', there is indeed a pattern waiting to become apparent once we develop the means to reveal it. This simple Platonism is the founding principle of an effort to order society: 'patterns' are nets of order into the anarchic ocean of social interaction. Discovering order and controlling the ordered society are parts of a single process.

Finally, the analysis machinery designates politics as a techno-scientific procedure, and reinforces the representation of the state as a depository of rationality. The decision to change the HSAS level, which affected daily life in so many ways, was reached through automated, scientific processes. It was an issue of technical know-how.

The politics of insulated intelligence

Once the decision to alter the threat level was made, it was communicated separately to sub-national governments, private businesses and the public. There have been nine public statements on nationwide or regional alerts: four communicating decisions to heighten the threat level to Orange and five for lowering it again to Yellow.[2] Another couplet was issued to inform on the raising and lowering of the level between Orange and Red in relation to incoming UK flights.

2 There has been no public statement on raising the level on 21 December 2004 (US House of Representatives 2004c: 46).

The latter two statements admit that changing the alert level was not based on intelligence, and that the US was simply mirroring developments in the UK. On the contrary, all statements regulating Orange-Yellow traffic claim that the decision to raise the threat level was based on: 'specific intelligence received and analysed by the full intelligence community [...] corroborated by multiple intelligence sources' (US Department of Homeland Security 2003a). Still, what this undeniable authority states is rather vague: Al Qaeda (US Office of Homeland Security 2002b); groups sympathetic to it; other anti-American terrorist groups; regional extremist organisations; ad hoc groups; or 'disgruntled individuals' unconnected to terrorist organisations (US Department of Homeland Security 2003c; 2003e) may proceed to attack US people or interests, at home or abroad, possibly aiming at soft targets. The method of the attack may involve: assault teams equipped with small arms; vehicle-born explosive devises; suicide bombers; radiological, biological or nuclear devices; or weapons of mass destruction. False alarms are justified, since 'intelligence knows' that alertness causes terrorists to alter or abandon their plans (US Department of Homeland Security 2002a; 2003b; 2003d; 2003f; 2004a; US Senate 2003a: Ashcroft).

Astonishingly, all that specific, corroborated, algorithmically generated, self-learning, perpetually reviewed intelligence, could only inform that *someone* might carry out attacks *somewhere*, using *something dangerous*. Given the impact of changing the threat level, these statements can be seen as attempts to condition the population in a political reality where crucial decisions are taken through incomprehensible procedures, and must be obeyed due to the superior knowledge possessed by the decision-makers.

Interestingly, the only specific information communicated by the statements concerns *time-frames*. Most statements mention the coming (or passing) of particular dates as co-determining the change of the threat level. The first alert covers the period of the 9/11 anniversary (US Department of Homeland Security 2002a); the second covers the 'Hajj, a Muslim religious period ending in mid-February' (US Department of Homeland Security 2003a); the fourth brackets the Iraq invasion (US Department of Homeland Security 2003c; 2003d); the fifth covers the Memorial Day weekend (US Department of Homeland Security 2003e; 2003f); and the sixth coincides with the Christmas season (US Department of Homeland Security 2004a). This indicates that something more mundane than the interrogation of social data by automata may have helped inform the decision.

Focusing on dates, we note that four out of six alerts coincide with major political events. The first alert coincided with UN discussions about launching the war on Iraq. The second covered the days of the global wave of anti-war protests, and led to the prohibition of the US flagship march in New York. The third bracketed the Iraq invasion, and included the dates for which the banned US marches were rescheduled. And the sixth (North-Eastern) alert was issued at the moment John Kerry was nominated presidential candidate by the Democrats' convection, stole his thunder, and dragged on to shield the 30 August 2004 Republican Convection from protests. Actively manipulated or not, it is clear that intelligence can be a powerful political weapon (US House of Representatives 2004b: Shays testimony; Shapiro and Cohen 2007).

Along these lines, the 17 March 2003 statement is astonishing. There, the basis of the decision to change the threat level was the belief of the intelligence community that 'terrorists' (ranging from Al Qaeda to random individuals), would attempt multiple attacks against US targets, 'claiming they defend Muslims or the "Iraqi people", rather than Saddam Hussein's regime' (US Department of Homeland Security 2003c). Thus, the corroborated intelligence which hitherto could not tell north from south, is suddenly extremely knowledgeable, eloquent, and specific about the *motivation* and *justification* of the threat. As this statement was issued on the eve of mass protests against the war; as the protestors' rationale was 'to defend the Iraqi people' and not, of course, 'Hussein's regime'; and as it clearly states that the 'terrorists' are not necessarily Al Qaeda, but even random individuals, this statement shows the potential of invoking intelligence to stigmatise and criminalise social opposition.

Indeed, politicians and security experts point out that the decision-taking process is far from dehumanised or depoliticised. First, critics and proponents agree that the overall object of security is the protection of the existing social order (e.g. Boukalas 2008; Caudle 2009; Neocleous 2011: 42). Second, security measures are the outcome of negotiations among social groups with vested interests. Third, maximising the surveillance and analysis capabilities is not a natural course of things, but a strategic decision. It is questionable regarding its effectiveness, but fully aligned to a trajectory of biopolitical control. Fourth, the quality of input material on which analysis depends; the supposition of what constitutes normal situations; the development of analytical models on its basis, etc, are outcomes of contingent processes in which political considerations and economic calculations are important factors (Schneier 2006: 33–35; US House of Representatives 2004b: 48–49; 2004c). Fifth, as the analysis of complex, uncertain situations necessarily contains a degree of indeterminacy, the political 'customers' tend to 'cherry-pick' from the intelligence estimates, 'naturally opting for the interpretation that is most congenial given their current agenda, bias, or policy favourite' (Treverton 2009: 153). Lastly, given that there are no criteria regarding the threshold of intelligence required to shift the alert level, the decision is 'subjective' and 'arbitrary', frequently triggered by political estimates and calculations (Shapiro and Cohen 2007: 128, 132; US House of Representatives 2004b: 14, 23, 39–41).

The System vs the public

The key addressee of HSAS was the general public. This is evident in its prominent coding in natural primary and secondary colours, as colours are unmediated communicators of emotion (van Leeuwen 2011). This mode of communication would be superfluous if the main addressee were governmental agencies or large private corporations, which were anyway contacted through other channels.

The main purpose of the System was to provide an 'inescapable reminder that

Table 10.1 Prescriptions to individuals and families

Condition	Prescriptions
Green- Low Risk	a. Develop a family emergency plan. Share it with family and friends, and practice the plan. b. Visit www.Ready.gov for help creating a plan. c. Create an 'Emergency Supply Kit' for your household. d. Be informed. Visit www.Ready.gov or obtain a copy of 'Preparing Makes Sense, Get Ready Now' by calling 1-800-BE-READY. e. Know how to shelter-in-place and how to turn off utilities (power, gas, and water) to your home. f. Examine volunteer opportunities in your community, such as Citizen Corps, Volunteers in Police Service, Neighborhood Watch or others, and donate your time. g. Consider completing an American Red Cross first aid or CPR course, or Community Emergency Response Team (CERT) course.
Blue- Guarded Risk	a. Complete recommended steps at level green. b. Review stored disaster supplies and replace items that are outdated. c. Be alert to suspicious activity and report it to proper authorities.
Yellow- Elevated Risk	a. Complete recommended steps at levels green and blue. b. Ensure disaster supply kit is stocked and ready. c. Check telephone numbers in family emergency plan and update as necessary. d. Develop alternate routes to/from work or school and practice them. e. Continue to be alert for suspicious activity and report it to authorities.
Orange- High Risk	a. Complete recommended steps at lower levels. b. Exercise caution when travelling, pay attention to travel advisories. c. Review your family emergency plan and make sure all family members know what to do. d. Be Patient. Expect some delays, baggage searches and restrictions at public buildings. e. Check on neighbours or others that might need assistance in an emergency.
Red- Severe Risk	a. Complete all recommended actions at lower levels. b. Listen to local emergency management officials. c. Stay tuned to TV or radio for current information/instructions. d. Be prepared to shelter-in-place or evacuate, as instructed. e. Expect traffic delays and restrictions. f. Provide volunteer services only as requested. g. Contact your school/business to determine the status of the work day.

Source: DHS, http://www.dhs.gov/xlibrary/assets/citizen-guidance-hsas2.pdf; last accessed, 30 March 2010.

the Nation is engaged in a global war on terror' (US House of Representatives 2004b: Cox). The permanent state of agitation codified in the Yellow condition is considered the 'new normalcy' (US House of Representatives 2004b: 21, Brennan). Concerns were expressed that HSAS may impose a condition of fear, especially when the population was not given instructions on how to act in an alert. To rectify this, the DHS requested the Red Cross to develop a set of measures the public should adopt at each threat level. The prescriptions (Table 10.1) enjoyed wide circulation, through the Ready.gov website, a telephone hotline and nationwide distributed brochures (US House of Representatives 2004c: 12).

The imposition of a domesticated and personalised regime of safety with emphasis on self-protection constitutes a governmental technology, one that offloads the responsibility for surviving onto the victim (Andrejevic 2006; Hay 2006). Still, this atomisation renders the individual entirely dependent on the state. Most of her interactions are either referring directly to the security apparatus or materialising through state projects. The prescriptions juxtapose an impotent individual to an impending lethal threat, and the state defines and mediates this relation. Individuals can but conform to a reality they cannot influence (Monahan 2010: 93). The only way to act is by becoming an accessory to the state mechanism. Vigilance was promoted through public statements urging the public to observe and report, highlighted as a key aim ('every citizen is a sensor'), and remains the focal point of the alert system which succeeded HSAS (US House of Representatives 2004b: 21; US Department of Homeland Security 2011a).

Nevertheless, the HSAS was 'very problematic' with the public. The Red Cross was disheartened to find that '60% of Americans are wholly unprepared for a disaster', terrorism-specific preparedness was even lower (substantially), and politicians and analysts were concerned that its failure to connect with the population would render HSAS irrelevant (Kano et al. 2011; Shapiro and Cohen 2007; US House of Representatives 2004c: 74, 104). This could be a reaction (conscious or not) of those dispossessed of influence to subscribe to a traumatic life-perception of total impotence and dependence. One problem the System had in relating to the public was a difficulty in making the 'imminent threat' doctrine biomatic, i.e to instill it as part of the daily lived experience. The other was that the quality of information in public statements alienated the public. Even when the decision to change the threat level was not based on 'vague, limited, or simply unavailable' information, the government determined that its disclosure would be 'foolhardy', since the terrorists may exploit it. Hence, 'the general public may have been the beneficiary of the actions of the official government without generally knowing if there was a great threat to them' (US House of Representatives 2004c: 61; US Office of Director of National Intelligence 2011: 59). Indeed, the only thing which a population deprived of collective resources (including knowledge) can do is to stand in the way of the security mechanism which strives to rescue them.

Government by experts vs democracy

The overarching effect of HSAS is the imposition of a mode of government based on expertise. Political decision making, and the legitimacy of authority, are premised on the superior knowledge of those in command. This type of government, focused on effectiveness, is in constant tension with democratic aspirations for freedom and equality. Ancient political thought had identified it as incompatible with democracy, and pertinent to oligarchic (or aristocratic) rule.

Despotism and democracy

Most societies, for most of history, have been organised politically into some form of despotism. In abstract, despotism is a mode of political organisation characterised by a dichotomy between the political system and society. All effective power to organise, direct and administer society is monopolised by the political system, which in turn is privately appropriated by an incarnate owner. The relationship between the political system and society is *force*: the despot can only rule inasmuch as he can impose his will onto the population (and, reversely, he can only be purged by removing his physical body). This relation is based on the belief that society is ordered according to a divine master plan – the despot is a divinity, or represents one. Despotism is therefore an order of *heteronomy*, for the organisational principles of society derive from beyond it. On this basis, social organisation becomes an issue of knowledge, interpretation and implementation of the divine plan (Castoriadis 1983b: 281–282; Contogeorgis 2007: 41–43; see also Oakley 2006).

Antipodal to despotism is democracy. Democracy signifies the absorption of politics into society, thus cancelling its separation from the political system. The social body is constituted and organised as the dominant political institution (*demos*), and assumes full political competence. With political functions assumed by a society organised into a continuous political institution, society as such determines – and can question – its institution *in toto*. The constitutive principles of democracy are social and personal *freedom* and political *equality*. Freedom refers to the effective (as opposed to merely formal) capacity of the individual to co-determine the norms of collective life (the law) and the directions of collective efforts (the modalities and objectives of social power); and equality refers to the effectively equal sharing of this capacity among all citizens (Castoriadis 1983b: 275, 281–282; 1988b: 158–162, 168–169; 1990; Colombo 2011; Contogeorgis 2007: 21–38; Saña 1991; see also Aristotle 1962: VI-2). The core of democratic political culture is the acknowledgment that all social norms and institutions are the work of society itself. This premise rejects the possibility that an extra-social source might be responsible for social norms, practices and institutions: society is autonomous (Castoriadis 1983b).

Modernity: autonomy, capitalism and the state

Modern political systems represent a departure from despotism, but do not constitute democracies. Politics ceases to be the personal affair of a despot, but remains institutionally separated from society. It is the terrain of competence of the state as a legal entity. Society is contractually linked to the state, providing it with personnel and legitimacy. The relationship between the political system and society is *power*. While force remains operative at a final analysis, the compulsion of the political system upon society is limited, set in advance, and depends on consent. Accordingly, the political culture of power is characterised by its constitution in/through law and the existence of legal rights which describe the relationship between the political system and society (Contogeorgis 2007: 41–43).

Society is not instituted as a political entity, thus politics is not undertaken by society as such, but has to be mediated by the state. Suffrage, recognised as the mark of a democratic political system, is a practice which legitimises the separation between the social and the political, and authorises the appropriation of politics by state officials. Society cannot recall its representatives, or control their actions. Controlling functions are instead incorporated in the state through the separation of powers. In modern political organisation there is complete lack of political organs under the control of the *demos*. While the state would formally be such a mechanism, representation – the delegation of authority to individuals permitted to act to their own discretion, without effective popular control – cancels this possibility (Bertolo 1999; Castoriadis 1983b; 2008; Levine 1993; Rousseau 1994: II-1, III-1-5, 12, 15). While the creation of socio-political associations and organisations 'outside' the formal state is tolerated or encouraged to varying degrees, the population is unable to take *collectively binding decisions* in matters of social organisation and direction. This capacity is monopolised by the state, and civil-society organisations pressure the latter to give their views and interests binding character. The lack of political organs not only means that the *demos* cannot implement its will, but that it does not exist at all. The *demos* is constituted as a subject inasmuch as it materialises in a set of political organs; in their absence the notion of a *demos* is meaningless.

Modern political organisation incorporates democratic and despotic elements. Its socio-political significations comprise a dynamic tension between the principle of autonomy and that of capitalist rationality. The former consists of the aspiration of social and personal self-determination. It is forged through the questioning of existing social orders, it dispenses of divine projects, and institutes humanity as the sole creator of its history. It is developed through myriad social movements and struggles. The principle of capitalist rationality consists of the quest for unlimited dominance over people and nature. It tends to reduce social values and relations into quantified input-output calculi geared towards unlimited growth; and to reinstate alien, extra-social rule in the form of objective laws – of nature, history, the economy, etc – which allegedly determine social organisation (Castoriadis 1990a: 37–39; 1990b).

The tension between autonomy and capitalist mastery is incorporated in the institution of the modern state, in the shape of its two main legitimacy frameworks: general will and techno-rationality. While largely antithetical, they are not incompatible, and co-inhabit the modern state. The state claims to constitute the unity of a fragmented civil society, ripped with conflicting interests, and it is therefore the only entity knowledgeable of the general will (or interest), hence it can provide its only legitimate definition (Bratsis 2007: 39–48; Contogeorgis 2007: 73–75; Poulantzas 1973: 125–141; 1976b: 314; 1978: 63–75). Its monopoly of knowledge over public affairs constitutes the state as society's depository of expertise over things social. This construes a techno-rational legitimacy platform, based on the state's capacity to deliver what is socially necessary (Castoriadis 1957: 92; 1980: 242; 1987: 221; Contogeorgis 2007: 645–652; Foucault 2008: 43; Poulantzas 1965: 110; 1978: 54–58).

Despite their interrelation, the two frameworks are analytically distinct, prevail at different degrees in different conjunctures, and their coexistence can entail tensions. The general will framework can provide the rallying point for popular-democratic action which would be difficult for the state to ignore or fully suppress without imperilling its legitimacy. The techno-rationality framework is unequivocally oligarchic: by constituting politics as a field of expertise, it negates the capacity of the population to practise it.

While in the political thought of early and high modernity (e.g. Machiavelli, Montesquieu, Rousseau, the Anarchists, and Marx) the two principles are present in dynamic tension, since the early twentieth century, institutional practice and political theory is increasingly tilting towards the techno-rationality framework. Modern political institutions are bent on devising limitations to popular sovereignty and will (Schmidt 2000: 51). Underlying this tendency is the separation of political activity from the question of social organisation. The latter is settled once and for all on the basis of private property and market-mediated relations. The political system becomes a mere servant of capitalism: its strategic planner and manager of its contradictions, side effects and crises. This arrangement entails the rise of technocracy as the main logic of politics, and of effectiveness as the main legitimacy for state power. While liberal democracy has already circumscribed the possibility of democratic organisation, the advance of technocracy constitutes a mutation of liberal democracy. It designates the decline of representative-parliamentary institutions; tips the balance of institutional power to the Executive and to informal networks parallel to the state; and introduces a disjunction between the public political scene and the real centres of power.

Government by the many vs government by experts

Technocracy implies that the state possesses expert knowledge of political affairs. This postulates that such expertise is possible. Contemporary political culture treats both postulates as natural facts. Ancient political significations were different, and merit mention as they challenge the foundations of technocratic rule.

In his monumental refute of democracy, Plato broke with the dominant political significations of his time, and claimed the possibility of political expertise. He postulated the existence of a true nature of all things – including of the Good – and an unequal, restricted, capacity among people to access knowledge thereof. The ideal polity would be one constituted and ruled by those capable of such knowledge (royal men or philosopher-kings) (*Republic*; *Statesman*). This *episteme* (scientific knowledge) of social affairs combines expertise in all sciences, crafts and arts which affect communal life, and transgresses levels of abstraction, from the absolute-universal (knowledge of the Good) to the absolutely specific (every action of every citizen) (Castoriadis 2002: 153–157).

Still, Plato accepted another common sense element of his society: the principle that the proper judge for expertise is not another expert, but the user of its products: the soldier (not a blacksmith) is the judge of the sword, the inhabitant (not an architect) the judge of a house, etc. This implies that the judge of political expertise is its user, the citizenry (Castoriadis 2008: 144–145, 192). The apparently inconsequential user-is-judge principle proves to be an essential prerequisite for a democratic politics, and a guarantee against the imposition of technocracy.

Plato's argument is premised on the ideal construction of the perfect polity on an extra-social plane which ought to serve as a model for actual polities and as the criterion on which they are judged. It introduces an abstraction that was hitherto foreign to Greek political thought. In Herodotus, Thucydides, the tragics, Isocrates, Democritus, Protagoras and Demosthenes, politics is always a pragmatic, contingent and antagonistic process, and political expertise is inconceivable (Castoriadis 2002: 112–114; Oikonomou 2003). Aristotle reconnects with this tradition. He rebuffs the notion of an ideal polity, and is instead preoccupied with the good fit between an actual *polis* and it polity (Aristotle 1962: IV-1; 1999: I). Moreover, politics is not an activity informed by *episteme*, but by *phronesis* (prudence). Based on experience and reasoning, *phronesis* is the capacity to deliberate and decide in specific conjunctures on things which can be acted upon by those who make the decisions (Artistotle 1999: VI). The rejection of political *episteme* stems from the nature of politics. Politics constitutes the higher synthesis of arts, crafts and sciences, and of forms of human association (Artistotle 1999: I; 1962: I). It is an activity of a different order, and the postulation of expertise therein constitutes the foundation of a power relation. Moreover, while 'science' designates expert knowledge of a particular field, politics is not a one-dimensional activity aiming towards a certain outcome, but one that refers to the universality of social existence (Castoriadis 1983b: 274–278; 1988a: 22–23; 2008: 142–143; Contogeorgis 2007: 660–665). In the absence of political *episteme*, Aristotle repeatedly admits that the many are likely to be, on aggregate, better suited for political decision-making than the excellent few (esp. Aristotle 1962: III-11).

In short, the claim to political expertise is incompatible with democratic politics. It is absurd given the universal character of politics as a process of instituting, organising, directing and administrating collective living. Rather than a matter of *episteme*, politics belongs to the realm of *doxa* (opinion). This acknowledgment is a necessary condition for democratic political organisation (Castoriadis 1990b: 127; Oikonomou 2003).

On this basis, the tension between autonomy and capitalist rationality which shapes modernity is recast as democracy vs government by experts. The increased political role of intelligence highlighted by the study of HSAS affects the balance between democratic and oligarchic tendencies in contemporary US political organisation. Its mode for doing so is acutely biopolitical.

A biopolitical system

In the late 1970s, Michel Foucault developed a seminal overview of liberal-capitalist power as one focused not on territory and the upholding of legal order therein, but on the condition of the population, on biological 'species life'. He termed this political modality 'biopolitics', and the associated organisation of power 'bio-power'. The System provides a staggering symptomatology of bio-power, especially if we consider 'species life' not as a given set of conditions of self-contained organisms, but as a relational process of formation, where the constitution of living beings is co-determined by that of others and their environment, and consists of transactions which set up each being. In this sense, biopolitics could refer to a governmentality concerned primarily with social relations, transactions and dynamics, rather than the enclosed, independent materiality of organisms. This interpretation may not be totally arbitrary. From the start, Foucault relates bio-power to the governing of populations through knowledge of, and intervention in, the aggregate phenomena their interactions produce. Exchange and circulation (of people, products, money, diseases) is the field where bio-power intervenes attempting to selectively facilitate or hinder certain potentials inherent in it (Foucault 2007: 18, 20–21, 319–326, 335–339, 351–354). Similarly, contemporary analysts, in emphasising the molecularisation and informationalisation of life, and setting code as its nucleus (Dillon and Reid 2001: 50, 53–56; 2009: 21, 59, 62) seem to conceptualise 'species life' as essentially transactional. Bio-power's key concern is the pluripotency of life and the selective facilitating/hindering of certain potentialities' actualisation. Its operational field is contingency, the determination of pluripotency's outcomes (Dillon and Lobo-Guerrero 2008: 288; Dillon and Reid 2001: 55; 2009: 31–33, 61). To deal with contingency, bio-power extends its remit beyond the observation of adherence to law and the *legal/illegal* dichotomy. It encompasses behaviours like industry, charity, civility, decency, safety, etc, to construe (and police) a *normal/abnormal* dichotomy. It is thus associated with the surveillance and analysis of behavioural patterns (Dillon and Lobo-Guerrero 2008: 267; Dillon and Reid 2009: 17; Foucault 2007: 319–323; see also Poulantzas 1980: 410).

The System is a case of biopolitics made-to-order. The confessed objective of the HSAS (and of all counterterrorism) is to 'save lives'. This opens up the problematic of certain lives being more worth-saving than others, of lives needing to be forcefully taken to the same end, of lives worth sacrificing, of 'collateral' lives that do not matter, etc – a calculus of life according to its social properties and potentialities. The mode of HSAS intervention consists in preventing certain of life's potentials from actualising – or to contingently prepare for such actualisation. Moreover, the HSAS, with its self-learning and deciding mechanisms, comprises an informational compound of organic and inorganic life. Its function is mass-surveillance of behaviour, its digestion into knowledge, and its arrangement into patterns. It de-codes and re-codes actualities and potentials. While it attempts to single out the odd pattern, it does so through mass surveillance aimed to effect (or prevent effects on) the general patterns of social life: while bio-power closes onto the singular-exceptional, it is concerned with the general-overall. Finally, the authority of its prescriptions lies in its claim to know the life it protects and the life-patterns which threaten it.

More broadly, security regimes are integral to broader configurations of power. Bio-security analysts insist that security paradigms are correlated to corresponding ways of rule; and that discourses of fear and danger are means through which programmes for social organisation are introduced, enacted, circulated and reproduced (Dillon and Reid 2001: 51; 2009: 17).

Finally, biopolitics is a form of government by experts. This is obvious in Foucault's exposition of liberal governmentality. It is founded on the separation between political power and its referent object, which lies outside it, in the economy. The latter is postulated as governed by its own objective laws. Government consists in guaranteeing the self-government of the economy by intervening only in order to prevent distortions and side-effects threatening the stability of the social formation. The legitimacy of authority lies in its success in doing so. To guarantee success, the state needs the fullest possible knowledge of society and of the effects of its actions therein. It pumps society for information, and hence claims expertise on all social things. The state claims to act on the basis of expertise, and its actions are judged not upon programmatic socio-political principles, but on their economic effectiveness (Foucault 2007: 349–350; 2008: 16, 30–32, 61–62, 246–247, 282–283). Thus, biopolitics is a form of government by experts. It postulates an extra-social source of social institution, authorises government on the basis of expertise, and judges it on results. As the scope of governmental expertise envelopes the bulk of social activity and relations in their singular detail, we curiously end up with a platonic *episteme* of the universal.

Despite fitting the HSAS case perfectly, biopolitical theory poses limitations to its analysis. While asserting that success in the realm of the economy is the criterion for governmental success or failure, it says nothing about what the measures of success or failure are, who sets them, who does the judging, and how. Biopolitics disregards the question of the user of governmental produce. It has *no consideration of the social forces* exercising (bio)power, and the forces it is exercised upon. This also means that it cannot consider the sources of the pluripotency, whose management is the sole purpose of bio-power. The disregard of social forces and dynamics results in a highly structural, reified account of 'liberal rule' regardless of subjectivities and strategies. It mystifies power (Boukalas 2012: 290–291). Thus, despite the centrality of political economy in Foucault's original account, an his emphasis on capitalism, bio-security analyses typically ignore the role of security in establishing, promoting and maintaining regimes of accumulation and exploitation. Consequently, they tend to miss the character of security projects as state strategies with inbuilt disposition to the use of force in defence of the social order (Neocleous 2008: 4–5, 22–23, 110–111; 2011: 42).

While biopolitical analyses can provide rich descriptions of power modalities and logics, they tend to hollow-out society as an analytical field. Their societies are uninhabited. They are reduced to operative technologies of power – or to mere power-effects. Therefore there is no conceptual scope in biopolitical approaches for a power-*less* society, hence the question of democracy cannot be conceived. To this question I now return, keeping the biopolitical perspective's insights on the connection between the HSAS and liberal governmentality; and its extremely important connotation that intelligence-driven governance does *not* constitute an exceptional state, but a form of capitalist rule plain and proper.

Intelligence as political expertise: the eclipse of democratic perspective

The governmental logic of homeland security's is encapsulated here:

> But scaring people – getting them to see the risk is real – may be the very condition of minimising or avoiding the danger. One weekend in 2003, the Prime Minister, after receiving intelligence information, decided to surround Heathrow [airport] with troops. He was criticised of scaremongering. Yet his actions may have stopped an attack.
>
> (Giddens 2005)

Cultivating fear to gain legitimacy for arbitrary exercise of power on the basis of secret information, is the political synopsis of homeland security. A key precondition for uttering the above statement is that technocratic effectiveness is entrenched as the basis for the legitimacy of authority – an authority Hobbesian n character and dismissive of democratic considerations.

Strictly speaking, this is nothing new. For Castoriadis, the rationality of capitalist mastery over people and things is co-constitutive of modernity. Foucault describes liberalism as expertise-based governmentality. Weber was concerned that 'secret knowledge' would make state bureaucracy an uncontrollable force (Weber 1994: 126, 156–159, 163–164). Since the 1930s, techno-rationality constitutes a coherent legitimating principle in the context of the corporate state, a trend related to the decline of classic liberal democracy – and recorded with intensifying urgency by the Frankfurt diaspora (Horkheimer 1940; Pollock 1941; Marcuse 1941; 1968). In the late 1970s, Marxist state theory noted that techno-rationality was becoming the predominant legitimacy basis, a development associated with the emergence of AS (Poulantzas 1978: 218–219). And, since the 1980s there is ongoing duplication between the operative logic of state agencies and commercial enterprise along the lines of efficiency-oriented managerialism, a trend accelerated during the 1990s with the proliferation of governance regimes.

What the HSAS examination shows is an *internal reconfiguration* of the techno-rationality principle. It departs from notions of economic performance and distribution (welfare, consumerism, 'great society', productivity, competitiveness) and is re-articulated on a security platform. This shift is crucial for insulating political decisions from scrutiny, critique and debate. The political process is not only based on secret information, but secrecy is its existential condition: if intelligence is made public, that intelligence and all consequent decisions become useless. This necessary concealment makes deliberation impossible, and this is a matter of major social concern. If we also consider the total scope of intelligence, we see that the population is rendered completely transparent vis à vis the state, while the latter's operation is thoroughly, and *openly*, concealed from the population – a perfect reversal of the classic liberal-democratic model.

The re-articulation of the techno-effectiveness principle on security grounds also constitutes a confirmation and a hardening of AS. A confirmation inasmuch as, in the context of intensified state control over every sphere of social life combined with radical decline of the democratic institutions and civil liberties, state authority is legitimated on the basis of instrumental effectiveness instead of notions of the general will or interest (Poulantzas 1978: 203, 218–219). And hardening, inasmuch as 'state control' becomes dramatically more expansive, detailed and outright coercive; and also because its reconfiguration on security grounds further undermines democratic principles and practices.

While the representation of politics as a sphere of technical expertise is anti-democratic as such, its original articulation under the sign of *economic* effectiveness was shadowed by a paradox: in order to be effective, economic expertise had to proliferate. Therefore, large parts of the population could claim relevant expertise; and everyone had everyday experience of economic realities. On this basis, society could demand a say in politics – as the debate and protest surrounding current crisis-management shows. On the contrary, political expertise organised on the platform of *security* puts the knowledge informing the political process beyond the reach of the population and under the exclusive control of the state summits.

While the secret character of relevant knowledge cancels the possibility of popular input in decision-making, its scientific nature renders it immune from accountability. The population can only judge it on its results. Still, the experts can lease responsibility for failure to faulty algorithms or fraud intelligence.

The increased political importance of intelligence reconfigures the state-population relations. They are now primarily coercive in character; set on the principle that everyone is a suspect (of uncommitted crimes); and prone to pre-emptive targeting according to class, race, ethnicity, social environment, personality traits and, of course, political disposition (Mattelart 2010: 184, Monahan 2010: 97–101; Ratcliffe 2008: 49–50, 56–57, 172).

Finally, the HSAS study indicates an obliteration of the notion of the 'people' from the viewpoint of the state. While in the context of modern politics 'the people' is conceived as an empirical, abstract mass of individuals/citizens partaking political status via communion with the state, the HSAS study shows the public conceptualised as a nuisance, hindering state effectiveness. It would be better if the public were not there at all, allowing the state to perform effectively in social vacuum. Counterterrorism policy establishes a platform for legitimising the exclusion of the population even from legitimising functions. Based on knowledge available only to political 'experts', legitimation becomes an act of faith from the people to its leaders, and therefore to a form of government which operates behind closed doors and behind the people's back.

The reconfiguration of government by experts on security grounds reduces the population to a political non-entity. Even its minimum prerogative of judging governmental actions becomes conceptually, practically and formally impossible. This confirms the predominance, and hardening, of a form of legitimacy pertinent to AS. It also signifies a resolution of the tensions inherent in modern political organisation: a retreat of democratic tendencies, and the univocal establishment of oligarchic government by experts.

Nevertheless, the demise of the HSAS indicates there may be limits to the political marginalisation of the population. It points to an unexpected confirmation of the user-is-judge principle: even when precluded from any judging capacity, the users ultimately determine the viability of the product. It seems that the moment government by experts is perfected (insulating political decision from popular input), is also the moment when policy collapses. This poses a direct challenge to the representation of the state as the depository of social expertise; and, broader still, questions whether the state can be insulated from social dynamics and struggles, however passive or 'remote' these may be (Poulantzas 1976a). It also highlights the inherent weakness of state projects premised on the exclusion of the population (Jessop 2011: 52). The more successful, the more brittle they are.

In May 2011, the HSAS was replaced by the National Terrorism Advisory System. The new System has neither colour coding, nor prefabricated instructions. Instructions will be case-specific, and distributed to the public only in the event of 'elevated' or 'imminent' threats (US Department of Homeland Security 2011a). In other words, the new System still attempts to engage the population by excluding it. This shows that government by experts remains undisrupted. So are its (self-destructive?) contradictions.

11 Citizen corps: homeland security citizenship[1]

Thus far we have examined how homeland security takes shape as a political project in several key areas of political activity: political discourse (Chapter 4), law (Chapters 5, 6 and 7) and policing (Chapters 8, 9 and 10). We have seen that the development of homeland security in and across these areas implicates the relation between the state and the population and, consequently, the place of the population in politics. Invariably, the role outlined for the population is one of political passivity, and of unity with, and dependence on, the state. Actions and behaviours which deviate from this condition are met with suspicion and the promise of repression.

The following chapters examine state-population relations in practice – when homeland security meets the people. Chapter 12 examines popular resistance to homeland security through a study of the 'community resolutions' movement. Chapter 13 looks at political repression as a systematic police practice. Before that, the present chapter looks at how popular support to homeland security is organised. It examines Citizen Corps, the main platform for citizens' participation in homeland security, and discusses its implications for citizenship.

Structure and organisation

Citizen Corps is a nationwide umbrella organisation for volunteers in homeland security: emergency response, police, and medical assistance. It is federally initiated, and the DHS assumes its overall direction. It is operated by local boards and agencies, in an effort to organise grassroots volunteers. Hence, the first question regarding Citizen Corps is whether it is a grassroots movement which builds upwards, compelling subsequent levels of government to accommodate it, or a federal enlistment project administered by sub-national governments.

In his 2002 State of the Union address, President Bush announced the creation of Citizen Corps as a platform to enhance a post-9/11 culture of citizenship, service and responsibility. As 'Americans are responding to the evil and horror of the terrorist attacks of September 11 with a renewed commitment to doing good',

---

[1] This chapter is an amended version of my article, 'US Citizen Corps: Pastoral Citizenship and Authoritarian Statism'. *Situations* 4 (2): 117–140, 2012.

he called each citizen to dedicate at least two years in voluntary service – seen as an integral part of the 'National Culture'. He also set its organisational principle: 'Our local mayors, council members and county commissioners know best what risks their communities face. They also know how best to use the talents and the time of their citizens [...]' (US President 2002a; FEMA 2002: 2; US House of Representatives 2007: 38). So, the foundation and raw material of Citizen Corps is the willingness of citizens to volunteer, a willingness inherent in national culture and activated by the catastrophe; and the best manner to accommodate this popular urge is through local officials. Similarly, the DHS stresses that while Citizen Corps' 'mission' is the same everywhere, mobilisation will be community-specific, given each community's uniqueness. Thus, Citizen Corps looks like a federally conceived, locally managed, citizen-practiced project, with the local level being crucial.

The DHS recommends to local officials some general 'strategies for success': maintenance of 'broad community representation' in the local Citizen Corps Councils (CCCs); development of 'knowledge of the community' and its 'security needs'; the filing of volunteers according to their skills; and liability arrangements, so that authorities can wave responsibility for volunteers' accidents (FEMA 2009). Furthermore, Citizen Corps is organised on a 'self-sufficiency' basis, by incorporating pre-existing volunteer groups in the Corps organisation, and with limited reliance on federal funding (US Department of Homeland Security 2002b). The DHS has especially appointed staff who work with senators, governors, mayors and representatives to propagate the project. It has established channels for popular outreach in order to create a nation-wide, locally based 'movement' to raise public awareness, provide preparedness training, and foster volunteer opportunities (US House of Representatives 2003b: 34–35, 70).

At the local level, the managing unit is the CCC. According to DHS guidance, CCCs should consist of: (a) elected local leadership: mayor, council members, commissioners; (b) emergency management leadership: police, fire, medical; (c) community and faith leaders; (d) leadership from major industries and educational institutions; (e) minority representatives; (f) local media executives. The purpose of the CCC is to tailor the national mission to the particularities of the local community, and to develop a local strategy to promote participation (US Department of Homeland Security 2002b). The CCC's duties are to: match the needs of first responders with the skills of volunteers; teach citizens what to do in a crisis; promote Citizen Corps' activities in the community; and report innovative practices so that they can be replicated by other communities. The DHS also provides a list of 'ideas for discussion' for the initial meetings of CCCs, and ideas on what to activities to plan (FEMA 2002: 5–9, 12–14).

At state level, each Governor has appointed a Citizen Corps State Coordinator, accompanied by a Council. They are charged with identifying needs, developing marketing strategies and strategies for collaboration between volunteers and security personnel – all in collaboration with the federal level (FEMA 2002: 5–6, 19).

The project is federally overseen by the CCC, which is chaired by the Federal Emergency Management Agency (FEMA) Deputy Director and includes federal first responders' leadership, emergency management agencies, volunteer organisations, and private sector representatives. The National Council's role is to promote the project nationwide, oversee its progress, develop training standards and materials for Citizen Corps' activities, and organise mentoring and idea-sharing. The National Council is not a governing body, nor does it set a national policy: its purpose is to 'foster collaboration' (FEMA 2002: 19; US Department of Homeland Security 2002c; US House of Representatives 2007: 6).

Local CCCs are usually appointed by the County Executive, and comprise about 25 members. Of them, the majority is local officials: political and judicial personnel (which among them assume the CCC's leadership), security experts, and heads of police and fire agencies. The 'non-governmental' compartment consists of business and church representatives; and representatives of schools, universities, media, and 'minority communities' often complete the set (Citizen Corps/Harris Unknown Date; Citizen Corps Fairfax Unknown Date; Citizen Corps/New York City Unknown Date).

The most striking feature of the directing bodies is that, at every level, and both in prescriptions and reality, there is *no representation whatsoever* of the volunteers. This suffices to shred any illusion of the Citizen Corps as a 'grass-roots' undertaking. The question is whether the federal or local governments are predominant.

The DHS describes the Citizen Corps' structure as an inverted pyramid. Local councils are situated at the top and are in charge of the creation, organisation and management of local volunteer groups, according to community needs and capacities. An intermediate (state) level provides regional collaboration. And the National Council is the general point of reference and facilitator of the project. A more careful reading reveals that the hierarchical pyramid is not inverted at all, but stands firmly on its base. Local groups are 'autonomous' inasmuch as they are constructed in a certain manner, consist of certain agents, perform certain functions, and perform them in certain ways to meet certain ends. The CCCs are not in charge, but *charged with* implementing a federal project at local level. Their degree of autonomy consists in devising the most effective ways for local implementation. Similarly, agents, strategies, ends and functions are federally prescribed to the state-level. And the National Council, composed by heads of federal agencies and whomever else they chose (business interests certainly, but *no* sub-national entities: US Department of Homeland Security 2002c; US House of Representatives 2003b: 71–72) defines, directs and oversees the effort from the top. The National Council has no direct authority upon sub-national ones, but given that it determines the Citizen Corps' purpose, structure, the players involved and their respective roles, assuming direct command would be redundant. Organisationally, the Citizen Corps is a metagovernance project.

This diagnosis, apart from implying crooked lines of hierarchy which cannot be retraced as lines of accountability, does not explain much. Jessop (2002a: 240–243) describes metagovernance as a broad organisational strategy, a context permitting wide internal differentiation, and notes that 'metagovernance should not be confused with some superordinate level of government in control of all governance arrangements nor with the imposition of a single all-purpose mode of governance' (Jessop 2002a: 242). Yet, the Citizen Corps strategy and organisation derive directly from such a 'superordinate' level. Examination of the metagovernance fauna shows that CCCs of all levels belong to the 'quango' (quasi autonomous non-governmental organisation) family. Such entities are nominally non-governmental, but they are created by, and depend upon, government agencies (Holland and Fallon 1978: 7). Their personnel are appointed by governing politicians on the basis of their expertise or their subscription to governmental agendas, and their boards are often dominated by private sector interests (Sullivan and Skelcher 2002: 18, 60; Skelcher 1998). The quango structure is especially attractive because it depoliticises and 'managerialises' public sector activity, resulting in dismissal of transparency and accountability in governmental workings (Sullivan and Skelcher 2002: 18, 137–138). As quangos, the CCCs pertain to the more statist variety of metagovernance. Like most quangos, the Citizen Corps was introduced by Executive *fiat*, without congressional authorisation. It can thus evade congressional review and public service regulations – hence exempting volunteers from insurance claims. Control from local legislatures is also bypassed, permitting the public-private Councils a free hand with the volunteers' governance.

Finally, at a couple of dozen million dollars per year, the project is cheap. The Citizen Corps runs on gratis labour, and cost effectiveness is inbuilt in its rationale. The mobilisation of volunteers for a couple of days is said to save a locality in wages more than its annual Citizen Corps budget – a 'phenomenal return on investment' (US House of Representatives 2007: 11, 23, 38; see also US Budget/DHS: http://www.gpo.gov/fdsys).

By late 2009, all states and over two-thirds of counties had developed CCCs, serving almost 80 per cent of the country's population (even if not all of them were active) (US House of Representatives 2009: 21). While information about the number of CCCs is abundant, there is none about the number of volunteers, and FEMA officials admit having no idea about the volunteers' social and demographic composition (US House of Representatives 2008a: 40)

Programmes and rationale

The Citizen Corps comprises five programmes, administered by three different Departments (the DHS, the DOJ, and the Department of Health & Human Services):

1. The *Community Emergency Response Team* programme (CERT) trains volunteers to respond to emergency situations. In an emergency, CERT members would give critical support to first responders, assist victims and organise spontaneous volunteers on the spot. In non-emergency situations, they would help improve the safety and preparedness of their community. CERT volunteers receive relevant training by teams of first responders. There are, approximately, 3,300 CERT programmes nationwide. The CERT is administered by the FEMA.

2. The *Fire Corps* utilises volunteers to enhance the capabilities of an overstretched fire and rescue force. There are an estimated 700 programmes nationwide. It is implemented by the International Association of Fire Chiefs, the International Association of Fire Fighters, and the National Volunteer Fire Council.
3. The *Neighbourhood Watch* programme is in its fourth decade. In collaboration with local police, residents look out for, and report, suspicious activity in their neighbourhood. Post-9/11, its focus shifted to disaster preparedness and terrorism awareness. Neighbourhood Watch counts approximately 15,000 groups, and is administered by the National Sheriff's Association.
4. The *Volunteers in Police Service* (VIPS) programme comprises local police departments' efforts to utilise volunteers. These efforts accelerated since 9/11, as demands on local law enforcement increased dramatically, causing serious overstretching. There are approximately 1,600 programmes nationwide. The VIPS is implemented by the International Association of Chiefs of Police (IACP).
5. The *Medical Reserve Corps* (MRC) programme enlists professional medical personnel and untrained citizens who wish to perform supporting functions. It has around 650 programmes nationwide, and is administered by the Department of Health (FEMA 2002: 6–7, 15–16; US Department of Homeland Security 2002d; US House of Representatives 2007: 10, 22–23, 29; 2009: 21).

All programmes operate independently of an emergency. In fact, only two (the CERT and the MRC) have a defined role in an emergency. Neighbourhood Watch is a citizens' policing initiative; and the VIPS and the Fire Corps are accessories to severely understaffed police and fire services.

Presenting the ways in which the Citizen Corps 'benefit the community', the DHS stresses that volunteerism enhances caring for oneself and others in a time of crisis; promotes the concept that everyone has a role to play in making the community safer, stronger and better prepared; and gives residents a greater sense of security, responsibility and personal control. Hence, Citizen Corps help to build a community's 'sense of cohesion, pride and patriotism' (FEMA 2002: 8, 11; Waugh 2003: 384).

This showcases the Citizen Corps' ideological premises. Facing a common Enemy and an imminent threat, state and population mobilise in unison, albeit in a 'mission' defined and organised by the former. Furthermore, volunteering appears as a half-measure to give the individual some of the sense of security and control that was taken away by the fear and neurosis cultivated by the state. In this context, popular mobilisation is only acknowledged when it occurs in a canvassed framework and according to prescription, while 'communal spirit' is identified with patriotism. According to the DHS, the post-9/11 environment provides an opportunity 'to reinvigorate our national identity' on the basis of a 'culture of service, citizenship and responsibility'. The opportunity lies in grasping the 'innumerable acts of kindness taking place in our communities everyday' to make them part of this 'profound cultural change' (FEMA 2002: 20; US President

2002a). The Citizen Corps is perceived as a way to co-opt practices of solidarity into a project whose structure, objectives, methods and meanings are defined by the state.

The local level reproduces the federal approach. To motivate citizens, the LA County CCC presents Citizen Corps' benefits to the volunteer: 'you have the opportunity to support an organisation and a cause you believe in'; to 'learn new skills and broaden your range of experience'; to 'meet new people'; and to 'strengthen your employment resume' (Citizen Corps/Los Angeles Unknown Date). Thus, in the Citizen Corps the authorities provide a platform in which citizens can somehow pursue crucial aspects of personal and social life, in concord with the exigencies of workfare.

This occurs against the backdrop of increasing difficulties with socialisation. Since the 1980s, there is rapid decrease of popular participation in formal politics (voting, party membership) and civic organisations, and practices of informal socialisation are also in decline. All forms of 'going out' are reduced almost by half, and so has the exchange of visits and the activities undertaken in common with neighbours (Putnam 2000: 31–62, 105–115). This decline results largely from work-related anxiety, long work hours and dwindling income (Boggs 2001; Putnam 2000: 189–190). Nonetheless, all aforementioned declining forms of socialisation are conformist ones (Boggs 2001). This provides an important insight into the Citizen Corps: they attempt to counter the decline of platforms of socialisation which inculcate people in the social order. They do so by constructing a 'community' under the aegis of the state, aiming to galvanise support to the social order of homeland security among inclined parts of the population.

Following this discussion of the Citizen Corps 'in general', I now examine them more substantially, by overviewing two programmes: the CERT, which is the par excellence 'emergency preparedness' scheme, and the VIPS, which provides for the closest collaboration between citizens and the coercive state apparatus.

CERT: a workforce for homeland security

Structure and organisation

The FEMA provides step-by-step guidance to local CERT Coordinators, detailing techniques for securing and maintaining the involvement of various 'key shareholders': local government officials, big business, media, and fire, police and medical services (FEMA 2003: 52–57). It also presents techniques to communicate with volunteers (bulletins, websites, surveys, newsletters), explains the merits of each, and even provides stylistic guidance – the issue is important because 'volunteers are priceless assets' (FEMA 2003: 108–118). The FEMA presents the training curriculum, and instructs on how to choose the trainers (FEMA 2003: 50, 86–92). Apart from the thorough instruction of the local link by the federal agency, a conscription to marketing concepts and discourse is apparent. The CERT Coordinator is a local dealer, with a (federal) product to sell.

The Los Angeles City CERT website (maintained by volunteers and by far the most complete of its kind), provides a unique insight on the programme's (pre) history. It began in 1986, when the LA Fire Department (LAFD) trained selected Neighbourhood Watch 'leaders'. The first CERT teams were developed a year later, and in 1993 the FEMA expanded the programme nationwide. In January 2002, the CERT was incorporated to the Citizen Corps and rapidly grew: from 100 programmes in 2002, to 900 in January 2004, and to 3,300 by mid-2009 (US Department of Homeland Security 2004c; US House of Representatives 2009: 21). Yet, CERT history somehow starts in 1985, with the Mexico City earthquake. At that event, large groups of untrained volunteers organised spontaneously and, in operations which lasted 15 days, rescued more than 800 people and lost 100 of their numbers. Capitalising on that experience, and with the knowledge that in emergencies bystanders are first to provide assistance and operate rescues (US House of Representatives 2007: 7), the LAFD formed the first CERT teams with the purpose to make volunteer groups safer and more effective.

Replicating Fire Department terminology, LA CERT units are called 'battalions'. Each battalion has a member appointed by LAFD to be its 'call-out contact'. Accordingly, 'CERT members will not self-dispatch to any incident', as only the teams requested by the LAFD may respond. The CERT call-out process runs as follows:

1. The LAFD calls the battalion's call-out contact;
2. She fills in the CERT Call-Out Assignment form;
3. The Contact calls the battalion members, repeating to each the information about the incident and recording their availability on the battalion's Call-Out List;
4. If the Contact cannot summon the number of volunteers requested by LAFD, she calls members of nearby battalions, until the number is met;
5. The Contact calls the CERT Battalion Coordinator and an assigned LAFD person to inform them of the incident call-out;
6. After the incident, the Contact will fax to LAFD both the completed Call-Out Assignment and the Call-Out List, complete with call results. All CERT members involved should 'use their CERT forms at the incident' and fax them completed within 48 hours after the call-out ends.

It is uncertain whether this process serves to mobilise volunteers, or to monitor them. It shows that citizens who underwent training in order to aid others are forced into inertia if the fire department does not call.

Once the teams arrive at the incident, they conduct themselves according to the CERT Incident Command System (ICS), a code providing a clear basic structure of command, permitting for added complexity when necessary. At the top of the hierarchy is the Fire Department's Incident Commander (IC); he assigns each CERT team an area and a task. Each team has a Group Leader who watches the others work. She is instructed to 'oversee and manage your resources. Do not get involved'. The Leader perpetually assesses the situation on the ground and reports it to the IC via a team member ('runner') assigned to messenger duty. If the deployment is big, the intermediate degrees of Division and Group Supervisors appear. These chiefs are instructed (apart from not getting involved with manual labour) to maintain documentation, which they submit to the IC at the end of the event (FEMA/Emergency Management Institute Unknown Date).

Thus, CERT teams are structured as perfect pyramids of hierarchy, reproducing those of the fire service: the 'culture of service and responsibility' is proving to be a cult of hierarchy and discipline.

Activity and rationale

Five modules, prescribed by the FEMA, seem to be common to all local CERT training programmes (Citizen Corps/Harris Unknown Date; Citizen Corps/Los Angeles Unknown Date; Citizen Corps/Miami-Dade Unknown Date; Citizen Corps/Orange Unknown Date): (a) *Disaster Preparedness*: preparing oneself and the community for a variety of hazards; (b) *Team Organisation and Disaster Psychology*: organising spontaneous volunteers and managing people's stress in an emergency; (c) *Medical Operations*: providing basic first aid; (d) *Fire Suppression*: extinguishing small fires; (e) *Light Search and Rescue*: locating and retrieving people trapped in debris; and (f) *Terrorism Awareness*: FBI agents teach the definition of terrorism, terrorist goals, weapons, indicators of an attack, and actions to be taken in a terrorist incident. The training concludes with a general simulation exercise. Some localities develop 'Continuing Education' courses, offering periodic 'refreshers' and advanced modules (Citizen Corps/Los Angeles Unknown Date; Citizen Corps/Miami-Dade Unknown Date).

The LA CERT website provides a synopsis of the local teams' activities since 1999, thus offering a diachronic view of the project. In 1999–2000, there were ten CERT events. All of them were either drills and 'refreshers', or conferences and fairs. Participants' numbers were low (one drill was effectuated by three people), and the public demonstrated perfect indifference.

In 2001–2002, CERT activity remained relatively modest, but was vested in patriotic spirit and grew in importance. Fairs enjoyed large turnout, and were attended by representatives of local and federal agencies and security-related firms.

In the 2003–2004 period activities multiplied. While most of them were exercises, the teams also participated in five real-life incidents: two election days, two marathons and the West Hollywood Christmas parade. In the three latter events the teams' task was to help people in the crowd and be ready to provide first-aid if needed. On the 20 May 2003 election they were dispatched in depots to count the ballot bags. On the 2 November 2004 election they looked after the fire stations and helped fire trucks enter and exit. There was also a genuine emergency in which the CERT participated. On 29 October 2003 one battalion was deployed at a fire, helped the traffic evacuating the area and distributed oxygen masks.

The previous period set the agenda of CERT activities. In 2005–2006, CERT events were exercises and marathons, while 2007–2008 saw them employed at peripheral tasks during wildfires (assessing damage, looking for missing pets). In

2009–2010, LA CERT activity reached its peak, comprising several exercises, monitoring the Hollywood Santa parade, helping with data entry for the marathon, promoting anti-flu vaccinations, etc. In this period, the California Governor inaugurated 'Disaster Corps', an elite unit of CERT veteran volunteers. Then, CERT activity seems to stop abruptly. In 2011, there was only a 'refresher' and some Fire Department babysitting. Activity has remained subdued ever since.

Apparently, volunteers have become an unpaid, jack-of-all-trades subunit of the Fire Department, performing any task it assigns them to (US House of Representatives 2007: 23, 42, 50–51). They are also uninsured for accidents they may suffer in training or in deployment. In a document adjunct to the volunteer application form, the applicant releases the County (its agencies, offices, etc) from any liability for discomfort, trauma, injury or death occurring to her while 'on service', and testifies that any medical treatment costs will be covered by her own means.

In sum, the CERT places the volunteer within concentric hierarchical structures: the team itself is one, the team's relation to emergency agencies is another, and the Citizen Corps structure a third. In this structure, the volunteers surrender to the unconditioned authority of the managing agency. The disciplined volunteer is moulded as an example of the ideal worker: obedient, gratis, flexible, skilled, uninsured, disposable.

Apart from providing a biomatic introduction – i.e. instilling it as part of the daily lived experience – into social life and work in a homeland security regime, there is not much else the CERT does. While in the wildcat groups of Mexico City 100 volunteers died saving 800 fellow citizens, in the efficiently trained and organised CERT case, both counts are zero. No CERT group was mobilised in Florida in the Autumn of 2004 when the state was ravaged by hurricanes. No CERT group was mobilised in Louisiana a year later, when Katrina visited (US House of Representatives 2007: 9, 51–52). And there is no mention of them near the Boston marathon bombings in April 2013. Los Angeles teams were having a 'great time' doing 'refreshers' during the October 2007 and the August 2009 wildfires. The contrast between Mexico and the CERT is one between spontaneous, self-organised citizen action, and an enlistment project. While in the former volunteers mobilise, deliberate, organise and act on issues which affect them; in the latter, citizens' participation mutates into a structure of authority, its initial purpose forgotten. Elaine Scarry draws similar conclusions by studying the unfolding of the 9/11 attacks. She juxtaposes the flight which hit the Pentagon with that brought down by its passengers in Pennsylvania, as exemplifying two different conceptions of national defence: the first, authoritarian, centralised and top-down; the other, distributed, inclusive and egalitarian. It was the latter which proved effective, despite the Pentagon's impossible technical, operational and organisational superiority (Scarry 2003: 4–7, 28). In fact, the CERT neutralises the spontaneous urge to assist in an emergency. Rather than doing what they volunteered for, volunteers are forced into inertia until they receive the Commander's call, and then spend their time filling reports. The CERT is a project which exploits the urge for mutual aid to forge disciplined, submissive citizens (hence the conceptual nervousness of disaster officials before the 'spontaneous volunteer': FEMA/Points of Light Foundation 2006). Democratic decision and action is faster because the participants are *de facto* interested in resolving the problem before them. The state's problem by contrast, is to subvert this dynamic into practices prescribed by its summits – not least, practices which would perpetuate a cult of authority.

VIPS: collusion with the force

Unlike the CERT, which has a clearly defined structure, from within the volunteer groups to the federal management, the VIPS is an umbrella programme covering all local police volunteering schemes. It is managed by the IACP, in partnership with the DOJ's Bureau of Justice Assistance. From 74 programmes at its inception in May 2002, the VIPS comprised 1,100 programmes in early 2004, and had grown to 2,200 by January 2012 (Citizen Corps 2004; VIPS 2012). It involves impressive numbers of volunteers, who make up from one-quarter to two-thirds of the local police workforce. contribute working hours which amount to hundreds of work years, and save their local force millions (VIPS 2005). There is remarkably little information on who these volunteers are. The roster includes doctors, teachers, students, businessmen, retirees, housewives, officers' relatives and college interns. The main reasons urging them to volunteer are: having a family member who is police, gratitude towards the police, staying busy, acquiring job skills and seeking employment. For their part, police departments seek to recruit people with strong interests in criminal justice, sociology, business, computer science, geography, journalism and aviation, with the overall purpose to improve public confidence in the Department (Citizen Corps/Miami-Dade Unknown Date; Citizen Corps/Harris Unknown Date).

The hiring process is entirely determined by the local force. Volunteers undergo background checks of varying intensity, and hiring requirements may range from production of a good character reference to a polygraph test. Volunteers are also subject to the code of conduct of the local force, and their tenure can be terminated at the discretion of the 'CEO': 'termination' is not 'subject to due process' (IACP 2004).

For as long as they are tolerated by their overlords, volunteers are at the bottom of the department's hierarchy: Chief of Police – Assistant Chief responsible for Support Services – Commander – Volunteer Coordinator – Volunteers. Their role is envisioned as auxiliary to professional officers, comprising supportive duties (clerical, parking fines, serving as 'eyes and ears', etc) (IACP 2004). In practice, it is much more varied. We can, generally, distinguish two broad approaches to using volunteers, an educational and an operational.

The rationale of the 'educational' approach is to provide volunteers with an intimate look in the Department's operation, enabling them to make informed judgments about it. Volunteers are instructed in the inner workings of the Department regarding patrol, criminal investigations, recruiting, training, crime prevention, traffic enforcement, use of force, narcotics, communications and gangs (Citizen Corps/Harris Unknown Date). They are also educated by officers on policing strategies, police science, law, and the criminal justice system (Citizen Corps/New York Unknown Date; Citizen Corps/Harris Unknown Date). They participate in role-play scenarios, and patrol alongside officers to gain first-hand experience of frontline duty. 'Ride-along' participants are prohibited to interact with the officers or with the suspects, and cannot take notes or record the experience. In addition, they release the Department from liability for anything that may happen to them during the programme (Citizen Corps/Harris Unknown Date). Youth volunteer programmes aim to familiarise college students with police operations, and provide specialised training in public safety and criminal justice concerns. There are also internship programmes which provide practical training in criminal justice to high school, college and graduate students (Citizen Corps/Montgomery Unknown Date; Citizen Corps/New York Unknown Date; Citizen Corps/Harris Unknown Date). Upon completing the course, volunteers are awarded a certificate, and in some cases are enrolled to further assist the department or start Neighbourhood Watch groups.

The 'operational' approach involves 'indoors' and 'outdoors' tasks. Volunteers are appointed a wide variety of administrative and technical jobs in order 'to augment labour resources' and to introduce new skills and expertise into the Department. They also patrol the neighbourhood on foot, cars, bikes and horses, covering commercial areas, parks, subway stations, etc, as well as mass gatherings. They are uniformed, and their primary function is to deter crime by being highly visible. In this manner it is said that the volunteers 'gain an appreciation of the hard work officers perform' (Citizen Corps/Miami-Dade Unknown Date; Citizen Corps/New York Unknown Date).

Lastly, volunteers are trained for 'eyes-and-ears' jobs. They are given lessons in 'observation' and code numbers to recite when they report to their Department. Many of the volunteers in these programmes are elderly or disabled people, who can 'observe' without venturing far from home.

The fundamental aim of both approaches is to inculcate the volunteer through identification-by-incorporation to the police. The embedded volunteer gets to see her town through the eyes of the police, to perceive its structure as a policing matrix, and its population as matter-for-policing. From there on, 'educational' programmes have pronounced public relations aspects, turning individuals who are positively inclined to the police into real 'fans' of the force. 'Operational' programmes intensify the embedding of the volunteer with the force, as volunteers are drawn inside the department, made colleagues of the officers, assigned uniforms and regalia, and are generally treated like officers. Like the CERT, the VIPS has a pronounced element of labour exploitation. They provide a large pool of totally gratis work, and outline a set of arbitrary working relations, determined unilaterally by the employer, and do not give the worker the slightest right or guarantee.

Neo-liberalism, neurosis and citizenship

Citizenship theorists focusing on the US tend to agree that the ideal type of citizen – the 'democratic-liberal', inclined to augment freedom and equality, and concerned with rights, government accountability and control – does not apply to contemporary US citizenship (Bhandar 2004; Brown 2006; Isin 2004). Over the last three decades, citizenship is increasingly organised on the basis of anxiety, fear and trauma, giving rise to a subject in constant awareness, alert and in anticipation of unexpected changes in her everyday life (Bhandar 2004). In line with the neoliberal policies which introduced it at the first place, confronting anxiety becomes a 'private' affair, undertaken by each individual in isolation and through marketised solutions. Neoliberal policies also cause a rise in volunteerism, as the state pressures charities to fill the void left by the dismantling of social welfare.

The overall effect of neoliberal policies on citizenship is to make anxiety its organisational basis. In its context, a sense of stability can be restored through the apparition of strong (state) leadership, requiring submission to its authority on the basis of the truth it represents. This 'pastoral' model legitimises inequality on the basis of perceived distance from the truth (Brown 2006).

The Citizen Corps looks like a test-tube case of such shifts in the nature of citizenship. It is a project based on anxiety management. It promotes a sublimation of the generalised anxiety caused by the violent neoliberal disruption of prior frameworks of social life, into the form of an imminent, physical disaster. At the same time, it provides a therapeutic channelling of this anxiety into ways beneficial to the social order which produces it, and forges a subject conditioned to live in it. Characteristically, in Congress (US House of Representatives 2004b: 97, 129) 'statesmen' and 'civil-society-men' concluded that the political imperative of homeland security faces a vital challenge in engaging citizens to live under the sign of a permanently imminent threat. To achieve this, they unanimously suggested introducing programmes which would make the condition of looming threat biomatic. This masquerades as a problem-solution technicality what in reality is a question of defining citizenship. And the preferred template for homeland security citizenship is Israel, the *par excellence* national security state (Elran 2009; McGee et al. 2009).

Inasmuch as the Citizen Corps testifies to the broader character of citizenship, it indicates tendencies in political culture, i.e. on how individuals contextualise the political world and their place therein. Here politics appears as a largely indecipherable system of lines of authority, uniting the President at the Olympian summit, and the citizen-volunteer at the bottom. From the top downwards, this is a system of command; from bottom upwards, it is a system of accountability. The citizen lives in, and develops affinities with, a form of socio-political organisation in which she is invariably an executant of decisions which do not involve her; and accountable to a structure of authority beyond her control.

In sum, the Citizen Corps is a platform for governance-through-neurosis (Isin 2004), premised on the postulation of an anxious citizen (Bhandar 2004) and the management of social anxiety. In homeland security the state installs anxiety, and defines it as an imminent threat of violent catastrophe. Through the Citizen Corps it provides a solution, the organisation, structure, and practice of which is state-determined. Finally, Corps is initiated by the President's call to a 'mission' defined by the morality of an eternal National Culture; and it constitutes a cult of authority, structured according to apportioned 'know-how' of the threat and of ways to counter it. It therefore seems that Brown's 'pastoral' citizenship, revering hierarchy and averted by democratic-egalitarian postulates, is indeed the point of arrival.

Citizenship is a relationship between the population and the state. Consequently, the forms of citizenship and shifts thereof, are related to forms of statehood and their change. This is not lost on analysts. Isin sees the shift towards the 'neurotic citizen' as the outcome of governmental projects, and Bhandar notes that the anxious citizen is the reproductive agent of a 'new normality' implemented by the state. Wendy Brown sees this connection as more developed and explicit. Her account of marketised citizenship echoes Foucault's (2008) analysis of liberalism; and her assessment of the 'pastoral' type is informed by Foucault's account of a pastoral modality of power based on 'pure obedience' to a leadership providing direction in the pursuit of truth (Foucault 2007: 163–185; Lemke 2001). Brown makes clear that successive reconfigurations of citizenship are components of state-driven governance projects: the neo-liberal, and the neo-conservative, respectively, with the latter being a version of the former (Brown 2005; 2006). The advance of neoliberalism signifies the cancelling of liberal democracy, as its specifying characteristics (representative democracy, civil society, public sphere free from repression, the rule of law, etc) are irrelevant to a mode of governance which imposes the logic of the market on all aspects of political and social activity.

While Brown's argument is valid and insightful, especially in establishing the interrelation between forms of citizenship, state projects and configurations of the state, there is some, potentially misleading, confusion in her analysis of these configurations. We gather, for instance, that the predominance of the Executive among state branches becomes an issue only with the advent of neoliberalism (while it is something highlighted by political and legal theorists since the 1930s); that we pass from an age of liberal normality to a state of permanent emergency; or that the liberal-democratic configuration is not restricted to the 'classic' features of parliamentary democracy, rule of law, etc, but also envelops the welfare state and redistributive policies. This makes the liberal configuration stretch, potentially, from the days of Adam Smith, to the days of Ronald Reagan. And, while this vast temporal expanse is treated as a continuum, the last three decades are marked by multiple shifts: from marketised, to pastoral, and now, with the state imposition of poverty, to a 'sacrificial' configuration of citizenship (Brown 2012). Moreover, the assessment of these configurations and their shifting is always observed, but never explained. While configurations (suddenly, in the last 35 years) come thick and fast, the questions of why this is happening, to what purpose, and to whose benefit or cost, remain un-asked. There is, therefore, concern with the periodisation of the phenomena Brown addresses; and with the apparent randomness of the 'emergences' she identifies.

The latter problem could be overcome by conceptualising the state as a parameter of social dynamics: as a creation, a terrain and an agent of social antagonism, rather than a dispositif of the abstract essence 'power'. Shifts in the character of the state and citizenship signify changes in the field of social dynamics, which are co-authored by the state and impact its form. Similarly, the notion of the state-form could remedy the problem of confused periodisation, as it refers to the socio-historically specific articulation among the state apparatus and state power, state structures and strategies, and the state and its social 'outside' (Chapter 2).

Thus, by being a citizenship project, the Citizen Corps can be conceptualised as pertinent to the contemporary US state-form, providing some partial indication of reconfigurations therein.

Citizen corps: crash-course in authoritarian statism

Brown (2005; 2006) affirms that the governmentality imposed by neo-liberal and neo-conservative projects disposes of liberal democracy, but does *not* constitute a fascist form. Rather, 'the substance of many of the significant features of constitutional and representative democracy have been gutted, jettisoned or end-run, even as they continue to be promulgated ideologically [...] [B]asic principles and institutions of democracy are becoming nothing other than ideological shells concealing their opposite ...' (Brown 2005: 52). For this new form of statehood 'we do not yet have a name' (Brown 2005: 51). Still, we may, '[f]or want of a better term', call it 'authoritarian statism' (Poulantzas 1978: 203).

In the late 1970s, Poulantzas coined the term 'authoritarian statism' to account for the systemic realignment of authoritarian elements within the increasingly hollowed democratic institutional shell. In a wavelength strikingly similar to Brown's, he insisted that AS is not a fascist state, nor a chrysalis form of such a formation: '*it rather represents the new "democratic" form of the bourgeois republic in the current phase of capitalism*' (Poulantzas 1978: 209, original emphasis). In other words, AS is a normal form of capitalist state, which nonetheless incorporates, normalises and *renders permanent* a variety of emergency-type features (Chapter 3), the combined effect of which is the drastic repression of the population's capacity to produce politics and influence the state. Instead, the state attempts to provide the population with platforms for 'appropriate' political participation: 'greater exclusion of the masses from the centres of political decision-making' is coupled with 'increased attempts to regiment the masses through "participation" schemes' (Poulantzas 1978: 238).

A crucial factor in the advent and transformation of AS is crisis. The advent of homeland security as a new AS phase was marked by the (by now prolonged and intensifying) crisis of the neoliberal/SWPR arrangement (Chapter 3). As the state and dominant capital opt to counter the crisis without touching its causes, homeland security effectuates a subterfuge. It conceals the political and economic character of the crisis and construes it as one of security. It thus helps the 'anxious citizen' to pin down the cause of his anxiety. And, in the Citizen Corps, it provides him a way to sublimate his neurosis in a politically appropriate way, and to share it with others.

While in the Citizen Corps the state constructs platforms for sublimation and socialisation, the volunteers are thoroughly excluded from defining their organisation and direction. This is mostly effectuated through the Citizen Corps' structure.

A distinction between structure *of*, and structure *in*, the Citizen Corps is useful here. 'Structure *of*' refers to the organisation of the project's managing entities: a quango pyramid formed by one national, 50 states, and thousands of local Councils, where the summit does not exercise direct command, but strategic planning and control over the base. At each level the directing entity is a conglomerate of government, capital, and the security mechanism. This structure puts completely unaccountable entities (business, churches, etc) in a position to co-direct the volunteering citizens.

'Structure *in*' refers to the structure of the teams, and the volunteers place therein. Here hierarchies and lines of command are not in a 'co-operative' limbo, but clear and hard, and invariably with the volunteer at the bottom. Additionally, the implementing authorities determine and introduce special intra-volunteer hierarchies, transforming the *groups* of volunteers to hierarchical *teams*. There is no operational need for, or benefit from, such hierarchisation. It is solely introduced to secure detailed control of the authorities over and inside the teams. Thus, the volunteers are under the boot of a clearly defined hierarchical structure, which is in turn situated within a twilight zone of accountability. The volunteers can have no impact upon these structures, or determine their own work.

Thus, the anxious, isolated individual is re-socialised in a statist matrix, where social relations are relations of authority, and social bonds are lines of command, and are passed down by a mysterious structure from above. In there, she is embedded with the coercive apparatus, identifies with the security personnel, and is indoctrinated to its logic. Finally, she is acclimatised to being the competent, submissive and devalued employee in a set of working relations that grants her nothing. She is *the ideal workfare labourer*.

To sum up, the Citizen Corps shows the coercive mechanism as a central platform for organising state-population relations. This, in turn, is symptomatic of the increased gravity of security policy and logic in the third phase of AS. The amalgamation of hierarchical command with 'governance' networks in the Citizen Corps' structure is typical of AS and effectuates the total exclusion of the volunteers from influencing their work. The work in question entails no rights (while it poses a lot of dangers), no remuneration, and its conditions are arbitrarily determined by the employer. The Citizen Corps are a pure form of workfarism. Operating at 'ground' level, the overall effect of the Citizen Corps is to condition the citizenry to the modalities of social life in an authoritarian workfarist context. Here the state operates at the deeply intimate level of the affinities of the psyche for survival, self-fulfilment and companionship, thus casting the Citizen Corps as a laboratory for the production of the type of citizen pertinent to the authoritarian republic in its 'homeland security' version.

While Bhandar notes that the citizen is the 'reproductive agent of the state' (Bhandar 2004: 265), the study of the Citizen Corps shows that it is also its *product*. Conditioned to live in the shadow of a permanent threat, in identification with the security mechanism, and under hard hierarchies and arbitrary rule, the volunteers are meant to be the first citizens of the authoritarian republic: its products and re-producers.

12 Resistance to homeland security

Community resolutions

Along with public protest against the Iraq war, the most important gesture of resistance to counterterrorism policy were the community resolutions against counterterrorist law and practices. As expressions of popular political opposition go, the 'resolutions movement' was peculiar. It lasted for an unusually long time (almost four years: 2002–2006), and it never developed a visible, mass presence in the streets. These peculiarities are due to its unusual character: the movement took an exclusively legal form. The resolutions are binding, legal decisions taken by city councils and state legislatures.

The first resolution was passed in January 2002, but they remained sporadic during that year. They took off, however, in early 2003, and increased exponentially over the next 18 months. They started slowing down from mid-2004; were less prevalent during the next year; and had practically ceased by 2006 (Table 12.1).

Over 400 communities and seven states (Alaska, California, Colorado, Idaho, Maine, Montana, Vermont) have passed resolutions, encompassing about 30 per cent of the US population. Regarding their geopolitical expansion, the most noticeable trend is that the larger the population of a locality, the more likely it is to have passed a resolution. The 15 largest US cities had all passed resolutions by late 2004, as had many big cities in the historic South. While there is a strong trend connecting large urban centres with Democrat majorities, the state-wide

Table 12.1 Resolutions per month/year

	Jan	Feb	Mar	Apr	May	Jun.	Jul	Aug	Sep	Oct	Nov	Dec	Total
2002	1	–	1	2	2	2	1	–	–	5	2	6	22
2003	10	22	25	22	27	15	10	10	25	21	13	12	212
2004	11	15	18	23	23	11	7	5	8	2	6	4	133
2005	1	4	3	3	7	2	1	1	1	2	2	2	29
2006	–	4	1	–	1	–	–	1	–	–	1	–	8

Source: compiled from data on the ACLU website, http://www.aclu.org/national-security/community-resolutions; last accessed, 4 May 2011.

resolutions in Republican strongholds like Alaska, Idaho, Montana and Colorado, mitigate any sense that party-affiliation is a determining factor.

While, as legal documents, the resolutions passed by local and state governments are binding on the agencies under their command, federal law overrules them, if conflict arises (ACLU 2003f; Herman 2008b: 80, 82; Young 2008: 59). Therefore, the significance of the resolutions is mainly political, a declaration of opposition to legal powers, prescriptions and practices.

Almost every resolution is divided in two parts. In the first (the 'whereas' section), it identifies the issues it addresses and explains its rationale. In the second ('therefore' section), it provides guidelines to various agencies under the control of the resolving authority. The 'therefore' section is the legally binding part of the resolution. Still, the 'whereas' section is of equal importance, as it identifies the legal provisions and policing practices which cause concern. The legal powers and counterterrorism practices opposed by the resolutions can be broken down into nine categories (Table 12.2).

There are, therefore, four main areas of popular concern with, and opposition to, counterterrorism:

(a) The Executive's surveillance powers, especially as they are unchecked by the Judiciary: electronic surveillance, secret searches and seizures, and access to records.
(b) The criminalisation of public political expression codified in the definition of domestic terrorism, and practiced through surveillance of political activity.
(c) Ethnic profiling.
(d) The absolute, arbitrary, *ius regis* coercive powers of the Executive.

While there is broad convergence among resolutions regarding the powers and practices targeted in the 'whereas' sections, the 'therefore' sections divide them into two large groups, a 'soft' and a 'hard' one. Soft resolutions are mostly oriented towards overview. A representative example is the resolution of Eugene, Oregon. It petitions the local Office of US Attorney, the local FBI office, and the Oregon State Police to report to the City Council monthly and publicly on the extent and manner in which they implement the Patriot Act. It asks for information on detentions, searches under §213, electronic surveillance, monitoring of political and religious activities, obtaining educational records under §507, and of library records and bookstore purchases under §215. Most resolutions are hard. They order local agencies to not implement the legal provisions specified in the resolution, and to refuse complying with federal requests to do so (e.g. Seattle, Hawaii, Baltimore, Alaska, Anchorage, Washington DC, Montana, Berkeley). Detroit is a characteristic example here. Its City Council directs the Police Department to refrain from enforcing federal immigration laws, from monitoring political and religious activities, and from co-operating with federal agencies when they do so. It also instructs the Director of the Library Commission to notify users of public libraries that their records may be obtained by the FBI.

Table 12.2 Content and targets of the resolutions

Categories of issues	Practice and/or legal statute opposed	Communities resolving against (examples)
Erosion of *probable cause of suspicion*	Patriot Act, §218; Attorney General's Guidelines of 30 May 2002	Berkeley, Seattle, Baltimore, Alaska, Anchorage, Austin, Chicago, Los Angeles, Washington-DC, Jerome
Erosion of *'due process'* on judicial proceedings	Patriot Act, §412;[1] the 'enemy combatant' Military Order; FBI treatment of the 9/11 2001 investigation detainees; interception of attorney-client communications	Denver, Berkeley, Seattle, Hawaii, Baltimore, Austin, Chicago, Los Angeles, Wendell
Social profiling in law enforcement practice	The FBI's 9/11 investigation; the FBI 'special registration' programme for US Muslims	Ann Arbor, Denver, Berkeley, Seattle, Vermont, Alaska, Philadelphia, Austin, Chicago, Los Angeles, Maine
Amplified powers for *electronic surveillance* and absence of judicial supervision	Patriot Act, §§206, 214, 207, 201–202,[2] 216	Berkeley, Seattle, Vermont, Philadelphia, Ann Arbor, Austin, Chicago, Los Angeles, New York, Maine, Syracuse
Secret *searches and seizures*	Patriot Act, §§206, 207, 213, 219	Denver, Berkeley, Seattle, Hawaii, Baltimore, Vermont, Philadelphia, Ann Arbor, Austin, Chicago, Los Angeles, New York, Maine, Syracuse
Enhanced access to personal records	Patriot Act, §§358,[3] 507–508,[4] 215, 505	Berkeley, Seattle, Hawaii, Vermont, Philadelphia, Ann Arbor, Austin, Chicago, Los Angeles, New York, Maine, Syracuse
Domestic terrorism: the overbroad definition can stifle public political expression through surveillance and penalisation	Patriot Act, §802	Berkeley, Seattle, Baltimore, Vermont, Philadelphia, Ann Arbor, Austin, Chicago, Los Angeles, Maine, Syracuse
Reversal of the requirement for compliance with petitions under the Freedom of Information Act	Attorney General's FOIA memorandum (2001); 2002 Intelligence Authorisation Act	Berkeley, Austin, Chicago, Los Angeles
Any furthering of the Executive's surveillance and coercive powers	In anticipation of the Domestic Security Enhancement Act	Baltimore, Austin, New York, Syracuse

[1] Authorises indefinite incarceration of non-citizens at Attorney General's discretion.
[2] Expand wiretap authority to broadly defined 'terrorism' and 'computer fraud' respectively; diminish legal standards and judicial overview.
[3] Access to financial records.
[4] Access to educational records.

Every resolution bases its authority on the Constitution and the Bill of Rights – and finds that this or that provision or practice contradicts it. The Constitution is often coupled as a source of authority with state constitutions, and sometimes with international law (e.g. Berkeley invokes the UN Human Rights Charter). Only in extremely rare cases (Tonasket, Washington; a community of approximately 1,000 people) the authority of the Constitution is seen as intermediate, and the citizenry ('People') named as the ultimate source of authority.

This disregard to popular will shown by a popular movement, and its emphasis on legal justification, is very unusual. Moreover, the legal provisions targeted by the resolutions are precisely those which were opposed by civil-libertarian lawyers' organisations. Characteristically, provisions which could be of immediate concern to local communities – like those in HSA (§§212–215) which provide impunity to 'critical infrastructure' corporations, even if their plants pose serious risk to personnel and neighbouring communities – are completely ignored by the resolutions. This indicates that civil-libertarian lawyers were involved in the resolutions movement, and that their involvement was decisive in identifying the issues of concern, the means for addressing them, and the prevailing justification.

Indeed, the contribution of lawyers was crucial to the movement. From early on, ACLU was hard at promoting the resolutions' tactic, its lawyers were at the centre of local efforts, and its local offices provided consultation and guidance throughout the process. It monitored developments closely, and taxonimised resolutions according to their character (binding or not), the specific issues they addressed, the date they were passed, the name and location of the resolving community, its population size, and its Representative or Senator.[1] Its local, regional and national directors issued numerous press releases (over 40 between early 2003 and mid-2005), stressing the rationale of the movement (protection of civil liberties and the Constitution), its non-partisan character and its nationwide scope (e.g. ACLU 2003b; 2003j; 2004a; 2004b; 2004c; 2004d; 2005a; 2005b). A dedicated, prominently displayed section of the ACLU website monitored and reported on developments on the resolutions nationwide, and featured relevant communiqués. These activities helped to galvanise the resolutions' (self-)perception as a singular, nationwide *movement* rather than a sum-total of mushrooming localised singularities; and contributed to delimiting (defining and limiting) this movement within a legal framework. Finally, and crucially in terms of enhancing the tactic and settling its agenda, the ACLU (2003g) produced a model-resolution, suggesting the issues to be addressed, the reasons for doing so, and the way to do it. From there on, community resolutions became uniform in they way they were set out, indicating that the ACLU's model was indeed used as a template. In another document titled *How to Pass a Community Resolution*, ACLU instructs those interested to: (a) scan for groups and organisations in their community *which* would support such effort; (b) scan for friendly representatives and get to know how local decision-making procedures work, and seek advice from nearby communities

---

1 Spreadsheets archiving the period between mid-2002 and late 2004 were kindly made available to the author by ACLU.

which have already passed resolutions; then (c) draft a proposal for the resolution, and inform and mobilise the community; and, lastly (d) start informal lobbying of local representatives (ACLU 2003c).

This testifies to the crucial role played by the ACLU as a collective 'cause lawyer' (i.e. a lawyer whose political and/or moral convictions determine her advocacy: Scheingold and Sarat 2004) in the resolutions movement. It also answers a most important question regarding the character of the movement: was it a *genuinely popular*, grassroots one or – given that resolutions were passed by City Councils, Municipal Assemblies, and State Congresses – an initiative of sub-national governments (Althouse 2008: 26; Young 2008: 51, 53)? The ACLU guidance, which starts with (groups of) concerned citizens, then opens to the broader community, and only at a final stage engages local political officials, leaves little doubt that the resolutions movement was a popular, grassroots project pushing upwards to the formal institutions. Indeed, the observation of a small number of communities shows that their resolving processes were bottom-up ones, largely conforming with ACLU guidance (Azulay 2003: 4–5). Most resolutions acknowledge that they were passed, in part, as a response to the concerns of specific groups in the community (students, 'minorities', librarians), and they salute other communities which have passed similar resolutions.

Finally, the resolutions resonated in the federal state. They caused the, thus far unique, occurrence of concerted Congress attempts to amend the Patriot Act. From early March to late October 2003, ten Bills attempted to restrict Patriot Act powers. They display clear alignment with the resolutions regarding Patriot Act provisions they target. Moreover, they coincide in time with the resolutions, which were also hailed by star Senators in the liberal camp (Kennedy, Leahy) (Chapter 7). Nonetheless, the congressional response considerably diluted the force of popular demands. Some of the most central points of popular opposition (the presidential 'Enemy Combatants' Military Order, the Attorney General's Guidelines, the unlimited detention of aliens, and the 'domestic terrorism' definition) were never taken up by Congress's resolutions. Furthermore, while popular resolutions sought to *abolish* legal provisions, the congressional Bills only sought to *amend*, so that they acquire legal standards and congressional review. And, while all community resolutions that we know of succeeded in becoming local law, all congressional motions failed.

Librarians: thorn in Patriot's side

While homeland security presents some anti-labour aspects, organised labour never reacted to its workfarist elements, or to the broader political project. The sole exception were the librarians. Librarians are directly implicated by the Patriot Act (§215 'access-all-records' provision), and have been frequently requested by the FBI (under §215 or, more routinely, NSL authority) to surrender their patrons' book borrowing and internet use records.

The librarians were the first to challenge (aspects of) homeland security long before the left-leaning lawyers, the general public, or Congress members did. Not a month from the Patriot Act's enactment, the first informative public meetings were held in libraries throughout the country (Scarry 2004: 10, n 25). As the first expression of popular resistance, those meetings left their mark on it. This is manifest in the sheer notoriety of §215. Moreover, about a third of the resolutions make special mention of libraries, and amending attempts in Congress focus disproportionately on libraries and the 'freedom to read'. Similar concern for financial, educational or medical records, also abundantly targeted by counterterrorism law, never materialised, for their custodians never raised the issue. On the contrary, through persistent, determined work, the librarians managed to translate the legal provisions of the Patriot Act into an impression that the FBI is spying on people's reading habits and internet usage. In doing so they managed to trigger anti-authoritarian reflexes from the population, thus turning a 'sectoral' issue to a political one.

The findings of the University of Illinois's Library Research Centre survey (2003) confirm the status of libraries as likely points of resistance. Sixty-five per cent of librarians declare themselves to be against governmental secrecy, even if it is employed to protect against terrorism. This is diametrically opposite to a 67 per cent of the general population, which finds it acceptable. Furthermore, only 10 per cent of libraries have amended their policies towards patrons in compliance with the Patriot Act provisions, and less than 2 per cent have co-operated with law enforcement voluntarily.

In January 2002, the librarians' central organisation, the American Library Association (ALA), issued its resolution targeting Patriot Act provisions and the Attorney General's Guidelines to the FBI (ALA 2002). This is definitely a 'hard' resolution. In the 'whereas' section, the ALA first defines the role of the government: to protect and preserve the fundamental democratic freedoms. Any sympathetic reference to the government's efforts to secure and protect, is resoundingly absent. Next, the ALA describes the librarians' social role: they are 'a critical force for promoting the free flow and unimpeded distribution of knowledge and information for individuals, institutions and communities'. Since 'the suppression of ideas undermines a democratic society', librarians are guardians of democracy. It is this work ethic, their self-perception as political and democratic actors *by profession*, which urges librarians to take an active stance in public affairs, and explains their particularity as the only workers to take on homeland security (ALA 1999; 2002).

On the basis of the definition of their respective roles, the ALA proceeds to launch a fierce attack on the administration. Legislation like the Patriot Act and directives like the Attorney General's Guidelines signify the government's departure from its proper role, and this forces the librarians to resist its commands. They refuse to comply with law enforcement requests, and justify their refusal on constitutional grounds: said requests violate the right to privacy and rights to free expression and association (ALA 2002).

Specifically resisted is the government's augmentation of surveillance on patrons' reading habits and internet use, and 'any use of governmental power to suppress the free and open exchange of knowledge and information or to intimidate individuals exercising free inquiry'. The ALA urges librarians 'to defend and support user privacy and free and open access to knowledge and information', by filing patron activity exclusively in accordance with the ALA's privacy policy, meaning that libraries should retain records independently of security concerns, and only in order to improve their function. The ALA promises to monitor and publicise police intrusion in libraries, and urges Congress to overview and amend the laws which threaten free expression and inquiry.

The ALA resolution has been endorsed by 41 state library associations, while another seven (Oregon, Pennsylvania, Michigan, New York, California, Delaware and Connecticut) have passed their own ones. These are essentially the same as the ALA's resolution, to which they add their explicit concern with the Patriot Act provisions for surveillance and detention outside the library context. They also touch on two further points. First, Michigan and California express concern with national security secrecy – the increasingly widespread official practice of redacting 'essential information' from governmental websites to 'avoid the perception of abetting terrorism' (see also ALA 2003). Second, they all refer to the discriminating effects of the legislation, since it is mostly the 'poor and unemployed' whose only access to computer services is through public libraries. This is the *only* reference to the class aspects of homeland security by opposition movements.

Apart from the formal reaction through resolutions, librarians have also been employing shop-floor guerrilla tactics. They warn their patrons about what can happen under the Patriot Act rules: 'Due to national security concerns, we are unable to tell you if your internet surfing habits, passwords and e-mail content are being monitored by federal agents. Please act appropriately'. This warning sign appears in public libraries (e.g. Killington, Vermont; Skokie, Illinois), forcing citizens to confront in concrete terms the force of the legal text – and thus enabling librarians to deliver a decisive blow in their ideological battle with the administration. Furthermore, librarians take active steps to protect patrons from surveillance. Some engage in record destruction, where the librarians who hold the last shift shred the daily records (e.g. Santa Cruz, California). Some delete from their computers the details of a book borrower at the moment the book is returned (Spokane, Washington; Santa Cruz, California). Others, at the end of the working day, eliminate all information on the day's activity from internet terminals, and purge on a monthly basis the names of whoever has borrowed books (e.g. Berkeley, California; see ACLU 2003f). However sporadic they may be, such actions demonstrate a determination to resist the homeland security regime on the basis of personal commitment and responsibility for the consequences.

Librarians managed to rattle the feathers of the almighty administration so much that the Attorney General took it upon himself to set things straight. Two years after 9/11, with the librarians' resistance and community resolutions in full swing, John Ashcroft went on an abundantly televised tour of 16 major cities, where he would explain the merits of the Patriot Act to audiences consisting of local police personnel. The core element of this propaganda effort was to create a cleavage between 'patriots' and 'scum', citizens who undermine the nation and hence do not deserve to be part thereof (Chapter 7). Regarding the librarians, the Department's preferred tactic was to mock their concerns and actions out of existence: 'If you were to listen to some [...] you might believe the hysteria behind this claim: "Your local library has been surrounded by the FBI." [...] Like the *X-Files*, [agents] are dressed in raincoats, dark suits, and sporting sunglasses. They stop patrons and librarians and interrogate everyone like Joe Friday [...] Agents are checking how far you have gotten on the latest Tom Clancy novel'. This 'baseless hysteria' diverts attention from 'the most important issues'. Hence, the Attorney General vigorously dismisses it: 'the hysteria is ridiculous. Our job is not' (US Attorney General 2003b). Thus, the patriots vs scum cleavage is coupled by another, between the brave, robust cop and the sissy, neurotic librarian. The critique and resistance of the librarians is swept aside in a manner of manly arrogance and in the midst of sarcastic contempt. As discussed below, this speaks volumes not only (and obviously) of the gender bias of homeland security, but also of its nature as a political project, and of the state's democratic credentials.

Legalism, politics and popular resistance

As social movements go, the resolutions present unusual characteristics in almost every turn. For a protest movement, it was unusually persistent and prolonged. For a popular movement, it was too reliant on lawyers to lead and define it. Most importantly, for a political movement, it showed disregard to (explicitly) political demands and justifications, and relied exclusively on legal ones. Lastly, for a grass-roots movement, it enjoyed extraordinary success at local and state level, but failed at the federal level.

Starting with the latter, the resolutions movement has met almost unqualified success at local level, considerable success at state level, but made no inroads with the federal institutions. As they climbed up the scales of government, the resolutions not only had their success rates diminished, they were also watered down. The comparison of local resolutions with congressional amendment proposals shows that the latter were narrower in content, and ignored some of the most important powers targeted by the resolutions. They were also lacking intensity: whereas sub-national resolutions effectively repealed the provisions they targeted by banning their organs from implementing them, congressional amendments sought only to introduce some processes of review and overview, i.e. to ameliorate the arbitrariness of counterterrorism powers, rather than abolish them.

These differences – in intensity, content and success – between the local and the federal level, contrast the ability of sub-national (especially local) governments to respond to popular demands, with the rigidity of federal-level politics. This may, in turn, result from uneven capacity of popular movements to organise and act at a local scale, as opposed to a national one. In any case, federal rigidity signifies that access of popular demands to national scale politics is heavily restricted – the DC is a fortressed town. This casts the centralisation of policing powers in the homeland security context (and almost every case of up-scaling of decision-making and control) in a new light: they are not technical-managerial solutions to a 'coordination' problem, but *aspects of a project of political exclusion and de-democratisation*.

A second irregularity of the resolutions is the role of the ACLU in the movement. The ACLU played a crucial part in its organisation, and also identified its objectives, methods, and justification. The ACLU is a 'prototypical voice' of left-liberal lawyering. The overall thrust of left liberal lawyers is to maintain the institutional shape of liberal democracy. They are focused on protecting the rule of law, individual and property rights, representative government, and a pluralist, independent civil society. Liberal lawyers fashion their advocacy in terms of defending the Constitution. They pursue their causes exclusively through the courts – 'litigation is very much the hallmark of liberal-democratic cause lawyering'. The triad of rights-legality-constitutionality is both means and goal of their advocacy. As their activity is compatible with the established juridico-political order, left-liberal lawyers tend to enjoy peer respect, elevated professional status, and good career prospects (Scheingold and Sarat 2004: 15–17, 102–103, 107–112).

The question here is why would a liberal organisation like the ACLU abandon the institutional safety of the courtroom and the comfort of professional and social status, and start organising grassroots political mobilisations, becoming effectively *the* party of opposition to homeland security? The answer is that, in all probability, the ACLU did not jump, but was pushed. It did not opt for an all-out grassroots strategy, but was forced to adopt it, given the failure of its attempts to challenge counterterrorism provisions in court, counting 24 failures in as many lawsuits between September 2001 and October 2002 (Boukalas 2013: 413). The inability of even liberal organisations to manoeuvre in the justice system highlights the synergy of the latter in the hardening of the broader state-form, which is by now intolerant to even liberal and systemic demands. Ironically, this hardening forced ACLU to reverse its strategic, century-long choice of abandoning grassroots mobilisation for litigation (Zackin 2008).

A third peculiarity of the resolutions movement was its duration. The low-profile, localised resolutions movement went on for almost four years, unlike the other main gesture of popular resistance to counterterrorism policy, the movement against the Iraq war, which was massive, dynamic, globally linked, but only lasted a few weeks and had disappeared by the time the first bombs fell on Baghdad. Much of this longevity was due to its form. The process of passing a resolution is a relatively long one, and their local character meant that the movement's forces were not all active at the same moment, but each locality resolved in its own time, thus spreading the overall duration of the movement.

Yet, another (double) factor for the persistence of the resolutions is the mutual relevance between the issue protested and the people protesting. The wars had severe impact on the daily life of the US population, as they caused oil prices to skyrocket, and led to excessive Defense appropriations causing severe public debt problems, which meant that the population could forget about welfare for the foreseeable future. Yet, these implications were not highlighted by the anti-war movement. The platform of protest was one of moral indignation, and once the protestors had expressed their anathema ('not in my name'), the movement evaporated. On the contrary, the resolutions movement framed the issue of 'FBI spying' and other counterterrorism powers as something affecting aspects of everyday life (the librarians' contribution was a catalyst here), and thus the issues it addressed were not remote, abstract ones, but pertained to lived reality.

The war was not only, so to speak, irrelevant to the population; the population was also irrelevant to it. The deployment of the armed forces is something held firmly beyond the reach of popular influence. As the US military is not based on general conscription, the population is unable to influence war-making. By contrast, in the resolutions case, the implementation of counterterrorism law depends on the collaboration of local officials, law enforcement, and professional and private sector entities: the FBI cannot collect library records if the librarians shred them. Along with the biomatic relevance of counterterrorism powers, i.e instilling it as part of the daily lived experience, it is this capacity to 'do something' about them that mobilised and maintained the resolutions movement (Scarry 2004: 14).

Still, the greatest anomaly of the resolutions movement is its very character. Why did a popular, *political* mobilisation take an exclusively *legal* form? Again, a great part of the answer can be provided by the anti-war movement. Although the first resolutions were passed before the anti-war protests, the latter gave momentum to the resolutions by challenging the consensus on war on terrorism, revitalising social opposition, and providing it with a focal demand. Characteristically, the moment the resolutions movement took off (early 2003) coincides with the moment the anti-war movement broke through. Yet, it was not only impetus that the anti-war demonstrations provided to the resolutions, but also a warning. In order to surface, the anti-war movement had to overcome the undermining of mass propaganda openly produced by the Administration against it; ignore 'Orange alerts'; defy court-issued prohibitions; suffer mass arrests and bestial violence by the police (ACLU 2003h; ACLU-New York 2003). In short, the resolutions movement took an exclusively legal-institutional form for reasons of self-preservation – because an overkill of state violence was awaiting protest in public space. This points anew to an authoritarian hardening of the state. It shows that, in the current phase of AS, the exclusion of popular input into politics is effectuated through the *shutting down of the streets* for popular politics, and the occupation of public space by the coercive mechanism.

The combined contribution of these two movements, the global, spectacular, dynamic anti-war protests, and the persistent, localised, slow-burning resolutions, marks a watershed in the story of homeland security. They invigorated the 'afflicted powers' of the US Left (Retort 2005), and smashed the state monopoly over homeland security truth. It is the moment that the convincing power of the war on terror discourse declines (Chapter 4), thus providing a possibility for the re-negotiation of the homeland security project. We now know that this possibility was never taken up, and that today homeland security has deepened, expanded and become neutralised and irreversible. Possibly, a part (however small) of the responsibility for this, lies with the resistance – or, rather, its limitations.

A brief comment on the modality of resistance completes my previous critique of constitutionalism as a basis for social opposition (Chapter 7), by assessing its political horizon in terms of autonomy and heteronomy.

The choice to oppose law (the Patriot Act) by law (resolution) only seems unproblematic at first glance. There is no reason why the form of the response must match that of the assault. More importantly, it raises questions on the scope and effectiveness of this kind of resistance. On the one hand, increasing parts of the population refuse to comply with legal requirements which, after scrutiny, deliberation and experience, they found unacceptable. The decision to defy legality when it is found intolerable is a profoundly political (and autonomous) stance. By placing the will of a population above its institutions, it acknowledges that this will creates, transforms and abolishes the institutions. But, at the same moment, this creative will is concealed, and the responsibility which springs from its expression is evaded. It seeks accommodation in a legal-constitutional framework, rather than one of political, democratic demand. This would be acceptable as a tactic to facilitate a political effort whilst protecting it from unnecessary casualties, especially when the state's coercive mechanism is hyperactive. It becomes problematic when it is the only tactic, the end of the effort. In the latter case, it upholds and galvanises the existing legal order and, through it, the political order, and limits political creation within the framework they provide. It is oriented to the past, and that is the only future it can envision. The rejection of counterterrorism powers occurs not on political or moral grounds – because we do not want to live like this – but on legal ones: because they contravene the Constitution. So what? What if the population wanted something which clashed with the Constitution? Recent administrations have run a horse and cart through it anyway, and they are none the worse for it. Does a rearguard action, based on the interpretation of sacred texts, have any chance of disrupting a state galloping towards authoritarianism? A dozen years of constitutionalist struggle have failed to reverse, or even ameliorate, a single counterterrorism provision. Instead, homeland security has deepened its roots, expanded its reach, and established its modalities as the normal configuration of state power.

Denying self-determination and concealing political will under legal scripture extinguishes the heart of political praxis, i.e. conscious determination and full responsibility. It subjects society to an absolute limit of what it can aspire, think and do with itself. Constitutionalism prevails as yet another order of alien rule, of heteronomy.

A last, important, lesson from the discussion of the resistance is provided by the state reaction it provoked. The fact that popular resistance – by however small a part of the population – is dismissed by the head of the relevant state authority in such a, boastful of its chauvinism, fashion, is yet another symptom of raging authoritarianism. Much worse, this brute official arrogance was met by no reaction from anywhere in civil society. Ashcroft's statements were reported in the press (*New York Times*, *Washington Post*) merely as 'the Attorney General mocks the librarians' without any comment on their sheer unacceptability as utterances of a democratic statesperson. Apparently, in the Land of the Free, the population sees nothing untoward in being treated like serfs. Even the primitive form of representation which currently passes for democracy holds as its founding premise that the sovereign entity is 'the People'. The elected representatives and the government are servants of the people's will. Now, if the servant treats the master in such terms, and the master accepts the treatment as normal, this can only mean that the roles are reversed. The non-reaction to Ashcroft's roaring signifies the shredding of even the pretence of a democratic culture.

Finally, the DOJ's tactics betray that *the objective of homeland security is not the security of the population*. In effect, parts of the population express concerns, or reject the measures the state imposes for their protection. Instead of negotiating with the 'protected' the terms of their security, the state ridicules and coerces them into accepting them. *Protection is an obligatory offer* by the state: the people must accept it whether they like it or not. This means that the protection of the population is irrelevant to the adopted policies. By pushing forward in the face of popular concern, the state betrays itself as motivated by factors other than the declared ones. If it indeed seeks to protect something, this is not the population, but something else. Security policy is independent from its publicly declared purpose, subject to other motivations, and serving other goals, and homeland security is an ideological subterfuge, a pretext for the advancement of strategies irrelevant to the security of the population. In this context, the only course of action for the latter is not to 'balance' security and liberty, but to reject security altogether, to decline the offer of obedience in exchange for protection, to 'return the gift' (Neocleous 2008: 185–186).

13 Repression

We do not appreciate your anti-American attitude

In May 2003, the ACLU published a miscellanea of post-9/11 coercion. Without being an exhaustive account – it only includes incidents reported to the ACLU – it was alarming for two reasons: incidents of repression cover the entirety of social space – from public and privatised public space, to intimate, personal space. And, second, the agents of repression are not only personnel of the coercive state mechanism, but also other public functionaries, and civil society actors. Diffused throughout the social nexus, what unifies these instances of repression is that they closely associate political critique with terrorism. They are, therefore, incidents of coercion typical to homeland security politics.

It started early. On 27 October 2001 in North Carolina, a student's house was raided by the Secret Service and local (Durham) police, in response to an anonymous tip about an 'anti-American' wall poster. (The poster was taking issue with the President's death-row record when he was Texas Governor.) The student was questioned about the Taliban, and never discovered which of her friends snitched her (ACLU 2003d: 5–6).

Universities are privileged sites of 'counterterrorist' action. In Iowa, in September 2002, police officers and a County Attorney threatened to arrest two students for hanging the US flag upside down from their dormitory window. In March 2003, the police thrashed an anti-war rally at the University of New Mexico, involving tear gas, beating and 17 arrests. The University of Maryland prohibited 'public speaking' and leafleting on its campus (ACLU 2003d: 5–7).

In April 2003, two teachers and a chancellor were suspended without pay from their public school in New Mexico, for displaying in class artwork expressing diverse opinions on the Iraq war – including some against it. At the same time, school officials were permitting army recruitment in its premises, and pro-war posters were prominently displayed. In Michigan (February 2003) a pupil was dismissed for wearing a t-shirt that framed the President as 'international terrorist' (ACLU 2003d: 14–15).

While its inbuilt coercive potential, ideological role, population synthesis and history of political production, make the educational system a locus of special attention, another setting deserving special mention is privatised public space.

This category is important for two reasons. First, it is constantly expanding, and threatens to absorb all public space. And second, whilst in it, citizens have to comply not only with the law, but also with privately issued rules. In March 2003, at a shopping mall in Guilderland, New York, a 61-year-old lawyer was arrested for trespassing, after he defied the private guards' order to remove his t-shirt, which was displaying a 'peace' sign. In Seattle, on the day of the large anti-war demonstration (15 February 2003), a woman waiting for the metro refused to lower her anti-war banner, and was consequently evicted from the station. Again in Seattle, in March 2003, a security officer ordered a man in a soup kitchen to remove his anti-war badge or leave the building (ACLU 2003d: 5–7). And, in March 2003, a passenger found in his baggage a card from the TSA, notifying him that his bags had been inspected in Seattle airport. Accompanying it was a hand-written note: 'we do not appreciate your anti-American attitude'. The bags contained two anti-war banners (ACLU 2003d: 17).

What makes these incidents noteworthy is that they are principally effectuated not by the official state apparatus (which is often absent), but by a motley set of, often private or self-appointed 'authorities' which rule over a fragmented, feudalised social space. Their rule is perfectly arbitrary, based on a quasi-feudal conception of ownership of the social site they are in charge of. They do not act through law, nor do they target activities on their illegal basis. And, obviously, what they target is the public display of certain political views. Thus, through the cultivation of patriotic bigotry, homeland security creates an environment of a (state-determined) 'legal pluralism' which replicates and outbids formal measures in thrashing antagonistic political expressions.

The peaceful streets of Pleasantville

Turning our attention from privatised, pseudo-public sites to public space 'proper', we find it under police curfew. Immediately after 9/11, the state of Illinois decided to close Chicago's Federal Plaza, the city's main site of public congregation, to all public activities (ACLU 2003d: 11). In Pleasantville, New Jersey, a demonstration against the Afghanistan war (9 October 2001) was not allowed to 'pass, congregate, or be in or over any of the streets, highways, alleys or any other public place in the city of Pleasantville' (ACLU 2003d: 3). The City of New York denied access to Central Park to demonstrations against the 2004 Republican convention, to avoid damage to the grass (*New York Times* 2004). And famously, New York City in conjuncture with a federal Court banned the central (15 February 2003) anti-war demonstration. When the people came out despite it, they faced massive police force, aiming to prevent the gathering. It resulted in 350 arrests. The arrested suffered a wide variety of adverse detainment conditions, and virtually all of them were interrogated about their political conviction (ACLU-New York 2003: 10, 20–22).

Outright prohibition, preferably involving a judge, of public protest is the ideal tactic. It classifies protestors as *de facto* 'illegal', and legitimates the police's violent conduct and arrests. Moreover, the police itself imposes prohibitions, both on assembly and on the space in which it can occur. This is the preferred, heavily used, tactic, and was codified in law to counter the Occupy movement (Chapter 5). This means that 'legal' demonstrations are treated no differently to banned ones. In New York, the 'outlawed' February event was rescheduled for March. The 200,000 participants faced the same inflated police presence and hundreds of arrests. Again, the arrested were interrogated on their political views, and the information extracted was fed into police databases (ACLU 2003d: 2).

In St Louis, during a presidential visit to the local Boeing plant (16 April 2003), the police herded the protestors to a remote, enclosed 'protest zone' which could not accommodate their numbers. Those refusing to comply were arrested, received rough treatment and their bail was set too high for them to cover (ACLU 2003d: 11). In Washington DC (27 March 2003), the police besieged a group of 400 demonstrators, and proceeded to arrest them on resisting a dispersal order (ACLU 2003d: 3). At the port of Oakland (7 April 2003), rubber bullets, tear gas and wooden pallets were used against an anti-war demonstration. In St Louis (30 March 2003), the police trapped and assaulted a group of about 60 young people after an anti-war rally. The beating was accompanied by cries of 'traitors', 'anti-Americans' and 'unpatriotic', and ended with eight youths arrested and one in hospital (ACLU 2003d: 8–10).

These early incidents point towards repressive overkill. This is directed against all kinds of public protest, and continues, unrelenting, to this day (ACLU 2012c). Still, special, intensified treatment is reserved for anti-systemic protests. The February 2002 New York protest against the World Economic Forum (WEF), and the November 2003 Miami protest against the Free Trade Area of the Americas (FTAA, an attempt to expand NAFTA to South America), were early testimonials of this.

The New York anti-WEF protest was the first in the US after 9/11. Marking a sharp reversal of the hitherto trend of 'anti-globalisation' events to grow and intensify, it was sparsely attended. The bulk of unions, NGOs and unaffiliated people had withdrawn, leaving only anti-capitalist elements (the Anarchists being the defining presence). In the build-up to the event, the New York Police Department (NYPD) was eloquent about its tactics. It reassured the public that its further post-9/11 traumatisation would be prevented, as numerous blue collar and three Secret Service divisions, two FBI and two NYPD battalions, helicopters and horse-riding units would be employed to secure the WEF convention. To secure it, certainly not from the bulk of 'peaceful protestors', but from 200 anticipated Anarchists, whom the Chief of NYPD was not expecting to 'cause trouble'; and from a terrorist assault, the possibility of which was not anticipated either. These 'anticipations' were produced by hundreds of FBI and NYPD officers monitoring intelligence on 'terrorists' and 'potentially violent protesters' (Esposito 2002; Scahill 2003).

It is worth noting how the police public relations assaults deliberately blur the radical difference between socialist revolutionaries and religious fundamentalists. The extreme incompatibility between these groups in terms of worldview, objectives, organisation and practice, is ignored. Since they both seem to reject the liberal-capitalist social order, and they both sometimes engage in some form of 'violence' against it, they are treated as two of a kind. On this basis, the police openly advertises its spying on political activity as essential in securing public peace.

The New York protest weekend concluded with 200 arrests. The police pressed some half-hearted charges ('parading without permit') and, after up to 60 hours' detention, released the arrested, after the demonstration had taken place (Kaplan 2002). Each of these arrests was *pre-emptive*. They were made not for any deed of the arrested, but because the police determined that they could proceed to illegal activity in the course of the protest. While within police powers, pre-emptive arrest in the context of public demonstrations was hitherto rare in democratic societies, after 9/11 it has become commonplace and systematic, as it aligns with the dominant pre-emptive trends in counterterrorism law.

Thus, the key parameters set by counterterrorism law already materialise during the first post-9/11 event of public protest. First, policing has become intelligence-determined, and this entails arbitrariness in its practice, as it acts upon the potentiality of social phenomena (not their illegality), informed by knowledge it claims to have but it cannot disclose. Second, a main recipient of this treatment is the political activity of the population, which is closely associated to terrorism. And, through its stirring towards the – essentially military – logic of pre-emption, the main consideration of the use of law is not the distribution of justice, but the neutralisation of threats.

These elements, featured in nascent form in New York, were fully developed in Miami. There, police infiltrators acted not only as informers, but also as agents-provocateurs. Pre-march arrests were the order of the day, but pre-emption went further, as some 10,000 protesters were simply not allowed to enter the city (Crumpacker 2003). Miami completed the post-9/11 model of policing protest. It did so by adding a crucial element alongside intelligence and pre-emption: *violence*.

In Miami, the police were out in numbers, dressed in military overalls, and armed to the teeth. They subjected the protesters to an orgy of violence: beatings, tear gas, concussion grenades, electroshocks (tasers) and rubber bullets (Crumpacker 2003; Scahill 2003; Starhawk 2003). They pressed serious charges against those they arrested, which meant that bail was set too high and most demonstrators could not afford it. The events were covered by embedded journalists, dressed in police uniforms and roaming the city as members of police squads. Further implying that Miami was a full-scale *military* operation, its funding derived from the DHS, private donations and a congressional appropriation for the Iraq war (Crumpacker 2003; Scahill 2003; Starhawk 2003).

The Miami MOUT (Military Operation in Urban Terrain) was designed to serve as a model for policing protest. The Mayor hailed it as a 'model for homeland security', and several cities had sent observers to study the operations (Scahill 2003). The relevance of this model to counterterrorism is rather stretched. An attempt at mass-assassination deriving from within a demonstration is historically non-existent, and logically absurd. Moreover, the 'Miami model' emerged before 9/11 – but *after Seattle*: most of its features were established in Philadelphia 2000

(Anonymous 2002). And, as testified by the Occupy protesters, it has become the default mode of dealing with 'difficult' crowd gatherings (e.g. Ciccariello-Maher 2011; Freedom Road Socialist Organisation 2012; Paul 2011; RCP 2012). The predominance of the 'Miami model' indicates that the purpose of homeland security is to prevent not another 9/11, but 'another' Seattle.

This treatment is premised on the systematic association of antagonistic politics and forms of popular resistance to terrorism, and is geared towards the imposition of full-blown repression against the real enemy: popular revolt. Thus, at the top of the 'domestic terrorism' list, we find the radical ecology of the Earth Liberation Front and the Animal Liberation Front whose combined action over 15 years amounts to US$110 million in damaged property and has never resulted in death or injury; and the anarchist Food Not Bombs, which disavows even property destruction. The FBI (Deputy Assistant Director for Counterterrorism) identified them as the single major source of 'violent crimes and terrorist actions', while a Senator noted they are 'just like al-Qaeda or any other terrorist organisation' (Senator J. Inhoffe, cited in Halperin 2005). Joint police-academy ventures are mobilised to rent some 'scientific' clout to the association of antagonistic (especially anarchist) politics to terrorism, bypassing the fact that, for a century, anarchist activity in the US has not caused death or serious injury. This results in some breathtaking language acrobatics which assume the 'violent' nature of property destruction and from it deduce a 'mentality', which, if aggravated, may proceed to harming humans (Borum and Tilby 2005).

This justifies (indeed, dictates) the constant harassing of anarchist groups by the police which continues unabated to this day. It comprises raids, detentions (always pre-emptive), interrogations, disruption of events, etc. And, it seems that in the northwest (Washington and Northern California) there is a systematic attempt underway to map out, and crash the anarchist movement. In most cases, people are arrested for possessing 'anarchist literature', are interrogated on their political beliefs, and asked to name their comrades. These pogroms are often effectuated by the 'counterterrorism' mechanism (the 'intelligence-led' FBI and JTTFs), and draw their legal authority from post-9/11 counterterrorism law. They belong to a well-drilled tactic (initiated immediately after 9/11 in relation, initially, to 'aliens') of pre-emptive detention, whereby the suspect is arrested not on criminal charges, but pending testimony before a grand jury (ACLU 2005a; Committee Against Political Repression 2013; Green 2005; Kiley 2012; Potter 2011; 2012a–d; 2013; Roach 2011: 188–189).

We are starting to decipher the real significance of terrorism – and the terrorist – in homeland security. A brief account of specific persecution cases will help to identify concrete modalities of repression.

Metamorphosis: Greenpeace's rowdy sailors

On 12 April 2002, two Greenpeace members climbed up a vessel which was approaching Florida with a cargo of illegally harvested mahogany from Brazil. Attempting to notify port authorities of the approach of illegal cargo, they hung a banner which read 'President Bush Stop Illegal Logging' at the side of the ship. They were arrested, sentenced and served their sentence. Yet, in July 2003, a federal grand jury issued an indictment against Greenpeace Inc, charging it with conspiracy to violate 18 USC §2279.

It was the first time in US legal history that an entire organisation was prosecuted on the basis that some of its members engaged in civil disobedience. The prosecution was based on a nineteenth-century statute, unused in over 130 years, which was meant to counter 'sailor mongering', a practice where pimps would board the ship, without permission and while it is still en route, in order to incite crew members to desert their posts and come ashore. Incredibly, 'sailor mongering' was the only charge in that lawsuit (ACLU/People for the American Way Unknown Date; Nimmo 2003). This astonishing case highlights the sheer determination of the homeland security state in dealing with political opposition of even the most systemic kind. Even though it was acquitted (Roig-Franzia 2004), Greenpeace got the message. Ever since, its US branch has refrained from the spectacular activism associated with the organisation, and is reduced to a mere think-tank (Griscom-Little 2005).

The castle: Indymedia's close encounters

On 7 October 2004, two Independent Media Centre (IMC or Indymedia) servers were seized, resulting in websites in 20 countries disappearing from the internet. Indymedia are self-managed online forums where politically active people post action reports, opinion and announcements. They are a main source of information for social movements, especially for those of left wing, anti-systemic character.

The seized servers were property of a Texas-based ISP (Rackspace Managed Hosting). They were located at Heathrow, UK. The ISP issued a statement explaining that it handed the servers 'acting as a good corporate citizen' in compliance to a court order pursuant to a Mutual Legal Assistance Treaty (MLAT), and that it was legally restrained from commenting further. The Treaty in question 'establishes procedures for international mutual assistance in investigations such as international terrorism, kidnapping and money laundering'. It is difficult to associate Indymedia with kidnapping, money laundering or similar organised crime activities. Indymedia was targeted in relation to 'international terrorism'.

A spokesperson stated that the FBI seized the servers after a request by Italian and Swiss authorities. Reportedly, Swiss authorities had previously launched investigations of Indymedia coverage of the 2003 protests in Evian against the G8. Also, a judge in Bologna had requested an investigation in Italy's Indymedia, in a period that the Italian IMC was dominated by communications between victims of Carabinieri violence in Genoa 2001, and their Italian comrades and lawyers. Italian authorities implied that they had requested US aid, but had not asked for a seizure. The British Home Secretary (David Blunkett) assured Parliament that UK law enforcement was not involved in the seizure, but refrained from clarifying whether the British government knew of the operation or whether agencies other than 'law enforcement' were involved.

Seven days after their seizure, the servers were returned to the ISP. (For a chronicle of the Indymedia seizure, see BBC 2004; Bunyan 2004; EFF 2004; 2005; Lettice 2004a; 2004b; 2004c; Indymedia 2004a; 2004b; 2004c; 2004d; Mattelart 2010: 155).

Apart from the fact of the servers' seizure from the UK, on the basis of a US Court order, nothing is clear about this case. And this is possibly its most important feature. Starting with the legal clause underlining the court order, it is unclear whether it was US Code, Title 28, §1782 – which would be the natural clause for such an order, but cannot be activated when legal privilege applies (in this case, freedom of speech or press-related protections). In all probability, the Patriot Act provisions (most likely §§215, 220) were either used to override these constitutional blocks or formed the sole legal authority of the order. In the latter case, the issuing court would be the FISA Court, and the secrecy of the order points in this direction. The order gained validity in the UK through MLAT. Yet, under MLAT, it is the host country's police which implements US court orders. Hence, the seizure should have been made by a UK police agency, possibly accompanied by FBI personnel. But the Home Office stressed that UK law enforcement had no involvement, again indicating an intelligence job, on FISA rules. Moreover, MLAT is activated by political personnel – in this case the British Home Secretary would approve a request by the US Attorney General. Indeed, the Home Secretary stopped short of declaring ignorance of the case.

This case raises as many questions, legal and political, as one cares to count: which court issued the order; who were the implementing authorities; on whose behalf were they acting; were they acting according to law – what law, of which state; can MLAT be used to bypass a country's legal and constitutional protections by having another country dealing with its citizens; what was the reason for the investigation; and what determined that the investigation was satisfied? Astonishingly, *no one* in authority expressed any interest about all this. In homeland security, 'seizures happen'.

While being a sign of political and legal pathology, this spectral operational style which defies legality, sovereignty and accountability, also showcases the competence of the intelligence mechanism. Here we see it in rude health, targeting political expression, transnationally and in a blanket manner.

The trial: the State vs citizen Austin

While in the Greenpeace case political repression occurred outside the counterterrorism legal framework, so that counterterrorism is not tarnished by attacking a well-respected organisation, and in the Indymedia case it occurred in a legal and political twilight zone, in the case of Sherman Austin homeland security law, police, and ideology act openly and in tandem.

On 24 January 2002, the Los Angeles JTTF, involving the FBI, the Secret Service, the Los Angeles Police Department and the Los Angeles Sheriff personnel in full gear, surrounded and invaded Sherman Austin's house. They effectuated a violent search, interrogated Austin for six hours about his relationships and political views, and confiscated all print material of political character and every computer in the house. Austin was, then, the 18-year-old administrator of 'Raise the Fist', an anarchist online forum.

The JTTF was acting in accordance with a 29-page search warrant ordering the investigation on the grounds that the target distributed 'anti-government [...] anti-capitalism, and militant messages that promoted communism'.

About ten days after the raid, Austin was in New York to demonstrate against the WEF. He was pre-emptively arrested and handcuffed along with 25 of his comrades. During 60 hours in custody, he was interrogated about his political views, and 'terrorism allegiances'. While in custody, he was officially charged in California for felony under 18 USC §842(p), a 1997 law activated for the very first time. It makes an offence 'to teach or demonstrate the making or use of an explosive, destructive device [...] or to distribute by any means information pertaining to [...] the manufacture or use of an explosive, destructive device' either knowing or intending 'that the teaching, demonstration, or information be used for [...] an activity that constitutes a Federal crime of violence'. The crime resides not on the act of publication, but on its reception by an audience. It thus creates a situation where people of certain political persuasions considered unlikely to utilise explosives are allowed to publish relevant material, while those of political persuasions considered likely to use them are prohibited (Anonymous 2003; Donohue 2008: 305–306; Touretzky Unknown Date).

The charges were pressed because Austin's website included a link to *another* website ('Break the Bank'), and the latter contained rudimentary information on making explosives. The police had interrogated the other site's administrator, but never pressed charges against him. (An interesting sub-plot here: Austin is an Anarchist. He is also poor, black and from a single-parent family. The 'Break the Bank' administrator is also an Anarchist. He is relatively well-off, white and from a Republican-leaning family. A racial selectivity of the prosecution is decipherable. So is a class-selectivity. Still, these are secondary (aggravating or ameliorating) conditions. The primary one is the targeting of political conviction, on dubious legal grounds. Thus, Austin downplays the importance of the class and race factors in his prosecution, and draws attention to the political one (Chowkwanyun 2003).)

Then, due process took over. Austin was denied bail because his arrest at the New York demonstrations and his possession of 'anarchist literature' proved he was 'a man on a mission', and hence 'all the factors inexorably lead to the conclusion that this defendant will be convicted'. Crucially, despite the blatant violations of the rule of law, the ACLU refused to offer any assistance, stating that it would not undertake criminal cases. This betrayal proved critical for Austin. Without the means to hire a barrister, he was stuck with the court-appointed one. The latter, in conjunction with the prosecutor, were pressing him to enter a plea agreement, a preferred tactic for the government in order to display counterterrorism results. Initially, Austin resisted the plea, but gave up when the lawyers pointed out that his crime could be aggravated by the Patriot Act, causing the maximum sentence to rise from 4 to 20 years (Anonymous 2003; Chowkwanyun 2003).

Austin was judged by a Reagan appointee, Judge Wilson, who interrupted the plea offer (four months in prison, another four in a mid-way house and three years' probation), asked the prosecutor if he had consulted the Attorney General and the FBI Director before the trial, and ordered him to contact these officials to get their recommendations for Austin's sentencing. He expressed wonder on the kind of message a four-month sentence would send to 'some other revolutionary who wants to change the world'. A few hours earlier, in the eastern coast, the Attorney General had issued guidelines to prosecutors, urging them to aim for longer sentences (US Attorney General 2003a).

On 4 August 2003, Austin was sentenced: one year in prison, followed by three years' probation. The terms of the probation obligated him to surrender his computer for weekly inspection, and prohibited him to associate with any anarchist group or person, or any other group or person advocating social, political or economic change.

California Senator Dianne Feinstein, author of the Patriot Act's *significant* FISA amendment, wrote to the Attorney General congratulating him for sentencing Austin under the law she authored in 1997. She complained that federal prosecutors were not taking 'this important anti-terrorism tool' seriously, and insisted that the DOJ should be 'aggressively enforcing it' (Feinstein 2003). The Senator seems determined to impose a crime based on the authorities' interpretation of intention. Bomb-making instructions can be found on mainstream websites, such as CNN, Wikipedia, etc. The only thing that Feinstein's amendment criminalised was its hosting by Anarchists and other 'likely to use' audiences. To prove the point, Professor D.S. Tourzesky, a self-proclaimed Republican, published on his own website, without any consequences, the information which led to Austin's incarceration (Donohue 2008: 306; Touretzky Unknown Date).

This case exposes homeland security law and justice as the authoritarian delirium of state managers bent on repression of social opposition. Everyone involved (the FBI, the JTTF, the local police, the prosecution, the defence, the judge, the press, the Senator) knew that Austin had not committed the crime he was prosecuted for, and everyone treated this as irrelevant to the 'case'. And rightly so: 'the case' was filed against the defendant's (*and others*') *political conviction*, using a law which penalises the 'intention' of an assumed audience as the factor determining criminality. From beginning (the initial search warrant) to end (the admonitory character of the sentence, and the probation terms), it is made clear that political conviction is the sole reason for the prosecution. The authorities were open about it; the only entity which failed to see it was the ACLU.

More than a concrete confirmation of the trends inherent in counterterrorism law, Austin's case shows the full cast of homeland security actors outdoing each other to deliver the greatest punishment to this anarchist-therefore-terrorist. Local police (New York) arrest him on suspicion he might do something illegal. The FBI-led JTTF put on an extravagant show of force against him. The lawyers arrange his punishment without trial or defence. The Judge sends them to consult their bosses, and, together with the Attorney General and the FBI Director, determines an admonitory penalty. The Senator complains there is not enough 'aggression' in implementing her law. The media omit to mention that the 'bomb-making instructions' were hosted on someone else's website. And, the constitutionally sensitive 'cause lawyers' are satisfied with the 'due process'.

Working class, black, young, raised by a single mother, Anarchist: *in the face of Sherman Austin, the authors of homeland security recognise their enemy.*

The universal adversary

The full counterterrorism arsenal – blanket surveillance, repression, collective and individual targeting by a police mechanism which is both pronounced and spectral – is aimed against the Universal Adversary (UA).

The UA is an abstraction referring to the overall enemy against which homeland security is mobilised. In an exhaustive report, the HSC produced a quantity of detailed attack scenarios the UA might realise. They include nuclear detonation, radiological attacks, a variety of bio-chemical attacks, explosives and cyber attacks. The homeland security objective is that the mechanism composed by all intelligence, law enforcement and emergency agencies, at the federal, state and local level, will prevent and respond to all such attacks. The UA is author of all threat, and target of all policing.

Even if abstract, the UA is not undefined. Unlike other central categories of counterterrorism, the UA is identified: 'foreign terrorists; *domestic radical groups*; state-sponsored adversaries; or in some cases *disgruntled employees*' (US Homeland Security Council 2004: iv, emphasis added).

The discussion could stop here: the Enemy is finally identified, and the object of homeland security defined. Popular political and labour action is bagged together with jihad, and the 'counterterrorism' machinery is designed to be used against them. The incidents and cases discussed above leave no doubt that this is happening. The Planning Scenarios show that the crashing of political and labour opposition is not an occasional side-effect, but a core, systemic feature of the homeland security state (US Homeland Security Council 2004; 2006).

Operationally, these 'scenarios' lack plausibility. Even the FBI notes that anarcho-nuclear and bio-labour attacks are quite unlikely (US Homeland Security Council 2004: iv). Their value resides in that they orient the vast, trans-scalar, policing mechanism to identify these parts of the population as the Enemy, and target them with the firmness and urgency pertinent to an existential threat.

The security personnel inculcated through exercises based on the Planning Scenarios, the DHS-led TOPOFF (Top Official) exercises. These take place throughout the country, sometimes also involving Canadian and Mexican personnel, and can engage over 15,000 officers. They involve simulation of warnings deriving from intelligence collection and analysis (based on actual counterterrorism databases), followed by an emergency situation, and inevitably ending with mass arrests of UAs (Chossudovsky 2005; US Department of Homeland Security 2007; FEMA Unknown Date).

The double institution of the US polity

The above show how popular politics are a priority target for the homeland security regime – its official mechanism, and assorted sectors of civil society. This occurs in three, interwoven, levels. First, homeland security attempts to repress the slightest antagonistic gesture; second, it exercises full and systematic repression of organised forms of struggle, especially those with anti-systemic objectives; and, third, political repression is inscribed in its structure as the UA arch-Enemy. The repression is a continuum expanding across intimate, feudalised and public space. The latter is occupied by the vast security mechanism, which can (and does) deny access therein at will.

This treatment started immediately after 9/11 – indeed, most of its elements predate it. It was captured into a comprehensive operational model within a year, and is mobilised with abandon every time a mass, antagonistic form of popular politics materialises in the streets: anti-war and anti-capitalist (Occupy) gestures have been its main victims thus far.

This shows that the re-alignment of the police mechanism and its legal powers so that it can effectively repress popular politics, were not exercises on paper. The police-ownership of public space effectively granted by 'counterterrorism' legislation; the capacity for total intelligence and pre-emptive action against 'troublemakers'; the guilt by association dogma; and, more than anything, the association of popular political struggles with terrorism, are the, now dominant, legal concepts on which political repression is based. Reversely, this also means that this type of repression is not a blip, but the conscious outcome of an institutional design; it is a *permanent condition of US politics* – ergo, it transcends two administrations and has already dealt with two different social movements in the context of two different crises.

The systematisation of repressive overkill points to 'open war against the popular masses' (Poulantzas 1976a: 129), to dictatorship. Exceptional-dictatorial forms of the capitalist state tend to 'freeze' social dynamics. They congeal the configuration among social forces as it was at the moment they are established, and crystallise it in the institutionality of the state. This results in a rigid state, unable to accommodate transitions in the balance of forces, whether within the power bloc or between the latter and the subaltern classes. For this, exceptional state-forms are inherently brittle (Poulantzas 1976a: 49–50, 57, 81, 83–84, 91–93). An indicator of this 'rigidity' with regards to homeland security is the extremely low level of tolerance it displays towards popular struggles. High-intensity force is unleashed towards movements which hardly challenge the social order. On the contrary, social opposition has become meek and defensive in its petitions. It is the reaction of the state which transforms even the least token into an 'act of resistance'.

Along these lines, we can divide the first phase of homeland security (the era of its ascendance, 2001–2008) in two periods. The first, 2001–2004, is a dictatorial one, marked by a tremendous projection of state force (domestically and abroad) to establish, first, the dominance of the A&E sectors in the power bloc and, second, the subjugation of the population to capital in the context of a new accumulation regime. This is a period when political struggles seem acute mainly due to the overtly muscular repression of them. Characteristically, in the second period (2004–2008), and while homeland security was constantly losing legitimacy (Chapter 4), political struggle became blunter, not sharper. This was a period of stabilisation: the Iraq war had consolidated A&E predominance in the power bloc by involving the US in a Middle East crisis which would last for decades – securing robust armaments orders and high oil prices; and the 2004 election secured that the new arrangements would take root domestically. Thus, the state-generated intensity of the political struggle receded.

The legacy of that early dictatorial moment is still with us, in the establishment of a mammoth policing mechanism designed to thrash popular resistance whenever its political directorate determines necessary, while infiltrating, monitoring and harassing political groups as a matter of course. Popular opposition faces a mega-apparatus of repression unheard of in a capitalist-democratic context. This is so because homeland security seeks to protect policies which advance extreme concentration of wealth, to the detriment of virtually the entirety of the population. The path it lays is rife with economic crises and possibilities for popular revolt, especially as the open collusion of the state with dominant capital has eroded its legitimacy.

In this context, periods of stabilisation (like the 2004–2008 one, or the one we are in today in relation to the – now normalised – economic crisis) mean different things to different people. In relation to dominant capital, they mark a return to institutional democratic normality, albeit with a different power bloc configuration. The grip of the state upon rival sectors can be loosened, their treatment does not have to be arbitrary, their agents can have their voices heard in the press, the academy and in Congress. The balance of forces in the power bloc can safely be determined through the flexible, democratic, channels which are more likely to secure its smooth operation and the stability of its dominance.

While the relations (political, economic, ideological, etc) of dominant capital are smoothly elaborated within the democratic mechanisms, political expressions of the population remain under the boot of dictatorship. This means that the present state-form is capable of accommodating intra-capitalist dynamics (and therefore has no fear of a violent *coup* or any such measure from capital's side). But, at the same time, it cannot accommodate change in the balance of forces between dominant capital and everyone else. Opting for violent repression of popular struggles means that the state-population relation becomes military in nature – a relationship of force. It may result in either the eternal suppression of popular resistance to successive waves of capitalist attacks, or a profound political crisis whose result is open.

14 Homeland security: capital in full armour

This study shows homeland security as a relatively unified political project, advanced by the state (branches and parties) in unison, and taking shape in and across the main areas of political activity: political discourse and culture; law and legal dynamics; institutional design and operational modality; state-population (and state-capital) relations. In doing so, homeland security is transforming legal and political outlooks, institutions, practices, modalities and relations – it redefines the law-form and the state-form.

Homeland security is the contingent outcome of social dynamics, mediated by the state and law. The overarching term describing these dynamics is 'crisis'. Homeland security was promoted as a response to the crisis of the workfare postnational governance regime, and the associated hegemonic decline of finance-led neoliberal arrangements. It involved a change of guard in the power bloc, from finance and IT to A&E. It took its shape through the contingent mobilisation (for and against) by forces in the power bloc, the state personnel and the broader population. And, while homeland security significantly altered the political and legal forms which were thrown into crisis in 2000, the legal and political forms it established are now attempting – thus far successfully – to preserve workfarism and wealth-concentration in the face of another round of crisis.

In this last chapter, I draw the overall conclusions of this study, and sketch out a perspective of homeland security in the context of the current economic crisis. Still, given that the juridico-political forms associated with homeland security are designed to combat crises, it is important to clarify that homeland security is not a 'permanent state of exception'.

No exceptions: authoritarian statism

Much of the debate regarding homeland security and the 'war on terror' is entrenched in a 'normality vs exception' framework, where 'normality' refers to liberal-democratic, constitutional forms of government, while 'exception' pertains to unrestrained, dictatorial rule. In this context, homeland security is seen as a consolidation of a state of exception, at the expense of liberal democracy and the rule of law. While this conclusion is not unreasonable, its underlying premises are problematic.

In Chapter 6, I discuss the state of exception as a legal concept, premised on a dichotomy between politics-violence and law-order, and argue that it does not correspond to the homeland security realities and that it is analytically blunt. The legal-political dichotomy corresponds, in turn, to that between the capitalist economy and the state, which too is subject to a plethora of 'exceptions' (Bates 2007: 17). Thus, as a political concept, the normality-exception dichotomy is discussed here in terms of the capitalist type of state (rather than the state in general). In this context, it pertains to the distinction between democratic and dictatorial state-forms.

There is certainly an (historical and structural) affinity between capital rule and liberal-democratic forms. The latter enable the smooth, orderly adjustment of forces amongst capital fractions, and the organisation of alliances with subordinate classes. Still, there is no incompatibility between capitalism and dictatorial forms. On the contrary, when the capitalist order is under threat (or under construction), constitutional niceties go out of the window (Bonefeld 2006; Bates 2007: 21, 28). This was obvious to the classics of liberalism (Locke, Rousseau), and it approaches self-parody in some 'realists': 'No sacrifice is too great for our democracy, least of all the temporary sacrifice of democracy itself' (Rossiter 1948: 314). The resort to exceptional forms can occur even in the absence of popular-democratic pressures, to resolve political impasse among power bloc fractions (Poulantzas 1974: 61, 71–72; see also Marx 1926; Gramsci 1998: 219–226).

Exceptional forms are an unwelcomed option and used sparsely, not due to capitalists' democratic ideals, but because they entail danger. Dictatorial forms cannot accommodate changes in the configuration of forces in the power bloc, or between the bloc and the subaltern classes. This makes them extremely unstable and fragile. When significant changes in the configuration of forces occur (necessarily) outside the state-form, the latter, once its coercive capacity is overcome, is smashed, producing a moment of radical indeterminacy that may threaten the continuation of capitalist rule (Poulantzas 1976a: 90–93).

Rather than abstract questions regarding a suspected 'state of exception', we may then ask whether the juridico-political forms associated with homeland security are exceptional-dictatorial or normal-democratic. Along these lines, it is hard to argue that the US is currently a dictatorship. The institutions of political democracy keep their shape and continue to function normally. There is no attempt to cancel constitutional democracy, but rather to transform it towards more oligarchic forms. This attempt is undertaken by both dominant parties: it is the outcome of political consensus, not of acute antagonism. In addition, there is no failure of existing political parties and networks to represent the dominant class (Belandis 2004: 122–123; Poulantzas 1974).

Still, it is equally difficult to disregard the findings of this study, which show an authoritarian hardening of the state across its areas of activity – from legal powers and modalities to political representations, from policing modalities to construction of citizenship platforms, and from institutional restructure to smashing social opposition. Not only fully anti-democratic, these tendencies are far from occasional; they are persistent and systematic. We are therefore in the realm of AS, the normal, constitutional-democratic, state-form which organically incorporates, and renders permanent, exceptional-authoritarian elements. In this sense, AS is the normal state-form which renders exceptional forms redundant.

Authoritarian statism, crisis and 9/11

Pertinent, ultimately, to the field of social dynamics, AS is a state-form forged by crisis – i.e. by intensification of social struggle which cannot be accommodated in the existing institutional arrangements. We have seen (Chapter 3) that it was first shaped to preserve the Keynesian welfare state during its 1970s political and economic crisis. Most of its key characteristics were forged by the need for flexible, *ad-* and *post-hoc* state intervention to secure continuing accumulation in the face of acute popular challenge and intra-capitalist antagonism. Drastically reconfigured, AS in its second, SWPR, phase provided the political platform for the destruction of welfare strategies, and the advance of the trans-national, finance-led, neoliberal governance, based on workfare. Its third reconfiguration in the context of homeland security occurred as an attempt to preserve this trans-national workfarist governance regime, which was facing a severe crisis on the eve of 9/11. The finance-led, neoliberal economic strategies and political organisation faced acute opposition from populations throughout the world, while the 1999–2000 burst of the 'new economy' bubble caused panic and capitalist unease with the accumulation regime (Chapter 3).

Against this global background, a US-specific development was a shift in the power bloc, as A&E could promise the entire capitalist class an escape from economic meltdown, by advancing an alternative accumulation mode based on stagflation. The new mode of accumulation signified intra-capital debauchery and a frontal attack on the subaltern classes. As a mode of 'accumulation by dispossession' (Harvey 2003; 2010), it would generate new crises. In anticipation, and with the license granted by 9/11, a hardened, martial reconfiguration of AS was installed.

Homeland security

Homeland security is a unified project operating in and across different contexts of political practice. Its political discourse describes a framework for perceiving politics and society, and for relating the state with the population. Its legislation outlines and imposes new modalities and objectives for state power, compatible with the discursive representation. It further redesigns the institutional outlook of the state so that it can correspond to strategic orientations of state power. This includes changes to the character of the law itself, and its importance. The restructuring of the coercive mechanism follows the blueprint set by the legislation, and draws its rationale and justification from political discourse. Discursive representations, legal powers and institutional capabilities converge, in contrasting modes, in relating to the population: to galvanise support and set a new citizenship model; and to delimit resistance and crash social opposition.

Further confirming the unity of the project, and its agenda, are certain motifs that recur throughout it. The premium on security as a dominant rationale and justification for state activity and authority; the collateral character of terrorism considerations in determining 'counterterrorism' policy; the management of potentiality through pre-emption and the acceleration of state activity; the state-capital fusion; the promotion of expertise as the sole justification of authority; the inclusion of the entire population in a coercive continuum; and the politicisation of the targets and objectives of policing – these trends tell the implicit story of homeland security as a new design of state power. They all converge into a singular trend: the *complete exclusion of the population from politics*, from influencing the forms of social life.

Three stages are decipherable in the life of the homeland security project thus far. The first extends, roughly, between 2001 and 2004. In this stage the project took shape and was imposed on US political and social life. This stage is marked by hectic state activity (hence termed the 'dictatorial moment': Chapter 13). The augmented role of the state was necessary to define the project, the imposition of which involved an epic struggle to reset political ideology, legislative design, the structures, powers and modalities of the state, the professional culture of state personnel – as well as embarking on two full-scale wars. It also involved a difficult transition of dominance in the power bloc, from IT and finance to A&E, and a change of accumulation regime. These shifts were made through 'counterterrorism' policy, and largely defined it. Their imposition was driven by the coercive state apparatus (the Department of Defense and the DOJ), which assumed the dominant role among state institutions, replacing the Treasury. This reconfiguration of political, economic and social life was made possible by the exceptional degree of popular backing for homeland security. For over a year the project enjoyed full support, and even when (since early 2003) some dissent appeared, it remained limited (Chapter 4) and was violently crushed (Chapter 13).

The second stage extends, roughly, between 2004 and 2008, and is one of stabilisation. State activity did not attempt to introduce ideologies, legal powers and institutional structures, modalities or cultures any longer, but to establish and fine-tune those imposed in the previous stage, so that they become operational and take root in the political system. The institutions of liberal democracy (especially Congress, but also the courts and the Executive) largely regained their shape, rhythm and functions, albeit with the power-relations among them recalibrated. With the major work of reshaping the power bloc done, its internal relations could again be regulated peacefully in the state and the parallel network. While there was little friction in the power bloc, the situation regarding the broader population is paradoxical. Homeland security was losing consensus, but very little popular resistance materialised, and when it did, it was extremely cautious. Moreover, almost invariably (with the exception of anarchists and other socialists, and librarians), it remained internal to the security logic. It sought to ameliorate some of its aspects, but was acknowledging its primacy. This points to a decisive ideological victory of the project, and to a drastic narrowing of the horizons of political contemplation and action.

While both these stages pertain to the ascendance of homeland security, the third one signals its normalisation. Partly due to a change of guard in the White House, but mostly due to the advent of a severe economic crisis which threatened the continuation of accumulation, homeland security is no longer the dominant state strategy. To begin with, it is no longer a project, but has taken its place in the political, legal and cultural constellation – it is part of the furniture. Second, security, while remaining extremely important, is not the top state priority, neither does its logic dictate and condition all state activity. Instead, the logic of accumulation – of the very preservation of the accumulation process – becomes primary. In this context, the coercive apparatus, while strengthened, ceases to be dominant among state mechanisms, and the economic apparatus (the Treasury and the Federal Bank) regains its usual place. And, thanks to its near collapse, finance is back in the driving seat in the power bloc. In short, homeland security is incorporated in the state, in a supporting role. Still, despite its relative decline in importance, *not a single domestic aspect of homeland security is reversed or cancelled*. Instead, this phase is one of further fine-tuning of practices, and of deepening and expanding of repressive powers.

Still, the most lasting impact of the homeland security project is the transformation of the state-form and the law-form. The forms which homeland security established remain operative today, and it is through them that the current economic crisis is being managed.

Ius regis and authoritarian statism III

The incorporation, combination and organic development of authoritarian objectives and dictatorial modalities in the institutional shell of liberal democracy signifies that the present form of the US state is an AS configuration. Indeed, homeland security reproduces and intensifies almost all the key AS features. Within the formal confines of the state, the Legislature's deliberative, overviewing and even rubber-stubbing capacities are severely curtailed. The legislating process migrates from the congressional assemblies to closed, *ad hoc* groups combining administration personnel and select Congress barons. Its rhythm is accelerated, as representatives are often limited to yes or no votes. The main author of its decline is Congress itself, as it unceasingly grants the Executive powers to circumvent it. There is no Executive coup against the Legislature, but an inter-branch synergy in concentrating power at the Executive summits.

The deliberation and policy-determination functions traditionally associated with the Legislature are undertaken by a parallel network of *ad hoc* and permanent, national and international, official and unofficial committees, working groups, organisations, etc. These have become the dominant policy-making fora, and comprise Executive personnel and agents of select capitals (Demirović 2012: 241; Klein 2007: 316–322). In homeland security, these networks are statalised, as the Executive asserts its power to arbitrarily select its interlocutors from the world of capital. Moreover, parallel networks are institutionalised. Their existence is recognised and protected (but not regulated) by law, especially regarding their secrecy and their decision-making authority. These powerful political platforms are, by law, insulated from the population.

If the Legislature, with its powers reduced and is functions overtaken, increasingly resembles political pantomime, the Judiciary is threatened with extinction. Having already lost much overview and adjudication powers over important economic processes and relations in the context of the *lex mercatoria* form, under homeland security it loses its core functions of controlling the process of criminal investigation and overviewing police work.

The eclipse of the Judiciary is symptomatic of a deeper trend that also came to prominence with the previous law-form: the instrumentalisation of law. The specifying logic of law is abandoned, and law is guided by non-legal logics (economic effectiveness; criminal pre-emption). This cancels its formal, functional and conceptual distinctness. Law is whatever the state designates and imposes as such, whether or not it fits with the legal system, resulting in a 'dummy of legality'. 'Law becomes nothing but the technical instrument for the execution of certain political objectives. It is nothing but the command of the ruler' (Neumann 1937: 61). This collapse of law to mere instrumentality threatens the very constitution of the capitalist *type* of law, leaving us with the mere resemblance of law in a capitalist society (Buckel 2011: 164–165). This is symptomatic of a loss of gravitas of law as such. 'Mission-led' governing, concerned with effectiveness, displaces principle-led politics codified in legal concepts. The demise of law as the basis of government entails reduced capacity to regulate social dynamics in an orderly manner, and to forge a stable equilibrium between social groups and classes (Paye 2007: 253). The current law-form, and the state-form which includes it, are therefore prone to political crisis.

The decline of law results largely from the turn to pre-emptive targeting of (potential) criminality. The trend towards pre-emption was already present in the first (1970s) AS phase, but has now become the dominant mode of policing, and its scope expands to envelop everyone and everything. It overcomes both the legal/illegal, and the normal/abnormal dichotomies, to inculcate all types of behaviour into statistically anticipated probabilities (Mattelart 2010: 184). Coercion becomes the main relation between the population and the state.

The police, almost fully emancipated from judicial control, monopolises the investigation process. It gains augmented capacity to dictate legislation and to determine social policy in relation to 'high risk' groups, and it assumes a role of moral leadership (Paye 2007: 185–188; Wacquant 2009).

Finally, the decline of law-based government and the retreat of the Judiciary and the Legislature signify an extreme concentration of power at the hands of the Executive. The latter is the principal political planner and actor. It regulates social relations directly (bypassing legal mediation), and occasionally assumes legislating functions (as in TARP) and even institutionalises its own legal system (as in Guantanamo). Moreover, power is not only concentrated at, but also within the Executive. Characteristic here is the restructuring of the all-important police apparatus in the shape of a perfect pyramid, culminating in the concentrated authority of presidential knowledge and control.

The intensification of these AS features enables us to speak of an authoritarian hardening of the AS form. Yet, what enables us to speak of AS in the first place is the general direction of these developments, i.e. increased state control over social life, combined with the decline of liberal-democratic freedoms and the political exclusion of the population. This general tendency is reproduced – and aggravated – even when the current configuration of AS departs from previous ones.

The homeland security version of AS is significantly different from its previous SWPR configuration. The (narrative of an) innovation-driven economy is emphatically replaced by one heavily dependent on state subsidies to stumble its way out of crises. The economic role of the state changes. From general administrator of networks of contractors and facilitator of the self-regulation of market forces, it becomes a venture capitalist. It provides select sectors with seed money, becomes their main (or only) consumer, and bails them out of bankruptcy (Klein 2007: 12).

Moreover, the economic and political strategies of the state are now anchored on the national scale. This is pronounced in the partiality of homeland security economy to US capital and workforce. In the context of the current economic crisis, the prevailing strategies of invigorating industrial production, promoting exports and re-balancing trade deficits are distinctly national. The national scale becomes the ultimate horizon of state activity, even when the latter involves international engagements. This is also evident in security policy – including war. In the context of the SWPR configuration of AS, the war in Kosovo was conducted under a human rights – universal and global – justification, whereas the wars in Iraq and Afghanistan were justified by the need to protect the homeland. (And the 'humanitarian' intervention in Libya was not instigated or led by the US.)

The national scale is also strengthened in relation to sub-national ones, something indicated by the jurisdictional unification of the country, the capture of sub-national police personnel by the federal Executive, its involvement in privileging select capitals at sub-national level, and the decline of the legal autonomy of sub-national governments.

Finally, the amorphous regime of joint public-private governance is undergoing a statist transformation. These mechanisms become legalised and more powerful than ever, but their composition, purpose and function are directly determined by the Executive. The state determines what governance mechanisms do, how, and, crucially, who participates therein.

The revival of statism is also evident in the law-form, as the withdrawal of state-law from the regulation of social and economic affairs is now coupled with its emphatic resurgence in relation to crime. This radically augments the powers of the state (concentrated in the Executive) in relation to the population, to the extent that the latter enjoys very little protection from state coercion. This occurs through the expansion of the state's legal powers, the erosion of legal standards and guarantees, and the production of vague, open-ended legislation. It culminates to the establishment of a legal regime which leaves designated individuals ('enemy combatants') at the mercy of state force. While introduced in the context of criminal law as part of security policy, the legal trend to augmented, arbitrary, Executive power metastasised since 2008 to economic practises. This re-statalisation of law is somewhat paradoxical: the *ius regis* form consists of 'more state', but 'less law'.

Thus, the dominant trends of the SWPR arrangement are transformed and even reversed by the advent of homeland security. All except one. Workfare is drastically intensified, as is shown in the conceptualisation of the worker as a security hazard, the imposition of flexible working relations in the public sector, the total exploitation of the volunteer, or the association of 'disgruntled employees' with terrorism. This social devaluation of labour resulted in intensification and expansion of exploitation in the homeland security years. The downward pressure on wages and on welfare continued, working hours got even longer, forms of precarious employment proliferated, as did the inculcation of submissiveness through insecurity (Liodakis 2010: 25, 32–33, 49–50, 90) – all this before we even consider the imposition of planned poverty in the context of the current crisis.

I argue (Chapter 3) that workfare was the determining element of the SWPR configuration, and that the other trends were developed to support it. As the SWPR was caught in popular and capitalist crossfire the hour before 9/11, homeland security redefined the supportive trends, so that workfare could continue relentlessly.

The reconfiguration of the state- and law-forms by the homeland security project took place through a monumental shift in state logic. Instead of accumulation, security became the state's top priority. Security was the key criterion for state action in other areas, thus helping state power to achieve coherence. And the coercive apparatus was driving state action, as its logic and objectives were helping inform the activities of all state mechanisms (Chapter 8).

This de-throning of the accumulation logic and the economic apparatus is rare in the context of the capitalist state. While the two logics often conflict as security policy can undermine accumulation, they are not fully incompatible. In abstract, we have seen that the constitutions of capitalist states typically predict and provide for the taking over by security logic and the coercive apparatus when popular struggles threaten the continuation of capital accumulation. In post-9/11 US, the shift to security occurred precisely at the moment of acute crisis of accumulation; and the homeland security project was essential in securing its continuation: both by turning the accumulation regime on its head and imposing a change of guard in the power bloc; and by setting up a draconian (legal, political, and technical) mechanism to neutralise popular struggles. In short: *in order to be guaranteed*, the process of accumulation was subjected to the logic and the mechanism of security. Since then, a devastating economic crisis caused the return of the accumulation logic and the economic apparatus in charge of the state. Yet, the state- and law-form which the homeland security project established are still in place, and the current crisis is managed through their modalities. This is not surprising. The reconfiguration of the law- and the state-form in the context of homeland security was made in order to combat the crisis of the neoliberal, finance-led, workfarist economic and political arrangement. This is what it is still doing today.

Authoritarian statism and accumulation through crisis

The reconfiguration of AS in the context of homeland security recasts the trends of the previous SWPR arrangement into a nationally anchored, statist framework, so that the workfare trend can continue unabated. In the context of the current economic crisis, the key modalities introduced in relation to security are replicated in the realm of economic policy. These inter-loans between security and economy are symptomatic of the overall function of AS. In all its configurations, this form is designed to secure capital accumulation in an unstable socio-political environment. The current attempt to manage the crisis uses homeland security modalities because it is still managing the ongoing crisis of finance-led, neo-liberal, workfare-based accumulation. This state-form seems to be constantly fire-fighting, and capital accumulation seems to be in permanent turmoil. The suspicion that accumulation is not only facing permanent crisis, but *occurs through crisis*, is worth consideration. A crisis-based accumulation regime was, after all, established by the A&E sector through homeland security, and it may be a different crisis (in finance rather than in oil-prices; in the core capitalist countries rather than the Middle East) which drives accumulation today.

Much like AS, the story of the present accumulation regime begins with the 1970s economic crisis. That was a crisis of over-accumulation, where capital remained idly amassed because it could not find profitable investment outlets. The various tactics developed to ameliorate overaccumulation were the ones that eventually combined into the finance-led, neoliberal, workfarist strategies which were prominent on the eve of 9/11 as they are today. The first of these tactics was the forceful introduction of assets, social wealth, relations and practices in the capitalisation circuit, so that they become profitable sites for investment and exploitation. This process, termed by David Harvey 'accumulation by dispossession', has been materialising through the private appropriation of state-owned assets, of land and water, of genetic material, of art and culture, of communal science, etc. (Harvey 2003: 147–149). Financialisation – the expropriation of personal income (wages and pensions) by financial institutions through expenditures for health, education, housing, etc – is a particular strand of this strategy, which gradually became the primary source of capitalist profitability (Lapavitsas 2013).

While these forms of forceful expropriation are often imposed upon society in the context of, usually orchestrated, 'crises' (Klein 2007), a different tactic of accumulation by dispossession indicates that crisis itself can be the vehicle for accumulation. In this case, accumulation is achieved not by expropriating new pastures for capital, but from drastic devaluation of existing capital and labour through crisis. This is achieved through rounds of austerity imposed by national states and international organisations, and through controlled financial crises, each invariably resulting in rapid concentration of wealth (Demirović 2009: 56; Harvey 2003: 150; 2010: 246; Nitzan and Bichler 2013a). This is a tactic of expansive exploitation: wage and pension reduction, precarious employment, rise of unemployment, decline of welfare provision, erosion of legal protections and rights. The state budget becomes a lever for the concentration of wealth: the subaltern classes contribute disproportionately to state income, as dominant capital becomes increasingly exempt from taxation; and state investment is concentrated to areas which favour capital's dominance – not education or welfare, but subsidies, bailouts, police, military and a health system designed to serve the interests of big pharmaceuticals rather than the needs of the citizenry (Demirović 2009: 46).

This mode of accumulation not only depends on crisis, it threatens to impose it as a permanent socio-economic condition. There is no longer economic restoration after a crisis, due to their depth and the accelerating frequency with which they occur (Demirović 2009: 56; Irvin 2008: 138–140). Marketisation undermines long-term capitalisation, as it weakens the education system, thus undermining the reproduction of a skilled workforce. Private corporations do not invest in research and development projects which do not have immediate commercial potential, and thus production cannot be revolutionised and remains stuck in a quagmire of falling profitability and overaccumulation. Similarly, the reduction of state income results in the dereliction of material infrastructure (Demirović 2009: 50; 2012: 242).

Moreover, this arrangement is acutely prone to political crisis. The collusion of state and capital in AS (especially since phase II), and the decline of law as a mediation of state force, makes state authority increasingly hard to justify, and deprives the state from the capacity to plan for capitalist reproduction in the long term.

Similarly, this mode of accumulation is crisis-generating in economic terms. The boosting of capital profitability by supply-side economic policies, and the drastic devaluation of the work and life of the population, entail a decline in demand. This, in turn, hinders profitability and causes overaccumulation – it recasts the process of accumulation as a circle of crisis. The financial bubble which, when it burst, caused the current economic crisis, was a response to a sharp fall in profitability between 1995 and 2001. With labour already devalued, credit became the main means to resolving the problem of weakening demand, thus creating the phenomenon of fincialisation. This was combined with the arrival of petro-dollars and mass state subsidies in security industries, resulting in immediate danger of a severe overaccumulation crisis. To avoid, or at least postpone, such an outcome, speculation – the investment on the anticipated value of assets – became the main engine for accumulation. Speculation-driven accumulation is extremely volatile as any fall-off in expectation can generate a full-blown crisis (Brenner 2009: 30–73; Harvey 2010: 112–114; Norfield 2012: 115–122).

Thus, while the state and the financial system are the epicentre of the current crisis, its underlying cause is the excessive capitalist empowerment over labour. Credit-powered consumption and speculation-driven accumulation temporarily evade the crisis-generating problem of weak demand, while at the same time exasperate it by perpetuating the concentration of wealth (Harvey 2010: 118). The successive accumulation strategies since the 1970s – dispossession, fincialisation, crisis – are designed to advance accumulation without the subaltern classes sharing in the production of wealth (hence recovering economic growth in the face of a starving population). Accumulation becomes synonymous with concentration of wealth, and this means that the power of capital over society has reached its zenith. Yet, in doing so, capital has exhausted its very source of power – society – so that its further accumulation has nothing to offer but crisis (simply put: who will bailout the financial sector in its next crisis, now that there is no public money left?) (Nitzan and Bichler 2013a; 2013b).

In short, it seems that the AS form is organically developing to manage recurring capitalist crisis. Its configurations at each of its three phases largely correspond to the specific features of the crisis erupting each time. The contradiction here is that, in helping repress, ameliorate, and manage a crisis, it generates a new one. This is because AS is a form developed to guarantee the core element that generates crisis: the overpowering of the population by dominant capital.

Since both the crisis and the state-form pertain, ultimately, in the field of social dynamics, it is useful to examine homeland security from that perspective.

Social antagonism

Conceptualising the state as a condensation of the power-relations between social forces, a field of social struggle and a site for the development of strategies implies that changes in state-form are related to social antagonism: they are symptomatic of (attempted) shifts therein.

In these terms, the third phase of AS can be summarised as a form intended to fortify and advance the power of dominant capital over all other social classes through the management of crisis. Through the third phase of AS, capital operates a sustained attack on the economic and political interests of all subaltern classes, from the sub-proletariat to small and medium dependent capitalists. The middle class is at the forefront of this assault, as its members become proletarianised.

Since 9/11, the reconfiguration of AS goes hand in hand with the imposition of accumulation through crisis. The latter was installed by forceful state leadership on behalf of the A&E sectors and, through the homeland security project, led to a reconfigured state-form. The predominance of security logic (and coercive functions) under homeland security corresponded to the interests of the A&E sector, and locked them in place. It was also instrumental in galvanising support by the population, and by the capital fractions which lost out in the power bloc and were intimidated by the prospect of a crisis-prone accumulation mode.

From the point of view of the power bloc, the reluctant fractions were gradually won over by the prospect of accumulation through crisis. Crucial in this was their gradual re-admission (from 2003/2004) into the formal and informal fora of policy determination, and their benefiting from (generous, if arbitrary) state subsidies. Also important were the credentials presented by the homeland security state. The latter displayed the capacity to: (a) smoothly organise power bloc reconfigurations, through normal institutionalised channels; (b) secure continuing capitalisation by dispossessing the population and concentrating social wealth at the hands of dominant capital; and (c) defend the accumulation process from popular challenges, by installing a repressive mega-apparatus designed to monitor the entire population and crush antagonistic activity.

The capacity of the state-form to safeguard accumulation was displayed at the onset of the 2008 financial crisis. The sudden re-shuffling of the power bloc in the context of a threatened catastrophe occurred quickly and without frictions. Finance was reinstalled in the driving seat virtually overnight and without resistance. This points to an alignment of interests between finance and the A&E sector, whose long-term differential accumulation is secured by crisis, and whose petro- and armo-dollars had been introduced into the financial bloodstream. It also indicates that, in the context of accumulation through crisis, the overall 'ecologically dominant' sector is the one whose weakness and volatility cause the most problems to other sectors and to non-economic social systems (Jessop 2010).

The smooth transition in power bloc leadership showcases the adequacy of the state-form to accommodate such shifts. It was immediately reflected in a shift in state logic and an institutional rearrangement where the power centres of A&E gave way to the power centres of finance. The unhindered function of established formal and informal fora guarantees that shifts in power among capital fractions are reflected in state policy and institutional hierarchy and the king-maker role of the White House guarantees a rapid transition in times of crisis. In short, from the point of view of dominant capital, the present state-form is perfectly capable to reflect, accommodate and advance competing interests in an orderly manner, while still able to rapidly act in an emergency. Similarly, the shift in prominent state logic and mechanism (from the coercive to the economic) which accompanied the shift in power bloc leadership, occurred without a change of the state-form.

From the point of view of the population, homeland security and accumulation through crisis signify a drastic intensification of economic dispossession and political exclusion. The years of homeland security ascendance (2001–2008) saw drastic intensification of workfarism leading to further deprivation of the population and concentration of wealth at the hands of top capitalists. Generous tax cuts were awarded to the highest earners, while social benefits were further reduced and access thereto was further restricted. Wages remained stagnant between 2000 and 2005, and real wages made record drops. Household income decreased continuously for five years, causing a 35 per cent rise in household debt and record numbers of personal bankruptcies. During all this, the US economy was growing, and productivity, profits, stocks and CEOs' remuneration were rising. This registers as a leap in inequality. The ratio between the highest and the average salary jumped from the already stratospheric 121:1 in 1997, to 431:1 in 2005. At the end, the top 5 per cent of the US population owned more that the 'other' 95 per cent (Borosage and Peters 2006; Collins and Yeskel 2005: 17–21, 43; CRS 2004d; 2005j; Irvin 2008: 149, 164; Reid Mandell 2006). Moreover, the cost of the A&E sectors' wars, estimated at about US$2 trillion (Bilmes and Stiglitz 2006), combined with similar expenditure in buying the financial sector's debts, produced vast public debt and crippled future public expenditure.

Crucial for organising and sustaining this prolonged, intense attack on the material interests of the population, is the political attack against it. The latter is analytically and temporarily prior to the former: without political exclusion, dispossession is impossible. It is effectuated through the reconfiguration of the law- and state-forms.

The political exclusion of the population is at the heart of homeland security. The representations in political discourse, the advance of government by experts in intelligence-led governance, and the organisation of citizenship through enlistment projects, allocate the population a perfectly passive political role. The concentration of power in the hands of the federal Executive at the expense of the other federal branches and sub-national governments, and the legal acknowledgement, and protection, of the parallel networks of power, institutionalise the exclusion of the population from influencing politics. This is encapsulated in the legal definition of terrorism, and accompanied by repression for those who defy the terms of their exclusion. To this purpose, the law provides augmented, sometimes limitless, coercive powers to the state, and a vast police apparatus, controlled by the political centre, is engaged in monitoring all social activity with a view to disrupting popular political organisation and action.

In short, in the third phase of AS, *the state assumes the monopoly of legitimate politics*. Only state (or state-sanctioned) authorities can carry out legitimate political actions (Paye 2007: 251). Given that AS is a state-form charged with managing accumulation crises while exasperating their underlying cause, homeland security is nothing but *the pre-emptive shielding of capitalist rule from anticipated popular struggles against political exclusion and economic dispossession*.

The management of the present economic crisis indicates that the state-form is, thus far, fit for purpose. It is successful in making the crisis profitable for dominant capital, while further intensifying dispossession and wealth concentration. Thus, the crisis-ridden financial sector achieved record profits in 2009–2010 and, through a new wave of mergers, it seems to have come out of the crisis strengthened (Demirović 2012: 247). This was achieved largely by the absorption of corporate (especially financial) losses into public debt. The soaring public debt meant a radical new round of dispossession: rise in unemployment, precariousness, poverty, collapse of living standards, deterioration of working relations, deregulation of the labour market, stagnation and cuts in wages, pensions and welfare expenditure (Demirović 2009: 53–55).

At the same time, the state is doing next to nothing to restrict or regulate the speculative practices which triggered the crisis (Norfield 2012: 127). This may be a pointer to a new capitalist dilemma. Dominant capital realises the extreme volatility of speculation-led accumulation, but resists restrictions, as they would lead to overaccumulation. It marches on towards the next crisis, hoping that the state will again suppress popular resistance and guarantee a profitable outcome.

As the state shutters all pretence to represent society as a whole, and openly colludes with capital in its brutal attack against the population, the most surprising development is the meekness of popular resistance. The latter is low in numbers and intensity, and defensive in its demands, which are mainly expressed in a neoliberal conceptual and discursive framework (Petras 2013). This is possibly the most important, lasting contribution of homeland security: it provides the state the means to destroy social opposition, not only by a mega-machine of repression, but by devaluating social antagonism through conceptual and legal association with terrorism. It has thus managed to close the horizon of what is socially desirable and feasible, and reduce politics into a perpetual rehashing of the present situation.

To sum up a rather long conclusion: the turn from the 1999–2001 crisis to homeland security and, from there, to the management of the current economic crisis, points to a mode of accumulation which depends on crisis. It necessitates a state-form (including a law-form) which can stave off the threatening impact of social antagonism. Homeland security, no longer a predominant state project, but incorporated into the state- and law-forms, *is the support mechanism of neoliberal social organisation and accumulation*. It has reshaped the state and law, endowing them with the ultimate solution to social antagonism: a legal, ideological and military mechanism designed for open warfare against social opposition, actual and anticipated.

Bibliography

Abel, Richard. 1989. *American Lawyers*. Oxford: Oxford University Press.
Abrahms, Max. 2012. 'The Political Effectiveness of Terrorism Revisited'. *Comparative Political Studies* 45 (3): 366–393.
Ackerman, Bruce. 2004. 'The Emergency Constitution?'. *Yale Law Journal* 113: 1029–1091.
Ackerman, Bruce. 2006. *Before the Next Attack*. New Haven: Yale University Press.
ACLU. 2001. 'Upsetting Checks and Balances', 1 November.
ACLU. 2002a. 'Civil Liberties After 9/11', 20 September.
ACLU. 2002b. 'Section 215 FAQ', 24 October.
ACLU. 2003a. 'Bigger Monster, Weaker Chains: the Growth of American Surveillance Society', 15 January.
ACLU. 2003b. 'Civil Liberties Protest Resolutions Reach Milestone; ACLU Hails 50th City to Resist Intrusive Federal Actions', 28 February.
ACLU. 2003c. 'How to Pass a Community Resolution', 20 May.
ACLU. 2003d. 'Freedom Under Fire: Dissent in Post-9/11 America', May.
ACLU. 2003e. 'Seeking Truth from Justice', July.
ACLU. 2003f. 'Independence Day 2003', July.
ACLU. 2003g. 'Draft Resolution', 14 July.
ACLU. 2003h. 'Freedom Under Fire: Dissent in post-9/11 America', 25 August.
ACLU. 2003i. 'Unpatriotic Acts: the FBI's Power to Rifle through your Records and Personal Belongings Without Telling you', 30 July.
ACLU. 2003j. 'Pro-Civil Liberties Local Government Resolutions Now Top 200, Milestone Vote Comes on Eve of PATRIOT Act Second Anniversary', 24 October.
ACLU. 2004a. 'Largest City to date Passes Community Resolution; Los Angeles Rejects Bush's Call to Continue Civil Liberties Curtailment', 21 January.
ACLU. 2004b. 'Largest City in America Passes Pro-Civil Liberties Resolution; New York City Becomes 250th to Join Call to Keep America Safe and Free', 4 February.
ACLU. 2004c. 'ACLU Welcomes Maine Statewide Patriot Act Resolution; Becomes Fourth State to Vote for Civil Liberties'. 23 March.
ACLU. 2004d. 'Pittsburgh City Council Rebuffs Bush Patriot Act Misinformation Tour; Pro-Civil Liberties Resolutions Now Cover 50 Million Americans', 26 April.
ACLU. 2005a. 'ACLU Applauds Colorado's Call to be Safe and Free; Nationwide Patriot Act Resolution Movement Still Gaining Momentum', 17 May.
ACLU. 2005b. 'Local Communities Join ACLU to Urge Patriot Act Reform in New Phase of National Campaign', 17 June.
ACLU. 2009. 'Reclaiming Patriotism – a Call to Reconsider the Patriot Act', March.

ACLU. 2012a. 'Indefinite Detention, Endless Worldwide War and the 12 National Defense Authorisation Act', 22 February.
ACLU. 2012b. 'Ready to Occupy? What you Need to Know About H.R. 347, the "Criminalizing Protest" Law', 26 April.
ACLU. 2012c. 'Spying on First Amendment Activity – State by State', 19 December.
ACLU/People for the American Way. Unknown Date. 'Amicus Brief of the ACLU of Florida and People For the American Way Foundation, in Support of Defendants Greenpeace's Motion for Discovery on Claim Selective Prosecution'.
ACLU-New York. 2003. 'Arresting Protest', 28 April.
Agamben, Giorgio. 1998. *Homo Sacer: Sovereign Power and Bare Life*. Stanford: Stanford University Press.
Agamben, Giorgio. 2005. *State of Exception*. Chicago: University of Chicago Press.
Aglietta, Michel. 2000. *A History of Capital Regulation: the US Experience*. London: Verso.
ALA. 1999. 'Libraries: an American Value', 3 February.
ALA. 2002. 'Resolution Reaffirming the Principles of Intellectual Freedom in the Aftermath of Terrorist Attacks', 23 January.
ALA. 2003. 'Restrictions on Access to Government Information Report', 9 June.
Allen, Charles. 2011. 'Intelligence Community Contractors: Are We Striking the Right Balance?', Statement to the *Senate Subcommittee on Oversight of Government Management, the Federal Workforce, and the District of Columbia*, 20 September.
Allen, Francis A. 1996. *The Habits of Legality: Criminal Justice and the Rule of Law*. Oxford: Oxford University Press.
Allen, Thad. 2012. 'Testimony' before the Subcommittee on *Oversight, Investigations and Management; Committee on Homeland Security*. House of Representatives, 22 March.
Althouse, Ann. 2008. The Vigour of the Anti-Commandeering Doctrine in Times of Terror. In: S. Herman and P. Finkelman (eds) *Terrorism, Government, and Law*. Westport: Praeger.
Amey, Scott. 2011. 'Intelligence Community Contractors: Are We Striking the Right Balance?'. Testimony before the *Senate Subcommittee on Oversight of Government Management, the Federal Workforce, and the District of Columbia*, 20 September.
Amstutz, Marc, Abegg, Andreas and Karavas, Vaios. 2007. 'Civil Society Constitutionalism: the Power of Contract Law'. *Indiana Journal of Global Legal Studies* 14 (2): 235–258.
Anderson, Nate. 2007. 'The Demise of ADVISE; DHS Data Mine Boarded Up'. Ars Technica, 6 September. http://arstechnica.com/security/2007/09/the-demise-of-advise-dhs-data-mine-boarded-up/; last accessed, 13 April 2012.
Andrejevic, Mark. 2006. 'Interactive (In)security'. *Cultural Studies* 20 (4–5): 441–458.
Anonymous. 2002. 'The Law of the Fist: New York Police Vow to Crash Protesters Against the World Economic Forum'. *Democracy Now*, 25 January.
Anonymous. 2003. 'The Persecution of Sherman Austin'. *Revolutionary Worker*, 26 October.
Arendt, Hannah. 1973. *The Origins of Totalitarianism*. San Diego: Harcourt Brace & Co.
Aristotle. 1962. *Politics*. R. Robinson (ed.) Oxford: Clarendon.
Aristotle. 1999. *Nicomachean Ethics*. T. Irwin (trans) Indianapolis: Hackett.
Arkin, William. 2006. 'The Department of Homeland Security's Unlimited Priorities'. *Washington Post*, 13 July.
Aronowitz, Stanley. 2002. Global Shift – A New Capitalist State? In: S. Aronowitz and P. Bratsis (eds) *Paradigm Lost*. Minneapolis: University of Minnesota Press.
Asgary, Ali. 2009. 'Review of Homeland Security and Private Sector Business: Corporations Role in Critical Infrastructure Protection'. *Journal of Homeland Security and Emergency Management* 6 (1): art. 61.

Associated Press. 2005. 'FBI Chief Won't Mandate Terror Expertise'. *New York Times*, 21 June.
Azulay, Jessica. 2003. 'Resolutions as Resistance'. *Z Magazine*, March.
Baker, Stewart. 2012. 'Department of Homeland Security: an Assessment of the Department and a Roadmap for its Future'. Hearing before the *House of Representatives Committee on Homeland Security*, 20 September.
Balbus, Isaac. 1977. 'The Commodity Form and the Legal Form'. *Law and Society Review* 2 (3): 571–578.
Ball, Kirstie et al. 2010. Surveillance Politics and Practices of Democratic Governance. In: K. Haggerty and M. Samatas (eds) *Surveillance and Democracy*. Abingdon: Routledge.
Barger, Harold. 1984. *The Impossible Presidency: Illusions and Realities of Executive Power*. Illinois: Scott, Foresman.
Barr, Stephen. 2005a. 'Homeland Security Employees Voice Uncertainty, Scepticism about Performance-based Pay'. *Washington Post*, 10 May.
Barr, Stephen. 2005b. 'All Sides Wrestle with Homeland Security's New Labour Relations System'. *Washington Post*, 10 June.
Barrow, Clyde W. 2005. 'The Return of the State: Globalisation, State Theory and the New Imperialism'. *New Political Science* 27 (2): 123–145.
Barthes, Roland. 1982. 'Writing Degree Zero'. In: S. Sontag (ed.) *A Barthes Reader*. London: Jonathan Cape.
Bates, David. 2007. 'Constitutional Violence'. *Journal of Law and Society* 34 (1): 14–30.
Baxi, Upendra. 2006. *The Future of Human Rights*. Oxford: Oxford University Press.
BBC. 2004. 'FBI Returns Seized News Servers', 14 October. http://news.bbc.co.uk/1/hi/technology/3742284.stm; last accessed, 22 June 2013.
Belandis, Dimitris. 2004. *In Search of the Internal Enemy*. Athens: Proskinio [in Greek].
Benjamin, George. 2012. 'The National Preparedness Report: Assessing the State of Preparedness'. Testimony, *House Committee on Homeland Security*, 6 June.
Beresford, Annette. 2004. 'Homeland Security as an American Ideology: Implications for US Policy and Action'. *Journal of Homeland Security and Emergency Management* 1 (3): art. 301.
Berger, Klaus Peter. 1999. *The Creeping Codification of the Lex Mercatoria*. The Hague: Kluwer Law International.
Bertolo, Amedeo. 1999. 'Democracy and Beyond'. *Democracy and Nature* 5 (2): 311–324.
Best, Michael H. 2000. Silicon Valley and the Resurgence of Route 128: Systems Integration and Regional Innovation. In: J.H. Dunning (ed.) *Regions, Globalisation and the Knowledge Based Economy*. Oxford: Oxford University Press.
Bhandar, Davina. 2004. 'Renormalising Citizenship and Life in Fortress North America'. *Citizenship Studies* 8 (3): 261–278.
Bilmes, Linda and Stiglitz, Joseph. 2006. 'The Economic Costs of the Iraq War: an Appraisal Three Years After the Beginning of the Conflict'. Working Paper 12054, *National Bureau of Economic Research*. Cambridge, MA.
Blair, Dennis and Leiter, Michael. 2010: 'Intelligence Reform: the Lessons and Implications of the Christmas Day Attack'. Statement for the Record for the *US Senate Homeland Security and Governmental Affairs Committee*, 20 January.
Blair, Dennis. 2011. 'Ten Years After 9/11: is Intelligence Reform Working?' Opening Statement before the *US Senate Homeland Security and Governmental Affairs Committee*, 19 May.
Block, Fred. 1987. *Revising State Theory*. Philadelphia: Temple University Press.
Boggs, Carl. 2001. 'Social Capital and Political Fantasy: Robert Putnam's Bowling Alone'. *Theory and Society* 30: 281–297.

Bonefeld, Werner. 2006. 'Democracy and Dictatorship: Means and Ends of State'. *Critique* 34 (3): 237–252.
Borosage, Robert and Peters, Troy. 2006. 'State of the People's Union'. *Tom Paine*, 26 January.
Borum, Randy and Tilby, Chuck. 2005. 'Anarchist Direct Actions: a Challenge for Law Enforcement'. *Studies in Conflict and Terrorism* 28: 201–223.
Boukalas, Christos. 2008. 'Counterterrorism Legislation and the US State Form'. *Radical Philosophy* 151: 31–41.
Boukalas, Christos. 2012. 'Government by Experts: Counterterrorism Intelligence and Democratic Retreat'. *Critical Studies on Terrorism* 5 (2): 277–296.
Boukalas, Christos. 2013. 'Politics as Legal Action/Lawyers as Political Actors: Towards a Reconceptualisation of Cause Lawyering'. *Social and Legal Studies* 22 (3): 395–420.
Bourdieu, Pierre. 1987. 'The Force of Law: Toward a Sociology of the Juridical Field'. *The Hastings Law School Journal* 38: 805–853.
Brand, Ulrich and Heigl, Miriam. 2011. 'Inside' and 'Outside': the State, Movements, and 'Radical Transformation' in the Work of Nicos Poulantzas. In: A. Gallas et al. (eds) *Reading Poulantzas*. Pontypool: Merlin Press.
Bratich, Jack. 2006. 'Public Secrecy and Immanent Security'. *Cultural Studies* 20 (4–5): 493–511.
Bratsis, Peter. 2003. Over, Under, Sideways, Down. Globalisation, Spatial Metaphors, and the Question of State Power. In: S. Aronowitz and H. Gautney (eds) *Implicating Empire*. New York: Basic Books.
Bratsis, Peter. 2007. *Everyday Life and the State*. London: Paradigm.
Brecher, Jeremy. 2003. Globalisation Today. In: S. Aronowitz and H. Gautney (eds) *Implicating Empire*. New York: Basic Books.
Brenner, Robert. 2009. What is Good for Goldman Sachs is Good for America – The Origins of the Current Crisis. Prologue to the Spanish translation of R. Brenner, *Economic of Global Turbulence*. London: Verso, 2006; Spanish translation, Madrid: Akal, 2009.
Brinkley, Alan. 2003. 'A Familiar Story: Lessons from Past Assaults on Freedoms'. In: R.C. Leone and G. Anrig Jr (eds) *War on Our Freedoms*. New York: Century Foundation.
Brooks, Ronald. 2011. 'Ten Years After 9/11: a Status Report on Information Sharing'. Statement for the Record, *Senate Committee on Homeland Security and Governmental Affairs*, 12 October.
Brown, David and Gray, Janice. 2007. 'Devils and Dust': Extending the 'Uncivil Politics of Law and Order' to the War on Terror. In: J. Hocking and C. Lewis (eds) *Counterterrorism and the Post-Democratic State*. Cheltenham: Edward Elgar.
Brown, Wendy. 2005. Neoliberalism and the End of Liberal Democracy. In: *idem, Edgework: Critical Essays on Knowledge and Politics*. Princeton: Princeton University Press.
Brown, Wendy. 2006. 'American Nightmare: Neoliberalism, Neoconservatism, and De-democratisation'. *Political Theory* 30: 690–714.
Brown, Wendy. 2012. 'Sacrificial Citizenship: Neoliberal Austerity Politics'. Roundtable discussion. http://globalization.gc.cuny.edu/events/sacrificial-citizenship-neoliberal-austerity-politics/; last accessed, 3 May 2012.
Brzezinski, Mathew. 2004. 'Red Alert'. *Mother Jones*, September/October.
Buckel, Sonja. 2011. The Juridical Condensation of Relations of Forces: Nicos Poulantzas and Law. In: A. Gallas et al. (eds) *Reading Poulantzas*. Pontypool: Merlin Press.
Bunyan, Tony. 2004. 'Was the Seizure of Indymedia's Servers in London Unlawful or Did the UK Government Collude?'. *Statewatch*, October. http://database.statewatch.org/article.asp?aid=26091; last accessed, 22 June 2013.

Burger, Timothy. 2005. 'Sidelining the CIA'. *Times Magazine*, 5 June.
Calliess, Gralf-Peter. 2007. 'The Making of Transnational Contract Law'. *Indiana Journal of Global Legal Studies* 14 (2): 469–483.
Carbonneau, Thomas. 1990. The Remaking of Arbitration: Design and Destiny. In: *idem* (ed.) *Lex Mercatoria and Arbitration*. Dobbs Ferry: Transnational Juris.
Cassese, Sabino. 1998. 'Administrative Law Without the State? The Challenge of Global Regulation'. *International Law and Politics* 37: 663–694.
Castoriadis, Cornelius. 1957. On the Content of Socialism. Reprinted in D.A. Curtis (ed.) *The Castoriadis Reader*. Oxford: Blackwell, 1997.
Castoriadis, Cornelius. 1965. Autonomy and Alienation. Reprinted in D.A. Curtis (ed.) *The Castoriadis Reader*. Oxford: Blackwell, 1997.
Castoriadis, Cornelius. 1980. From Ecology to Autonomy. Reprinted in D.A. Curtis (ed.) *The Castoriadis Reader*. Oxford: Blackwell, 1997.
Castoriadis, Cornelius. 1983a. The Logic of Magmas and the Question of Autonomy. Reprinted in D.A. Curtis (ed.) *The Castoriadis Reader*. Oxford: Blackwell, 1997.
Castoriadis, Cornelius. 1983b. The Greek Polis and the Creation of Democracy. Reprinted in D.A. Curtis (ed.) *The Castoriadis Reader*. Oxford: Blackwell, 1997.
Castoriadis, Cornelius. 1987. The Crisis of Culture and the State. Reprinted in D.A. Curtis (ed.) *Philosophy, Politics, Autonomy*, Oxford: Oxford University Press, 1997.
Castoriadis, Cornelius. 1988a. The End of Philosophy? Reprinted in D.A. Curtis (ed.) *Philosophy, Politics, Autonomy*. Oxford: Oxford University Press, 1997.
Castoriadis, Cornelius. 1988b. Power, Politics, Autonomy. Reprinted in D.A. Curtis (ed.) *Philosophy, Politics, Autonomy*. Oxford: Oxford University Press, 1997.
Castoriadis, Cornelius. 1989c. Done and to Be Done. Reprinted in D.A. Curtis (ed.) *The Castoriadis Reader*. Oxford: Blackwell, 1997.
Castoriadis, Cornelius. 1990a. The Retreat of Autonomy: Postmodernism as Generalised Conformism. Reprinted in D.A. Curtis (ed.) *The World in Fragments*. Stanford: Stanford University Press, 1997.
Castoriadis, Cornelius. 1990b. What Democracy? Reprinted in *idem*, *Figures of the Thinkable*, Stanford: Stanford University Press, 2007.
Castoriadis, Cornelius. 1994. Radical Imagination and the Social Instituting Imaginary. Reprinted in D.A. Curtis (ed.) *The Castoriadis Reader*. Oxford: Blackwell 1997.
Castoriadis, Cornelius. 2002. *On Plato's Statesman*. Stanford: Stanford University Press.
Castoriadis, Cornelius. 2008. *The Greek Particularity Vol. 2*. Athens: Kritiki [in Greek].
Castoriadis, Cornelius. 2012. *The Possibility of an Autonomous Society*. Athens: Stasei Ekpiptontes [in Greek].
Caudle, Sharon. 2009. 'National Security Strategies: Security from What, for Whom, and by What Means'. *Journal of Homeland Security and Emergency Management* 6 (1): art. 22.
Caudle, Sharon. 2011. 'Centralisation and Decentralisation of Policy: the National Interest of Homeland Security'. *Journal of Homeland Security and Emergency Management* 8 (1): art. 56.
Center for Democracy and Technology. 2003. 'Setting the Record Straight: an Analysis of the Justice Department's Patriot website', 27 October.
Chang, Nancy. 2002. *Silencing Political Dissent*. New York: Open Media.
Charteris-Black, Jonathan. 2005. *Politicians and Rhetoric: the Persuasive Power of Metaphor*. Basingstoke: Palgrave-Macmillan.
Chesnais, Francois. 2001. Facing Two Enemies. In: R. Herera (ed.) *L'Empire en Guerre*. Paris: Les Temps des Cherices [in French].
Chesney, Robert. 2007. 'Federal Prosecution of Terrorism-related Offenses'. *Lewis & Clarke Law Review* 11 (4): 851–901.

Chossudovsky, Michael. 2005. 'Emergency Preparedness against the Universal Adversary'. *Global Research*, 7 June.
Chowkwanyun, Marlin. 2003. 'An Interview with Sherman Austin'. *Counterpunch*, 16 August.
Ciccariello-Maher, George. 2011. 'The Coming War on the Occupy Movement: Repression Breeds Resistance', 29 November. http://www.peopleofcolororganize.com/activism/coming-war-occupy-movement-repression-breeds-resistance/; last accessed, 22 June 2013.
Cillufo, Frank. 2012. 'The Department of Homeland Security: an Assessment of the Department and a Roadmap for its Future'. Statement before the *House of Representatives Committee on Homeland Security*, 20 September.
Citizen Corps. 2004. 'Citizen Corps Celebrates Success at Two-Year Anniversary'. Press Release, 23 January. http://www.ok.gov/homeland/News/2004/January_2004/CITIZEN_CORPS_CELEBRATES_SUCCESS_AT_TWO_YEAR_ANNIVERSARY.html; last accessed, 4 June 2012.
Citizen Corps/Fairfax, Virginia. Unknown Date. http://www.fairfaxcountycitizencorps.org and links; last accessed, 6 June 2011.
Citizen Corps/Harris, Texas. Unknown Date. http://www.harriscountycitizencorps.com and links; last accessed, 6 June 2011.
Citizen Corps/Los Angeles, California. Unknown Date. http://www.cert-la.com and links; last accessed, 4 June 2011.
Citizen Corps/Miami-Dade, Florida. Unknown Date. http://www.miamidade.gov/homeland and links; last accessed, 6 June 2011.
Citizen Corps/Montgomery, Maryland. Unknown Date. http://www.montgomerycountymd.gov/mcgtmpl.asp?url=/Content/Volunteer/VO.asp and links; last accessed, 4 June 2011.
Citizen Corps/New York City. Unknown Date. http://www.nyc.gov/html/programmes/citizencorps.html and links; last accessed, 4 June 2011.
Citizen Corps/Orange, Florida. Unknown Date. http://www.ocoem.com/citizen_corps.ht and links; last accessed, 6 June 2011.
Clayton, Mark. 2006. 'US Plans Massive Data Sweep'. *The Christian Science Monitor*, 9 February.
CLS Center on Law and Security. 2010. *Terrorist Trial Report Card: September 11 2001 – September 11 2010*. K.J. Greenberg (ed.) New York University School of Law.
CLS. 2011. *Terrorist Trial Report Card: September 11 2001 – September 11 2011*. K.J. Greenberg (ed.) New York University School of Law.
Clunan, Anne. 2006. 'The Fight Against Terrorist Financing'. *Political Science Quarterly* 121 (4): 569–596.
Clune, William. 2011. 'Legal Disintegration and a Theory of the State'. *German Law Journal* 12 (1): 186–205.
Cmar, Thomas. 2002. 'Office of Homeland Security'. *Harvard Journal on Legislation* 39 (2): 455–474.
Cobain, Ian. 2013. 'Obama's Secret Kill List – the Disposition Matrix'. *The Guardian*, 14 July.
Cohen, Stanley. 1985. *Visions of Social Control*. Cambridge: Polity Press.
Colangelo, Philip. Unknown Date. 'The Secret FISA Court: Rubber-Stamping on Rights'. *Covert Action Quarterly*. http://rense.com/general5/fisacourt.htm; last accessed, 7 May 2011.
Colatrella, Steven. 2011. 'Nothing Exceptional: Against Agamben'. *Journal for Critical Education Policy Studies* 9 (1): 97–125.
Cole, David. 2003. *Enemy Aliens: Double Standards and Constitutional Freedoms in the War on Terrorism*. New York: New Press.

Cole, David and Dempsey, James. 2002. *Terrorism and the Constitution*. New York: New Press.
Cole, David and Lederman, Marty. 2006. 'The NSA Surveillance Program'. *Indiana Law Journal* 81: 1355–1425.
Collins, Chuck and Yeskel, Felice. 2005. *Economic Apartheid in America*. New York: New Press.
Colombo, Eduardo. 2011. *Changing Paradigm: Anarchism, Social Obligation, and the Duty of Obedience*. Athens: Stasei Ekpiptontes [in Greek] (Originally: 'Anarchisme, Obligation Sociale et Devoir d'Obéissance'. *Refractions* 2, Spring 1998).
Committee Against Political Repression. 2013. 'Never Surrender: Kerry Cunneen Subpoenaed to the NW Grand Jury', 9 January. http://nopoliticalrepression.wordpress.com/2013/01/09/never-surrender-kerry-cunneen-subpoenaed-to-the-nw-grand-jury/; last accessed, 22 June 2013.
Contogeorgis, George. 1985. *Political System and Politics*. Athens: Polytypo [in Greek].
Contogeorgis, George. 2007. *Democracy as Freedom*. Athens: Patakis [in Greek].
Contogeorgis, George. 2011. *Politics as a Phenomenon*. http://contogeorgis.blogspot.com/2011/02/blog-post_3629.html; last accessed, 14 November 2011.
Cox, Michael. 2004. The Bush Doctrine and the Lessons from History. In: D. Held and M. Koening-Archibugi (eds) *American Power in the 21st Century*. Cambridge: Polity Press.
Croft, Stuart. 2006. *Culture, Crisis, and America's War on Terror*. Cambridge: Cambridge University Press.
Cronin, Thomas. 1977. The Presidency and its Paradoxes. In: T. Cronin and R. Tugwell (eds) *The Presidency Reappraised*. New York: Praeger.
Crouch, Colin. 2004. *Post-Democracy*. Cambridge: Polity Press.
CRS. 2001. 'Terrorism: Section by Section Analysis of the USA PATRIOT Act'. RL31200. Charles Doyle, 10 December.
CRS. 2004a. 'FBI Intelligence Reform Since September 11 2001: Issues and Options for Congress'. RL32336. Alfred Cumming and Todd Masse, 6 April.
CRS. 2004b. 'Risk Management and Critical Infrastructure Protection: Assessing, Integrating and Managing Threats, Vulnerabilities and Consequences'. RL32561. John Moteff, 2 September.
CRS. 2004c. 'Critical Infrastructure and Key Assets: Definition and Identification'. RL32631. John Moteff and Paul Parfomak, 1 October.
CRS. 2004d. 'Welfare Reform: An Issue Overview'. IB93034. Vee Burke, 28 October.
CRS. 2004e. 'Intelligence Issues for Congress'. IB10012. Richard Best Jr, 9 December.
CRS. 2004f. 'Data Mining – an Overview'. RL31798. Jeffrey Seifert, 16 December.
CRS. 2005a. 'Information Sharing for Homeland Security: A Brief Overview'. RL32597. Harold Relyea, 10 January.
CRS. 2005b. 'Homeland Security: Final Regulations on Classification, Pay and Performance Management Compared with Current Law'. RL32261. Barbara Schwemle, 2 February.
CRS. 2005c. 'Homeland Security: Data on Employees and Unions Affected'. RS21268. Gail McCallion, 9 February.
CRS. 2005d. 'Homeland Security Advisory System: Possible Issues for Congressional Oversight'. RL32023. Shawn Reece, 11 January.
CRS. 2005e. 'The National Counterterrorism Centre: Implementation Challenges and Issues for Congress'. RL32816. Todd Masse, 24 March.
CRS. 2005f. 'Science and Technology Policy: Issues for the 109th Congress'. RL32837. Frank Gottron, 28 March.
CRS. 2005g. 'The Interagency Security Committee and Security Standards for Federal Buildings'. RS22121. Stephanie Smith, 22 April.

CRS. 2005h. 'Homeland Security Department: FY2006 Appropriations'. RL32863. Jennifer Lake and Blas Nuñez-Neto, 29 June.
CRS. 2005i. 'State and Local Homeland Security: Unresolved Issues for the 109th Congress'. RL32941. Shawn Reece, 9 June.
CRS. 2005j. 'Welfare Reauthorisation: an Overview of the Issues'. IB10140. Gene Falk, Melinda Gish and Carmen Solomon-Fears, 1 July.
CRS. 2006. 'Department of Homeland Security Grants to State and Local Governments: FY2003 to 2006'. RL33770. Steven Maguire and Shawn Reese, 22 December.
CRS. 2009a. 'The Emergency Economic Stabilisation Act and Recent Financial Turmoil: Issues and Analysis'. RL34730. Baird Webel and Edward V. Murphy, 23 January.
CRS. 2009b. 'Troubled Asset Relief Programme: Legislation and Treasury Implementation'. RL34730. Baird Webel and Edward V. Murphy, 24 March.
CRS. 2010. 'The Military Commissions Act of 2009: Overview and Legal Issues'. R41163. Jennifer K. Elsea, 6 April.
CRS. 2011a. 'Amendments to the Foreign Intelligence Surveillance Act (FISA) Extended Until June 1 2015'. R40138. Edward C. Liu, 16 June.
CRS. 2011b. 'Critical Infrastructures: Background, Policy, and Implementation'. RL30153. John Moteff, 11 July.
CRS. 2011c. 'Intelligence Issues for Congress'. RL 33539. Richard Best, 28 December.
CRS. 2012a. 'The National Defense Authorisation Act for FY2012: Detainee Matters'. R42143. Jennifer K. Elsea and John Garcia, 11 December.
CRS. 2012b. 'Troubled Asset Relief Program (TARP): Implementation and Status'. R41427. Baird Webel, 18 May.
Crumpacker, Tom. 2003. 'Anarchists on the Beach-Some Impressions from Miami'. *Counterpunch*, 26 November.
Cutler, A. Claire. 1995. 'Global Capitalism and Liberal Myths: Dispute Settlement in Private International Trade Law'. *Millennium: Journal of International Studies* 24: 384.
Cutler, A. Claire. 2003. *Private Power and Global Authority –Transnational Merchant Law in the Global Political Economy*. Cambridge: Cambridge University Press.
Dalmer, Bert. 2005. 'List of Assets has Some Surprises'. *The Des Moines Register*, 5 June.
Daniels, Stephen and Martin, Joanne. 2009. 'Legal Services for the Poor: Access, Self-interest, and Pro Bono'. *American Bar Foundation Research Paper* Series 09-02.
Davies, Jonathan. 2011. *Challenging Governance Theory*. Bristol: Policy Press.
Day, Richard. 2005. *Gramsci is Dead. Anarchist Currents in the Newest Social Movements*. London: Pluto.
De Young, Karen. 2006. 'A Fight Against Terrorism-and Disorganisation'. *Washington Post*, 9 August.
Debord, Guy. 1967. *La Societé du Spectacle*. Paris: Buchet-Chastel.
Della Porta, Donatella. 2006. *The Global Justice Movement: Cross-national and Transnational Perspectives*. New York: Paradigm.
Demirović, Alex. 2009. 'Postneoliberalism and Post-Fordism – Is there a New Period in the Capitalist mode of Production?'. *Development Dialogue*, January: 45–58.
Demirović, Alex. 2011. Rule of the People? Democracy and the Capitalist State in the Work of Nicos Poulantzas. In: A. Gallas et al. (eds) *Reading Poulantzas*. Pontypool: Merlin Press.
Demirović, Alex. 2012. The Inter-nationalisation of the State and the Crisis of Financial Capitalism. In: C. Golemis and I. Oikonomou (eds) *Poulantzas Today*. Athens: Nissos [in Greek].

Democratic Members of the House Select Committee on Homeland Security. 2004. 'America at Risk. A Homeland Security Report Card. Initial Findings', January.

Dezalay, Yves and Garth, Bryant G. 1996. *Dealing in Virtue: International Commercial Arbitration and the Construction of a Transnational Legal Order*. Chicago: University of Chicago Press.

Dickinson, Laura. 2012. 'Outsourcing Covert Activities'. *Journal of National Security Law and Policy* 5: 521–537.

DiGrazia, Christine. 2003. 'Memo from Derby: Just in Case, Because it Can Happen Here'. *New York Times*, 30 March.

Dillon, Michael and Lobo-Guerrero, Luis. 2008. 'Biopolitics of Security in the 21st Century: an Introduction'. *Review of International Studies* 34 (2): 265–292.

Dillon, Michael and Reid, Julian. 2001. 'Global Liberal Governance: Biopolitics, Security, and War'. *Millennium* 30 (1): 41–66.

Dillon, Michael and Reid, Julian. 2009. *The Liberal Way of War – Killing to Make Life Live*. Abingdon: Routledge.

DiMatteo, Larry A. 2010. 'Strategic Contracting: Contract Law as a Source of Competitive Advantage'. *American Business Law Journal* 47 (4): 727–794.

Dobner, Petra. 2010. More Law, Less Democracy? Democracy and Transnational Constitutionalism. In: P. Dobner and M. Loughlin (eds) *The Twilight of Constitutionalism?* Oxford: Oxford University Press.

Donohue, Laura K. 2008. *The Cost of Counterterrorism*. Cambridge: Cambridge University Press.

Donohue, Laura K. 2009. 'The Perilous Dialogue'. *California Law Review* 97: 357–392.

Donohue, Laura. 2012. 'The Limits of National Security'. Georgetown Public Law and Legal Theory Research Paper No. 12-118.

Douzinas, Costas. 2013. 'The Paradoxes of Human Rights'. *Constellations* 20 (1): 51–67.

Drury, Shadia. 1988. *The Political Ideas of Leo Strauss*. New York: St Martin's Press.

Dunmire, Patricia. 2005. 'Pre-empting the Future: Rhetoric and Ideology of the Future in Political Discourse'. *Discourse and Society* 16 (4): 481–513.

Easton, David and Hess, Robert. 1962. 'The Child's Political World'. *Midwest Journal of Political Science* 6 (4): 229–246.

Easton, David and Hess, Robert. 1969. *Children in the Political System*. New York: McGraw-Hill.

EFF. 2001. 'Analysis of the Provisions of the USA PATRIOT Act that Relate to Online Activities', 31 October. http://w2.eff.org/Privacy/Surveillance/Terrorism/20011031_eff_usa_patriot_analysis.php; last accessed, 1 March 2010.

EFF. 2004. 'Indymedia Server Seizures', October. https://www.eff.org/Censorship/Indymedia/; last accessed, 20 May 2011.

EFF. 2005. 'Indymedia Server Takedown', August 2005. https://www.eff.org/cases/indymedia-server-takedown; last accessed, 20 May 2011.

Eggen, Dan and Pincus, Walter. 2005. 'Report: FBI Analyst Jobs Remain Vacant'. *Washington Post*, 5 May.

Ehrlich, Eugen. 1936. *Fundamental Principles of the Sociology of Law*. Cambridge, MA: Harvard University Press.

Ellman, Jesse, Herman, Priscilla and Sanders, Gregory. 2012. 'US Department of Homeland Security Contract Spending and the Supporting Industrial Base, 2004–2011'. Washington DC: Centre for Strategic and International Studies.

Elran, Meir. 2009. 'Review of "Public Role and Engagement in Counterterrorism Efforts: Implications of Israeli Practices for the US"'. *Journal of Homeland Security and Emergency Management* 6 (1): art. 69.

Emerson, Catherine. 2012. 'Testimony' before the Subcommittee on *Oversight, Investigations and Management; Committee on Homeland Security*. House of Representatives, 22 March.
EPIC. 2003. 'Report to Congress Regarding the Terrorism Information Awareness Programme', 20 May 2013.
EPIC. 2005. 'Total "Terrorism" Information Awareness'. http://epic.org/privacy/profiling/tia/; last accessed, 20 May 2013.
EPIC. Unknown Date. 'Foreign Intelligence Surveillance Act Orders 1979–2011'. http://www.epic.org/privacy/wiretap/stats/fisa_stats.html; last accessed, 17 November 2012.
Erdely, Sabrina Rubin. 2012. 'The Plot Against Occupy'. *Rolling Stone*, 26 September.
Ericson, Richard. 2007. *Crime in an Insecure World*. Cambridge: Polity Press.
Esmeir, Samera. 2007. 'The Violence of Non-violence: Law and War in Iraq'. *Journal of Law and Society* 34 (1): 99–115.
Esposito, Richard. 2002. 'Law of the Fist'. *Village Voice*, 22 January.
Etzioni, Amitai. 2004. *How Patriotic is the Patriot Act?* New York: Routledge.
Fairclough, Norman. 1989. *Language and Power*. London: Longman.
Fairclough, Norman. 1992. *Discourse and Social Change*. Cambridge: Polity Press.
Fairclough, Norman. 1995. *Critical Discourse Analysis: the Critical Study of Language*. London: Longman.
Fairclough, Norman. 2003. *Analysing Discourse*. London: Routledge.
Fairclough, Norman, Jessop, Bob and Sayer, Andrew. 2001. 'Critical Realism and Semiosis'. Working Paper, *International Association for Critical Realism Annual Conference*, Roskilde.
Feinstein, Dianne. 2003. 'Senator Feinstein Urges Department of Justice to Aggressively Enforce Bombmaking Statute'. https://votesmart.org/public-statement/20372/senator-feinstein-urges-department-of-justice-to-aggressively-enforce-bombmaking-statute#.UcX3wBxLEpQ; last accessed, 23 June 2013.
FEMA. 2002. 'Citizen Corps: a Guide for Local Officials'.
FEMA. 2003. 'Starting and Maintaining a CERT Programme'.
FEMA. 2009. Citizen Corps Volunteer Liability Guide'.
FEMA. Unknown Date. 'Fact Sheet: Universal Adversary Program'.
FEMA/Emergency Management Institute. Unknown Date. 'CERT Incident Command System'.
FEMA/Points of Light Foundation. 2006. 'Managing Volunteers in Times of Disaster'.
Fine, Ben. 2010. Zombienomics: the Living Death of the Dismal Science. In: Birch and Mykhnenko (eds) *The Rise and Fall of Neo-Liberalism*. London: Zed.
Fine, Bob. 2002 [1984]. *Democracy and the Rule of Law*. Caldwell, NJ: Blackburn Press.
Foucault, Michel. 2007. *Security, Territory, Population*. Basingstoke: Palgrave Macmillan.
Foucault, Michel. 2008. *The Birth of Biopolitics*. Basingstoke: Palgrave Macmillan.
Freedom Road Socialist Organisation. 2012. 'Occupy Wall Street Movement: Repression and Resistance', 10 January. http://www.fightbacknews.org/2012/1/10/occupy-wall-street-movement-repression-and-resistance; last accessed, 22 June 2013.
Gallup. 2001a. 'Americans See Terrorist Attacks as Act of War'. David Moore, 12 September.
Gallup. 2001b. 'Bush Job Approval Highest in Gallup History'. David Moore, 24 September.
Gallup. 2001c. 'Personal Impact on Americans' Lives'. Lydia Saad, 24 September.
Gallup. 2001d. 'Americans' Priorities for President and Congress Shift After Attacks'. Jeffrey Jones, 10 October.

Gallup. 2001e. 'What Has Changed and What Hasn't'. Frank Newport, 29 October.
Gallup. 2001f. 'Public Overwhelmingly Backs Bush in Attacks on Afghanistan'. David Moore, 8 October.
Gallup. 2001g. 'Americans View Afghans Favourably, but not Taliban Government'. Jeffrey Jones, 19 October.
Gallup. 2001h. 'Americans Showing Patience in War on Terrorism'. Jeffrey Jones, 16 October.
Gallup. 2001i. 'On a Mission'. Susan Ellingwood, 15 December.
Gallup. 2002a. 'American Opinion: Should Saddam be Worried?'. Ben Klima, 15 January.
Gallup. 2002b. 'Taking the War Beyond Afghanistan'. Frank Newport, 4 February.
Gallup. 2002c. 'A Passion for Work'. Kenneth Tucker, 18 February.
Gallup. 2002d. 'North Korea Below Iran and Iraq on Americans' Evil List'. Frank Newport and Joseph Carroll, 19 February.
Gallup. 2002e. 'Nearly Nine in Ten Americans Believe Bin Laden Associates in the US'. Jeffrey Jones, 17 September.
Gallup. 2002f. 'Public Supports Bush Positions on UN Involvement in Iraq'. Frank Newport, 18 September.
Gallup. 2002g. 'Post 9/11, Compassionate Companies Had Highly Engaged Employees, Reports Gallup Management Journal'. 15 March.
Gallup. 2003a. 'Public Rallying Around Bush's Call for War'. David Moore, 11 February.
Gallup. 2003b. 'Latest Update Shows No Change in Support for Invasion of Iraq'. Jeffrey Jones, 7 March.
Gallup. 2003c. 'Public Approves Bush's Ultimatum by More than 2–1 Margin'. David Moore, 18 March.
Gallup. 2003d. 'Special Release: American Opinion on the War', 21 March.
Gallup. 2003e. 'War Makes Americans Confident, Sad'. David Moore, 26 March.
Gallup. 2003f. 'Speech Watchers Believe Iraq Victory Aids US in War on Terrorism'. Jeffrey Jones, 2 May.
Gallup. 2003g. 'Americans Feeling More Patriotic this Independence Day'. Mark Gillespie, 3 July 2003.
Gallup. 2003h. 'Seven in Ten are "Extremely" Proud to be Americans this Independence Day'. Joseph Carroll, 3 July.
Gallup. 2003i. 'Terrorism Tops List of Key 2004 Election Issues'. Jeffrey Jones, 29 December.
Gallup. 2004. 'Bare Majority Supports War Effort After *Mission Accomplished* Speech'. Jeffrey Jones, 30 April.
Gallup. 2005a. 'Confidence in Institutions'. Gallup Poll News Service.
Gallup. 2005b. 'Who's Proud to be an American?'. Joseph Carroll, 8 February.
Gallup. 2005c. 'Despite Bush Push, Little Change in Views on Social Security'. Frank Newport, 9 February.
Gallup. 2005d. 'Flash Poll: Instant Reaction to Bush's Iraq Speech'. Jeffrey Jones, 29 June.
Gallup. 2005e. 'Post-9/11 Patriotism Remains Steadfast'. Joseph Carroll, 19 July.
Gallup. 2005f. 'Basic Attitudes Toward Iraq War Slightly More Positive'. Jeffrey Jones, 14 December.
Gallup. 2005g. 'Iraq and Terrorism Are Top Priorities for President and Congress'. Frank Newport, 19 December.
Gallup. 2005h. 'Negative Attitudes on Iraq Prove Hard to Change'. Lydia Saad, 20 December.

Gallup. 2010. 'One in Three Americans Extremely Patriotic'. Lymari Morales, 2 July.
Gallup. 2012. 'Americans Want Next President to Prioritize Jobs, Corruption'. Jeffrey Jones, 30 July.
Gallup. 2013. 'Confidence in Institutions'. Gallup Poll News Service, 4 January.
Gallup. Unknown Date. 'Osama Bin Laden' (questionnaire series).
Gannon, John. 2011. 'Ten Years After 9/11: is Intelligence Reform Working?' Opening Statement before the *US Senate Homeland Security and Governmental Affairs Committee*, 12 May.
Garland, David. 2002. *The Culture of Control*. Oxford: Oxford University Press.
Gearty, Connor. 2006. *Can Human Rights Survive?* Cambridge: Cambridge University Press.
Gessner, Volkmar. 1998. Globalisation and Legal Uncertainty. In: V. Gessner and A.C. Budak (eds) *Emerging Legal Certainty: Empirical Studies on the Globalisation of Law*. Aldershot: Dartmouth.
Giddens, Anthony. 2005. 'Scaring People May Be the Only Way to Avoid the Risks of New-style Terrorism'. *New Statesman*, 10 January.
Gilliard-Matthews, Stacia and Schneider, Anne. 2010. 'Politics or Risks? An Analysis of Homeland Security Grant Allocations to the States'. *Journal of Homeland Security and Emergency Management* 7 (1): art. 57.
Golder, Ben and Fitzpatrick, Peter. 2009. *Foucault's Law*. Abingdon: Routledge.
Golder, Ben and Williams, George. 2004. 'What is "Terrorism"? Problems of Legal Definition'. *University of New South Wales Law Journal* 27 (2): 270–295.
Graeber, David. 2002. 'The New Anarchists'. *New Left Review* 13, January–February.
Gramsci, Antonio. 1998. *Selections from the Prison Notebooks*. London: Lawrence & Wishart.
Green, Bruce A. 1999. 'Forward: Rationing Lawyers: Ethical and Professional Issues in the Delivery of Legal Services to Low-income Clients'. *Fordham Law Review* 67 (5): 1713–1748.
Green, Jordan. 2005. 'Released Files Indicate FBI Spying on Activists'. *Yes Weekly*, 24 May.
Greenstein, Fred. 1965. *Children and Politics*. New Haven: Yale University Press.
Greenwald, Glenn. 2013a. 'NSA Collecting Phone Records of Millions of Verizon Customers Daily'. *The Guardian*, 6 June.
Greenwald, Glenn. 2013b. 'X-Keyscore: NSA Toll Collects "Nearly Everything a User Does on the Internet"'. *The Guardian*, 31 July.
Griscom-Little, Amanda. 2005. 'Greenpeace Gives Peace a Chance. Greenpeace Shifts Tactics as it Looks Ahead to Four More Years of Bush'. *Grist Magazine*, 8 February.
Gross, Oren. 2003. 'Chaos and Rules: Should Responses to Violent Crises Always be Constitutional?'. *Yale Law Journal* 112: 1011–1134.
Gruppe Krisis. 1999. 'Manifesto Against Labour'. http://www.krisis.org/1999/manifesto-against-labour; last accessed, 14 June 2012.
Hacker, Jacob S. 2004. 'Privatising Risk Without Privatising the Welfare State: the Hidden Politics of Social Policy Retrenchment in the United States'. *American Political Science Review* 98 (2): 243–260.
Hadfield, Gillian and Talley, Eric. 2006. 'On Public Versus Private Provision of Corporate Law'. *Journal of Law, Economy, and Organisation* 22 (2): 414–441. http://ssrn.com/abstract=883705; last accessed, 24 July 2012.
Hadfield, Gillian. 2001. Privatising Commercial Law. *Regulation* 24 (1): 40–45.
Haggerty, Kevin and Ericson, Richard. 2000. 'The Surveillance Assemblage'. *British Journal of Sociology* 51 (4): 506–522.
Hall, Stuart et al. 1978. *Policing the Crisis: Mugging, the State and Law and Order*. London: MacMillan.
Hall, Stuart. 1980. *Drifting Into a Law and Order Society*. London: Cobden Trust.

Halperin, John. 2005. 'FBI: Radical Activist Groups are Major Threat'. *Associated Press*, 19 May.
Handler, Joel F. 2004. *Social Citizenship and Workfare in the United States and Western Europe*. Cambridge: Cambridge University Press.
Hanlon, Gerard. 1997. 'A Profession in Transition? – Lawyers, the Market, and Significant Others'. *Modern Law Review* 60 (6): 798–822.
Harman, Jane. 2011. 'Ten Years After 9/11: is Intelligence Reform Working?'. Testimony before the *US Senate Homeland Security and Governmental Affairs Committee*, 12 May.
Harvey, David. 2003. *The New Imperialism*. Oxford: Oxford University Press.
Harvey, David. 2005. *A Brief History of Neoliberalism*. Oxford: Oxford University Press.
Harvey, David. 2010. *The Enigma of Capital*. London: Profile.
Harvey, Frank. 2007. 'The Homeland Security Dilemma: Imagination, Failure, and the Escalating Costs of Perfecting Security'. *Canadian Journal of Political Science* 40 (2): 283–316.
Hay, James. 2006. 'Designing Homes to be the First Line of Defence'. *Cultural Studies* 20 (4–5): 349–377.
Hayden, Michael. 2011. 'Testimony' before the *US Senate Homeland Security and Governmental Affairs Committee*, 12 May.
Hayek, Friedrich A. 1960. *The Constitution of Freedom*. London: Routledge.
Hayek, Friedrich A. 1979. *Law, Legislation, and Liberty: a New Statement of the Legal Principles of Justice and Political Economy*. London: Routledge.
Hayes, James and Ebinger, Charles. 2011. 'The Private Sector and the Role of Risk and Responsibility in Securing the Nation's Infrastructure'. *Journal of Homeland Security and Emergency Management* 8 (1): art. 13.
Henderson, N.C. 2003. 'The Patriot Act's Impact on the Government's Ability to Conduct Electronic Surveillance of Ongoing Domestic Communications'. *Duke Law Journal* 52 (1): 179–209.
Heng, Yee-Kuang and McDonagh, Ken. 2008. 'The Other War on Terror Revealed: Global Governmentality and the Financial Action Task Force's Campaign against Terrorist Financing'. *Review of International Studies* 34: 553–573.
Herman, Suzan. 2008a. Introduction: National Authority and Local Autonomy in the War on Terror. In: S. Herman and P. Finkelman (eds) *Terrorism, Government, and Law*. Westport: Praeger.
Herman, Suzan. 2008b. Collapsing Spheres: Joint Terrorism Task Forces, Federalism, and the War on Terror. In: S. Herman and P. Finkelman (eds) *Terrorism, Government, and Law*. Westport: Praeger.
Herszenhorn, David. 2003. 'Crisis Plans being Redrawn by Schools Across Nation'. *New York Times*, 12 April.
Hetherington, Marc and Nelson, Michael. 2003. 'Anatomy of a Rally Effect: George W. Bush and the War on Terrorism'. *Political Science and Politics*, January.
Higgott, Richard and Weber, Heloise. 2005. 'GATS in Context: Development, an Evolving Lex Mercatoria and the Doha Agenda'. *Review of International Political Economy* 12 (3): 434–455.
Hirsch, Joachim. 1978. The State Apparatus and Social Reproduction. In: J. Holloway and S. Picciotto (eds) *State and Capital*. London: Arnold.
Hobbes, Thomas. 2008 (1651). *Leviathan*. Oxford: Oxford University Press.
Hofstadter, Richard. 1965. *The Paranoid Style in American Politics*. New York: Vintage.
Holland, Philip and Fallon, Michael. 1978. 'The Quango Explosion'. Conservative Political Centre, London.

Hooghe, Liesbet and Marks, Gary. 2003. 'Unravelling the Central State, but How? Types of Multilevel Governance'. *American Political Science Review* 97 (2): 233–243.
Hopkins, Nick. 2013. 'UK Gathering Secret Intelligence via Covert NSA Operation'. *The Guardian*, 7 June.
Horkheimer, Max. 1940. The Authoritarian State. In: A. Arato and E. Gebhardt (eds) *The Essential Frankfurt School Reader*. Oxford: Blackwell, 1978.
Huddy, Leonie and Feldman, Stanley. 2011. 'Americans Respond Politically to 9/11 – Understanding the Impact of the Terrorist Attacks and their Aftermath'. *American Psychologist* 66 (6): 455–467.
Huysmans, Jef. 2008. 'The Jargon of the Exception – on Schmitt, Agamben, and the Absence of Political Society'. *International Political Sociology* 2: 165–183.
IACP. 2004. 'Model Policy – Volunteers'. http://www.theiacp.org/LinkClick.aspx?fileticket=t2v48YSSlh0%3d&tabid=392; last accessed, 4 June 2011.
IACP. 2005. 'From Hometown Security to Homeland Security', 17 May.
Indymedia. 2004a. 'FBI Seizes IMC Servers in the UK', 7 October. http://www.indymedia.org/en/2004/10/111999.shtml; last accessed, 22 June 2013.
Indymedia. 2004b. 'Italy and Switzerland Requested Indymedia's Server Seizure', 9 October. http://www.indymedia.org/en/2004/10/112047.shtml; last accessed, 22 June 2013.
Indymedia. 2004c. 'Indymedia's Hardware is Returned, but Many Questions Remain', 21 October. http://pittsburgh.indymedia.org/news/2004/10/15938.php; last accessed, 22 June 2013.
Indymedia. 2004d. 'IMC: FBI and Other Legalbreaking News', 28 October. http://indymedia.org/en/static/fbi; last accessed, 22 June 2013.
Inigo-Mora, Isabel. 2004. 'On the Use of the Personal Pronoun *We* in Communities'. *Journal of Language and Politics* 3 (1): 27–52.
Irvin, George. 2008. *Super Rich*. Cambridge: Polity Press.
Isin, Engin. 2004. 'The Neurotic Citizen'. *Citizenship Studies* 8 (3): 217–235.
Jakobs, Günther. 2003. *Derecho Penal del Enemigo*. Madrid: Civitas [in Spanish].
Jakobs, Günther. 2011. *Coercion and Personhood in Law*. Athens: Eurasia [in Greek].
Jappe, Anselm. 2009. 'Crédit à Mort'. *Lignes*: n. 30.
Jessop, Bob. 1982. *The Capitalist State*. Oxford: Blackwell.
Jessop, Bob. 1985. *Nicos Poulantzas: Marxist Theory and Political Strategy*. London: Macmillan.
Jessop, Bob. 1990. *State Theory*. Cambridge: Polity Press.
Jessop, Bob. 1992. The Economy, the State, and the Law: Theories of Relative Autonomy and Autopoietic Closure. In: G. Teubner and A. Febrajo (eds) *State, Law, and Economy as Autopoietic Systems – Regulation and Autonomy in a New Perspective*. European Yearbook in the Sociology of Law (1991–1992). Milan: Dott. A. Giuffre Editore.
Jessop, Bob. 2002a. *The Future of the Capitalist State*. Cambridge: Polity Press.
Jessop, Bob. 2002b. Globalisation and the National State. In: S. Aronowitz and P. Bratsis (eds) *Paradigm Lost*. Minneapolis: University of Minnesota Press.
Jessop, Bob. 2008. *State Power: a Strategic-Relational Approach*. Cambridge: Polity Press.
Jessop, Bob. 2009. The Spatiotemporal Dynamics of Globalising Capital and their Impact on State Power and Democracy. In: H. Rosa and W.E. Scheuerman (eds) *High-Speed Society*. University Park: Pennsylvania State University Press.
Jessop, Bob. 2010. From Hegemony to Crisis? The Continuing Ecological Dominance of Neoliberalism. In: K. Birch and V. Mykhnenko (eds) *The Rise and Fall of Neo-Liberalism*. London: Zed.

Jessop, Bob. 2011. Poulantzas's *State, Power, Socialism* as a Modern Classic. In: A. Gallas et al. (eds) *Reading Poulantzas*. Pontypool: Merlin Press.
Jessop, Bob. 2012. *The State*. Cambridge: Polity Press.
Johns, Fleur. 2005. 'Guantanamo Bay and the Annihilation of the Exception'. *European Journal of International Law* 16 (4): 613–635.
Johnston, David. 2005. 'FBI Counterterror Officials Lack Experience, Lawyer Says'. *New York Times*, 20 June.
Jones, R.J. Barry. 2002. Governance and the Challenges of Changing Political Space. In: Y.H. Ferguson and R.J. Barry Jones (eds) *Political Space: Frontiers of Change and Governance in a Globalising World*. Albany: State University of New York Press.
Kano, Megumi et al. 2011. 'Terrorism Preparedness and Exposure Reduction since 9/11: the Status of Public Readiness in the United States'. *Journal of Homeland Security and Emergency Management* 8 (1): art. 37.
Kaplan, Esther. 2002. 'Spies in Blue'. *Village Voice*, 13–19 February.
Kapstein, Ethan. 1994. *Governing the Global Economy: International Finance and the State*. Cambridge, MA: Harvard University Press.
Kiley, Brendan. 2012. 'Political Convictions? Federal Prosecutors in Seattle are Dragging Activists into Grand Juries, Citing their Social Circles and Anarchist Reading Materials'. *The Stranger*, 8 August. http://www.thestranger.com/seattle/political-convictions/Content?oid=14397498; last accessed, 22 June 2013.
Kimmitt, Robert. 2007. 'The Role of Finance in Combating National Security Threats'. *The Washington Institute*, 10 May.
Kinsey, Richard. 1979. Despotism and Legality. In: *Capitalism and the Rule of Law*. National Deviancy Conference/Conference of Socialist Economists. London: Hutchinson.
Klein, Naomi. 2002. *Fences and Windows*. London: HarperCollins.
Klein, Naomi. 2007. *The Shock Doctrine*. London: Allen Lane.
Koch, Max. 2011. 'Poulantzas's Class Analysis'. In: A. Gallas et al. (eds) *Reading Poulantzas*. Pontypool: Merlin Press.
Koerner, Brendan. 2002. 'The Security Traders.' *Mother Jones*, September/October.
Krasner, Stephen D. 1978. *Defending the National Interest*. Princeton: Princeton University Press.
Kriegel, Blandine. 1995. *The State and the Rule of Law*. Princeton: Princeton University Press.
Kris, David S. 2007. 'Modernising the Foreign Intelligence Surveillance Act'. Working Paper on Counterterrorism and American Statutory Law. Brookings Institution, Georgetown University Law Centre, and Hoover Institution.
Krisch, Nico. 2010. *Beyond Constitutionalism – the Pluralist Structure of Postnational Law*. Oxford: Oxford University Press.
Laclau, Ernesto and Mouffe, Chantalle. 1975. *Hegemony and Socialist Strategy*. London: Verso.
Laliotou, Ioanna. 2005. Aspects of the National Imaginary in the US. In: P. Voglis, I. Laliotou and Y. Papatheodorou (eds) *The Temptation of Empire*. Athens: Metaihmio [in Greek].
Lanier, Cathy. 2011. 'Ten Years After 9/11: a Status Report on Information Sharing'. Testimony to *Senate Committee on Homeland Security and Governmental Affairs*, 12 October.
Lapavitsas, Costas. 2009. 'Financialised Capitalism: Crisis and Financial Expropriation'. *Historical Materialism* 14 (1): 129–154.
Lapavitsas, Costas. 2013. Financialised Capitalism: Crisis and Financial Expropriation. In: C. Lapavitsas (ed.) *Financialisation in Crisis*. Chicago: Heymarket.
Larsen, Randall. 2005. 'Years After 9/11'. *Washington Post*, 20 May.

Lasry, Lex. 2007. Military Justice: David Hicks and Guantanamo Bay. In: J. Hocking and C. Lewis (eds) *Counter-terrorism and the Post-democratic State*. Cheltenham: Edward Elgar.
Lawyers' Committee for Human Rights. 2002. *A Year of Loss*, September.
Lee, Jennifer. 2004. 'Fireworks and Sharpshooters Welcome 2004'. *New York Times*, 1 January.
Leigh Brown, Patricia. 2003. 'Prosaic San Mateo Bridge across San Francisco Bay is Now a Possible Terror Target'. *New York Times*, 23 March.
Lemke, Thomas. 2001. '"The Birth of Biopolitics": Michel Foucault's Lecture at the College de France on Neo-liberal Governmentality'. *Economy and Society* 30 (2): 190–207.
Lenin, Vladimir Illitch. 1932. *State and Revolution*. New York: International Publishers.
Leone, Richard. 2003. The Quiet Republic. In: R.C. Leone and G. Arnig (eds) *The War on Our Freedoms*. New York: Century Foundation.
Lettice, John. 2004a. 'Home Office in Frame Over FBI's London Server Seizures'. *The Register*, 11 October.
Lettice, John. 2004b. 'Indymedia Seizures: a Trawl for Genoa G8 Trial Cover-up?'. *The Register*, 14 October.
Lettice, John. 2004c. 'Indymedia: the Tale of the Servers Nobody Seized'. *The Register*, 21 October.
Leurs, Koen. 2007. *Framing Terrorism – Good vs. Evil?* MA Dissertation, University of Utrecht.
Levine, Andrew. 1993. *The General Will: Rousseau, Marx, Communism*. Cambridge: Cambridge University Press.
Lichtblau, Eric. 2003. 'Americans Order Foreign Airlines to Use Marshals'. *New York Times*, 30 December.
Lichtblau, Eric. 2004. 'Flight Sent Back on Terror Fear US Officials Say'. *New York Times*, 1 January.
Likosky, Michael B. 2003. 'Compound Corporations: the Public Law Functions of Lex Mercatoria'. *Non-State Actors and International Law* 3: 251–281.
Liodakis, George. 2010. *Totalitarian Capitalism and Beyond*. Burlington: Ashgate.
Locher, James. 2009. 'Statement' before the *Senate Committee on Homeland Security and Government Affairs*, 12 February.
Loughlin, Martin. 2000. *Sword and Scales – an Examination of the Relationship Between Law and Politics*. Oxford: Hart.
Loughlin, Martin. 2010. What is Constitutionalisation? In: P. Dobner and M. Loughlin (eds) *The Twilight of Constitutionalism?* Oxford: Oxford University Press.
Lowenthal, Mark. 2011. 'Intelligence Community Contractors: Are We Striking the Right Balance?'. Statement before the *Senate Subcommittee on Oversight of Government Management, the Federal Workforce, and the District of Columbia*, 20 September.
Lyon, David. 2003. *Surveillance after September 11*. Cambridge: Polity Press.
MacAskill, Ewen et al. 2013. 'The National Security Agency: Surveillance Giant with Eyes on America'. *The Guardian*, 6 June.
Mackleavy, Julie. 2010. Remaking the Welfare State: from Safety Net to Trampoline. In: K. Birch and V. Mykhnenko (eds) *The Rise and Fall of Neo-Liberalism*. London: Zed.
Manitakis, Antonis. 2003. Prologue. In: A. Manitakis and A. Takis (eds) *Terrorism and Rights*. Athens: Savalas [in Greek].
Manoledakis, Ioannis. 2003. State Security or Freedom? In: A. Manitakis and A. Takis (eds) *Terrorism and Rights*. Athens: Savalas [in Greek].
Marcuse, Herbert. 1941. Some Social Implications of Modern Technology. In: A. Arato and E. Gebhardt (eds) *The Essential Frankfurt School Reader*. Oxford: Blackwell.
Marcuse, Herbert. 1968. *Negations*. London: Penguin.

Mariner, Joanne. 2009. 'A First Look at the Military Commissions Act 2009'. *Find Law*, November–December 2009. http://writ.news.findlaw.com/mariner/20091104.html; http://writ.lp.findlaw.com/mariner/20091130.html; http://writ.lp.findlaw.com/mariner/20091229.html; last accessed, 22 August 2012.

Marks, Susan. 2008. Exploitation as an International Legal Concept. In: S. Marks (ed.) *International Law on the Left*. Cambridge: Cambridge University Press.

Marx, Karl. 1926 [1851]. *The 18th Brumaire of Louis Bonaparte*. London: Allen & Unwin.

Marx, Karl. 1936 [1847]. *The Poverty of Philosophy*. London: M. Lawrence.

Mattelart, Armand. 2010. *The Globalisation of Surveillance*. Cambridge: Polity Press.

Max, D.T. 2001.'The Making of the Speech'. *New York Times*, 7 October.

Mazzone, Jason. 2008. The Security Constitution. In: S. Hernan and P. Finkelman (eds) *Terrorism, Government, and Law*. Westport: Praeger.

McAllister, Ted. 1996. *Revolt against Modernity. Leo Strauss and Eric Voegelin and the Search for a Post-liberal Order*. St Lawrence: University Press of Kansas.

McEvoy, Kieran. 2007. 'Beyond Legalism: Towards a Thicker Understanding of Transitional Justice'. *Journal of Law and Society* 34 (4): 411–440.

McGee, Sibel et al. 2009. Public Role and Engagement in Counterterrorism Efforts: Implications of Israeli Practices for the US – Final Report for Department of Homeland Security, Office of Science and Technology. Homeland Security Institute.

McVea, Harry. 2004. 'Legal Disciplinary Practices – Who Needs Them?'. *Journal of Law and Society* 31 (4): 563–577.

Michaels, Ralf. 2007. 'The True Lex Mercatoria: Law Beyond the State'. *Indiana Journal of Global Legal Studies* 14 (2): 447–468.

Miéville, China. 2008. The Commodity-form Theory of International Law. In: S. Marks (ed.) *International Law on the Left*. Cambridge: Cambridge University Press.

Miliband, Ralph. 1969. *The State in capitalist Society*. London: Weidenfeld & Nicolson.

Missouri School of Journalism. 2002. *Journalism and Terrorism: How the War on Terrorism has Changed American Journalism*. First Amendment Center.

Monahan, Torin and Palmer, Neil. 2011. 'The Emerging Politics of DHS Fusion Centres'. *Security Dialogue* 40 (6): 617–636.

Monahan, Torin. 2010. Surveillance as Governance: Social Inequality and the Pursuit of Democratic Surveillance. In: K. Haggerty and M. Samatas (eds) *Surveillance and Democracy*. Abingdon: Routledge.

Moran, Jon. 2005. 'State Power and the War on Terror: a Comparative Analysis of the UK and USA'. *Crime, Law and Social Change* 44 (4 and 5): 335–359.

Morreale, Stephen and Lambert, David. 2009. 'Homeland Security and the Police Mission'. *Journal of Homeland Security and Emergency Management* 6 (1): art. 68.

Mueller, Robert. 2011. 'Statement' before the *US Senate Homeland Security and Governmental Affairs Committee*, 13 September.

Napolitano, Janet. 2010. 'Statement for the Record' before the *Senate Committee on Homeland Security and Governmental Affairs*.

Napolitano, Janet. 2012. 'Statement for the Record' before the *Senate Committee on Homeland Security and Governmental Affairs*, 21 March.

Neocleous, Mark. 2000. *The Fabrication of Social Order: A Critical Theory of Police Power*. London: Pluto Press.

Neocleous, Mark. 2006a. 'The Problem with Normality: Taking Exception to "Permanent Emergency"'. *Alternatives* 31: 191–213.

Neocleous, Mark. 2006b. 'The State of Emergency and the Rule of Law'. Paper delivered to the *Studies in Modern Capitalism Conference*, Nanjing University.

Neocleous, Mark. 2008. *A Critique of Security*. Edinburgh: Edinburgh University Press.
Neocleous, Mark. 2011. Security as Pacification. In: M. Neocleous and G. Rigakos (eds) *Anti-security*. Ottawa: Red Quill.
Neumann, Franz. 1936 [1986]. *The Rule of Law – Political Theory and the Legal System in Modern Society*. Leamington Spa: Berg.
Neumann, Franz. 1937. The Change in the Function of Law in Modrn Society. In: *idem, The Democratic and the Authoritarian State: Essays in Political and Legal Theory*. Glencoe: Free Press, 1957.
New York Times (Editorial Desk). 2004. 'Lawn vs. Demonstrators', 11 May.
NIAC. 2008. 'Critical Infrastructure Partnership Strategic Assessment – Final Report and Recommendations'. http://www.dhs.gov/xlibrary/assets/niac/niac_critical_infra structure_protection_assessment_final_report.pdf; last accessed, 15 March 2013.
Nimmo, Kurt. 2003. 'Ashcroft's War on Greenpeace'. *Counterpunch*, 24 October.
Nitzan, Jonathan and Bichler, Shimshon. 2004a. 'Dominant Capital and the New Wars'. *Journal of World-Systems Research* 10 (2): 255–327.
Nitzan, Jonathan and Bichler, Shimshon. 2004b. 'Clash of Civilisations or Capital Accumulation?'. *News from Within* 10 (3), July.
Nitzan, Jonathan and Bichler, Shimshon. 2006. 'New Imperialism or New Capitalism?'. *Review* 29 (1): 1–86.
Nitzan, Jonathan and Bichler, Shimshon. 2009a. *Capital as Power*. Abingdon: Routledge.
Nitzan, Jonathan and Bichler, Shimshon. 2009b. 'Contours of Crisis II: Fiction and Reality'. *Dollars and Sense*, 28 April.
Nitzan, Jonathan and Bichler, Shimshon. 2009c. 'Contours of Crisis III: Systemic Fear and Forward Looking Finance'. *Dollars and Sense*, June.
Nitzan, Jonathan and Bichler, Shimshon. 2013a. 'Capitalism as a Mode of Power'. Interview by Piotr Dutkiewics. In: P. Dutkiewics and R. Sakwa (eds) *22 Ideas to Fix the World: Conversations with the World's Foremost Thinkers*. New York: New York University Press.
Nitzan, Jonathan and Bichler, Shimshon. 2013b. 'Can Capitalists Afford Recovery?'. Working papers on *Capital as Power*, no. 2013/01.
Noctiummes, Tania and Page, Jean-Pierre. 2000. La Croisade de George Bush Junior. In: R. Herrera et al. (eds) *L' Empire en Guerre*. Paris: Les Temps des Cerises.
Nordlinger, Eric. A. 1981. *On the Autonomy of the Democratic State*. Cambridge, MA: Harvard University Press.
Norfield, Tony. 2012. 'Derivatives and Capitalist Markets: the Speculative Heart of Capital'. *Historical Materialism* 20 (1): 103–132.
Norton, Marc. 2004. 'Supreme Court and Enemy Combatants'. *Counterpunch*, 28 June.
Notes from Nowhere. 2003. *We are Everywhere: the Irresistible Rise of Global Anti-capitalism*. London: Verso.
Nunn, Sam. 2005. 'Preventing the Next Terrorist Attack: the Theory and Practice of Homeland Security Information Systems'. *Journal of Homeland Security and Emergency Management* 2 (3): 1–28.
Oakley, Francis. 2006. *Kingship*. Oxford: Blackwell.
Odom, William. 2005. 'Why the FBI Can't Be Reformed'. *Washington Post*, 29 June.
Offe, Claus. 1974. 'Structural Problems of the Capitalist State: Class Rule and the Political System – On the Selectiveness of Political Institutions'. *German Political Studies* 1: 31–57.
Offe, Claus. 1984. *Contradictions of the Welfare State*. London: Hutchinson.
Oikonomou, Yorgos. 2003. 'Plato and Castoriadis: the Concealment and the Unveiling of Democracy'. *Democracy and Nature* 9 (2): 247–262.

Olsen, Matthew. 2011. 'Ten Years after 9/11: Are We Safer?'. Testimony before the *Committee on Homeland Security and Governmental Affairs*, 13 September.
Oppenheimer, Martin and Canning, Jane. 1979. 'The National Security State: Repression within Capitalism'. *Berkeley Journal of Sociology* 23: 1–33.
Packer, Jeremy. 2006. 'Becoming Bombs'. *Cultural Studies* 20 (4–5): 378–399.
Palan, Ronen, Abbott, Jason and Deans, Phil. 1996. *State Strategies in the Global Political Economy*. London: Pinter.
Panitch, Leo. 1994. Globalisation and the State. In: R. Miliband and L. Panitch (eds) *Socialist Register 1994: Between Globalism and Nationalism*. London: Merlin Press.
Panitch, Leo. 2000. 'The New Imperial State'. *New Left Review* 2, March/April.
Papacharalambous, Charis. 2009. 'God, the State, and the Sovereign: the Recurrence of Carl Schmitt'. In: *Carl Schmitt On the Three Kinds of Legal Thought*. Athens: Papazisis [in Greek].
Papacharissi, Zizi and Oliveira, Maria de Fatima. 2008. 'News Frames Terrorism: a Comparative Analysis of Frames Employed in Terrorism Coverage in US and UK Newspapers'. *International Journal of Press and Politics* 13 (1): 52–74.
Paraskevopoulos, Nicos. 2004. 'Security of the Sate, Insecurity of Justice'. In: A. Manitakis and A. Takis (eds) *Terrorism and Rights*. Athens: Savalas [in Greek].
Pashukanis, Evgeny. 1924 [1987]. *The General Theory of Law and Marxism*. London: Pluto.
Paul, Bruce. 2011. 'National Day of Action against State Repression of the Occupy Movement', 17 November. http://occupyoakland.org/2011/11/national-day-of-action-against-state-repression-of-the-occupy-movement/; last accessed, 22 June 2013.
Paye, Jean-Claude. 2007. *Global War on Liberty*. New York: Telos.
Pear, Robert and Janofsky, Michael. 2005. 'Students to Bear Big Burden under the Final Budget Bill'. *New York Times*, 21 December.
Petras, James. 2013. The Politics of Language and the Language of Political Regression. In: R. Fisher (ed.) *Managing Democracy, Managing Dissent*. London: Freedom Press.
Pew Research. 2001a. 'American Psyche Reeling from Terror', 19 September.
Pew Research. 2001b. 'Military Action a Higher Priority Than Homeland Defence', 27 September.
Pew Research. 2002a. 'Unusually High Interest in Bush's State of the Union', 17 January.
Pew Research. 2002b. 'Americans Favour Force in Iraq, Somalia, Sudan', 22 January.
Pew Research. 2002c. 'Bush Engages and Persuades Public on Iraq', 19 September.
Picciotto, Sol. 1992. *International Business Taxation: a Study in the Internationalisation of Business*. London: Weidenfeld & Nicholson.
Pincus, Walter. 2005. 'Counterterrorism Centre Awaits Presidential Action'. *Washington Post*, 3 June.
Plato. 1966. *Republic*. I.A. Richards (ed.) Cambridge: Cambridge University Press.
Plato. 1952. *Statesman*. J.B Skemp (trans.) London: Routledge.
Pollock, Friedrich. 1941. State Capitalism: its Possibilities and Limitations. Reprinted in A. Arato and E. Gebhardt (eds) *The Essential Frankfurt School Reader*. Oxford: Blackwell, 1978.
Poole, Patrick. 2000. 'Inside America's Secret Court'. http://fly.hiwaay.net/~pspeaople/fiscshort.html; last accessed, 14 August 2008.
Potter, Will. 2011. 'FBI Says Activists who Investigate Factory Farms Can be Prosecuted as Terrorists'. *Green is the New Red*, 20 December. http://www.greenisthenewred.com/blog/fbi-undercover-investigators-animal-enterprise-terrorism-act/5440/; last accessed, 18 November 2012.
Potter, Will. 2012. 'Today is October 10th, 2012 and I am Ready to Go to Prison'. *Green is the New Red*, 10 October. http://www.greenisthenewred.com/blog/leah-plante-grand-jury-seattle-anarchist/6448/; last accessed, 18 November 2012.

Potter, Will. 2012a. '3 NATO Protesters Charged with "Terrorism" in Chicago – Identical to Other FBI Plots'. *Green is the New Red*, 21 May. http://www.greenisthenewred.com/blog/three-nato-protesters-terrorists/6119/; last accessed, 22 June 2013.

Potter, Will. 2012b. 'Breaking: FBI and JTTF Raid Multiple Homes, Grand Jury Subpoenas in Portland, Olympia, Seattle'. *Green is the New Red*, 25 July. http://www.greenisthenewred.com/blog/home-raids-grand-jury-subpoenas-portland-olympia-seattle/6233/; last accessed, 22 June 2013.

Potter, Will. 2012c. 'FBI Agents Raid Homes in Search of "Anarchist Literature"'. *Green is the New Red*, 30 July. http://www.greenisthenewred.com/blog/fbi-raid-anarchist-literature-portland-seattle/6267/; last accessed, 22 June 2013.

Potter, Will. 2012d. '3 People Now in Jail for Refusing to Talk about Other Anarchists'. *Green is the New Red*, 11 October. http://www.greenisthenewred.com/blog/3-young-people-now-in-jail-for-refusing-to-talk-about-other-anarchists/6467/; last accessed, 22 June 2013.

Potter, Will. 2013. 'Gerald Koch Hasn't Been Accused of a Crime, But the Feds Put Him in Jail Anyway'. *Vice*, June. http://www.vice.com/read/gerald-koch-is-in-jailfor-being-an-anarchist; last accessed, 22 June 2013.

Poulantzas, Nicos. 1964. Marxist Examination of the Contemporary State and Law and the Question of the 'Alternative'. Reprinted in J. Martin (ed.) *The Poulantzas Reader*. London: Verso 2008.

Poulantzas, Nicos. 1965. Preliminaries to the Study of Hegemony in the State. Reprinted in J. Martin (ed.) *The Poulantzas Reader*. London: Verso 2008.

Poulantzas, Nicos. 1973. *Political Power and Social Classes*. London: NLB.

Poulantzas, Nicos. 1974. *Fascism and Dictatorship*. London: NLB.

Poulantzas, Nicos. 1975. *Classes in Contemporary Capitalism*. London: NLB.

Poulantzas, Nicos. 1976a. *The Crisis of Dictatorships*. London: NLB.

Poulantzas, Nicos. 1976b. The Political Crisis and the Crisis of the State. Reprinted in J. Martin (ed.) *The Poulantzas Reader* London: Verso (2008).

Poulantzas, Nicos. 1976c. The Capitalist State: a Reply to Miliband and Laclau. Reprinted in J. Martin (ed.) *The Poulantzas Reader* London: Verso (2008).

Poulantzas, Nicos. 1978. *State, Power, Socialism*. London: NLB (Reprinted by Verso 2000).

Poulantzas, Nicos. 1980. Research Note on the State and Society. In: J. Martin (ed.) *The Poulantzas Reader* London: Verso (2008).

Press, Daryl. 1999. 'Urban Warfare: Options, Problems and the Future'. *Marine Corps Gazette* 83 (4): 14–18.

Progressive Policy Institute. 2003. 'America at Risk. A Homeland Security Report Card', July.

Putnam, Robert. 2000. *Bowling Alone. The Collapse and Revival of American Community*. New York: Simon & Schuster.

Ragavan, Chitra. 2005. 'Fixing the FBI'. *US News*, 28 March.

RAND, 2004. 'Collecting the Dots: Problem Formulation and Solution Elements'.

RAND, Unknown Date. 'Out of the Ordinary. Finding Hidden Threats by Analysing Unusual Behaviour'.

Ratcliffe, Jerry. 2008. *Intelligence-Led Policing*. Cullompton: Willan.

RCP. 2012. 'The Repression of the Occupy Movement Must not Stand'. *Revolution* #261, 26 February.

Reese, Stephen and Lewis, Seth. 2009. 'Framing the War on Terror – the Internalisation of Policy in the US Press'. *Journalism* 10 (6): 776–797.

Reid Mandell, Betty. 2006. 'Reply to Christopher Jencks on Welfare Reform'. *Z Net*, 28 March.

Retort. 2005. *Afflicted Powers*. London: Verso.
Ridge, Thomas. 2009. 'Testimony', before the *Senate Committee on Homeland Security and Government Affairs*, 12 February.
Roach, Kent. 2011. *The 9/11 Effect*. Cambridge: Cambridge University Press.
Roberts, Simon. 2005. After Government? On Representing Law Without the State. *Modern Law Review* 68 (1): 1–24.
Robin, Corey. 2003. 'Fear American Style – Civil Liberty After 9/11'. In: S. Aronowitz and H. Gautney (eds) *Implicating Empire*. New York: Basic Books.
Robin, Corey. 2004. *Fear – the History of a Political Idea*. Oxford: Oxford University Press.
Robinson, Linda and Whitelaw, Kevin. 2006. 'Seeking Spies'. *US News*, 13 February.
Rogoff, Kenneth and Reinhart, Carmen. 2008. 'Banking Crises: an Equal Opportunity Menace'. http://scholar.harvard.edu/files/rogoff/files/banking_crises.pdf; last accessed, 4 June 2012.
Roig-Franzia, Manuel. 2004. 'Judge Dismisses Greenpeace Charges'. *Washington Post*, 20 May.
Rossiter, Clinton. 1948. *Constitutional Dictatorship – Crisis Government in the Modern Democracies*. Princeton: Princeton University Press.
Rousseau, Jean-Jacques. 1994. *The Social Contract*. C. Betts (trans.) Oxford: Oxford University Press.
Rutherford Institute. 2003. 'Memorandum: Life, Liberty, and the Pursuit of Terrorists', 27 August.
Samples, John. 2010. 'Lawless Policy – TARP as Congressional Failure'. *CATO Institute*, Policy Analysis no. 660.
Saña, Heleno. 1991. *Oppressors and Oppressed – Material for a Theory of Emancipation*. Las Palmas: Ayuntamiento [in Spanish].
Sanguinetti, Gianfranco. 1978. *On Terrorism and the State*. http://www.notbored.org/on-terrorism.html; last accessed, 14 December 2012.
Santos, Boaventura de Sousa. 1993. The Postmodern Transition: Law and Politics. In: A. Sarat and T. Kearns (eds) *The Fate of Law*. Ann Arbor: University of Michigan Press.
Santos, Boaventura de Sousa. 1995. *Toward a New Common Sense: Law, Science, and Politics in Paradigmatic Transition*. London: Routledge.
Santos, Boaventura de Sousa. 2002. *Toward a New Legal Common Sense – Law, Globalisation, and Emancipation* (2nd edn). London: LexisNexis Butterworths.
Santos, Boaventura de Sousa. 2005. Beyond Neoliberal Governance: the World Economic Forum as Subaltern Cosmopolitan Politics and Legality. In: B. Santos and C. Rodriguez-Garavito (eds) *Law and Globalisation from Below*. Cambridge: Cambridge University Press.
Sarafianos, Dimitris and Tsaitouridis, Christos. 2003. Defending Democracy from Terrorist Crimes, and Defending Freedom from Counterterrorism Legislation. In: A. Manitakis and A. Takis (eds) *Terrorism and Rights*. Athens: Savalas [in Greek].
Scahill, Jeremy. 2003. 'The Miami Model: Paramilitaries, Embedded Journalists and Illegal Protests'. *Z-Net*, November.
Scarry, Elaine. 2003. *Who Defended the Country?* Boston: Beacon Press.
Scarry, Elaine. 2004. 'Resolving to Resist: Local Governments are Refusing to Comply with the Patriot Act'. *Boston Review*, February–March.
Scheingold, Stuart and Sarat, Austin. 2004. *Something to Believe in: Politics, Professionalism, and Cause Lawyering*. Stanford: Stanford University Press.
Scheingold, Stuart. 2001. Cause Lawyering and Democracy in Transnational Perspective. In: A. Sarat and S. Scheingold (eds) *Cause Lawyering and the State in a Global Era*. Oxford: Oxford University Press.

Scheuerman, William E. 1999. 'Economic Globalisation and the Rule of Law'. *Constellations* 6 (1): 3–24.
Scheuerman, William E. 2000. 'The Economic State of Emergency'. *Cardozo Law Review* 21: 1890.
Scheuerman, William E. 2001. 'Reflexive Law and the Challenges of Globalisation'. *Journal of Political Philosophy* 9 (1): 81–102.
Scheuerman, William E. 2002. 'Rethinking Crisis Government'. Constellations 9 (4): 492–505.
Scheuerman, William E. 2004. *Liberal Democracy and the social Acceleration of Time*. Baltimore: Johns Hopkins University Press.
Schmidt, Manfred. 2000. *Demokratietheorien: Eine Einfuhrung*. Opladen: Verlag Leske + Budrich.
Schmitt, Carl. 1985 [1926]. *The Crisis of Parliamentary Democracy*. Boston: Massachusetts Institute of Technology.
Schmitt, Carl. 1988 [1922]. *Political Theology*. Boston: Massachusetts Institute of Technology.
Schmitt, Carl. 1996 [1932]. *The Concept of the Political*. Chicago: University of Chicago Press.
Schmitt, Carl. 2004 [1932]. *Legality and Legitimacy*. Durham: Duke University Press.
Schmitt, Carl. 2007 [1964]. *Theory of the Partisan*. New York: Telos.
Schneier, Bruce. 2006. *Beyond Fear*. New York: Copernicus.
Schubert, James, Stewart, Patrick and Curran, Margaret-Ann. 2002. 'A Defining Presidential Moment: 9/11 and the Rally Effect'. *Political Psychology* 23 (3): 559–583.
Schulhofer, Stephen. 2003. 'No Checks, No Balances: Disregarding Bedrock Constitutional Principles'. In: R.C. Leone and G. Anrig (eds) *The War on Our Freedoms*. New York: Century Foundation.
Scott, Robert E. 2004. 'The Death of Contract Law'. *University of Toronto Law Journal* 54 (4): 369–390.
Sena, Mike. 2012. 'The National Preparedness Report: Assessing the State of Preparedness'. Statement before the *House of Representatives Subcommittee on Emergency Preparedness, Response, and Communications*, 6 June.
Shapiro, Jacob and Cohen, Dara. 2007. 'Colour Bind: Lessons from the Failed Homeland Security Advisory System'. *International Security* 32 (2): 121–154.
Shenon, Philip. 2003a. 'Air Patrols are Resumed over City'. *New York Times*, 25 March.
Shenon, Philip. 2003b. 'Ridge Says US May Need Pay to Install Anti-missile Devices on Airliners'. *New York Times*, 9 April.
Showstack-Sassoon, Anne. 1987. *Gramsci's Politics*. London: Hutchinson.
Siperco, Ian. 2006. 'Marshalling the Great Arsenal of Democracy: Engaging the Private Sector to Secure the Public Good'. *Journal of Homeland Security and Emergency Management* 3 (4): art. 5.
Skelcher, Chris. 1998. *The Appointed State: Quasi Governmental Organisations and Democracy*. Buckingham: Open University Press.
Skinner, Richard. 2012. 'The Department of Homeland Security: an Assessment of the Department and a Roadmap for its Future'. Statement before the *Committee on Homeland Security*, US House of Representatives, 20 September.
Skocpol, Theda. 1979. *States and Social Revolutions: a Comparative Analysis of France, Russia and China*. Cambridge: Cambridge University Press.
Sommerlad, Hilary. 2002. 'Women Solicitors in a Fractured Profession: Intersections of Gender and Professionalism in England and Wales'. *International Journal of the Legal Profession* 9 (3): 213.

Sommerlad, Hilary. 2004. 'Some Reflections on the Relationship between Citizenship, Access to Justice, and the Reform of Legal Aid'. *Journal of Law and Society* 31 (3): 345–368.

Sommerlad, Hilary. 2008. 'Reflection on the Reconfiguration of Access to Justice'. *International Journal of the Legal Profession* 13 (3): 179–193.

Sowińska, Agnieszka. 2012. 'Toward an Axiological-Semantic Approach to the Analysis of Political Discourse'. Working Paper, Toruń: Nicolaus Copernicus University.

SRI International. 2004. *Link Analysis Workbench*.

Starhawk. 2003. 'Miami: a Dangerous Victory'. *Infoshop*, 9 December.

Steyn, Johan. 2003. 'The Legal Black Hole'. 27th F.A. Man Lecture, 25 November. http://www.statewatch.org/news/2003/nov/guantanamo.pdf; last accessed, 23 August 2012.

Stier, Max. 2012. 'Testimony' before the Subcommittee on *Oversight, Investigations and Management; Committee on Homeland Security*. House of Representatives, 22 March.

Stone Sweet, Alec. 2006. 'The New Lex Mercatoria and Transnational Governance'. *Journal of European Public Policy* 13 (5): 627–646.

Strange, Susan. 1987. 'The Persistent Myth of "Lost" Hegemony'. *International Organisation* 41 (4): 551–574.

Strange, Susan. 2002. Finance in Politics: and Epilogue to *Mad Money*. In: Y.H. Ferguson and R.J. Barry Jones (eds) *Political Space: Frontiers of Change and Governance in a Globalising World*. Albany: State University of New York.

Strauss, Leo. 1968. *On Tyranny*. New York: Cornell University Press.

Strauss, Leo. 1983. *Studies in Platonic Philosophy*. Chicago: University of Chicago Press.

Strossen, Nadine and Elgar, Timothy. 2004. Written Statement before the US Commission on Civil Rights at Hearing on 'Security and Liberty', 19 March.

Sugarman, David. 2000. Is Company Law Founded on Contract or Public Regulation: the Law Commission's Paper on Directors' Duties. In: M. Andenas and D. Sugarman (eds) *Directors' Conflicts of Interest: Legal, Socio-legal, and Economic Analysis*. London: Kluwer Law International.

Sullivan, Helen and Skelcher, Chris. 2002. *Working Across Boundaries: Collaboration in the Public Services*. Hampshire: MacMillan.

Sullivan, Kathleen. 2003. Under a Watchful Eye: Incursions on Personal Privacy. In: R.C. Leone and G. Anrig (eds) *The War on Our Freedoms*. New York: Century Foundation.

Talanian, Nancy. 2003. 'The Homeland Security Act: the Decline of Privacy, the Rise of Government Secrecy'. Bill of Rights Defence Committee.

Tassis, Theophanis. 2008. *Castoriadis – A Philosophy of Autonomy*. Athens: Eurasia [in Greek].

Tavernise, Sabrina. 2004. 'In Packed Square, Fear is Pushed Out by the Big Party'. *New York Times*, 1 January.

Teubner, Gunther. 1983. 'Substantive and Reflexive Elements in Modern Law'. *Law and Society Review* 17 (2): 239–285.

Teubner, Gunther. 1985. After Legal Instrumentalism? Strategic Models of Post-Regulatory Law. In: *idem* (ed) *Dilemmas of Law in the Welfare State*. New York: de Gruyter.

Teubner, Gunther. 1997. Global Bukowina: Legal Pluralism in the World Society. In: *idem* (ed.) *Global Law Without a State*. Aldershot: Dartmouth.

Teubner, Gunther. 2002. 'Breaking Frames: Economic Globalisation and the Emergence of Lex Mercatoria'. *European Journal of Social Theory* 5 (2): 199–217.

Thucydides. 2011. *History*. N.M. Skouteropoulos (ed.). Athens: Polis [in Greek].

Tomlinson, Jim. 1990. *Hayek and the Market*. London: Pluto.

Touretzky, David. Unknown Date. 'What the FBI Doesn't Want You to See at RaisetheFist. com'. http://www-2.cs.cmu.edu/~dst/raisethefist/; last accessed, 4 February 2007.

Trenkle, Norbert. 2008. 'Tremors on the Global Market'. http://www.krisis.org/2009/tremors-on-the-global-market; last accessed, 1 June 2012.

Treverton, Gregory. 2009. *Intelligence for an Age of Terror*. Cambridge: Cambridge University Press.

Tsoukalas, Constantine. 2002. Relative Autonomy and its Changing Forms. In: S. Aronowitz and P. Bratsis (eds) *Paradigm Lost*. Minneapolis: University of Minnesota Press.

Tuschling, Burkhard. 1976. *Rechtsform und Produktionsverhaeltnisse*. Frankfurt: EVA.

Unger, Roberto. 1976. *Law in Modern Society*. New York: Free Press.

University of Illinois–Library Research Centre. 2003. 'Public Libraries and Civil Liberties: a Profession Divided'.

US Attorney General. 2001. *Attorney General John Ashcroft's testimony before the House Judiciary Committee*, 24 September.

US Attorney General. 2002a. *Memorandum: Intelligence Sharing Procedures for Foreign Intelligence and Foreign Counterintelligence Investigations Conducted by the FBI*, 6 March. https://www.fas.org/irp/agency/doj/fisa/ag030602.html; last accessed, 17 November 2012.

US Attorney General. 2002b. *The Attorney General's Guidelines on General Crimes, Racketeering Enterprise and Terrorism Enterprise Investigations*, 30 May. http://www.fas.org/irp/agency/doj/fbi/generalcrimes2.pdf; last accessed, 18 November 2012.

US Attorney General. 2003a. 'Memorandum: Departmental Guidance on sentencing Recommendations and Appeals'. *US Department of Justice, Office of Attorney General*, 28 July.

US Attorney General 2003b. 'The Proven Tactics in the Fight Against Crime'. *Prepared Remarks of AG John Ashcroft*. Washington DC, 15 September.

US Department of Defense. 2005. *Strategy for Homeland Defence and Civil Support*, 24 June.

US Department of Homeland Security. 2002a. 'Threat Level Raised to Orange', 11 September.

US Department of Homeland Security. 2002b. 'Citizen Corps Councils'. http://www.citizencorps.gov; last accessed, 3 May 2011.

US Department of Homeland Security. 2002c. 'National Citizen Corps Council'. http://www.citizencorps.gov; last accessed, 3 May 2011.

US Department of Homeland Security. 2002d. 'Citizen Corps Programmes'. http://www.citizencorps.gov; last accessed, 3 May 2011.

US Department of Homeland Security. 2003a. 'Remarks by Secretary Ridge, Attorney General Ashcroft and Director Mueller', 7 February.

US Department of Homeland Security. 2003b. *Joint statement of Attorney General and Secretary of Homeland Security*, 27 February.

US Department of Homeland Security. 2003c. *Operation Liberty Shield/Threat Level Up*, 17 March.

US Department of Homeland Security. 2003d. *Threat Level Lowered*, 16 April.

US Department of Homeland Security. 2003e. *Raising the Threat Level*, 20 May.

US Department of Homeland Security. 2003f. *Lowering the Threat Level*, 30 May.

US Department of Homeland Security. 2003g. 'A Day in the life of Homeland Security', 19 June.

US Department of Homeland Security. 2004a. *Remarks by Secretary Tom Ridge on Lowering the Threat Level to Yellow*, 9 January.

US Department of Homeland Security. 2004b. *Homeland Security Advisory System Increased to Orange for Financial Institutions in Specific Geographical Areas*, 1 August.

US Department of Homeland Security. 2004c. *Citizen Corps Celebrates Success at Two-Year Anniversary*. http://www.citizencorps.gov; last accessed, 9 July 2008.

US Department of Homeland Security. 2006. *DHS Intelligence Enterprise Strategic Plan*, January.
US Department of Homeland Security. 2007. 'The TOPOFF 4 Full Scale Exercise'. http://www.dhs.gov/topoff-4-full-scale-exercise; last accessed, 21 June 2012.
US Department of Homeland Security. 2009a. 'Leftwing Extremists Likely to Increase Use of Cyber Attacks over the Coming Decade', 26 January.
US Department of Homeland Security. 2009b. 'Rightwing Extremism: Current Economic and Political Climate Fuelling Resurgence in Radicalisation and Recruitment', 7 April.
US Department of Homeland Security. 2009c. 'National Infrastructure Protection Plan'. http://www.dhs.gov/xlibrary/assets/NIPP_Plan.pdf; last accessed, 15 March 2013.
US Department of Homeland Security. 2011a. 'National Terrorism Advisory System Public Guide', April.
US Department of Homeland Security. 2011b. 'Domestic Terrorism and Homegrown Violent Extremism Lexicon', 10 November.
US Department of Homeland Security. 2012. 'DHS Announces More Than $1.3 billion in Fiscal Year 2012 Preparedness Awards'. http://www.dhs.gov/news/2012/06/29/dhs-announces-more-13-billion-fiscal-year-fy-2012-preparedness-grant-awards; last accessed, 13 March 2013.
US Department of Homeland Security. Unknown Date I. 'National Infrastructure Advisory Council Members'. http://www.dhs.gov/national-infrastructure-advisory-council-members; last accessed, 15 March 2013.
US Department of Homeland Security. Unknown Date II. 'Department of Homeland Security Prime Contractors'. http://www.dhs.gov/xlibrary/assets/opnbiz/OSDBU-DHS_Prime_Contractors_List.pdf; last accessed, 24 March 2013.
US Department of Homeland Security. Unknown Date III. 'Science and Technology Directory Centres of Excellence'. http://www.dhs.gov/st-centers-excellence; last accessed, 8 January 2006.
US Department of Homeland Security. Unknown Date IV. 'Understanding the Homeland Security Advisory System'.
US Department of Homeland Security/Office of Inspector General (US DHS/OIG). 2003a. 'Semi-annual Report for the Congress', 1 April–30 September.
US Department of Homeland Security/Office of Inspector General. 2003b. 'Semi-annual Report for the Congress', 30 April.
US Department of Homeland Security/Office of Inspector General. 2004. 'Semi-annual Report for the Congress', 1 October 2003–31 March 2004.
US Department of Homeland Security/Office of Inspector General. 2006. 'Progress in Developing the National Assets Database', June.
US Department of Homeland Security/Office of Science and Technology. Unknown Date. 'Fact Sheet: DHS Programmes to Increase the Numbers of American Students'.
US Department of Homeland Security/Privacy Office. 2007. 'DHS Privacy Office Review of the Analysis, Dissemination, Visualisation, Insight, and Semantic Enhancement (ADVICE) Programme', 11 July.
US Department of Homeland Security Secretary. 2009. 'Statement for the Record' before the *Senate US Security and Governmental Affairs Committee*, 12 May.
US Department of Justice. 1988. 'Terrorism in the United States'. Terrorist Research and Analytical Center, Counterterrorism Section, 31 December.
US Department of Justice. 2002. 'Justice Dept. answers to the questions of the House Judiciary Committee (submitted 13 June 2002) regarding the use of Patriot Act', 26 July 2002.

US Department of Justice. 2003a. 'Office of the Assistant Attorney General Answers to Questions Submitted (on April 1 2003) by the House Judiciary Committee to the Attorney General on USA PATRIOT Act Implementation', 13 May.
US Department of Justice. 2003b. 'Office of the Assistant Attorney General Answers to Questions Submitted (on April 1 2003) by the House Judiciary Committee to the Attorney General on USA PATRIOT Act Implementation', 26 August.
US Department of Justice. 2004. 'Delayed Notice Search Warrants: a Vital and Time-honoured Tool for Fighting Crime', 22 September.
US Department of Justice. 2007. 'A Review of the Federal Bureau of Investigations' Use of Section 215 Orders for Business Records'. Office of Inspector General, March.
US Department of Justice. 2009. 'Investigating Terrorism and Criminal Extremism – Terms and Concepts'. Bureau of Justice Assistance, US Department of Justice.
US Federal Bureau of Investigation. 2003. *FBI Intelligence Bulletin no. 89*, 15 October.
US Federal Register. 2011. Volume 76, No. 176, Monday 12 September, 56227–56242.
US Foreign Intelligence Surveillance Court. 2002. 'Memorandum Opinion'. Washington DC, 17 May.
US Foreign Intelligence Surveillance Court. 2013. 'Secondary Order'. Washington DC, 25 April.
US Government Accountability Office. 2012a. 'Preliminary Observations on DHS's Efforts to Improve Employee Morale'. Testimony before the Subcommittee on *Oversight, Investigations and Management; Committee on Homeland Security*, House of Representatives, 22 March.
US Government Accountability Office. 2012b. 'Department of Homeland Security: an Assessment of the Department and a Roadmap for its Future'. *Hearing before the House of Representatives Committee on Homeland Security*. Janet Napolitano, 20 September.
US Government Accountability Office. 2012c. 'Department of Homeland Security – Continued Progress Made Improving and Integrating Management Areas, but More Work Remains', 20 September.
US Homeland Security Council. 2004. 'Planning Scenarios – version 2.0', July.
US Homeland Security Council. 2006. 'National Planning Scenarios – version 21.3, Final Draft', March.
US House of Representatives. 2003a. 'Hearing: Anti-terrorism Investigations and the Fourth Amendment after September 11, 2001'. *House Subcommittee on the Constitution*, 20 May.
US House of Representatives. 2003b. 'Hearing: How is the Department of Homeland Security Improving Our Capabilities?'. *Select Committee on Homeland Security*, 19 June.
US House of Representatives. 2004a. 'America at Risk. A Homeland Security Report Card. Initial Findings'. *Democratic Members of the House Select Committee on Homeland Security*, January.
US House of Representatives. 2004b. 'Hearing: The Homeland Security Advisory System'. *Select Committee on Homeland Security*, 4 February. Washington DC: US Government Printing Office.
US House of Representatives. 2004c. 'Hearing: Homeland Security Advisory System: Threat Codes and Public Responses'. *Subcommittee of National Security, Emerging Threats and International Relations*, 16 March. Washington DC: US Government Printing Office.
US House of Representatives. 2006. 'Waste, Abuse, and Mismanagement in Department of Homeland Security Contracts'. Report by the Committee on Government Reform.

US House of Representatives. 2007. 'Hearing: Citizen Preparedness: Helping Our Communities Help Themselves'. *Subcommittee on Emergency Communications, Preparedness, and Response*, 13 June.

US House of Representatives. 2008a. 'Hearing: Moving Beyond the First Five Years: Ensuring FEMA's Ability to Respond and Recover in the Wake of a National Catastrophe'. *Subcommittee on Emergency Communications, Preparedness, and Response*, 9 April.

US House of Representatives. 2008b. 'Hearing: Oversight Concerns Regarding Treasury Department Conduct of the Troubled Assets Relief Program'. *Committee on Financial Services*, 10 December.

US House of Representatives. 2009. 'Hearing: Preparedness (Part I and II)'. *Subcommittee on Emergency Communications, Preparedness, and Response*, 1 and 27 October.

US Office of Director of National Intelligence. 2011. *U.S. National Intelligence – an Overview*.

US Office of Homeland Security. 2002a. *National Strategy for Homeland Security*, July.

US Office of Homeland Security. 2002b. *Threat Level Raised to Orange*, 10 September.

US President. 2001a. 'Statement by the President in His Address to the Nation', 11 September, 8:30 pm.

US President. 2001b. 'Remarks by the President In Photo Opportunity with the National Security Team', 12 September, 10:53 am.

US President. 2001c. 'Radio Address of the President to the Nation', 15 September.

US President. 2001d. 'Address to a Joint Session of Congress and the American People', 20 September, 9.00 pm.

US President. 2001e. 'Radio Address', 20 October.

US President. 2001f. 'Economy an Important Part of Homeland Defence', 24 October.

US President. 2001g. 'Radio Address: President Discusses Job Creation Package', 1 December.

US President. 2001h. 'Radio Address', 8 December.

US President. 2001i. 'Radio Address: President Calls Senate to Bring Economy Package to Vote', 15 December.

US President. 2002a. State of the Union Address, 29 January. http://georgewbush-whitehouse.archives.gov/news/releases/2002/01/20020129-11.html; last accessed, 6 June 2013.

US President. 2002b. 'Radio Address: President's Priorities', 14 August.

US President. 2002c. 'Radio Address', 20 July.

US President. 2002d. 'Radio Address', 17 August.

US President. 2002e. 'The Department of Homeland Security', June.

US President. 2002f. 'Securing the Homeland, Strengthening the Nation'.

US President. 2003. 'President Bush Signs Partial Birth Abortion Act of 2003', 5 November.

US President. 2005. 'Radio Address', 9 July.

US President. 2006. 'Radio Address: President's Trip to Southeast Asia/APEC', 18 November.

US President. 2010a. 'Weekly Address: President Obama Outlines Steps Taken to Protect the Safety and Security of the American People', 2 January.

US President. 2010b. 'Weekly Address: President Obama Invites all Americans to Honor America's Fallen Heroes this Memorial Day', 29 May.

US President. 2010c. 'Weekly Address: President Obama Commemorates the Ninth Anniversary of the September 11th Attacks', 9 September.

US President. 2011a. 'Weekly Address: Remembering September 11th', 10 September.

US President. 2011b. 'Weekly Address: Honoring those who Served in Iraq, as the War Comes to an End', 17 December.
US President. 2012a. 'Weekly Address: A New Chapter in Afghanistan', 26 May.
US President. 2012b. 'Weekly Address: Honoring Our Nation's Service Members and Military Families', 1 September.
US President. 2012c. 'Weekly Address: Coming Together to Remember September 11', 8 September.
US President. 2012d. 'Weekly Address: Carrying on the Work of Our Fallen Heroes', 15 September.
US President. 2013. *Presidential Policy Directive 21: Critical Infrastructure Security and Resilience*, 12 February.
US Senate. 1995. *National Defence Authoriasation Act for Fiscal Year 1996 Report* (S.R. 104–112). Senate Committee on Armed Services, 12 July.
US Senate. 2001. 'Department of Justice Oversight: Preserving our Freedoms While Defending Against Terrorism'. *Hearing before the Senate Judiciary Committee*, 6 December.
US Senate. 2002a. 'Reforming the FBI in the 21st Century'. *Hearing before the Senate Judiciary Committee*, 8 May.
US Senate. 2002b. 'The Patriot Act in Practice: Shedding Light in the FISA Process'. *Hearing before the Senate Judiciary Committee*, 10 September.
US Senate. 2002c. 'Tools against Terror: How the Administration is Implementing New Laws in the Fight to Protect Our Homeland'. *Hearing before the Senate Judiciary Committee*, 9 October.
US Senate. 2003a. 'The War Against Terrorism: Working Together to Protect America', *Hearing before the Senate Judiciary Committee*, 4 March.
US Senate. 2003b. 'Oversight Hearing: Law Enforcement and Terrorism'. *Hearing before the Senate Judiciary Committee*, 23 July.
US Senate. 2003c. 'America after 9/11: Freedom Preserved or Freedom Lost?'. *Hearing before the Senate Judiciary Committee*, 18 November.
US Senate. 2006. 'FBI Oversight'. *Hearing before the Committee on the Judiciary*, 6 December.
US Senate. 2011a. 'The USA PATRIOT Act Sunset Extension Act of 2011'. *Senate Judiciary Committee Minority Report*, 5 April.
US Senate. 2011b. 'Ten Years after 9/11: Are We Safer?'. *Hearing before the Committee on Homeland Security and Governmental Affairs*, 13 September.
US White House/Office of Press Secretary. 2004. 'President Signs Intelligence Reform and Terrorism Prevention Act', 17 December.
van Leeuwen, Theo. 2011. *The Language of Colour*. Abingdon: Routledge.
Vergopoulos, Kostas. 2002. *The End of the Circle: Coercion and Hegemony in the 21st Century*. Athens: Livanis [in Greek].
VIPS. 2005. *VIPS in Focus*, vol. 1. http://www.policevolunteers.org/pdf/Neighborhood%20Watch.pdf; last accessed, 4 June 2011.
VIPS. 2012. 'Celebrating 10 Years of VIPS'. Podcast, 3 January. http://www.policevolunteers.org/resources/podcasts/; last accessed, 4 June 2011.
von Bogdandy, Armin, Dann, Phillip and Goldman, Mattias. 2008. 'Developing the Publicness of Public International Law: Towards a Legal Framework for Global Governance Activities'. *German Law Journal* 9 (11): 1375–1400.
Wacquant. Loïc. 1999. *Les Prisons de la Misere*. Paris: Liber.
Wacquant, Loïc. 2009. *Punishing the Poor*. Durham and London: Duke University Press.
Walker, Nigel. 1986. Introduction. In: K. Heal and G. Laycock (eds) *Situational Crime Prevention*. London: Her Majesty's Stationery Office.

Walkin, Daniel. 2003. 'A City of Silver Bells, Orange Alerts, and Shrugs'. *New York Times*, 23 December.
Wallance, Lorna H. 2000. Foreign Direct Investment in the USA: a Subnational Investigation. In: J.H. Dunning (ed.) *Regions, Globalisation, and the Knowledge-Based Economy*. Oxford: Oxford University Press.
Warren, Robert. 2004. City Streets – the War Zones of Globalisation: Democracy and Military Occupation on Urban Terrain in Early Twenty-first Century. In: S. Graham (ed). *Cities, War and Terrorism*. Oxford: Blackwell.
Waugh, William. 2003. 'Terrorism, Homeland Security, and the National Emergency Management Network'. *Public Administration Review* 3: 373–385.
Waxman, Matthew. 2009. 'Police and National Security: American Local Law Enforcement and Counterterrorism After 9/11'. *Journal of National Security Law and Policy* 3: 377–407.
Weber, Max. 1919 [1948]. Politics as a Vocation. In: *Essays from Max Weber*. London: Routledge and Kegan Paul.
Weber, Max. 1978. *Economy and Society*. Berkeley: University of California Press.
Weber, Max. 1994. *Political Writings*. Cambridge: Cambridge University Press.
Weiler, J.H.H. 2001. 'The Rule of Lawyers and the Ethos of Diplomats: Reflections on the Internal and External Legitimacy of WTO Dispute Settlement'. *Journal of World Trade* 35 (2): 191–207.
Wheeler, Marcy. 2013. 'How the US Congress Lost the Plot on Secrecy, Surveillance and Accountability'. *The Guardian*, 7 June.
White, Lucie. 1999. 'Specially Tailored Legal Services for Low-income Persons in the Age of Wealth Inequality: Pragmatism or Capitulation?'. *Fordham Law Review* 67 (5): 2573–2580.
Whyte, David. 2010. The Neoliberal State of Exception in Occupied Iraq. In: W.L. Chambliss et al. (eds) *State Crime in the Global Age*. Portland: Willan.
Willer, Robb. 2004. 'The Effects of Government-issued Terror Warnings on Presidential Approval'. *Current Research in Social Psychology* 10 (1): 1–12.
Williams, James W. 2006. 'Private Legal Orders: Professional Markets and the Commodification of Financial Governance'. *Social and Legal Studies* 15 (2): 209–235.
Wissel, Jens. 2011. The Transnationalisation of the Bourgeoisie and the New Networks of Power. In: A. Gallas et al. (eds) *Reading Poulantzas*. Pontypool: Merlin Press.
Wodak, Ruth. 2001. What Critical Discourse Analysis is About: a Summary of its History, Important Concepts, and its Developments. In: R. Wodak and M. Mayer (eds) *Methods of Critical Discourse Analysis*. London: Sage.
Wolff, Edward N. 2000. 'Recent Trends in Wealth Ownership 1983–1998'. *Jerome Levy Economics Institute*, Working Paper 300.
Wood, Ellen. 2003. *Empire of Capital*. London: Verso.
Wormuth, Christine. 2009. 'Structuring National Security and Homeland Security in the White House'. Statement before the *Senate Committee on Homeland Security and Government Affairs*, 12 February.
Young, Ernest. 2008. Welcome to the Dark Side: Liberals Rediscover Federalism in the Wake of the War on Terror. In: S. Herman and P. Finkelman (eds) *Terrorism, Government, and Law*. Westport: Praeger.
Zackin, Emily. 2008. 'Popular Constitutionalism's Hard When You're Not Very Popular: Why the ACLU Turned to Courts'. *Law and Society Review* 42 (2): 367–395.
Zumbansen, Peer. 2006. 'The Law of Society: Governance Through Contract'. *Indiana Journal of Global Legal Studies* 14 (2): 191–233.

List of Legislation

Anti-Terrorism and Effective Death Penalty Act 1996
Authorisation for the Use of Military Force, 14 September 2001
Detainee Treatment Act 2005
Emergency Economic Stabilization Act 2008
Executive Order 13224. 'Blocking Property and Prohibiting Transactions With Persons Who Commit, Threaten to Commit, or Support Terrorism'
Executive Order 13355. 'Strengthened Management of the Intelligence Community'
Executive Order 13567. 'Periodic Review of Individuals Detained at Guantanamo Bay Naval Station Pursuant to the Authorization for Use of Military Force'.
Federal Restricted Buildings and Grounds Improvement Act 2011
Faster and Smarter Funding for First Responders Act 2005
Foreign Intelligence Surveillance Act 1978
Foreign Intelligence Surveillance Amendments Act 2008
Freedom of Information Act 1966
Intelligence Authorization Act 2002
Intelligence Enhancement Act 2003
Intelligence Reform and Terrorism Prevention Act 2004
International Emergency Economic Powers Act 1977
Military Commissions Act 2006
Military Commissions Act 2009
Military Order of November 13, 2001. Detention, Treatment, and Trial of Certain Noncitizens in the War Against Terrorism
National Defense Authorization Act 2012
Patriot Improvement and Reauthorization Act 2006
Personal Responsibility and Work Opportunity Act 1996
Pre-trial Detention and Lifetime Supervision Act 2003
Protect America Act 2008
Terrorist Penalties Enhancement Act 2003
Uniting and Strengthening America by Providing Appropriate Tools Required to Intercept and Obstruct Terrorism (USA PATRIOT) Act, 2001
Whistleblowers Protection Act 1989

List of Cases

Arar v. Ashcroft (414 F.Supp.2d 250, ED NY 2006)
Boumediene v. Bush
Hamdi v. Rumsfeld
Khaled el-Masri v. George Tenet (1:05-cv-01417-TSE-TRJ ED VA 2006)
Rasul v. Bush

Index

access to justice, 24, 35, 39–40
accumulation, 7, 14–15, 27–28, 29–31, 43–44, 130, 210, 212, 215–216, 218–219, 221
   by dispossession, 210, 216–217
   logic, 28, 30, 212, 215
   mode, 27, 38, 43–45, 210, 217–218, 221
   process, 25, 43, 212, 215, 218
   regime, 27, 43–45, 165, 207, 210–211, 215–216
   strategy, 28, 42, 217
   through crisis, 216–219, 221
   vs. law, 20
   vs. the state, 14–15, 216, 219
   see also: differential accumulation, crisis of accumulation
Ackerman, Bruce, 96
advisory committee, 86
Agamben, Giorgio, 25, 97–99
alien, 8, 51, 76–78, 80, 96, 188, 200
American Civil Liberties Union (ACLU), 104, 109, 111, 113, 187–188, 192, 196, 203–204
American Libraries Association (ALA), 189–190
anarchist, 10, 41–42, 104–105, 112, 145, 162, 198, 200, 203–205, 211
anti-democratic policy, 2–3
anti-democratic relation, 151
anti-democratic tendency, 209
anti-democratic trends, 32
Anti-Terrorism and Effective Death Penalty Act, 77
anti-war
   gesture, 206
   movement, 10, 192–193
   demonstration, 193, 197–198
   protest, 156, 193
   rally, 196, 198
arms and energy sector (A&E), 43–44, 109, 206–208, 210–211, 216, 218–219
Arar v. Ashcroft, 109

Arendt, Hannah, 149
Aristotle, 163
Ashcroft, John, 67, 102, 104, 190, 194–195
Attorney General's Guidelines to the FBI, 104, 186, 188–189
Austin, Sherman, 202–205
Authorisation for the Use of Military Force (AUMF), 73, 78, 81, 96, 110
authoritarian statism (AS), 10, 32–35, 99–101, 116, 146, 182–183, 208–210, 212–218, 220
   phase I, 32, 100, 210, 213
   phase II, 33–35, 100, 210, 214–215, 217
   phase III, 99, 182, 210, 212–216, 218, 220
   vs. crisis, 32, 146, 182, 210
autonomy, 8, 12, 21, 24, 76, 92, 135–136, 160–161, 163, 171, 193, 214

Bichler, Shimshon, 42
biopolitics, 9, 146, 157, 163–165
bio-power, 164–165
bio-security, 123, 164–165
Boumediene v. Bush, 80
Brown, Wendy, 181–182
burden of proof, 83–85, 149
Bush, George W., 46, 60, 63, 65, 113, 169, 201
Bush administration, 63, 65, 68, 96, 103, 105, 112, 122–123, 142, 144

capital, 6–7, 9, 15, 27–28, 30–34, 37–41, 43–44, 61, 63, 83–87, 92, 101, 106, 115, 128–129, 131, 134–135, 146–147, 183, 206–208, 212, 214, 216–218, 220
   entity, 36–37, 42, 86, 89, 92, 101, 128
   financial, 30–31
   fractions, 4, 30, 34, 109, 209, 218–219
   sectors, 30, 42–44, 109, 147
   transnational, 31, 34, 37, 39, 92
   (*see also*: accumulation, dominant capital, state vs. capital)

Capital, 25
capitalism, 11, 20–21, 25, 32, 160, 162, 165, 182, 203, 209
capitalist class (*and*: capitalists), 21, 27, 38, 42, 209–210, 215, 218–219
capitalist interests, 33
capitalist mastery, 161, 166
capitalist rationality, 161, 163
capitalist relations, 15, 20
capitalist rule (*and*: capital rule), 82, 114, 116, 165, 209, 220
capitalist society, 21–22, 82, 203
capitalist type of law (*and*: capitalist law), 19–23, 25, 213
capitalist type of state (*and*: capitalist state), 14–18, 20–21, 32, 41, 101, 146, 149, 182, 206, 209, 215
Castoriadis, Cornelius, 7, 13, 166
Central Intelligence Agency (CIA), 71, 81, 123–124, 137, 139–142, 153
cause-lawyers, 188, 192, 205
Citizen Corps, 9, 158, 169–175, 177, 180, 182–183
citizenship, 6, 9, 27, 36, 38–39, 41, 80, 111, 169, 173, 179–182, 209–210, 220
    (*see also*: state-population relations)
civil-libertarian lawyers (*and*: liberal lawyers), 8, 111–112, 187, 182
coercive state apparatus (*and*: mechanism), 76, 81, 85, 95, 101, 103, 105, 134–135, 144, 146–148, 152, 174, 183, 193–194, 196, 210–212, 215, 219
    logic of, 134, 183, 215
Cohen, Stanley, 146–147
Community Emergency Response Team (CERT), 158, 172–179
community resolutions, *see*: resolutions
congress, 8, 47, 56–57, 61, 67–70, 73, 77–80, 86–89, 94, 96, 100, 104 fn.1, 106–108, 111–112, 118, 124–125, 132, 137–140, 143–144, 180, 188–190, 207, 211–212 (*see also*: legislature)
conjuncture, 15, 24, 26, 42, 98, 127, 162–163, 197
constitution, 6, 23, 36, 41, 44, 47, 160, 164, 187, 213, 215
Constitution (US), 68, 96, 111–116, 187, 192, 194
constitutionalism, 8, 21, 24, 35, 113–115, 193–194
counterterrorism, 1–6, 8, 11–12, 61, 65, 78, 82, 84–85, 89, 91–92, 100, 106, 108–109, 112, 120, 123–125, 136–141, 143, 149, 164, 185, 199–200, 202–203, 205

law (and: legislation), 5–6, 8, 62, 65, 67–69, 73, 75–76, 78, 81, 84, 86, 88, 90–92, 94–97, 99–100, 104–106, 108–112, 116, 144, 148, 189, 193, 199–200, 202, 204, 206
    measure, 68, 106, 109, 113, 122
    policy, 1–3, 18, 65–66, 97, 105, 108, 167, 184, 192, 211
    powers, 78, 191, 193–194
    provisions, 75, 192, 194
    vs. democracy, 3
    vs. law-form, 6, 90–94
    vs. popular politics, 1, 4–5
    vs. rule of law, 94
    vs. state-form, 18
courts, 8, 38, 40, 70, 73–74, 79–81, 85, 83, 102, 105, 109–112, 126, 192, 211
    see also: judiciary
crisis, 7, 10, 27, 30–33, 41, 43–44, 65, 84, 86–87, 94, 99–100, 117, 130, 146, 170, 173, 182, 207–208, 210, 215–218, 220
    accumulation, 27, 215, 220
    economic, 1, 8, 10, 27, 31–32, 41, 66–67, 92, 94, 99, 101, 120, 134, 182, 207–208, 210, 212, 214–217, 219–221
    financial, 42, 86, 100, 216, 218
    permanent, 32, 99, 216–217
    political, 10, 33, 35, 41–42, 99, 182, 207, 210, 213, 217
    security, 86, 182
    systemic, 42
    vs. social antagonism, 32, 210
    see also: accumulation through crisis, authoritarian statism vs. crisis
crisis-generating, 10, 217–218
crisis-management, 10, 88, 117, 167, 215–216, 218, 220–221
crisis-tendencies, 45
crisis-prone, 34–35, 44, 213, 217–218
critical discourse analysis (CDA), 7, 47
critical infrastructure (CI), 86, 119, 121–122, 126–129, 148, 187
    vs. power bloc, 128–129

Debord, Guy, 31
democracy, 1–2, 7, 9, 12, 32, 41, 49, 52, 54, 60, 64, 108, 111, 113, 159–160, 162–163, 165–166, 182, 189, 194, 209
    capitalist, 109, 207
    constitutional, 209–210
    liberal, 33, 162, 166, 179, 181–182, 192, 208, 211–212
    parliamentary, 181
    pluralist, 149

representative, 33, 181–182
  see also: government by experts vs. democracy; state-form
democratic actor, 189
democratic aspirations, 159
democratic channels, 32, 207
democratic consideration, 36, 166
democratic culture, 160, 195
democratic demand, 194
democratic freedoms, 112, 189, 214
democratic institutions, 10, 111, 167
democratic institutional shell, 10, 99, 182
democratic model, 166
democratic normality, 207
democratic organisation, 162–163
democratic politics, 163
democratic polity, 10, 12, 111
democratic political system, 161
democratic practice, 3, 167
democratic principles, 9, 167
democratic society, 189, 199
democratic state-form, 10, 149, 182, 209–210
democratic tendencies, 163, 167
Democrat, 57, 107, 118, 122–123, 156, 184
Democratic Party, 118
demos, 160–161
Department of Defense, 103, 120–121, 129, 131, 139, 192, 211, *see also*: Pentagon
Department of Homeland Security (DHS), 8–9, 73, 76, 86, 89, 104–105, 117, 119–136, 139, 141–142, 144–145, 151, 153, 158, 169–173, 199, 205
Department of Justice (DOJ), 62–63, 69–71, 102–106, 110, 120, 123, 130–131, 138–139, 145, 172, 178, 195, 204, 211
despotism, 132, 160
Detainee Treatment Act, 79
dictatorship, 206–207, 209, *see also*: state-form
differential accumulation, 42–43, 219
Director of National Intelligence (DNI), 9, 73, 139–142, 145
data mining, 73, 119, 154–155
domestic terrorism, 8, 67, 77, 81, 83, 107, 112–113, 185–186, 188, 200
dominant capital, 7, 10, 41, 43–44, 182, 207, 217–220
connecting the dots, 154
doxa, 163

ecology, 10, 105, 145, 200
economic security, 120, 126
economic state apparatus (*and*: mechanism), 33, 101, 212, 215, 219

economy, 12, 15, 20, 23, 30–32, 34, 37–38, 40, 43–44, 58, 60–61, 64, 66, 85–86–89, 91–93, 99, 113, 118, 129–130, 134, 148, 161, 165, 214, 216, 218
  international, 61
  knowledge-based, 28, 30
  logic of, 15, 101
  national, 61, 101, 131
  new, 42, 210
  political, 6, 22, 30, 44, 165
  US, 43, 88, 219
  vs. law, 20–22, 209
  vs. government, 165
  vs. the state, 14–15, 20, 99
  see also: homeland security economy
effectiveness, 2–3, 9, 36, 75, 76, 91–93, 119, 125, 133–134, 157, 166, 167, 172, 194, 213
  as legitimation, 166–167
  logic of, 93
  vs. democracy, 9, 159, 162
  vs. general will, 166–167
  vs. legal logic, 95, 213
  vs. socio-political principles, 165
emergency, 56, 61, 65, 68–69, 78–81, 84, 86, 94, 96, 98–100, 115, 120–121, 125, 152, 158, 169, 172–174, 176–177, 182, 205, 219
  economic 8, 94, 99
  existential, 96
  permanent, 181
  state of, 22, 97, 100
  vs. legal framework, 78, 80–81, 88, 94, 99
emergency agencies, 152, 177, 205
emergency law (and legislation), 94, 99
emergency management, 170–171
emergency personnel, 76, 131
emergency powers, 88, 94, 96
emergency services, 124, 126
Emergency Economic Stabilisation Act (EESA), 86–88, 100–101
enemy, 7, 48–55, 58–60, 62–65, 76–77, 94–95, 105–106, 117–120, 129, 143, 149–150, 173, 205–206
  existential, 51, 148, 150
  internal (and: ~within), 94, 106, 145, 148–149
  real, 94, 200
enemy belligerent, 80–81
enemy combatant, 8, 79–81, 92 95, 109–110, 186, 188, 214
episteme, 162–163, 165
essentialism, 97–98

256   *Index*

Executive, 8, 32, 37, 40, 49–50, 56, 59, 69, 73, 79–81, 83–85, 87–91, 94, 96, 100–102, 108, 113, 115, 120, 123, 129, 134, 162, 181, 211–213
  authority, 75, 99, 112
  coup, 69, 212
  determination, 90, 214
  discretion, 76, 94, 101, 134
  federal, 8, 75–76, 123, 131, 135, 214, 220
  fiat, 79, 172
  infringement, 68, 113
  licence, 90–91
  logic, 75
  monopoly, 74, 84, 90, 93–94
  personnel, 84, 123, 212
  power, 8, 32, 73, 84–85, 88, 93–94, 96, 100, 107–108, 135, 162, 185–186, 212–215, 220
  sub-national (and: state/local), 126, 135
  vs. capital, 37, 89, 128–129, 134, 212
  vs. emergency, 94, 100, 115
  vs. judiciary (and: courts), 31, 37–38, 50, 74–75, 88, 109–111
  vs. legislature (and: Congress), 31–32, 37–38, 61, 68, 88, 108, 111, 212
  vs. power bloc, 131
Executive Order, 8, 80, 84–85, 140
exception, 25, 78–79, 90, 94–98, 208–209
  permanent, 99
  vs. normality, 78, 96–99, 208–209
  (*see also*: state of exception)
exceptional case, 96
exceptional category, 77, 96
exceptional mode, 98
exceptional moment, 98
exceptional powers, 67, 78, 97
extrajudicial assassination (*and*: targeted assassination, presidentially authorised assassination), 81, 96, 100,
extraordinary rendition, 109
Extremism and Radicalisation Branch, 104

Fairclough, Norman, 47
Faster and Smarter Funding for First Responders Act, 125
Federal Bureau of Investigations (FBI), 56, 68, 70–74, 76, 83, 102–104, 106, 119, 123, 126, 135–139, 141–142, 144, 149, 153, 176, 185–186, 188–189, 193, 198, 200–202, 204–205
  as an intelligence agency, 136–139
Federal Emergency Management Agency (FEMA), 170, 172, 174–176, 178

Federal Reserve (Fed), 86, 88, 100
Federal Restricted Buildings and Grounds Improvement Act, 84
finance, 29, 219, *see also*: capital
financialisation, 216
Fine, Bob, 25
fishing expedition, 104–105
flexibility, 14, 27, 37, 88, 119, 132–133
force, 11, 14, 19, 21, 23, 30, 35, 39, 47, 50, 53–55, 59, 61, 69, 78–80, 82–83, 93–94, 96–98, 104, 108, 115, 152, 160, 165, 166, 178–179, 188–190, 204, 206–207
  driving, 12, 29–30, 108
  instituting, 12
  see also: state force
freedom, 48–50, 52–53, 55–56, 58–60, 62, 64, 107, 114, 117, 159, 179, 189
  of association, 114
  constitutional, 111–113
  legal, 21
  personal, 108
  political, 115
  of speech, 48, 202
  vs. democracy, 159–160
  vs. security, 113–114
  (*see also*: liberty)
Freedom of Information Act (FOIA), 186
Foreign Intelligence Surveillance Act (FISA), 69–72, 74–77, 102–103, 107, 110, 112, 139, 145, 202, 204
Foreign Intelligence Surveillance Amendments Act, 74
Foreign Intelligence Surveillance Court (FISC), 70, 71n, 72, 102–103, 110, 202
Foreign Intelligence Surveillance Court of Review, 70, 110
Foucault, Michel, 146, 149, 163–166, 181
fusion centres, 125

Garland, David, 147
general interest, 15, 17, 33
general will, 161–162, 167
Giuliani, Carlo, 42
Goldman, Emma, 112
governance, 26, 28–30, 34–37, 40–42, 101, 128, 134, 147, 165, 171–172, 180–181, 210, 214, 220
  legal, 38–40, 91
  mechanism, 29–30, 32, 34–36, 214
  network, 150, 183
  project, 181
  regime, 28–29, 38, 41, 91, 166, 208, 210
  strategy, 29

vs. statism, 134–135
  see also: metagovernance
government by experts, 9, 12, 54, 151, 159, 162–163, 165, 167–168, 220
governmental logic, 166
Gramsci, Antonio, 7
Greenpeace, 104, 200–202
Greenspan, Alan, 42
Gross, Oren, 96
Guantanamo, 67, 79–81, 96, 112, 213
  treatment, 78–81, 92–93, 110, 112
guilt by association, 54, 77, 84, 94, 206

habeas corpus, 79–80, 109–110
hegemony, 26, 31, 33, 35
Hall, Stuart, 146
heteronomy, 12, 59, 116, 160, 193–194
Hamdi, Yaser, 110
Hamdi v. Rumsfeld, 79–80, 110
homeland security, 1, 3–10, 45, 54, 58–61, 66, 84, 86, 92, 94, 98–99, 101, 107, 111, 113–114, 117–124, 126–127, 129–132, 137, 139–140, 143, 148–149, 151, 153, 166, 169, 174, 180, 182, 184 188–195, 197, 199–200, 202, 204–209, 211–212, 216, 219, 221
  logic, 101
  phases of, 206–207, 211–212
  vs. citizenship, 169, 180, 183
  vs crisis, 208, 210, 215–216
  vs. law-form, 1, 5, 8, 45, 208–209, 213, 215
  vs. social dynamics, 208, 218–221
  vs. state-form, 1, 5, 10, 45, 99, 149, 182, 208–209, 212–215
homeland security law (*and*: legislation), 69, 94, 101, 202, 204, *see also*: counterterrorism law
homeland security modalities, 1, 216
homeland security logic, 101, 166
homeland security policy, 67, 124
homeland security politics, 59, 196,
homeland security project, 58, 63, 66, 110, 118–119, 122, 169, 193, 208, 210–212, 215, 218
homeland security regime, 59, 101, 177, 190, 206
homeland security state, 106, 201, 205, 218
Homeland Security Act (HSA), 8, 69, 73, 76, 86, 89, 92, 120, 126, 130, 187
Homeland Security Advisory System (HSAS), 9, 119, 125, 151–152, 155, 157–159, 163–168
Homeland Security Council (HSC), 123–124, 139, 153, 205

homeland security economy, 9, 126, 129–131, 134, 141, 214
Hoover, Edgar J., 70, 112, 138, 150
human rights (HR), 36, 38–41, 92–93, 187, 124
  vs. citizenship-based rights, 38–41

indymedia, 201–202
information technology (IT), 73, 124, 126, 129–130, 137–138, 144
  sector 43, 63, 128–130, 208, 211
intelligence, 8–9, 56, 58, 64, 67, 69–73, 75–76, 81, 84, 90, 93, 105, 110, 119, 121–125, 127, 132, 136–145, 148–151, 153, 155–157, 163, 166–167, 198–200, 202, 205
  as a mode of government, 9, 151, 163, 165–167, 220
  strategic, 138
  tactical, 138
  vs. law enforcement, 102–103, 105, 110, 137–139
  see also: intelligence-led policing, total intelligence
intelligence agency, 9, 71, 100, 102–103, 136–140, 205
intelligence mechanism (*and*: apparatus, machine), 9, 136, 139, 143, 145, 149, 151, 202
intelligence modus operandi, 54, 136
intelligence operation, 70, 104, 136–138, 140–141, 143
intelligence personnel (*and*: agent, operative), 56, 69–70, 137, 141
intelligence-led policing, 136, 146, 148, 199
Intelligence Enhancement Act, 69
Intelligence Reform and Terrorism Prevention Act (Intelligence Reform Act; IRTPA), 8, 72, 140
International Emergency Economic Powers Act, 84
Iraq, 3–4, 65, 108–109, 123, 139, 149, 156, 184, 192, 196, 199, 207, 214,
ius regis, 78–79, 81, 90, 93, 99, 185, 212, 215
  (*see also*: law-form)

Jakobs, Günther, 95
Jessop, Bob, 7, 14, 29–30, 171
Joint Terrorism Task Force (JTTF), 104n, 125–126, 138, 200, 202–204
Judiciary, 19, 24, 37, 59, 70, 74–75, 79, 85, 88–91, 93–94, 109–111, 113, 115, 185, 213
  logic, 24, 75
  see also: courts, Executive vs Judiciary

258   *Index*

Keynesian welfare national state (KWNS), 27, 32, 100
Khaled el-Masri v. George Tenet, 109

labour force, 15, 31–32, *see also*: workforce
law, 1, 3–7, 11, 18–26, 28, 35–41, 43–44, 50, 54, 67–68, 71, 73–82, 84–88, 90–93, 95–99, 102, 111, 114–116, 126, 133, 137, 144, 148, 160, 164, 169, 194, 197–198, 202, 203–205, 208, 210, 212–213, 215, 217, 220–221
   as instrument, 8, 36, 91, 134, 213
   as social relation, 5–7, 18–19, 21, 26, 98
   criminal (and: criminal justice), 78, 81–82, 90–93, 95, 146, 178–179, 214
   federal, 88, 185
   international, 3, 37, 80, 187
   logic of, 8, 19–20, 22–24, 26, 35–36, 38, 41, 91, 213
   state/local, 88, 188
   vs. social dynamics, 6–7, 19, 22, 39, 98, 102
   vs. state-dynamics, 22–23, 26, 102
   vs. state, 4–6, 14, 18–26, 39–41, 91–93, 99, 115–116, 217
   vs. politics, 18, 21, 67, 97–98, 115, 208
   vs. violence, 97–98, 115
   see also: capitalist type of law, counterterrorism law, homeland security law, strategic-relational approach, type of law
law-abiding citizens, 104, 148
law-abiding protesters, 104
law-form, 1, 5, 7, 23–27, 35, 37–40, 75, 79, 85, 89–93, 99, 134, 208, 212–215, 221
   normal vs. exceptional, 8, 99
   vs. state-form, 5, 7, 26, 39–41, 99, 213
   vs. type of law, 25
   see also: ius regis, lex mercatoria
law enforcement, 51, 64, 71, 74–76, 84–85, 102–105, 121, 123, 125, 135, 137–138, 140, 144, 152, 173, 186, 189, 193, 201–202
   agency, 102, 105, 110, 139, 201, 205
   mechanism, 70
   personnel, 69–70, 102, 110, 137
   see also: intelligence vs. law enforcement
legal dynamics, 67, 208
legal system, 5–6, 22–24, 26, 35, 37, 82, 90–92, 95, 213
legislature, 32–33, 37, 59, 68–69, 88, 100, 111, 115, 212–213, *see also*: congress, executive vs. legislature
legitimacy (*and*: legitimation), 33, 36, 42, 45, 66, 159–162, 165–167, 207
Lex Mercatoria, 36–37, 40, 92–93

lex mercatoria (as a law-form), 35, 37–39, 90–93, 213
liberal lawyers, see civil-libertarian lawyers
liberty, 50, 61–62, 79, 112, 114, 116, 119
   vs. security, 3, 113–114, 195
   see also: freedom
librarian, 9, 108, 188–191, 193–194, 211
lone wolf amendment, 71–72, 77
Lyon, David, 144

McCarthy, Joseph, 150
McCarthysm, 112
market forces, 214
market logic, 40, 181
market relations, 162
market strategies, 170
Marx, Karl, 7, 25, 162
marxist, 22, 166
material support, 58, 76–77, 79, 83–84, 106, 109
metagovernance, 28, 34, 41, 92, 171–172
military commission, 78–80
Military Commissions Act (MCA), 79–80
Military Order, 8, 78–80, 186, 188
Mueller, Robert, 102, 106, 138
mutual aid, 21, 177

National Defense Authorization Act (NDAA), 69, 80–81
National Security Agency (NSA), 69, 73, 75, 103, 109, 141, 145
national security, 61, 66, 78, 84–85, 94, 109–110, 113–114, 124–125, 132–133, 136, 138, 142–143, 190
National Security Council, 47, 49, 81, 124, 141
National Security Letter (NSL). 72–73, 103, 188
nationalism, 21, 113, 116
Neocleous, Mark, 149
neoliberalism, 30–31, 181
neoliberal arrangement, 41, 182, 208, 215
neoliberal economics, 60
neoliberal framework, 220
neoliberal governance, 26, 42, 210
neoliberal hegemony, 33
neoliberal ideology, 30, 42
neoliberal order, 100
neoliberal policy, 60, 180
neoliberal politics, 148
neoliberal social organisation, 221
neoliberal state, 141
neoliberal strategy, 31, 41–42, 210, 216
Nitzan, Jonathan, 42

Obama, Barack, 63–64, 80, 124, 142
Obama administration, 81, 96, 106, 123
Occupy movement, 10, 84, 198, 200, 206
oligarchic form, 209
oligarchic framework, 162
oligarchic government, 167
oligarchic relation, 151
oligarchic rule, 159
oligarchic tendency, 163

Padilla, Jose, 80, 109
parallel network of power, 31–34, 101, 134, 211–212, 220
part-whole paradox, 17, 22
partisan, 94–95
Pashukanis, Eugeny, 25
pattern, 37, 77, 94, 131, 144–145, 154–155, 164
   revelation, 144–145, 153–155
Patriot Act, 8, 67–79, 81, 83–86, 96, 100, 102–103, 107–110, 112, 124, 139, 144–145, 185–186, 188–190, 194, 202–204
   §213, 74, 102, 107, 185–186
   §215, 71–72, 86, 103, 107–108, 112, 145, 185–189, 202
   §218, 71, 102, 110, 186
   §802, 81–82, 186
   vs. FISA, 69–72, 74, *see also*: Foreign Intelligence Surveillance Act
Patriot Improvement and Reauthorization Act (PIRA), 69, 71n, 73, 84
patriotism, 45, 57, 65–66, 68, 113–114, 173
Personal Responsibility and Work Opportunity Act, 29
Pentagon (also: Department of Defense), 117, 123–124, 130, 139–142, 144, 153, 177
philosopher king, 148, 162,
phronesis, 163
Plato, 162–163
polemos, 58–59
police, 9, 19, 42, 56, 66, 69, 71, 75–76, 86, 106, 117, 120–121, 128, 135, 137–139, 140–141, 145, 147–149, 152–153, 164, 169–171, 173–174, 178–179, 185, 196–200, 202–203, 206, 213, 217
   local (and: sub-national), 76, 135, 138–139, 173, 178, 196, 203–204, 214
   logic, 149
   modus operandi, 136
   vs. Judiciary, 75–76, 213
police apparatus (*and*: mechanism), 75–76, 125–126, 135–136, 148, 205–206, 213, 220

police brutality, 42, 104n,
police curfew, 197
police department, 125–126, 178, 186, 198, 202
police infiltrator, 199
police intrusion, 190
police matter, 120
police personnel, 76, 83, 131, 190, 214
police powers, 63, 199
police practice, 3, 9, 84, 103, 105, 169
police presence, 100, 118–119, 198
police restructuring, 76, 117
police volunteering, 178
police violence (*and*: force), 193, 197
policing, 33, 35, 69–71, 75–76, 81, 90, 103, 105–106, 110, 136, 138, 146–149, 169, 173, 178–179, 185, 191, 199, 211
   logic, 76, 147
   modality (*and*: mode), 69, 71, 119, 143, 148, 209, 213
   model, 9, 146, 148, 199
   relation, 120
   pre-emptive, 33, 76, 94, 105, 139, 146, 148
   spatiality (*and*: space), 8, 69, 75, 103
   target, 10, 35, 205, 211
   temporality (*and*: time), 8, 69, 75
   see also: intelligence-led policing
policing mechanism (*and*: apparatus), 8, 70, 73, 76, 103, 136, 205, 207
political activity, 1, 9–10, 12, 23, 28, 93, 100, 103–104, 120, 125, 148, 162, 169, 185, 199, 208
political crime, 105
political exclusion (*and*: exclusion from politics), 10, 33–35, 66, 191, 214, 211–220
political expertise, 162–163, 166–167
political logic, 60, 162
political labour, 12–14, 18, 111
political targeting, 8, 106
political science, 11–13, 17
politics, 1, 4–7, 11–13, 16, 17–18, 21, 26, 33–35, 39, 41, 44, 46–47, 56, 59, 61, 65–66, 68, 94–97, 115–116, 119, 155, 160–163, 167, 169, 174, 180, 182, 191, 193, 206, 209–211, 213, 220–221 (*see also*: law vs. politics, popular politics, state vs. politics)
popular politics, 9, 84, 105, 115, 193, 206
   association with terrorism, 200
   criminalisation of, 9
   see also: political exclusion
post-national, 27–28, 31–36, 39–41, *see also*: Schumpeterian post-national workfare regime

260 *Index*

Poulantzas, Nicos, 7, 14, 32, 99, 146, 182
power, 5–7, 10, 12–13, 16, 21, 24–25, 32, 39, 41, 43–44, 47, 49, 53, 59, 67, 80, 89, 93, 97–99, 115, 146, 160, 163–166, 181, 218–219
   balance, 16, 19, 39, 75, 81–82, 100, 162
   concentration of, 34, 59, 135, 212–213, 220
   federal, 126
   foreign, 70–72
   modality (and: mode), 5, 15, 58, 66, 97, 101, 146, 165, 181
   national, 140
   political, 13, 44, 97, 165
   relations, 1, 4–5, 7–8, 16, 47, 59, 163, 211, 218
   social, 13, 41, 98–99, 160
   structural, 30
   see also: state power
power bloc, 7, 44, 92, 101, 109, 123, 128, 131, 134, 206–212, 215, 218–219
power centre, 47, 162, 219
precarious employment, 215–216
precarious worker, 28
precarious working relations, 39, 141
pre-emption, 8, 33, 51, 58, 76, 93, 119, 136, 138–139, 143, 147–149, 199, 211, 213
pre-emptive arrest (and: detention), 24, 199–200, 203
pre-emptive logic, 149, 199
presidentially authorised assassination, see: extrajudicial assassination
presumption of guilt, 94
presumption of innocence, 24, 83, 90
Pretrial Detention and Lifetime Supervision Act, 83
Protect America Act, 73–74

Rasul v. Bush, 79
ratchet effect, 76–78, 80, 96, 133
resolutions, 9, 108, 169, 184–193
resolutions movement, *see*: resolutions
right, 20, 23, 25, 28, 34, 38–39, 41, 50, 61–62, 66, 79–80, 92–93, 95, 111–112, 114, 131–132, 135, 160, 179–180, 183, 192, 218
   assembly, 35, 84
   association, 189
   civic trial, 112
   due process, 111
   expression, 189
   a natural judge, 79
   privacy, 72, 111, 189
   property, 111, 114, 192
   vote, 132
   see also: habeas corpus, human rights
right of the king, 79, 93
right of state, 95
roving warrant, 74–75
rule of law, 8, 20–21, 37–38, 68, 79, 81, 93–95, 97–98, 111, 181, 192, 203, 208
Rumsfeld, Donald, 140, 148

scale, 11, 28–29, 40, 44, 134, 191
   global, 11, 30, 92
   local, 28, 191
   international, 28
   national, 11–12, 28, 31, 36, 92, 134, 191, 214
   sub-national, 29, 36, 76, 92, 214
   supra-national, 29–30, 36, 92
   transnational, 30, 92
Scheuerman, William, 94
Schmitt, Carl, 51, 94–97, 150
Schumpeterian, 27, 30–31, 134, *see also*: Schumpeterian post-national workfare regime
Schumpeterian post-national workfare regime (SWPR), 27–32, 39–41–42
   as authoritarian statism, 32–35, 100–101, 182, 210, 214–216
secret searches, 73–74, 102, 107, 112, 185–186
Secret Service, 84, 120–121, 123, 196, 198, 202
security, 1, 3, 6, 28, 36, 54, 57, 60–61, 63–64, 66, 86, 89, 91–93, 114, 116, 119–120, 122, 124–131, 147, 149, 152–153, 157, 164–167, 170, 173, 190, 195, 211–212, 215–216
   crisis, 86, 182
   logic, 183, 211–212, 215, 218
   see also: homeland security, national security, liberty vs. security
security agency, 109, 120
security apparatus (and: mechanism), 56, 59, 64, 67, 120, 123, 135, 159, 183, 206, 215
security expert, 2, 46, 153, 157, 171
security firm (*and*: enterprise, industry), 129, 147, 176, 217
security measures, 2, 66, 119, 152–153, 157
security personnel, 2, 119, 170, 183, 205
security policy, 60, 67, 116, 122, 183, 195, 214–215
social antagonism, 5, 13, 15, 21, 32–33, 99, 102, 181, 218, 221, *see also*: social dynamics, social struggle

social dynamics 1, 3, 67, 12, 14–17, 19, 22–24, 26, 29, 31, 40, 44, 91, 98, 101, 108, 115–116, 168, 181, 206, 208, 210, 213, 218, *see also*: social antagonism, social struggle, law vs. social dynamics, state vs. social dynamics
social forces, 3–7, 13, 15–19, 21–23, 26–27, 39, 41, 44, 98–99, 165, 206, 218
social security, 28–29, 65–66, 85
social struggle, 17–18, 22, 44, 116, 146, 210, 218, *see also*: social antagonism, social dynamics
speed, 37, 66, 75, 88, 91, 94, 100
state, 2–35, 38–40, 43–44, 56–59. 62–67, 74–75, 77, 80–83, 91–93, 95–96, 98–102, 106, 111–112, 114–120, 124, 126, 128–130, 134–136, 141, 143, 147–149, 151, 155, 159–162, 165–169, 173–174, 178, 180–182, 191, 193–195, 202, 206–215, 220–221
  as an institutional mechanism, 14
  as a social relation, 5, 7, 14, 18–19, 26
  as a (legal) subject, 14, 21, 23, 39
state activity, 211–212, 214
state actor, 3, 23–24, 44, 111
state apparatus (and: mechanism), 14, 16–17, 21–22, 24, 28, 33, 59, 73, 85, 95, 101, 111, 134, 144, 148, 159, 182, 197, 212, 215 (*see also*: coercive state apparatus, economic state apparatus)
  force, 206, 214, 217
  institutionality (*and*: institutional design, institutional outlook), 5, 25, 29, 206, 210
  logic, 15, 22, 41, 166, 215, 219
  vs. capital, 33–34, 44, 85–86, 92, 101, }128–129, 207, 216–217
  vs. democracy, 160–162
  vs. economy, 15, 20, 34, 37, 40, 99, 101, 214
  vs. politics, 5, 12–14, 18, 119, 220
  vs. social dynamics, 6, 14, 17, 26, 98, 101, 116, 168, 181–182, 218–221
  vs. society 4–6, 16–17, 20, 41, 160–161, 165, *see also*: capitalist state, law vs. state, state-form
statehood, 19, 115, 181–182
state bureaucracy, 117, 166
state dynamics, 6, 18, 22–24, 26, 91, 102, 108
state-form, 1, 5, 7–10, 15–18, 25–33, 40–42, 45, 85, 89, 99, 101, 115, 134–136, 146, 149–150, 182, 192, 207–210, 212–213, 215–219
  exceptional, 10, 206, 209–210
  normal, 10, 15, 32, 182, 209–210
  (*see also*: authoritarian statism)

state institution, 1, 5–6, 17–18, 25, 81, 101, 211
state-law, 19, 23, 25, 35, 37, 39–40, 214
state manager, 4, 16, 86, 149, 204
state of exception 8, 25, 94, 98–99, 208–209
  permanent, 97, 208
  see also: exception
state personnel, 2, 14, 23, 110–111, 208, 211
state policy, 2–3, 16, 44, 219
state-population relations (*see also*: citizenship), 5, 8–9, 26, 34, 46–47, 56–59, 62, 64–66, 93, 100, 151, 166–167, 169, 173, 181–183, 207–208, 213
state power, 16–17, 19, 21–23, 25, 30, 33, 75–76. 81, 84–85, 93–94, 98–99, 135, 143, 162, 182, 194, 210–211, 215
state powers, 1, 10, 84, 108, 111–112, 115
state practice, 5, 116
state project, 159, 168, 181, 221
state priority, 117, 143, 212, 215
state strategy, 6, 16–17, 23, 26, 31, 34, 44, 47, 69, 73, 89, 145, 165, 182, 212, 214
state structure, 16–17, 182
state theory, 6–7, 166
state violence, 115, 118, 193
statism, 54, 66, 133, 135, 214
strategic-relational approach, 5–7, 11, 18, 44
  to law, 19, 22, 26
  to the state, 7, 14, 18, 26
Stiglitz, Joseph, 42
Strauss, Leo, 2
sub-national government, 8–9, 92, 119–120, 124–127, 139, 151–153, 155, 169, 188, 191, 214, 220
Supreme Court, 79–80, 109–110, 126
surveillance, 6, 8, 35, 58, 67, 69–70, 73–76, 94, 100, 103, 106–107, 112, 118–119, 121, 137, 144–145, 148–149, 152, 157, 164, 185–186, 189–190
  blanket, 76, 84–85, 103, 105, 119, 205
  electronic, 67, 74–75, 102, 185–186
  integrated, 144
  mass, 164
  roving, 73–75, 102
  total, 144, 155

targeted assassination, *see*: extrajudicial assassination
techno-rationality, 161–162, 166
terrorism, 1–3, 8–9, 49, 53, 55, 60–61, 66–67, 71–72, 76–78, 81–85, 88, 104–106, 118–119, 121, 124–125, 129, 135, 140, 144–145, 186, 189–190, 200, 203–204, 211, 215

terrorism (*cont.*)
  case, 102, 104–106
  crime, 77–78, 83, 103–105, 118
  definition, 81–83, 104, 118, 144, 176, 220
  international, 72, 77–78, 81, 201
  suspect, 95
  vs. common crime, 82–84
  vs. material support, 58, 77
  vs. social antagonism, 104–105, 135, 145, 196, 199–200, 206, 221
  see also: domestic terrorism, war on terrorism
terrorism awareness, 173, 176
terrorism expert, 2
terrorism investigation, 102, 106
terrorism preparedness, 159, 173
terrorism prevention, 136
terrorist, 7, 51, 62–63, 83, 95–96, 104, 144, 148, 196, 200, 204
terrorist act, 77
terrorist activity (*and*: action), 71, 77, 103, 119, 144, 153, 200
terrorist attack (*and*: assault, hit), 2, 55, 61, 65, 78, 117, 119, 144–145, 169, 198
terrorist challenge, 117
terrorist communique, 63
terrorist crime, 83
terrorist group, 1, 54, 156
terrorist incident, 78, 176
terrorist network, 60, 71
terrorist organisation, 53–54, 62, 67, 77, 104, 156, 200
terrorist suspect, 73, 78
terrorist sympathiser, 104, 106
terrorist target, 127
terrorist threat, 119, 123, 151
Terrorist Penalties Enhancement Act, 83
Title III, US Code, 69–72, 74, 102, 110

total intelligence, 9, 69, 105, 118, 136, 143–145, 206
Treasury, 84–85, 87–89, 100–101, 103, 134, 211–212
Troubled Asset Relief Program (TARP), 87–89, 213
type of law, 7, 19–25, 213, *see also*: capitalist type of law
type of state, 7, 13–16, 18, 149, 209, *see also*: capitalist type of state

unprotected enemy belligerent, 80–81
user-is-judge principle, 163, 168

volunteer, 9, 158, 169–180, 182–183, 215
Volunteers in Police Service (VIPS), 158, 173–174, 178–179
volunteerism, 173, 180
  Universal Adversary, 205–206

war on terror discourse, 46–48, 51, 53, 55, 59–65, 105, 118, 193
war on terrorism, 3, 108, 150, 193
Whistleblowers Protection Act, 86
White House, 44, 80, 117, 122–123, 134, 143, 212, 219
welfare, 27–30, 34–35, 66, 93, 118, 144, 147, 166, 180, 192, 210, 215–217, 220
welfare state, 25, 27, 30, 32–33, 35, 146, 148–149, 181, 210, *see also*: Keynesian welfare national state
workfare, 28, 32, 135, 148, 174, 183, 210, 215–216, *see also*: Schumpeterian post-national workfare regime
workfarism, 29–30, 133–135, 183, 208, 219
workforce, 28–30, 35, 131, 133, 144, 174, 178, 214, 217, *see also*: labour force